THE FAITH OF JUDAISM

THE
FAITH OF JUDAISM

an interpretation for our times

BY

Rabbi ISIDORE EPSTEIN

B.A., Ph.D., D.Lit.,

Principal of Jews' College, London

LONDON

THE SONCINO PRESS

1960

FIRST PUBLISHED 1954
SECOND IMPRESSION 1955
THIRD IMPRESSION 1960

PRINTED IN GREAT BRITAIN
BY THE HOLLEN STREET PRESS LIMITED
LONDON, W.I

לזכרון
נשמות הורי היקרים
אבי מורי ר׳ דוד בר׳ יעקב
ואמי מורתי מ׳ מלכה בת ר׳ יחזקאל
זכרונם לברכה

The Biblical references are according to chapter and verse
of the Hebrew Text

☆　　☆　　☆

ABBREVIATIONS

A.P.B.	*Authorised Daily Prayer Book*
B.T.	Babylonian Talmud
E.T.	English Translation
E.V.	English Version
H.U.C.A.	*Hebrew Union College Annual*
I.C.C.	*International Critical Commentary*
J.Q.R.(N.S.)	*Jewish Quarterly Review (New Series)*
J.T.	Jerusalem Talmud
M.G.W.J.	*Monatsschrift für Geschichte und Wissenschaft des Judentums*
n.d.	no date
R.E.J.	*Revue des Etudes Juives*

CONTENTS

PREFACE

This book is an attempt to describe the Faith of Judaism in the light of modern knowledge and in relation to our times. The aim is to present a rational exposition of the doctrinal foundations of the Jewish religion, and to vindicate their abiding validity, as well as their relevance to the individual and corporate life of the Jew of today. This book may thus be regarded as a sequel to my previous work entitled ' The Jewish Way of Life.' Whilst the earlier work deals with the ethical side of Judaism, the present one is concerned with the religious faith, in which the Jewish social and moral teaching is grounded and by which it is nourished and sustained.

The author, it may well be stated at the outset, is not in sympathy with the anti-intellectual and existentialist trends that characterize much of contemporary Jewish religious writings. On the contrary, he is convinced (*i*) that because Judaism is a way of everyday life, the faith upon which it is founded must make sense and answer to the rationality which is fundamental to human nature ; and (*ii*) that because Judaism claims the allegiance of the individual Jew not simply *as an individual* but as a son of his people, the validity of its faith cannot be established by reference to merely personal and subjective experience, in which the feelings and aspirations of the individual are the sole determining factors, but must be sought in an objective revelation of God in history involving the *whole* community of Israel.

The general arrangement of the book is broadly as follows :

Chapter I, which may be regarded as introductory, explains the need for a restatement of the Jewish faith.

Chapters II-III consider the importance of religion in general for the strengthening of morality—public and private—and for the satisfaction of the individual's personal life.

ix

Chapters IV-VII discuss the distinctive character as well as the revelational basis of the Jewish religion.

Chapters VIII-XV offer a systematic presentation and defence of the fundamental affirmations of the Jewish orthodox faith, in accordance with the language and thought of the present day.

Each chapter is followed by notes which, taken together, make up a substantial part of the work. In writing the book I have had in mind the natural preference of the general reader for continuity of presentation. For this reason I have left out of the main body of the work much relevant material, the inclusion of which would have tended to interrupt that continuity. All such matter has been placed in the notes, which, inasmuch as they serve *inter alia* to supplement the information given in the text and to develop the various subjects under discussion, form an integral part of the work—and should not be omitted by the reader. In order to ease the task of the reader the pages on which the notes are to be found are given on the opening page of each chapter.

The quotations and references in the text as well as in the notes will show the extent of my indebtedness to the writings of others. Taking my stand on the primary Jewish religious sources—the Bible, the Talmud and Midrash—I have derived additional instruction, inspiration and guidance from other treasuries of the Jewish spirit, ancient, mediaeval and modern. I have also drawn upon the armoury of non-Jewish writers— mostly contemporary—particularly in defence of positions held in common by all theistic religions. In every case I have done my best to acknowledge my debt.

With such an abundance of sources, the reader will perforce encounter in this work much that is familiar ; but in the present setting, what is familiar will be found to have assumed a new form and contributed to the exposition offered in the ensuing pages.

It may well be that what I have written will not receive

the approbation of all. I can only say that I have sought in these pages to give expression to thoughts which I, personally, found helpful in meeting squarely the modern challenge to Israel's ancient faith ; and it is in the hope that these will prove equally helpful to others that I present this work.

In sending this book to the reading public, I trust I will not be considered presumptuous if I attach to it the words of Abraham Ibn Daud (*c.* 1110-1180) in the introduction to his philosophic work *Emunah Ramah* (' Exalted Faith ') : ' *I advise every one who is perfectly innocent and who is not interested in philosophical questions and is entirely unconcerned about his ignorance—I advise such a person to refrain from opening a book of a similar nature. His simplicity is his bliss, for after all the purpose of philosophy is conduct. On the other hand, those who are learned in the principles of religion, and also well versed in philosophy, need not my book, for their own wisdom can give them more satisfaction than this work. It is the beginner in speculation who can benefit from this work—the man who has not yet been able to see the rational necessity of the beliefs and practices which he knows from tradition.*'

It only remains for me to acknowledge my obligations to Mr H. Vezey Strong, Director of The Soncino Press Ltd., for his unfailing courtesy as well as painstaking care in supervising the publication of this work through its various stages ; to Mr Maurice Simon, M.A., for his helpful criticisms and suggestions ; and to the compositors, readers, and craftsmen for their patience and skilled service.

Grateful thanks are also due to Mr Charles Clore for his generosity in assisting this publication ; and I have likewise to thank my dear wife, to whom my indebtedness is far too great to be expressed in words.

I. E.

October 1954
Tishri 5715

CHAPTER I

THE CRISIS OF FAITH

THESE are days of the gravest crisis for all religions. Many are the trials which the various faiths have had to undergo at one time or another; but this is the first time that the crisis lies in the fact that religion is by-passed, as if it were an obsolete fortress not even worth attacking. The religious wars that figure so largely in the history of Europe were critical periods, but the situation to-day is incomparably worse. Then it was a struggle in which the opposing creeds appeared as active forces taking part in mighty battles; now, although our social order is threatened, as never before, with complete disintegration, in vain do we look for religions among the actors on the global stage of history.

Many of those who still cling to their ancestral beliefs are deeply disturbed by this state of things. They are afraid of becoming isolated and, as it were, cut off from the main stream of contemporary thought. Even their own attachment to their religion is threatened; for, after all, it is easier to be religious in a religious world than in a non-religious one. What is more, they see in this drift away from religion one of the chief causes of that very social disintegration which is the object of such general concern. They therefore ask themselves anxiously whether anything can be done to stop the drift while there is yet time.

This phenomenon and its resulting problems are

I

common to all forms of religion, both Jewish and non-Jewish, in this and many other countries at the present day. But this work treats primarily of one particular branch, viz., the orthodox form of the Jewish religion, and is meant in the first instance for those who are concerned with Orthodox Judaism. Yet it should also be of interest to a much wider circle. For Judaism is the parent of both Christianity and Mohammedanism (Islam), and Orthodoxy is the parent of all other existing forms of Judaism. Hence an examination of the common malady as it affects Orthodox Judaism is more likely to go to its very root and to contain valuable instruction also for the other forms of religion.

The crisis in Orthodox Judaism is fundamentally one of faith or belief. It is true that Jewish Orthodoxy is primarily a religion of action, and its still faithful adherents are mostly concerned with the decay of Jewish practice. But on examination it is found that the principal and the most serious (though by no means the only) cause of this decay is the weakening of belief in the principles of Judaism.

The Jewish religion in its Orthodox manifestation appears to the average man of modern education to be moribund and tied to old formulas and conceptions which the growing mind of man has discarded long ago. It is looked upon as offering a blind resistance to the pressure of Western civilisation and the scientific spirit of the age. It seems to be entirely out of touch with the ideals, needs and problems of the day, and satisfied to remain where it has been for centuries. This *semper eadem* which Orthodoxy is said to exhibit is held responsible for the straying of educated men and women from the old paths.

Actually, of course, the unbeliever is no new phenomenon in Jewish history. Already over eighteen centuries ago, Rabbi Eleazar ben Arach enjoined on his disciples that they should know ' what answer to give to the *epikoros* (unbeliever).'[1] But the distinctive and disturbing character of the unbelief of the present age is its widespread character. Whereas in the past the sceptical and critical attitude was to be found mainly amongst thinkers and philosophers, to-day it affects the mind of the crowd. The majority of the people to-day have a vague feeling that the fundamentals of the Torah and Jewish teaching have been so seriously impugned by the latest criticism that Judaism has become irrelevant to daily life. Among the several causes producing this situation must certainly be included the poisonous atmosphere generated by the incessant output of a literature, written in a charming and captivating style, which attacks the foundations of religious ideals, shared by Judaism with other religions in common. Thus do men and women breathe a vitiated atmosphere which they mistake for fresh air, and insensibly suffer from a spiritual anaemia which is fatal to Jewish loyalty and Jewish life.

Most disquieting in particular is the emergence in our midst of a mass of standardised ' pocket-*epikorsim* ' who keep on repeating parrot-like the same stock phrases of scientific or pseudo-scientific character, with little knowledge of what they mean—and all the time imagining that they are learned, educated, bold, bright and independent, merely because they abuse what it is fashionable to abuse—the teachings of Israel, and the eternal truths of our faith.² This emotional ignorance, which is the source of much of the spiritual *malaise* of our days, is not without tragic results; it is responsible for the existence among us of a class of men and women who have been drawn into the vortex of non-Jewish life, losing thereby the old props without acquiring any solid new ones. They thus become moral and spiritual vagabonds—indeed the most forlorn and tragic figures in human life.

This spiritual disorder, however, because it is general and widespread must be treated with tolerance and sympathy. The old-fashioned way of administering a sharp rebuke to the restless and inquisitive mind can only serve to estrange this mind more and more. On the contrary, those who ask questions regarding Jewish beliefs, practices, hopes and aspirations, are asking fair questions, and are entitled to candid and courteous answers. The answer, however, while courteous, must be given with conviction, which alone can inspire confidence and calm the perplexed mind.

Those to whom we have to address ourselves are of three types. On the one hand, there is the unbeliever, or atheist, who for one cause or another rejects outright the affirmations of religion in general, and those of Judaism in particular. On the other hand, there is quite a large class of people whose sympathies are with Judaism, but whose loyalty has been stifled or undermined by anti-Jewish or anti-religious prejudices of varied nature and origin. And finally, there are many among the faithful whose mind is bewildered and uncertain, owing to the general rationalistic trend of the age.

4

These three types of Jews, too, are no new phenomena in Israel. Over one thousand years ago already,
the Jewish philosopher Saadia (892-942)[3] drew attention
in the Introduction to his philosophical work *Emunot
we-Deot* (' Beliefs and Opinions '), to the existence of
these three types, whom he sought to benefit by his
guidance. ' My heart ', he writes, ' grieved for mankind and my soul was moved on account of our own
people, Israel, as I saw in my time (*i*) many who
adhered to their faith, but entertained impure beliefs
and unclear ideas; while (*ii*) those who deny their faith
boast of their unbelief and triumphantly deride the men
of truth, although they themselves are in error. I saw,
furthermore (*iii*) men sink, as it were, in a sea of doubt,
and overwhelmed by the waves of confusion, and there
was no diver to bring them up from the depths and
no swimmer to come to their rescue.'

Each of these types demands a different treatment
and a distinct method of approach. Generally speaking,
our principal concern is with the doubtful rather than
with the denying, the hesitant rather than the defiant.
Our aim, in the first instance, should be to win the
doubter, and strengthen the faith of the believer who
is perplexed and confused.

A far more difficult problem is presented by the
atheistic man. There will be few to challenge the view
expressed by many Jewish religious teachers that
nothing short of divine discipline, through a soul-
shattering experience, can be of avail to bring back to
God and to Judaism the man who has no *emunah*, no
faith. We may cite in this connection the striking
declaration in the ethical work, *Sefer-ha-Yashar* of

B

5

Zechariah ha-Yewani (fourteenth century), commonly ascribed to Rabbenu Tam (Jacob b. Meir): ' As to him who has no faith, how difficult indeed it is to find a remedy for him, and a cure for his ailment, unless God in His judgment strikes him down and causes in him a change of heart . . . ; for there is no means for his improvement: even if he be afforded every manner of instruction and reproof, all will be accounted by him as naught.'[4]

From this point of view, it might be thought advisable to leave the atheist on one side and to confine our attention to the other two types. This, however, would be a mistake. For while it is doubtful whether any success can be expected from an offensive against this type of man, we must certainly be prepared to meet his challenge and defend ourselves against his attack. And if our defence is efficient we shall find that it is after all the most effective method of attack.

To be efficient, our defence need not be so strong as to be absolutely unassailable. All that we need to show is that our faith is not a blind faith, for which we can give no better reason than that we derive comfort from holding it, or that our fathers and forefathers held it; but that it is a rational faith, which can be supported on rational grounds, and that it claims our undivided loyalty, because it is in fact the only faith which gives a really reasonable explanation of existence, as well as of the fateful ròle played by the Jews in the world's history. Having submitted our case on those lines, we invite our questioner to give his interpretation, and we will find that he will invariably fail. We may, it is true, not be able to convince him; but we shall have done enough, not only to make him less cock-sure of himself, but also to secure his respect for our attitude. For he will have learnt to realise that the faith to which we adhere, and which we practise, is not a strange bundle and medley of inconsistencies, superstitions and peculiar customs, but a unique rational way of life, of an excellence and sufficiency which no other can equal or rival.

In this connection it may even be worth showing that the mere absence of demonstration in the mathematical sense does not invalidate in any way our claim; but that in fact, the truth and falsity of any proposition in science no less than in religion does not stand or fall by the logical proof that can be adduced in support of it. This line of approach has already been indicated by Saadia. Describing the process through which the knowledge of things is generally acquired,[5] Saadia shows that in dealing with ultimate reality and fundamental problems of existence, we move in regions beyond the range of human observation, experiment and experience, and where, if we are to arrive at any conclusion, we are forced into the acceptance of certain assumptions as matters of faith, rather than as things proven. As an example, he adduces the problem of Creation. ' Creation-out-of-nothing ' (which Judaism affirms) is, indeed, Saadia agrees, an occurrence which has never been observed. As far as our knowledge of physical phenomena goes, nothing comes out of nothing, *ex nihilo, nihil fit*. Yet, notwithstanding the absence of an analogy within experience, ' Creation-out-of-nothing ' is accepted by the believing Jew as a doctrine of his faith.[6] This, indeed, may appear as a chink in the armoury of Jewish teaching. But, Saadia rejoins, so does the eternity of the universe taught by the materialist philosophers contradict all that is known to us by observation, in that it supposes that something has come into being without having been caused. ' Thus it is ', concludes Saadia, ' that not only we alone have agreed to assent to something the like of which we have never observed, but all investigators and logicians have agreed to act in this manner.'⁷

Here we have the enunciation of a truth which has lost none of its validity to-day. It is common for people who refuse to accept the affirmations of religion to contrast religion with science to the disadvantage of the former. Science, they assert, walks by knowledge, whereas religion walks by faith. Science proves its principles by experience or by logical reasoning from experience, whereas religion assumes its principles without proof. This, in effect, was the objection which the poet Tennyson in his *In Memoriam*, under the influence of the mid-Victorian scientific way of thinking of his time, gave expression to in the well-known lines:

> ' We have but faith: we cannot know;
> For knowledge is of things we see.'

Now this argument, so often put forward and so readily accepted by the unthinking, is quite fallacious. Science is as much built upon faith as is religion, and can dispense with it as little. Before science can proceed to investigate a single question, it must perform a number of pure acts of faith. All scientific enquiry implies a belief that the world of objects is amenable to rational interpretation. Acceptance of the trustworthiness of human reason and the senses—a point already, by the way, emphasised by Saadia[8]—is another example of the part faith plays in science. For unless reason and the senses can be trusted, knowledge of the external world is impossible. A particular example in science of a deeper faith is the acceptance of the law of the uniformity of Nature. This law expresses the idea that the universe is an orderly whole, a rational system, with nothing freakish or chaotic in its composition. In accordance with this law we must conceive that the laws governing the little region of space and time open to us are directly related to the structural law of events in vastly remote spaces and distant time. Without this conviction science would have been impossible, except in the sense of establishing entirely arbitrary connections, which are not warranted by anything intrinsic in the nature of things. But this law of uniformity of Nature, which is the first article of the scientific creed, has never been proved.[9] This is admitted even by so thoroughgoing a scientist as T. H. Huxley, who declares in effect that faith, if only in the universality of order, is an essential condition for the study of Nature and the investigation of phenomena.[10] Here we have a declaration by one of the high priests of Science, that Science depends on faith no less than Religion. Professor Whitehead, too, speaks of ' faith in reason ' as the trust ' that the ultimate nature of things lies together in a harmony which excludes mere arbitrariness.' ' This faith,' he continues, ' cannot be justified by any inductive generalisation.'[11] Yet science goes forward with its tasks, untroubled by the reflection that its faith in the uniformity of Nature is incapable of demonstration. It is satisfied with the knowledge that this faith has provided science with the explanation of the things disclosed to us in a way which no other theory could have done; that it has made progress possible; and that the more we look for it the more of it we shall find. In the same way religion, and particularly the Jewish religion, can show that while its affirmations may be incapable of compelling proof in the mathematical sense, it is the one and only view of life which can offer an explanation to the meaning of existence, and to the riddle of Jewish history; and which has made human, spiritual and moral progress possible; and that the more we live by this faith the more confirmation of it do we find.

This briefly is as far as we can go in dealing with the atheist or unbeliever. As already stated, we may not be able to convince him, but this line of argument should help to blunt much of the point of his attack and make him recognise, in the words of Saadia, that ' deniers have no sound objection to raise against our Torah, nor have doubters any proof to invalidate our faith.'[12]

But, it will be asked, surely this kind of argument is liable to encourage agnosticism? Once admit that you cannot conclusively prove the teachings of faith, will it not be natural for the argumentative type of man to force us into the admission that the only rational attitude for a thinking mind to adopt is a suspension of judgment?

The answer to this question is quite simple. Religion is, after all, not a mere matter of speculation, like the ultimate constitution of the universe, in regard to which a suspension of judgment can have not the slightest effect on human conduct. Religion is inextricably bound up with action; and whenever we do anything worth while, we decide at once on the speculative question which determines our action. A doctor, for example, called in to treat a man seriously ill, has to decide at once what his patient suffers from and what remedies are to be employed. Life has to be lived, and since it has to be lived, it must be lived upon one principle or another. It may be lived upon the principle of religion, in which case it will follow a particular line of conduct, or upon the principle of atheism, in which case it will follow another line of conduct. Between these two alternatives there is no middle position. There can, indeed, be no neutrality in matters of religion. Either you lead a religious life, or you do not. The agnostic professes not to decide between these two alternatives, but in reality he does decide. He refuses to regulate his life as he would regulate it if he accepted the affirmations of religion, and therefore to all intents and purposes he denies them. He thus no longer suspends his judgment, but definitely decides against religion.

This argument against agnosticism is fully developed by William James, who speaks of religion as offering a ' forced *option* ' regarding which man must decide in one way or another. No one, he argues, really doubts. A man may think that he does, but he always acts as if he believes, whether in God, in immortality, in morality, or else the opposite. We may suspend judgment in theory, but we cannot in practice.[13]

This idea has already been advanced by Saadia in

the passage quoted, where he describes the agnostics of his age as ' men sinking in a sea of doubt.'[14] This metaphor is appropriate to the fact that in religion indecision is out of place, even as indecision is out of place in a raging sea; you either swim or sink. Either you float, drift and are carried away to perdition, or you make the great venture, leading to life, safety and salvation.

It must be admitted that even after we have vindicated the claims of our faith before the bar of reason, much of our religious perplexities will still remain unsolved. The spiritual *malaise* afflicting our generation is, after all, not in every case intellectual, derived from so-called logical and scientific difficulties. There are also other more subtle causes responsible for the prevailing unbelief and irreligion. Already Saadia, in the Introduction to his *Emunot we-Deot*,[15] passes in review a number of factors which contributed in his days to the lapse from Jewish religious life and observance. Of these he enumerates eight, which reduced to headings are as follows: (1) Aversion to truth; (2) Mental laziness; (3) The spirit of acquisitiveness; (4) Mental incapacity; (5) Pride; (6) Influence of environment; (7) Attitude of some religious people; (8) Grievance against a religious person. For people who have allowed their religious life to deteriorate through one of these causes, Saadia makes it quite clear that his work has not been written. His work was designed only for such as take life and the problems of religion seriously, and are prepared to be taught and convinced. But where unbelief is simply the reflection of self-interest, pride, prejudice, or any other emotional condition, his book, he warns, will prove of no avail. Saadia repeats this caution at the end of his work, where he writes, ' Nothing of this book will be of benefit save to him who is pure of heart and intent on moral elevation.'[16] And rightly so. It is futile to approach a person suffering from a nervous break-down with an argument. What he needs is not a logician but a physician. A defective argument may be corrected by a more accurate argument, but an emotional attitude can be adjusted only by some other treatment than the one which a philosophical treatise can provide.

Does not Saadia seem to be addressing himself here, across the space of ten centuries, to the men and women of this generation, directing our mind to the existence of other important factors which cannot be ignored when considering the spiritual crisis in our times ? These factors are as varied to-day as they were in the days of Saadia; and are in fact the very same.

There is the ' aversion to truth.' ' Truth,' as Saadia remarks, ' is bitter,'[17] and some people will turn their back on Judaism for the same reason as sufferers from a serious disease are apt to avoid consulting a doctor. They are afraid of being confronted with the truth. They are aware of the tremendous implications of Judaism, the severity of its demands, the change in their whole conduct which obedience to its claims involves; and they are unwilling to face the pain and responsibility of the change, and thus refuse to accept conclusions which their mind and conscience urge upon them in their better moments.

We also suffer from ' mental laziness.' The trouble

with many of us is that we want our Judaism to be offered on a platter, in the same way as are our meals, without being prepared to fulfil the necessary conditions for learning what Judaism really means. Walter Lippmann, the well-known American thinker, has already drawn attention to these two features, as affecting the whole of our present-day civilisation. ' We reject,' he writes, ' the religious heritage, first because to master it requires more effort than we are willing to make, and second because it creates issues that are too deep and too contentious to be faced with equanimity. We are afraid (he continues) to face any longer . . . the severe discipline and the deep disconcerting issues of the nature of the universe and of man's place in it and of his destiny.'[18]

Another cause is the ' spirit of acquisitiveness,' the urge of serving self, rather than the higher ideals in life.

We also suffer from an ' incapacity of thinking ' rationally and logically where matters of religious faith are concerned. ' The modern European,' writes John Macmurray, ' who rejects religion on scientific grounds is characteristically incapable of applying the objective standards of scientific judgment in the field of religion. He merely ignores it and tends to resent being reminded of it. One might suppose that this was due to reaction against his own religious upbringing. Even so, it would be evidence of an unconscious resistance to the recognition of an important field of actual fact which demands to be included in any truly scientific outlook.'[19]

Another factor is ' pride ', the overweening confidence in the self-sufficiency of human reason, power and achievement, that makes Judaism and its teachings superfluous for the right ordering of individual and corporate life.

Then again, there is the ' influence of environment ' which is inimical to a life of religious devotion and practice.

There is, furthermore, the ' attitude of some religious people,' which is apt to be narrowing, rather than enlarging, and which breeds intolerance, bitterness, estrangement and drift.

Finally, a ' resentment against a religious person ' is apt to be transferred to the religion he practises, in the same manner as the anti-Semite will blame the whole Jewish people for any grievance, real or imaginary, which he nurses against an individual Jew.

These varied attitudes which Saadia would regard as non-educable, do not, however, account for the general drift noticeable in our times. There are still many men and women ' pure of heart and intent on moral elevation,'[20] who nevertheless stray from the traditional path of Jewish observance and duty, as a result of genuine intellectual difficulties which they are unable to resolve. This is an undeniable fact; and it is a fact the broad implications of which must be definitely faced. Merely to drill into men, women and children, the bare facts of religious history and practice is not enough. If the soul of the child is to expand and religion is to take firm root in his being, the scheme of the Jewish faith must be set before him in its fulness, and its rational cohesion. Only when young people accept the Jewish religion as an intelligent interpretation of the Universe, will they be able to reject insidious doctrines which clamour on every side for their allegiance, and resist the subversive trends that seek to detach them from the faith of their fathers.[21]

There is no question that numberless men and women lapse from the Jewish faith, because, gradually or suddenly, they wake up to the fact that they do not know *what* they have to believe, and *why* they are to believe. Only if a greater effort is made to instruct people in the doctrinal aspects of the Jewish religion, and in its underlying philosophy, can there be any hope of stemming the tide of irreligion which sweeps away so many and of building up a generation of men and women of unflinching religious loyalty and sturdy faith. Then, gone will be the fear that the increase of knowledge will destroy the essence of our faith. On the contrary, equipped with a deep understanding of what Judaism teaches, the increase of knowledge will only serve to strengthen the faith in God, Who is the root and ground of all knowledge, and in challenging and ringing tones we shall exclaim with the poet:

> ' Let knowledge grow from more to more,
> But more of reverence in us dwell;
> That mind and soul, according well,
> May make one music as before,
> But vaster.'
> ALFRED TENNYSON, *In Memoriam.*

NOTES

[1] Ethics of the Fathers II, 19. *Epikoros* is an Hebraised form for Epicurean, originally denoting a follower of the Greek philosopher Epicurus (341-270), who taught, among other things, that there was no Providence and that the world was governed by chance, and

applied by the Rabbis to all such as denied God and His commandments.

[2] See John Macmurray, *The Clue to History* (1938), p. 86. ' This
(scientific world view) is not in any sense science. It is a speculative
metaphysics, supposed to be warranted by some of the findings of
modern science, repudiated by numbers of first-class scientists, and
mainly held for emotional reasons, by people who would be entirely
out of place in a laboratory and quite unable to pass the simplest of
scientific examinations.' *Cf.* also Abraham ibn Daud (*c.* 1110-1180),
Emunah Ramah, Introduction : ' In our days it sometimes happens
that one who studies a little of the philosophies is unable to hold in
his hands the two lamps, the lamp of religion in his right hand, and
the lamp of philosophy in his left; but no sooner does he kindle the
lamp of philosophy than he extinguishes the lamp of religion. And
this has happened not only in our generation; this also happened in
former times.' בזמננו זה יקרה לפעמים מי שיעיין בחכמות מעט ואין בו
כח שיאחז בשתי ידיו שני נרות. בימינו נר דתו ובשמאלו נר חכמתו. אך
כאשר ידלק נר חכמתו יכבה נר הדת. ולא בזה הדור בלבד קרה זה אך כבר
קרה זה בזמנים ראשונים. What in the time of Ibn Daud was considered more or less a rare phenomenon is in our days a common-
place.

[3] This date of Saadia's birth, given by Ibn Daud, and accepted
hitherto without question, has recently been disputed by Jacob Mann
on the basis of a *Genizah* fragment, which fixes Saadia's birth in 882.
Malter, however, disregards this evidence and adheres to the former
date, as the new date would involve a reconstruction of Saadia's
biography, which he is not prepared to entertain. See H. Malter,
Life and Works of Saadia Gaon (1921), pp. 421ff. Mann, however,
in *R.E.J.* lxxiii (1921), p. 107, refutes Malter and argues for the
new date. See also M. Ventura, *La Philosophie de Saadia* (1934)
p. 15, n. 1.

[4] *Sefer ha-Yashar,* vi. מי שאין בו אמונה מה מאוד קשה למצא לו
תרופה ולמכתו תעלה אם האלהים בראתו לא ידיחהו ויהפך לו לב אחר . . .
כי אין סבה לתקונו ואם ישימו לפניו כל עניני המוסר והתוכחות הכל
הוא לו לאיי ויחשבוהו ללעג.

[5] Saadia, *Emunot we-Deot, Introduction* (ed. Slucki, p. 7), shows that our general knowledge comes to us by means of (1) observation (ידיעת הנראה), (2) knowledge of reason (מדע השכל), and (3) knowledge inferred by logical necessity (ידיעת מה שההכרח מביא אליו). Saadia defines (2) as comprising axioms, or self-evident propositions, as for example, the knowledge that truth is good and falsehood reprehensible, which corresponds more or less with what is known as ' intuition ', whereas (3), which can be rendered ' discursive reasoning ', is based on (1) and (2). See I. Efros, *Saadia's Theory of Knowledge, J.Q.R.* (*N.S.*) XXXIII (1942-3), p. 140. See further, A. Heschel, *The Quest of Certainty in Saadia's Philosophy, ibid.*, p. 274, n. 44 and H. A. Wolfson, *The Double Faith Theory in Clement, Saadia, Averroes and St. Thomas, ibid.*, pp. 231ff., and *Notes on the Proof of the Existence of God in Jewish Theology*, in *H.U.C.A.* (1924), I, p. 578, n. 1.

[6] See *infra*, pp. 170ff.

[7] *Emunot we-Deot*, I, 1 (ed. Slucki, p. 15): ולא אנחנו בלבד הסכמנו עם נפשנו על הודאת דבר שלא ראינו כמוהו בתחלה, אך כל המעיינים, והמביאים ראיות הסכימו נפשם על כזה. See also J. A. Thomson, *Scientific Riddles* (1938), p. 369. ' Science cannot tell us anything about the beginning, for the moment we speak about the beginning scientifically, we are bound to think of something before that.'

[8] *Emunot we-Deot*, I (ed. Slucki, p. 36). See A. Heschel, *op. cit.* p. 270, n. 26.

[9] See A. N. Whitehead, *Science and the Modern World* (Pelican Books, 1938), pp. 14ff.

[10] ' The one act of faith in the convert to science is the confession of the universality of order and of the absolute validity, in all times and under all circumstances, of the law of causation. This confession is an act of faith, because by the nature of the case the truth of such propositions is not susceptible of proof. But such faith is not blind, but reasonable, because it is invariably confirmed by experience and constitutes the sole trustworthy foundation for all action.'—F. Darwin, *Life and Letters of Charles Darwin* (1888), II, p. 200. See also T. H. Huxley, *Evolution and Ethics* (1894), p. 121.

[11] A. N. Whitehead, *op. cit.* pp. 30-31.

[12] *Emunot we-Deot*, Introduction (ed. Slucki), p. 11: כי לא יתכן
שיהיה לכופרים עלינו טענה בתורתנו, ולא ראיה למספקים באמונתנו.

[13] William James, *The Will to Believe* (1899), pp. 26ff. See also
Nels F. S. Ferré, *Faith and Reason* (1946), p. 5: ' Agnosticism is
not open-mindedness, it is culpable inaction. Tentativeness in
morals and religion, except in terms of a humble and teachable
positiveness, is not a matter of humility and fair play; it is a matter
of stabbing the good in the back by treachery; it is an insidious
alliance with evil.'

[14] See *supra*, p. 15.

[15] *Emunot we-Deot*, Introduction (ed. Slucki), p. 13.

[16] *Ibid.* (ed. Slucki), p. 161, according to H. Malter's (*op. cit.*
p. 260) correction, reading כי אם עם זכות הלב instead of כי אם
לזכות הלב in accordance with the Arabic original: מע אכלאץ אלקלוב.
See S. Rosenblatt, *Saadia Gaon, The Book of Beliefs and Opinions*
(1948), p. 407, who translates the passage '. . . this entire book can
serve a useful purpose only when it is *coupled with sincerity of the
heart and an earnest striving for its improvement*" (italics ours).

[17] *Op. cit.* (ed. Slucki), p. 13.

[18] Walter Lippmann, *Address to the American Association for the
Advancement of Science* (1940) quoted by R. W. Livingstone,
Education for a World Adrift (1943), p. 111.

[19] John Macmurray, *op. cit.* p. 19. See also Nels S. F. Ferré,
op. cit. p. 83: ' Science can be, and is being made, into an escapist
philosophy—into a dodging of moral discipline and spiritual respon-
sibilities, without which no life can be full and satisfactory, and
without which society is bound to meet ever new disasters.'

[20] See *supra*, p. 23.

[21] See Isaac Melzen (1854-1914) *Sefat Emet* Introduction,
quoted by D. Katz, *Tenuat ha-Musar* (1950), I, p. 364: ' Those who
teach children without explanation or exposition of the subject
matter, so as to implant the faith in the heart of their pupils in a

manner acceptable to their intelligence, impart an instruction which cannot strike root . . . This indeed is one of the causes that there grows up in our midst a youth devoid of Torah and the fear of God. It is therefore necessary for the teacher to strive to reveal the lessons which flow alike in matters of morals and faith from the narratives of the Torah . . . in a manner which appeals to the mind.' Cf. also Moses Maimonides (1135-1204), *Tehiyyat ha-Metim*, in *Responsa* (Leipzig ed. 1859), p. 10a: ' Our endeavour and that of a number of individuals differs from the endeavour of the multitude. For the multitude of men of Torah find pleasure and foolish delight in making Torah and Reason two contraries, and they take out everything unusual and strange from the realm of the intelligible, and say that it is a miracle, for they eschew the thought that anything should follow the normal course of nature, whether it be something which is recounted of the past, or which is seen in the present, or what is foretold of the future. We, however, endeavour to combine the Torah and Reason, and in this way reduce everything as much as is possible to natural principles, except where it is clear that we are dealing with the miraculous and that it cannot be explained in any other way.' This view of Maimonides was shared on the whole not only, as he himself here tells us, by a number of his contemporaries, but also by many of the greatest of Jewish religious teachers both of those who preceded and who followed him. Admittedly there were some outstanding authorities who frowned upon the study of philosophy, even when defended by the plea that it led to a better knowledge of God. In this connection mention might be made of the attitude of the renowned Hai Gaon (939-1038), as registered in a responsum of his to Samuel ha-Naggid (993-1055), of which we have two versions. In the one, given by Moses Nahmanides (1194-1270), in a letter he addressed to the Rabbis of France with reference to the anti-Maimonidean controversy (1232-1236), the concluding passage reads: ' The fear of sin, humility and holiness can be found only among those who engage in the study of the Mishnah and Talmud, *together with Wisdom (philosophy); not in matters of Wisdom alone* '. ולא תמצא יראת חטא וענוה וקדושה אלא באותם המתעסקים במשנה ובתלמוד ובחכמה יחד, לא בדברי חכמה בלבד. See *Iggerot Kenaot* (ed. Leipzig 1859), p. 10c., and B. M.

Lewin, *Otzar ha-Geonim*, *Hagigah* (Jerusalem, 1930), pp. 65-66.
These words here italicised, and overlined in the Hebrew, implying
that the condemnation is reserved only for the *exclusive* study of
philosophy, but not when it is allied to Torah pursuits, are significantly absent in the version given by Isaac ben Sheshet Barfat (1326-
1408), *Responsa*, 45, and by Jacob ben Solomon ibn Habib (*c*. 1460-
1516), in his notes on the *En Jakob*, Hagigah 15b, thus making the
condemnation more sweeping. But whatever the correct version,
it is clear from the whole trend of Hai Gaon's way of thinking,
as we know it from his works, that he did not oppose philosophy
as such, but only because, when divorced from revelation, it was
a false teaching. He was, however, much in favour of the study
of the general sciences, which he considered to be an essential
equipment of a Jewish scholar. See I. H. Weiss, *Haasif* (Warsaw,
1886), III, pp. 148-152. Similarly Asher ben Yehiel (1250-1327),
one of the most famous Rabbis of his age, placed himself in opposition to philosophical studies because he feared their subversive
effects upon the immature and unsteady mind, not because he held
them in contempt. On the contrary, he recognised the value of
philosophy as a discipline, and praised its devotees, calling them
'great wise men' (חכמים גדולים), and he held that, provided a
man was well equipped by knowledge of Torah and staunchness of
faith to resist its seductive influences, there could be no harm in
engaging in its study and pursuit. See I. H. Weiss, *Dor Dor we-
Dorshaw* (Berlin ed. 1924) V, pp. 67-8. Even the author of the
Sefer ha-Yashar, who in his hostility to philosophical studies
declared that ' those who corrupt their faith and lose the hope of
the future are those who cleave to secular sciences, and attach themselves to those who study them ' (*Sefer ha-Yashar*, xiii): כל המשחיתים
אמונתם המאבדים תקותם מן הבא, הם אשר דבקו בחכמות החצוניות ואשר
התחברו ללומדיהם. did not deny the benefit accruing from such
studies, if pursued under an ' expert and pious teacher, capable of
offering guidance amid the pitfalls that might jeopardise the faith
of the student ' (*ibid*. vi). מלמד בקי וחסיד שיורהו וישמרהו מן המקומות
אשר תחלש אמונתו.
As against this attitude, however, may be cited that expressed by
Abraham Bibago (d. after 1489), in his *Derek Emunah*, III, viz.,

C

' that speculation, investigation, and knowledge of any kind do not turn away a man from perfection, nor do evil-doing and offences follow from them: but quite the reverse. And if we see men who are evil-doers, and at the same time students of the " wisdoms ", know that not the sciences are the cause of their evil, but their own evil constitution; and had they not been " wise " they would have been more evil and sinful, for " wisdom " can in no wise do harm, but only proves beneficial.' Striking too, in this connection, is the comment of the *Zohar*, on the verse ' wherein there is no blemish ' (Numbers xix. 2)—' This alludes to the kingdom of Greece, for it is near the path of faith.' דא מלכות יון דאינון קרבין לארחי מהימנותא This enigmatic statement is understood as referring to the Greek philosophers who ' in some of their teachings . . . approximate to the views of our teachers, of blessed memory '. See Joseph Ergas (1685-1730), *Shomer Emunim*, I, 37. A good, though far from exhaustive, account of the different attitudes of Jewish religious authorities to philosophy is given by I. S. Reggio (1784-1855) in his *ha-Torah we-ha-Philisophia*, I-III; see also D. A. Tursch, *Mozne Zedek* (Warsaw, 1895), pp. 39ff.

CHAPTER II

THE MORAL NEED FOR RELIGION

WE have seen that in religion, neutrality or suspension of judgment is a totally untenable position. Religion involves action, and where action is concerned there is no credit, least of all intellectual credit, in professing to have no opinion, when in fact we act all the time as if one opinion is true and the other false.

At the same time, it has also been intimated that as between belief and unbelief there is no theoretical (though there may be a practical) compulsion to choose either. That is to say, no arguments can be adduced in favour of either which have the force of a mathematical demonstration, and consequently the logical mind must be determined in favour of the one or the other by some extraneous considerations. The question then may be asked, Are there any extraneous considerations which should determine the mind to choose belief rather than unbelief? For instance, does belief procure for us benefits which we could not derive from unbelief ?

The answer is that there certainly are such considerations and benefits. One of them, with which this chapter is concerned, is the unique support which belief, and with it religion, lends to morality.

All that we are, it has been said, is the result of what we have thought. Men live in accordance with their philosophy of life, their conception of the world. Human action is, after all, profoundly influenced by

23

For notes on this chapter, see pp. 38-44.

the assumption man makes about the nature of ultimate reality.[1] The whole character of man's social no
less than his personal life is determined by his convictions about the existence of God and His relations
to His creatures.[2] In the realm of individual piety this
is too obvious to need remark; but it is hardly less
evident in the corporate realm. The world still recalls
to-day with horror the cruelties and beastliness per-
petrated by the Germans in the concentration camps
of the Nazi Reich. These nameless deeds in the camps,
it must be remembered, were not committed by
primitive barbarians and savages, but by civilised
and educated men and women. But these civilised
men and women had a false philosophy of life,
a philosophy founded on the doctrine of 'blood,
race, and soil,' and that brought their conduct to
a depth of degradation such as humanity had never
witnessed before.

Belsen, Buchenwald, Auschwitz, and all the rest of
the death-camps and gas-chambers, have indeed given
practical demonstrations, on a wider scale than any
man has ever seen before, of the vital connection
between creed and conduct, belief and practice. They
have helped a great number of people to realise that
what men or nations think and believe makes an
immense difference to the way they live and the things
they do.

It makes indeed all the difference in the world
whether we believe that the world is a machine, without
intelligence and without purpose, or whether we affirm
that it is the creation of God. A man who believes in
God will act on that faith, and will seek moral perfec-

tion. Once, however, the world is conceived as without God, life begins to be conceived as without honour, and acting on that assumption, as humanity has learnt to its cost, men will live selfishly, live brutally, live badly.[3]

This inseparableness of belief and action has ever been one of the fundamentals of the Jewish religion. Whilst its chief objectives are good conduct and obedience, it is in faith that it fixes the root of all training and moral development.

Before proceeding further, it may be advisable to point out that in speaking of religion we are concerned with religion in the higher sense. That is, religion which associates the deity with moral attributes. It is only of this type of religion, to which Judaism has given birth, that we can affirm that it assists morality. Other religions, on the other hand, have no such relation to moral life. One has only to recall the abominable practices associated with the old polytheistic cults,[4] and Plato's criticism of the Greek religion,[5] because of the great moral evils it bred, to realise that the relation of religion to morals is by no means of a uniform character. Even in our days Hinduism in its worship is said to encourage lust and cruelty; and so in India certain conceptions of the Divine are said to be current which are conducive to immorality. It was only in Israel that the idea of the inseparableness of religion and right living first arose; and from Israel this conception was taken over by her two daughters, Christianity and Mohammedanism, and shaped by them for their own ends.

This dependence of morality on religion has been

taught by Judaism throughout the ages with unbroken consistency. From the earliest days, the Jewish people have seen in religion the source of moral life and in the absence of religion the cause of moral depravity. One need only recall Abraham's plea: ' For I thought, surely the fear of God is not in this place and they will slay me for my wife's sake ' (Genesis xx. 11), as well as Joseph's declaration: ' I fear God ' (Genesis xlii. 18)— a declaration which was sufficient to assure his brethren that no harm would befall them—one need only recall this plea and this declaration to realise how early in Jewish history this vital ethical principle had been accepted and recognised.[6]

This idea of the unity of morality and religion suffuses the whole of the Bible. It underlies the whole of the Mosaic legislation, where religious laws appear side by side with the moral laws, as for example in the 19th chapter of Leviticus; and it is the dominant note running through the rest of the Biblical writings. Out of the numerous Biblical passages that could be quoted in support,[7] there is one striking verse to which attention should be drawn: ' The knave saith in his heart, ' "There is no God ", (and the result is) they are corrupt, they have done abominable works. There is no one that doeth good ' (Psalm xiv. 1). It is to be noted that the ' knave '[8]—this is the more correct translation of the Hebrew *nabal;* the English rendering ' fool ' has no warrant—does not actually proclaim openly that there is no God. In fact he invokes God and, as was the way of Hitler, the arch-knave of our generation, he even goes so far as to claim that Providence is on his side; but ' in his heart he says, " There is no God " ' with disastrous results—' they are corrupt; they have done abominable works; there is no one that doeth good.' And what is true of the Bible is equally true of Rabbinic literature. Unmistakable in this connection is the dictum: ' No man deals falsely with his neighbour until first he denies God.'[9]

The reason for this close connection of religion and morality is not far to seek. One of the essential elements in the religious consciousness is the sense of responsibility to God.[10] Such a sense must at all times provide the most effective restraint upon bad action and the most powerful incentive to virtue.[11] The fact that there are to be found agnostics and atheists of high moral life does not invalidate the claim of religion. One might just as well argue that work is not essential to the production of wealth because there are people who have wealth without ever having done any work ! We live after all in a world that has been fructified for thousands of years by religious ideas, and in such a world the fruits of religion are sufficiently rich and attractive to be shared by people who have neither worked nor done anything to contribute directly to their growth. This point is well brought out by Prof. E. S. Waterhouse in an article he contributed to the late Chief Rabbi, Dr. J. H. Hertz's Festival Volume, under the title, *The Religious Basis of Morality*. ' A parasite,' he writes, ' is an independent organism, but its existence is none the less dependent upon that of its host. If the host perishes, the parasite perishes with it.' ' Using the term,' he continues, ' in the scientific, and not in any offensive sense, may not the morality which is independent of religion be parasitic upon the religious system within which it has grown up ? Surely the question of morality independent of religion cannot be settled by reference to individuals whose moral life is lived in a community saturated with ideas of religion.'[12]   Whether morality could exist independently of all religious influences has yet to be discovered.

Apposite in this connection is the reply which Lord Bryce once gave when asked, ' What do you think would be the effect of the disappearance of religious education from schools ? ' ' I can't answer that,' he replied, ' till three generations have passed.' Sir Richard Livingstone, in his *Education for a World Adrift* in reporting this reply of Lord Bryce, makes the following pertinent comment: ' We have inherited,' he writes, ' good habits, and habits persist almost indefinitely, if there is nothing to destroy them. A plant may continue in apparent health for some time after its roots have been cut, yet its days are numbered.'[13] In truth, to use another simile, the religious impulse of hundreds of generations may carry a people along the paths of moral life for some time, even as the train glides along after the steam is shut off. But without the driving force of religion, stoppage is inevitable, and with that stoppage the moral and spiritual values of life must come to an end.

Besides, we must not overlook in this connection the fact that moral standards of non-educated agnostics or atheists are invariably lower than those of the educated agnostic or atheist. No such difference of moral sensitiveness between the educated and the non-educated exists among religious people. We all can count among our acquaintances simple folk of no education, but who, under the refining influences of religion, are possessed of a moral character which can serve as an example and inspiration to the more sophisticated and educated among their brethren.[14]

But even were agnosticism or atheism to succeed in substantiating its claim to be able to minister to the moral culture and improvement of mankind, merely on the basis of pure ethics, without appeal to religion, the resultant morality would still be, by its very nature, inferior to that which has its source in religion.

Let us examine the claims of non-religious ethical doctrine, which we may briefly refer to as 'ethics.' Taking its stand against all presumptuous self-serving, ethics comes to the conclusion that the Ego of the individual must be replaced by the Ego of mankind. Whoever has not this dominating conception cannot be considered a real social individual, for ethics recognises man only as part of mankind. The individual is the bearer of humanity, without as such losing the character of an individual. It is indeed humanity that confers upon him true individuality. The abstract ethical idea is partially embodied in the State, through the organism of which some of the highest activities of the individual are made possible; and through the State he is being led to associate with other States—an association of which UNO—with all its imperfections—is the latest expression.

Yet on closer examination ethics, in spite of the apparent fulness of its content, is found to suffer from a certain deficiency which forces it to yield primacy of place to religion as an instrument for the moral training alike of the individual, the nation, and humanity.

1. Ethics cannot take us further than this: that morality is law and precept, and that obedience is duty, to which the individual must submit in order that his own welfare along with that of others may be secured and furthered, not as an individual, but as a member of a community, the units of which are interdependent. This is truly an ideal which *may* inspire to the greatest efforts in the cause of duty. But will it for the ordinary man be more than an ideal ? Has it sufficient compelling force to turn a sinner into a saint ? Has it the power to supply man with what is called ' moral autonomy '—that is, the *will* to govern himself from within ? It is well and good to inculcate the highest moral principles, and to hold up the conception of the high-minded or great-souled gentleman as ideal; but how cure the vices, the evil dispositions and propensities, the deceitfulness and weakness of the human heart, making man disposed and willing to do, obey and live up to the ideal ? It is just this failure of ethics that is responsible for the records of Greece, exhibiting, as Lecky has already shown, ' a rather unusual number of examples of high professions falsified in action, and of men who, displaying in some forms the most undoubted and transcendent virtue, fell in others far below the average of mankind '.[15] If ethical ideals were powerless to cure the wickedness of human nature among the cultured and educated Greeks, of what avail could they have been to the masses ? Is it then a wonder that the Greeks, although the most splendidly gifted race that has ever lived, ended, as historians tell

us, by committing suicide, killing off each other in silly and unnecessary wars, and in savage faction fights.[16]

2. And not only is ethics unable to turn a sinner into a saint. It has no power of producing a saint. Ethics can, indeed, claim a number of goodly men of virtue; but no saints. The ideal of saintliness, the chief mark of which is humility and contrition of spirit, is alien to ethics. History hardly knows the existence of an atheist who was a real saint. ' Among all the men of the ancient heathen world,' writes J. R. Seeley, the author of *Ecce Homo*—and he might have added, ' as well as among all men of the modern world '—' there were scarcely one or two to whom we may venture to apply the epithet holy. In other words, there were not more than one or two, if any, who besides being virtuous in their actions, were possessed of an unaffected enthusiasm for goodness, and besides abstaining from vice regarded even a vicious thought with horror.'[17] How much the ancient Greeks were familiar with the ideal of saintliness can be gauged from Plato, who in his Symposium boasts of Socrates, his teacher, that he was not a homosexualist![18] Similarly, Diogenes Laertius (died 222 C.E.) in his life of Zeno, the founder of Stoicism, praises the philosopher for being little addicted to this vice![19]

This inability of ethics to produce saintly men has already been noted by Maimonides. After codifying in his *Hilekot Melakim*, the seven commandments of the Sons of Noah that constitute for all times the religion of humanity, Maimonides concludes with the following words: ' Whosoever accepts the seven commandments and is careful in the observance of them, belongs to the saints of the nations of the world, and has a share in the world to come. That is, provided he accepts and fulfils them because God has commanded them in the Torah . . . But if he observes them as a result of his own contemplation, he does not belong to the saints of the nations of the world, but to their sages.'[20]

Here we have Maimonides' declaration that ethics divorced from religion may well be productive of sages, wise men, *Hakamim*, but not of *Hasidim*, saints and pious men.

3. Not only is ethics powerless to supply man with 'moral autonomy'; it is even incapable of furnishing a motive for right action. If anyone doubts this let him read the chapter entitled 'Why act rightly?' in Viscount Samuel's *Belief and Action*.[21] Appeals to enlightened self-interest and expedience may be well and good; but very often self-interest may point to the opposite direction. It is not always the case that honesty is the best policy; that good ethics proves sound economics and safe politics. Hitler's Germany up to Stalingrad thought otherwise. It really believed that aggression, brutality, lying and deceit paid; and these would indeed have brought them in rich dividends but for the 'Miracle of Dunkirk,' and what Sir (then Mr.) Winston Churchill called, the 'Interfering Hand.' Viscount Samuel, after grappling with this problem, concludes that unless man's religious faith supplies him with a motive, he must act for some reason other than self-interest. 'He must act from kindness or love, from patriotism, or from a sense of duty of some other kind; he must act altruistically.'[22] But Viscount Samuel does

not tell us why, if religion is eliminated, man must act altruistically ? You may say, Reason ! Moral Law ! Well, ask the Nazi that was, what his reason told him and what his moral law dictated ? ' The Nazi,' as Professor Waterhouse, writing before the crushing defeat of Germany, states in the article already referred to, ' laughs at the argument of reason. Moral law, he replies, is, as the humanists say, derived from man, but he will be the man who shall lay down that law. If others dispute his right to do so, let them prove their views by the ordeal of battle.'[23] There is no question that decency cannot be produced without religious principles. It is useless to try to keep back the raging sea of human instincts and passions with the flimsy mud embankment of an appeal to altruism, moral law, and other ideals to which ethics has recourse.[24]

And what is true of individual moral conduct is equally true of the social order as a whole. However ingeniously we might plan or organise society and adjust human relationships, all our plans and efforts are bound to miscarry unless God is enthroned in the new order we seek to establish. Without God the very goods acquired become sources of moral and consequent social disintegration. As Lewis Mumford well remarks in his *Condition of Man:* ' At the very moment that mankind as a whole is clothed, fed, sheltered adequately, relieved from want and anxiety, there will arise new conditions calling equally for struggle, internal if not external conditions, derived precisely from the goods that have been achieved.'[25] And no wonder ! Without God, all human attempts to establish a world order of harmony and peace are attempts

33

to solve the problem of human relations in the wrong way. They are efforts to heal the disease of humanity by external remedies, and as futile as the application of a plaster to a festering sore fed by some internal disease. If society is to get rid of its diseases, there must be an inner cleansing of the heart of the individuals who make up the society, and whose vices and failures constitute the vices and failures of the society to which they belong. But this regeneration of the heart can come only through the power of God working on the spirit of man.

An illustration of the inadequacy of human resources to ensure moral conduct is afforded by Soviet Russia. Soviet Russia introduced all kinds of new incentives for establishing a Socialist State and paradise for workers. The new incentives were—to quote Arthur Koestler's *The Yogi and the Commissar*—' collectivism to replace the individual competition; voluntary discipline instead of economic and legal coercion; the consciousness of responsibility towards the community; international class-solidarity to replace chauvinism; the dignity of labour to replace dignity of birth or position; a spirit of fraternity among equals to replace the paternity of God and Leader; reform instead of retribution; persuasion instead of compulsion; in general a new spiritual climate permeated with the feelings of brotherliness, equality, solidarity—"All for one and one for all ".' And yet what do we find ? '. . . a generation after the experiment started, the new incentives have been replaced without exception and in all walks of life by the old, abandoned ones. The war has accelerated this development and brought

34

it to its completion. The crowning of the Orthodox Metropolitan Sergius in Moscow Cathedral and his official recognition as Patriarch of all Russians on September 12th, 1943, was a symbolic act in more than one respect; it was a confession of the Soviet regime's failure to create a new human creed, new ethical values, a new faith for which to live and die.' ' It may be argued by apologists ', continues Koestler, ' that one of the reasons for the revival of the Orthodox Church was to attract the people of the Balkans. This is very likely true, but it only proves our point. It signifies that the regime, in its appeals for support abroad and at home, had to fall back upon religious incentives, precisely because the kind of Socialism practised in Russia has no sufficient spiritual attraction.'[26]

4. Ethics, further, offers no assurance that human strivings after progress are not in vain, a mere illusion, a chasing of the will-o'-the-wisp. Granted that things continue to evolve and develop, it does not follow that things are bound to become morally better. Darwin long ago declared that there was no moral content in evolution. All that evolution does is to make things more and more complex, for better or for worse. Evolution thus offers no guarantee that civilisation will not one day go to pieces, the whole of mankind falling a prey to complete annihilation; and what would then become of all moral values and achievements which ethics seeks to cultivate ?

The grave lack in the plausible system of non-religious ethics will now have become evident; and it is precisely this lack which religion, particularly the Jewish religion, can make good. It alone is capable of providing man with ' moral autonomy.' It alone has the power of producing saints. It alone gives to morality a compelling motive. It alone offers the assurance that human moral strivings are not in vain, as well as a guarantee of the final victory of right over wrong, of the ultimate rule of the good and true on earth.

The need of religion is particularly acute in our own day when ethical thought is so much dominated by totalitarian doctrines. Fundamental to religion is its conception of the place of the *individual* in the scheme of things. By its root-declaration that man has been created in the image of God, the individual becomes endowed in the eyes of Judaism, as well as of its daughter religions, with a personality of infinite value and dignity. Man in himself is a moral being, independent of his society and environment, because of his relation with God; and his self-realisation is determined by the development of his personal character on moral lines often running counter to the interests of the society and group of which he is a member.

By contrast, Totalitarianism does not recognise the value of the individual as an individual. Human personality, *per se*, has no absolute value for it; nor are man's moral efforts of any value except in so far as they subserve the interests of the totalitarian state or society. Totalitarian ethics with its system of ' social-engineering ' looks upon men as mere parts of the industrial machine for whose feelings no consideration need be shown, even as no one considers the feelings of cogwheels or troubles about the emotions of pistons. Such is the degradation and devaluation of the individual brought about by a social ethic that seeks to establish for itself an autonomous existence in independence of religion.

To take an illustration from our own generation, which will help to clarify the distinction between religion and totalitarian ethics in their approach to this problem of the individual—Pastor Niemoeller, who for years defied the Nazi assault on the religious freedom of the individual, was from the point of view of ethics, as conceived by the Nazi State, a non-social and non-ethical individual; but, in the eyes of religion, notwithstanding his otherwise notorious Nazi sympathies, Niemoeller's stand was but a vindication of the moral worth with which religion invests the individual. Likewise, in considering the guilt of the German people for the crimes of their leaders—from the standpoint of ethics, the individual German cannot be held responsible for the offences he had committed as a *Volksgenosse* of the *Herrenvolk*, since he had no independent existence apart from the German state. Whereas in the eyes of religion, every individual German is accountable as an individual before God and man.

The place of the individual in the scheme of things was, in the last analysis, the issue for which, it must ever be remembered, humanity expended for almost six years much blood and treasure;[27] and it is an issue which still confronts the world to-day, and which will determine in the long course the fate of our civilisation.

Scientists and economists everywhere are busy planning some kind of new social and international order that would make this world of ours a place fit for ordinary men and women to live in. Much of what these planners recommend, so as to ensure to every

37

person enough food, adequate clothing and a satisfactory home, cannot but receive the unqualified approval of every one who loves his fellow-man. But these scientific and economic planners, because they only deal with man as a cog in the social and industrial machine, are unable to combat the assumption that the individual is nothing compared with the Race, State or Working Class. Here is the age-long problem of the value of man. Is he a mere puppet or a unique personality? Is he but the product of chance, here to-day and gone to-morrow, or a child of God, standing with Him in everlasting relationship?

Judaism leaves no doubt as to the answer to this question. By its central conception of man's relation to God, it affirms man to be a unique personality; and it is upon the acceptance of this truth, as Judaism conceived it from the very first, that the future of civilisation depends. If the individual is treated as something impersonal, there can in the long run be very little to choose between one programme of social reconstruction and another. If on the other hand his personality is respected and his spiritual and moral qualities are recognised, then society can safely stand those far-reaching measures of economic and social reforms which all the technological and scientific resources of our age can supply.

NOTES

[1] ' Man is made by his belief. As he believes so he is.' *Bhagavad Gita*, quoted in A. Huxley's *Perennial Philosophy* (1947), p. 28. See also A. I. Kook, *Iggerot Rayah* (1943), p. 19.

[2] See G. K. Chesterton, *Essays*, ' Heretics ' (1905), Preface,

' There are some people, and I am one of them, who think that the most practical thing about a man is his view of the universe. We think that for a landlady considering a lodger it is important to know his income; but still more is it important to know his philosophy. We must think that for a general about to fight an enemy, it is important to know the enemy's number; but still more important is it to know the enemy's philosophy. We think the question is not whether the theory of the cosmos matters, but whether in the long run anything else affects them.' William James, the American philosopher, quoting in one of his lectures with approval these words, declared, ' I think with Mr. Chesterton in this matter. I know,' he continued, addressing his audience, ' that you ladies and gentlemen have a philosophy each and all of you, and that the most interesting and important thing about you is the way in which it determines the perspective in your several worlds.'—W. James, *Pragmatism* (1907), pp. 3-4.

³ ' When a man denies and effaces the divine image in himself, he cannot long preserve the human image, and the animal then predominates in him. By losing the support of God he submits himself to the unstable elements of the world, which must sooner or later submerge him.'—N. Berdyaev, *Freedom and the Spirit* (1935), p. 217.

⁴ See Leviticus xviii. 3, 24; and Wisdom of Solomon xii. 3-6. In Rabbinic literature idolatry is frequently bracketed with bloodshed and incest, because of their close association with each other, see B.T. Sanhedrin, 74a, Arakin, 16a, Tosefta Peah I, 2.

⁵ See Plato's *Republic*, Jowett's translation, III, p. 250-1 and also G. F. Moore, *History of Religion* (1929), p. 470. Cf. also Ahad Ha-Am (Asher Ginzberg), *Parashat Derakim* (ed. Berlin, 1921) II, p. 84.

⁶ ' This was the strength of the Hebrew race as a whole—that they practically identified religion and morality. Among them a right faith was the inspiration of a right life; creed was the mould of conduct and character; the fear of the Lord created an atmosphere in which impure thoughts and unholy desires died a natural death. Among them the decadence of morality was never due to anything

but a decadence of religion, and every ethical revival sprang from a religious revival. They had the highest conceivable sanction of virtue, because the God whom they adored, being Himself morally beautiful, was the Archetype of purity, righteousness, truth and love. Among pagan races, theology was not less strikingly divorced from morality than among the Hebrews it was conjoined therewith. Jupiter, the highest god of Greece, was notoriously adulterous. Krishna, the favourite god of the Hindoos, is the incarnation of abandoned immorality. But it is impossible to think of the God of the Hebrews as other than spotlessly pure.'—J. Strachan, *Hebrew Ideals* (4th ed., 1922), pp. 292-3.

[7] E.g. Exodus xix. 18; Hosea iv. 1-2; Psalms cxi. 10; Job xxxi. 13-4. Significant too, is the juxtaposition of the law of blasphemy and that of killing a man, in Leviticus xxiv. 16-17; see A. I. Kook, *op. cit.*, p. 100.

[8] David Smith, *Man's need of God* (1910), p. 99, points out that the Hebrew word *nabal*, rendered 'fool,' means literally 'withered'. ' And so the fool here,' he writes, ' is one whose soul is withered, shrivelled and atrophied . . . it is not intellectual aberration, but moral depravity—the blight of uncleanliness, the canker of corruption . . . it is this that withers the soul; and it is the man whose heart has thus been eaten out of him that says and thinks that " there is no God ".'

[9] See Tosefta Shebuoth, III, 6; ' Chananya b. Kinai said: " It is written, If anyone sin and commit a trespass against the Lord, and deal falsely with his neighbour " (Leviticus v. 21); no man deals falsely with his neighbour until he denies first the Root (God). It happened once that R. Reuben spent Sabbath in Tiberias and a certain philosopher found him, and said to him, Who is most hateful in the world ? He replied, He who denies Him who created him. The other asked (further), How so ? He answered: Honour thy father and thy mother; thou shalt not murder; thou shalt not commit adultery; thou shalt not steal; thou shalt not bear false witness against thy neighbour; thou shalt not covet. Hence no man denies anyone of these derivative commandments until he has first denied the Root; and no man goes to commit a transgression until he first

denies Him who laid the commandment upon him.'   חנניא בן כינאי

אומר וכיחש בעמיתו אין אדם כוחש בעמיתו עד שכופר בעיקר, פעם אחת
שבת ר׳ ראובן בטבריא ומצאו פולוסיפות אחד אמר לו איזה שנאוי בעולם,
אמר לו זה הכופר במי שבראו, אמר לו האיך, אמר לו כבד את אביך ואת
אמך, לא תרצח, לא תנאף, לא תגנב, לא תענה ברעך עד שקר, ולא תחמוד,
הא אין אדם כופר בדבר עד שכופר בעיקר, ואין אדם הולך לדבר עבירה אלא
א״כ כופר במי שציוה עליה.

10 See G. F. Moore, *Judaism* (1927), I, p. 467, and III, p. 144,
n. 194. It is well to note that in the Bible as well as in the Talmud
the fear of the Lord stands for religion, and the religious man is
described as one who fears God. See G. F. Moore, *op. cit.*, II, p. 96.

11 See *Ethics of the Fathers*, II, 1: ' Reflect upon three things and
thou wilt not come within the power of sin: know what is above
thee—a seeing eye and a hearing ear and all thy deeds written in a
book.' See also B.T. Berakot 28b: ' When Rabbi Johanan ben
Zakkai was ill, his disciples went to visit him. . . . They said to
him, " O our master, bless us." He said to them, " May it be His
will that the fear of heaven shall be upon you (as real) as the fear of
flesh and blood." His disciples said to him, " Thus far ! " He
replied, " Would that it be so. For know ye, when a man commits a
transgression, he says (I hope), no man sees me." ' See further,
B.T. Baba Metzia 58b: ' All commands left to the heart—that is,
to conscience—are accompanied in Scripture by the words, " Thou
shalt fear thy God " ': כל דבר המסור ללב נאמר בו ויראת מאלהיך
[There are four such commands in the Bible: Leviticus xix. 14 and
32; xxv. 36 and 43.] So all-important is the principle of the fear of
the Lord for all Jewish life and action that it is given prominence in
the opening paragraph of the *Shulchan Aruch*. ' " I have set the
Lord always before me " (Psalm xvi. 9): This is a leading principle
in religion, and in the upward strivings of the righteous who walk
ever in the presence of God. For a man's mode of life, his demeanour
and his deeds when alone in the house, are unlike those which he
would exhibit when in the presence of a great king; nor are his
speech and general conversation in the circle of his family and
friends the same as when he is with the king. And how much more
considered will his demeanour be, if he reflect that there stands
over him the King of Kings, the Holy One, blessed be He, Whose

glory fills the whole earth, watching his conduct and surveying his deeds; even as it is written: Can any man hide himself in secret places that I shall not see him ? saith the Lord (Jeremiah xxiii. 24). Such contemplation must perforce imbue him with a true sense of reverence and humility and with a feeling of unworthiness before Him' (*Shulchan, Aruch* I, 1). Cf. Maimonides, *Guide*, III. 52.

[12] E. S. Waterhouse, *The Religious Basis of Morality*, in *Essays Presented to J. H. Hertz*, ed. by I. Epstein, E. Levine and C. Roth (1942), pp. 413-4.

[13] R. W. Livingstone, *Education for a World Adrift* (1941), p. 24.

[14] See C. H. Harris, *Pro Fide* (1930), p. 126, n. 1.

[15] W. E. H. Lecky, *History of European Morals* (ed. 1877), I, p. 193. 'The Greek *Sophia* was entirely devoid of power over the will and heart of mankind. It remained purely theoretical and abstract; it could do nothing for men. It was the property of a few and had no effect, or miserably inadequate effect, on the life and character of those few. Where it did in some degree touch the heart and affect the life of some rare individual it produced a philosophic and affected prig, rather than a true man; and in the case of some of its most elegant exponents, such as Seneca, there was a woeful contrast in spirit between their words and life '—William M. Ramsay in J. Hastings, *Dictionary of the Bible*, V, 150.

[16] ' The history of their (the Greek) cities is a long tale of faction which was apt to degenerate into that " competition in perfecting the fine art of conspiracies and atrocities " of which Thucydides writes in his account of the seduction in Corcyra.'—H. A. L. Fisher, *A History of Europe* (1936), p. 49. On Greek race-suicide see M. Rostovtzeff, *Social and Economic History of the Hellenistic World* (1941), II, p. 622 and p. 941. See also J. Kastein, *History and Destiny of the Jews* (1933), p. 89, quoting approvingly Nietzsche's description of the Greeks as ' the political fools of ancient history.'

[17] Quoted in C. H. Harris, *op. cit.*, p. 348. See also R. W. Livingstone, *The Greek Genius and its meaning to Us* (1924), p. 25: ' Even with men like Socrates and Plato it may be questioned how far moral striving was the centre of their soul.'

[18] See Plato *Symposium*, 216ff, Loeb Classical Library Edition (1925), trs. W. R. M. Lamb, pp. 223ff.

[19] See W. E. H. Lecky, *op. cit.*, Vol. II, p. 294, n. 2. Cf. also the nauseating statement of Socrates at a banquet concerning Charmides: ' Ah, my noble friend, I saw inside his cloak and caught fire, and could possess myself no longer; and I thought none so wise in love matters as Cydias, who in speaking of a beautiful boy recommends someone " to beware of coming as a fawn before a lion, and being seized as his portion of flesh "; for I too felt that I had fallen a prey to some such creature.'—Plato's *Charmides*, 155, Loeb Classical Library Edition (1927), trs. W. R. M. Lamb, p. 17. Socrates was also, as we are told by Xenophon, in his *Memorabilia of Socrates*, III, 11, more than an acquaintance of the courtesan, named Theodota, whom he saw first as she was posing in the nude for her portrait. After thanking her for having revealed her beauty, Socrates proceeded to give her some shrewd advice as to how to excite an appetite in her lovers and prevent it from becoming cloyed.

[20] Maimonides *Yad ha-Hazakah, Hilekot Melakim*, VIII, 11. כל המקבל שבע מצוות ונזהר לעשותן הרי זה מחסידי אומות העולם ויש לו חלק לעולם הבא. והוא שיקבל אותן ויעשה אותן מפני שצוה בהן הקב״ה בתורה... אבל אם עשאן מפני הכרע הדעת... אינו מחסידי אומות עולם אלא מחכמיהם. This is in accordance with the reading of Rabbi Moses Alashkar (1466-1542), *Responsa*, 117, which is generally accepted as a correct one, and which receives support from the *Mishnat Rabbi Eliezer* (ed. Enelow), p. 121. Our printed editions read, ' He is neither of the *Hasidim*, nor of the *Hakamim*.' ואינו מחסידי אומות העולם ולא מחכמיהם On the seven commandments of the Sons of Noah, see *infra*, p. 244.

[21] Viscount Samuel, *Belief and Action* (Pelican ed. 1939), pp. 107ff.

[22] *Op. cit.*, p. 121.

[23] E. S. Waterhouse, *op. cit.*, p. 423.

[24] C. E. M. Joad, *Decadence* (1948), pp. 42-3, quotes an interesting passage from Plato describing how a community which had once conducted its life on the basis of moral principles will continue to observe and maintain a minimum standard of moral behaviour, even

when the principles it was originally based on had been abandoned, so long as times are quiet and life is easy. But when the winds have changed, and the storms of adversity begin to blow, then the moral structure, lacking any foundation in moral principles, collapses.

[25] L. Mumford, *The Condition of Man* (1944), p. 337.

[26] A. Koestler, *The Yogi and the Commissar* (1945), pp. 194-5.

[27] This issue was emphasised by the late President Roosevelt in his message to the world shortly after America's entry into the second World War: ' We are inspired by a faith which goes back through all the years to the first chapter of the Book of Genesis: " God created man in his own image." We on our side are striving to be true to that divine heritage. We are fighting, as our fathers have fought, to uphold the doctrine that all men are equal in the sight of God. Those on the other side are striving to destroy this deep belief and to create a world in their own image—a world of tyranny, and cruelty and serfdom. That is the conflict that day and night now pervades our lives. No compromise can end that conflict. There never has been—there never can be—successful compromise between good and evil.'

CHAPTER III

THE PERSONAL NEED FOR RELIGION

THE support which religion lends to morality has its counterpart in the benefits it bestows on what may be called the personal life of the individual.

We read in the First Book of Kings, chapter xi, the vivid and impressive story of the young Edomite prince, Hadad, who fled his native country to escape the wrath of Joab, David's captain, who had vowed to kill every male person in Edom. Hadad reached Egypt in safety, was received by Pharaoh with favour, and finally married a sister of Pharaoh's queen, who bore him a son. Years went by, Hadad prospered and lived in plenty and in luxury, but when he heard that both David and Joab had died, he came to Pharaoh and asked him leave to depart and return to his own country. 'Why?' Pharaoh asked him in surprise. 'What hast thou lacked in Egypt with me, that thou seekest thine own country?' 'Nothing,' replied Hadad: 'howbeit, send me away.' That 'howbeit' revealed the call of the true fatherland which swept away all arguments of expediency.

This story was not written as a parable, but it is aptly used by Rufus Jones[1] in illustration of the mysterious pull of the human soul towards a domain where we can feel truly at home, and where alone we can find the satisfaction of all needs of our inner life. These needs of our inner life are varied, but they can be reduced to three: the need of security, the need of companionship and the need of achievement.

45

For notes on this chapter, see pp. 59-61.

We all need security. In this seemingly friendless universe where a bit of rock falling from a senseless cliff can cut off the creative genius of a Shakespeare, silence the music of the heart of a Beethoven, put out the light of the eyes of a Turner, with an indifference that is appalling, man feels the need of a security that is always final and absolute.

' What about a man who is run over by a tram-car?' is a question which André Malraux asked at a Communist Writers' Congress after hours of speeches about the brave new world in construction. This question was met with blank stares, and Malraux did not insist. ' But there is a voice within us which does insist . . . To be killed on a barricade or to die a martyr of science, provides some compensation, but what about a man who is run over by a tram-car? or the child who is drowned?' The answer which Malraux received after a long painful silence, was that ' in a perfect social transport-system there will be no accidents.'² This witty retort may have served a purpose in breaking the tension aroused by his question of questions, but surely it was no answer to this quest for security which is insistent in the heart of us all!

Related to the need of security is the need of companionship. Despite his human relations, man leads in his innermost self a very lonely existence. ' In all chief matters of life ', wrote the French poet Amiel in his *Journal*, ' we are alone: we dream alone; we suffer alone; we die alone.'³ ' We are all islands,' says George Eliot, in one of her letters, ' each in his hidden sphere of joy or woe, our hermit spirits dwell and roam apart. In all the deepest aspects of our life we are lonely

46

beings with desires and hopes and pain and raptures which we cannot tell and cannot share.'³   The human heart cries out for a companion who is always adequate, as it does for security.   In the words of the Psalmist ' I look at my right hand, and see, for there is no man that knoweth me; refuge faileth me, no man careth for my soul ' (Psalm cxlii. 5).

We also have the need of achievement and fulfilment. Achievement in some form or other is a goal to every normal person.   The desire to create something, to get something done, to be a success at something, is a desire which we all find unmistakably present in ourselves, when we are in good health.   We want to do something worth doing; something lasting and abiding; something which should give meaning and purpose to our existence; and the prayer offered by the Jew daily in the words, ' That we may not labour in vain, nor bring forth to confusion,'³ᵃ is but an expression of one of the most persistent needs of our human life.   Yet what mortal can truthfully claim to have this need satisfied ?   ' I suppose,' wrote G. J. Romanes, one of the greatest representatives of the Darwinian tradition, in his book *Thoughts on Religion*, ' the most exalted and least " carnal " of worldly joys consists in the adequate recognition by the world of higher achievements by ourselves.   Yet it is notorious that,

" It is by God decreed,
Fame shall not satisfy the highest need ".

' It has been my lot,' he continues, ' to know not a few famous men of our generation and I have always observed that this is profoundly true.   Like all other

" moral " satisfactions, this soon palls by custom, and as soon as one end for distinction is reached, another is pined for; there is no finality to rest in, while disease and death are always standing in the background. Custom may even blind men to their own misery, so far as not to make them realise what is wanting; yet the want is there.'[4]

Security, companionship, and achievement—it is with the baffling pursuit of these that religion has to do. Where all human resources fail, it comes to our rescue; when they have done their utmost, its work begins.

How does religion meet these deepest and most imperious of our needs ? One answer may be found in Schleiermacher's definition of religion as a ' feeling of dependence ' (*Abhängigkeitgefühl*). ' Piety ' (*Frömmigkeit*) . . ., he writes in *Der christliche Glaube* ('The Christian Faith '), ' is, considered purely in itself, neither a Knowing nor a Doing, but a modification of Feeling, or of immediate self-consciousness.'[5] ' The common element in all howsoever diverse expressions of piety, by which these are conjointly distinguished from all other feelings . . . is this: the consciousness of being absolutely dependent (*schlechthin abhängig*), or, which is the same thing, of being in relation with God.'[6]

Schleiermacher's definition of religion is more or less adequate. It will be noted that Schleiermacher speaks of religious dependence as being of an *absolute* character. This is evidently in order to distinguish between the feeling of religious dependence and purely natural feelings of dependence, which may arise in other connections as determined by circumstances and environment, such as the dependence of a child on the father and the servant on his master. Whereas elsewhere the dependence is purely of a relative character, in religion the dependence is absolute. Rudolf Otto, however, in his book *The Idea of the Holy*[7] points out that this distinction makes the difference between the feeling of religious dependence and other feelings of dependence merely one of degree, whereas it is actually a difference of intrinsic quality. Schleiermacher in Otto's view, in designating religion a ' feeling of dependence,' has failed to indicate that there is a distinctive type of feeling which is unique to religion. Otto cites as an example of the feeling of dependence as exhibited in religion the words of Abraham, when he pleaded with God for the men of Sodom, ' Behold, now I have taken upon me to speak unto the Lord which am but dust and ashes ' (Genesis xviii. 27). ' There,' he says, ' you have a self-confessed feeling of dependence which is yet far more than, and something other than, merely a feeling of dependence.' He proposes to rename it ' creature-consciousness ' or ' creature-feeling ' (*Kreaturgefühl*). ' It is the emotion of a creature submerged and overwhelmed by its own nothingness in contrast to that which is supreme above all creatures.'[8]

This definition is more satisfactory than Schleiermacher's and we shall have something to say about it on a later occasion.[9] Here we will only point out further that the idea of ' creature-feeling ' has long ago been singled out by the Sages of Israel as an essential element of the religious consciousness. In verse 2 in Psalm c,

49

' Know that He is the Lord, He is our God, and we are His ' (which the Jew recites with few exceptions every weekday) the word rendered ' and His ' is spelt with an *alef*, which makes it to mean ' and not '; and the Midrash, adopting the spelling, translates in the name of Rabbi Judah ben Simon: ' Know that the Lord is our God: He made us and not we ourselves.'[10] This idea of ' creature-consciousness ' gains a fuller expression in Psalm cxxxix., ' For Thou hast formed my reins. Thou hast knit me together in my mother's womb . . . my frame was not hidden from thee when I was made in secret ' (verses 13-15).

The conception of God as our Maker has a tremendous implication for our personal life. As God's special creature, man has his very being grounded in God, and the whole marvel of what he is goes back to God, and is laid bare before his Creator. ' O Lord, Thou hast searched me and known me . . . Thou understandest my thoughts from afar ' (Psalm cxxxix. 1-2). And through this all-searching knowledge, God enters with power into man's life, physical and moral, determining under every variation of condition and circumstances his fate and destiny. ' Thou hast set me behind and before, and laid Thine hand upon me ' (*ibid.* 5). Moreover, as His handiwork, every individual is God's concern, and He will not forsake the work of His own hands. All that is best in the life of man is His. It is He who made us, and not we ourselves, and He will surely not give man up before His work with man is finished. ' The Lord will perfect that which concerneth me. Thy mercy, O Lord, endureth for ever. Forsake not the work of Thy hand ' (Psalm cxxxviii. 8).

Religion thus understood can indeed satisfy the deepest longings of the heart. It meets first the need for companionship. ' For all those who somehow had a God ', wrote Nietzsche, ' what I know as solitude did not exist '. Religion, indeed, gives the feeling that man is not alone, in this seemingly friendless universe. When to all appearances all human resources fail, there is ever God's close inward presence to sustain and guide man in his isolation and loneliness. ' Whither shall I go from Thy spirit ? Or whither shall I flee from Thy presence ? If I ascend up into Heaven, Thou art there; If I make my bed in the netherworld, behold, Thou art there. If I take the wings of the morning, and dwell in the uttermost parts of the sea; even there would Thy hand lead me, and Thy right hand would hold me ' (Psalm cxxxix. 7-10).

Man is thus no longer a mere unit in the crowd, a mere speck in the ocean of existence, left to swim, to drift, to sink and die, but a precious object, under the special care of an Eternal Friend, Who alone survives the wreck of time and change, and to Whom man can turn when he feels he has no place whither to flee, and no man caring for his soul.

Besides giving man more than human companionship, religion gives him also a sense of security. It saves us, and all that matters most in our existence, not only from spiritual isolation, but also from transience and decay. This is what is meant when religion is spoken of by Höffding as the ' conservation of values.'[10a] In the heart of all those who steadfastly seek after the highest good, there has grown up the assurance that the power who made them will not play false by destroying them and all they have toiled for and striven to attain, but will rather see that nothing in them and of them that is worthy to survive shall ever be lost.

Religion also meets the human need of achievement. In every country and in every clime, men of every race and every tongue have felt that man can have no assurance that his striving after the good, the true and the beautiful in life is not in vain, unless there be one to guarantee its fulfilment. The sense of the presence of such a guarantor, the sense of the interest and care he takes in all we value and all we love, the promise of his eternal guardianship of the interests we hold most dear—that makes all the difference to us in the world. It makes for fulfilment and achievement. This is what religion does for man: ' Faithful is thy Employer to pay thee the reward for thy labour '[11]—such is the message of religion as announced by Judaism. There you have an assurance which enables us to pass over from the world of striving to the world of achievement, and to break through the narrow confines of our finiteness into the wider regions of self-determination and self-realisation.

This is the final answer of religion, through all the misgivings which the transitory character of life, and the changes and chances of existence, may give rise to in the human heart. Man is the handiwork of God, and as his Creator, Companion and Guarantor, God will keep that which man has committed to Him. ' They shall not labour in vain, nor bring forth for confusion, for they are the seed blessed of the Lord '' (Isaiah lxv. 23).

All this may appear too obvious to have required

elaboration, nor, it is to be confessed, would so much space have been devoted to the subject, but for the common tendency to assess the value of religion principally from the contribution it makes to the preservation and development of social values; whereas, if we consider the matter more closely, we shall find that what constitutes the secret of religion's overwhelming hold over the heart of man is the personal experience it involves. 'The pivot round which religion revolves, as William James remarked, is the interest of the individual in his private destiny.'[12] The same insight into the significance of religion as independent of any social implications is expressed in Professor Whitehead's definition of religion as, 'what the individual does with his own solitariness'.[13] The religion of every religious man belongs to him, not merely as a participator in an activity shared with others. It belongs to him first and foremost as an individual, with all his bodily senses, his emotions, his interests, his affections. Religion, writes Rufus Jones, in his *Testimony of the Soul*, is first, last and always bound to be an individual person's experience or appreciation or attitude. 'We are dealing with "a grin without a face" until religion *personalises* into the concrete. We cannot talk of beauty in the collective life of mankind, for whenever beauty is actually felt, it is felt by somebody in particular. No crowding of heads together ever fuses experiences into a composite experience, which exists over and above the persons who own the heads. There is no known contrivance by which we can get away from "inner experience." To the end of time, so long as we remain persons, religion will begin as an inner experience in somebody's soul. It will not be the operation of an entity called a "group-mind". We are, of course, powerfully affected by our relations to a group, and there is no such existing reality as "an isolated individual", but the moment we ask for the origin and basis of conscious experience, we are invariably sent to a concrete mind, which is *somebody's mind*, and what he experiences will be an "inner experience" within himself.'[14] All this does not mean that social values can be eliminated without emptying religion of its content, but it does signify that what gives religion its power of enriching the value of human personality in the social order is the personal element which is central to religious consciousness.

This personal experience which religion involves has its source according to Judaism, as has already been said before, in the relationship between individual and God. It is this close relationship between man and God, his Creator—which religion, with varying force and clearness, has ever sought to affirm—which imparts to religion its dynamic force as an instrument of moral training and culture. This awareness of the relation between man and God is of tremendous consequence for the personal life of the individual. When the whole of man's life and action is dominated by the sense of this divine relationship, happiness is achieved. This happiness is not merely expressive of an action or an emotion. It is an essential quality of the soul, a spiritual endowment which enriches the whole content of life, transforming human character, personality and existence. It inspires the most sublime faith and trust in God that burns undimmed at all times in adversity and

in prosperity. In the words of the *Sefer ha-Yashar*:
'The deeply pious men . . . who perform the will of
God . . . and endeavour to walk in His ways . . .
rejoice in their lot . . . In their heart there is no
grief, sorrow, unhappiness or distress . . . for they
trust in their Maker. Misfortune does not terrify
them, nor do alarms agitate them. When great trouble
comes upon them, or a day of wrath or anger, they do
not murmur against God, but on the contrary vindicate
His judgment upon them.'[15] Similarly William James,
in an essay on *The Gospel of Relaxation*, writes, ' The
really religious person is unshakable and full of
equanimity and calmly ready for anything that the day
may bring forth.'[16] And it spells a joy and gladness of
heart, body and mind, compared with which material
blessings count for nothing. ' Thou hast put gladness
into my heart more than they have when their wine
and corn are increased ' (Psalm iv. 3). Nay, it carries
with it the triumphant assurance of divine salvation
even in the darkest periods of an all-enveloping and
ever-deepening gloom, without a gleam of light or ray
of hope. ' Yea, though I walk through the valley of the
shadow of death, I fear no evil, for Thou art with
me ' (Psalm xxiii. 4).

This testimony of the Psalms has been enforced by
the witness of countless men and women in all ages
and climes. You may call it an illusion, but you
must give some kind of coherent and rational explanation of the fact that the illusion is there. Stoics, we
know, declared that suffering is an illusion which can
be overcome by will-power, and, as a consequence,
Stoics advocated indifference, even to social suffer-

ing.[17] This consistency is understandable. But how explain an attitude such as that which characterises the religious person and as exemplified in the Psalms, which, while refusing to ignore the existence of evil where others are concerned, and while stirred to battle manfully with the social ills of life, at the same time experiences amid all his personal sufferings a joy and serenity and peace that pass all understanding. Here you have a man, as in Psalm xci, who is beset by dangers and evil men, whose existence he does not ignore nor wish away; but at the same time declares that because his soul has set its hope on God, he will be delivered from all evil and can tread securely on the lion and the adder. God's angels will bear their charge upon their hands lest the man strike his foot against a stone. The Psalmist who wrote this knew all this to be at variance with experience. He knew that the lion before it springs and the adder before it strikes did not stop to consider whether their prey fears God or not. Yet set among the many hazards of the world and conscious, too, of his impotence to overcome them, the Psalmist feels secure, because he could reach up to Him who is over all and commit himself to the care of God.[18] How explain it ? It is a secret which is known to none but the religious in every generation. But sufficient is their claim to justify the validity of their testimony, even as the testimony regarding the beauties of nature given by those who can see is accepted by the blind; and if, for any cause, this evidence ever ceased to be available to the generality of mankind, religion would cease to be a force in human life, and retain its interest only for the antiquarian, philospher and historian.

Or again, how explain the attitude of the martyr who goes to meet death for his faith, with joy in his heart and song on his lips ? Well known is the story of Rabbi Akiba's martyrdom in the year 135 C.E. under the Hadrianic persecutions. The Romans tortured him to death by tearing his flesh from his living body with iron combs. As he lay in unspeakable agony, he suddenly noticed the first streaks of dawn flushing the eastern skies. This was the beginning of the time prescribed for the morning recital of the Jew's declaration of faith—the *Shema*. Oblivious of his pain, Rabbi Akiba proclaimed in a loud and steady voice—' Hear, O Israel, the Lord our God, the Lord is One. And thou shalt love the Lord thy God with all thine heart, and with all thy soul, and with all thy might.' Tineius Rufus, the Roman general, who supervised the horrible execution, cried out, ' Are you a sorcerer, insensible to suffering ? ' ' I am no sorcerer,' replied the martyr-Rabbi, ' but throughout my days I have been waiting for the opportunity when I might truly testify that I love God, not only with all my heart and all my might, but also with my very life itself. Should I not therefore rejoice that the opportunity has come ? ' And repeating the initial verse again, he expired as he reached the word ' One '.[19] How explain this ? It will not do to describe it as mere illusion or wish-fulfilment. It is absurd to say that Rabbi Akiba's state of mind was the outcome of wishful thinking; a wishful thinking that impels man to do what, by natural standards, he should have far from wished to do is self-contradictory. Perhaps it will be said that the soldier in time of war is equally prepared to renounce all, even life itself, in

57

the service of the State. Yes, but war with its motto ' kill or be killed ' does, in the last analysis, satisfy man's native instinct for self-assertion, and it is in the satisfaction of that instinct that the soldier dies. There is all the difference in the world between the soldier charging an enemy in the teeth of machine-gun fire— but all the time driven on by the urge to kill, and to fulfil his native human instinct for the destruction of the enemy—and the martyr facing martyrdom with nothing to gratify his natural inclinations.

A living witness to this peculiar quality of the soul which religion engenders is the Jewish people. The Jews have been described as a ' stubbornly optimistic people.' No people has suffered more cruelly from ' man's inhumanity to man ' than have the Jews. They endured such trials as no other people have been called upon to bear, and yet far from despairing and giving way to pessimism, they rejoiced in their lot. In sorrow as in joy, in adversity as in prosperity, their heart responded to the refrain, ' Happy are we, how good is our portion, and how pleasant is our lot ! '[20] How utterly different was the attitude of the Greeks. With all their great capacity for happiness they were afraid of it, for they knew it could not last, and thus they could not escape a sense of frustration, which in turn infected all Greek thought.[21] The thing that saved the Jewish people was the firm and unquenchable faith in God, which they brought to life, and which enabled them not only to overcome persecutions and temptations greater than any that have confronted other peoples, but also to triumph over death itself. ' Though he slay me, yet I will trust in him ' (Job xiii. 15). That was the shining faith that burnt steadily in the heart of the Jew, illumining his path throughout his long and chequered history.

The unique value of religion in satisfying the vital needs of our personal life will thus have become evident. Without the vision of God we lose the sense of stability and security. Once the thought of God grows dim, life loses its eternal background and its final meaning. The springs of life itself are sapped, and with nothing really worth living for, man becomes cynical or neurotic, a fit subject for a psycho-analyst. 'Among all my patients over thirty-five years,' writes C. G. Jung in his *Modern Man in Search of a Soul*[22], 'there has not been one whose problem in the last resort was not that of finding a religious outlook on life. It is safe to say that everyone of them fell ill because he had lost that which the living religions of every age have given to their followers. And none of them has been really healed who did not regain his religious outlook.' This contribution of religion to personal life, though mainly a product of the Jewish religious genius, is now shared to a greater or lesser degree by all higher religions, which Judaism has inspired, or to which it gave birth, but the specific implications of this aspect of religion for Judaism will become clear as we proceed with the presentation of our subject.

NOTES

[1] See Rufus Jones, *The Testimony of the Soul* (1930), p. 120.

[2] See A. Koestler, *The Yogi and the Commissar* (1945), pp. 126ff.

[3] Quoted in the *Speaker's Bible*, *Psalms* IV, ed. by E. Hastings (1932), p. 191.

[3a] *A.P.B.*, p. 74.

[4] G. J. Romanes, *Thoughts on Religion*, ed. by Ch. Gore (1895), p. 151.

[5] F. Schleiermacher, *The Christian Faith*, parag. 3, E. T. by H. R. Mackintosh and J. S. Stewart, from the second German edition (1830).

[6] *Ibid.*, parag. 4. See also Schleiermacher's *Speeches on Religion*, E. T. by John Oman (1893), p. 106.

[7] Rudolf Otto, *The Idea of the Holy*, E.T. by J. W. Harvey from the ninth German edition, 1st ed. 1923, 3rd impr., with additions 1925, second ed. 1950 (German original: *Das Heilige*, 1st ed. 1917).

[8] *Op. cit.*, p. 10.

[9] See *infra*, pp. 104f.

[10] Midrash Genesis Rabbah, C.1. הוא עשנו ולא אנחנו בראנו את נפשינו.

[10a] H. Höffding, *The Philosophy of Religion*, E. T., B. E. Meyer (1906), p. 6.

[11] *Ethics of the Fathers*, ii, 17.

[12] William James, *Varieties of Religious Experiences* (1902), p. 491.

[13] A. N. Whitehead, *Religion in the Making* (1926), p. 16.

[14] Rufus Jones, *op. cit.*, p. 47.

[15] See *Sefer ha-Yashar*, iii; עושי ... דע כי חסידי מעלה העליונה רצון האל ... ומתאמצים ללכת בדרכיו ... הם השמחים בחלקם ... אין בלבם לא תוגה ולא יגון. ולא אד ולא עצבון ... כי הם יבטחו על עושיהם. ולא יחרידם בבוא התלאות, ולא יבהילם חרדת התשואות. בבוא עליהם תוקף צרה, או יום חרון ועברה לא יקצפו על דין אלהיהם רק יצדיקו דינו (עליהם). see also Bahya ibn Pakuda (*c.* 1050), *Hobot ha-Lebabot*, ix, 4.

[16] William James, *Gospel of Relaxation*, in *Talks for Teachers on Psychology* (1911), p. 224.

[17] See E. Bevan, *Stoics and Sceptics* (1913), pp. 66-7.

[18] See A. C. Welch, *The Psalter* (1926), pp. 110-11.

[19] See B.T. Berakot 61b and J.T. IX, 5. See also Finkelstein, *Akiba* (1936), pp. 276-7. According to S. Liebermann this method of execution was employed instead of the normal execution by the sword in order to prevent Rabbi Akiba from reciting the Shema which was prohibited by decree because it implied the negation of the worship of the Emperor. See *The Martyrs of Caesarea*, Annuaire de l'Institut de Philologie, VI (1939-44), p. 47, quoted by M. Kadushin, *The Rabbinic Mind* (1952), p. 131, note.

[20] See *A.P.B.*, p. 8.

[21] See S. H. Butcher, *Some Aspects of the Greek Genius* (3rd ed. 1904), p. 133-176.

[22] C. G. Jung, *Modern Man in Search of a Soul* (1936), p. 264.

CHAPTER IV

THE DISTINCTIVE CHARACTER OF JEWISH RELIGIOUS CONSCIOUSNESS

WE have seen in the two previous chapters that the religious consciousness embraces three elements—the knowledge of God, the love of Him, and moral purpose. These three elements are derived respectively from the three attitudes which the human mind, according to current classification, adopts in the pursuit of its objectives—the cognitive or intellectual, the emotional and the volitional. These three attitudes often overlap, but even in such cases one of them usually stands out as prominent, in accordance with the end pursued. In science, the cognitive is most pronounced, in aesthetics the emotional, and the volitional in morals.[1] In religion, however, all three attitudes have free play, as can be seen from the presence in it of the three elements we have mentioned. The knowledge of God points to the operation of the cognitive attitude, the love of Him to that of the emotional, and moral action to that of the volitional.

Before we go further, it may be well to point out that there are thinkers who assert that one or other of these attitudes is alone sufficient to constitute a religion and to satisfy the religious consciousness. For instance, there are many who are of the opinion that religion is to be reckoned among the products of intellectual life pure and simple. Its deepest intention, it is held, is to dispel the darkness that broods over man and his

62

universe and to furnish a working solution of the great insistent problems of existence. 'The object of religion as well as that of philosophy,' says Hegel, ' is eternal truth in its objectivity.'[2] Philosophy and religion indeed have their thoughts cast in different moulds and address different audiences; but they deal with the same subject matter. Among the religions which make intellectual knowledge their aim are Brahmanism and Buddhism. To Brahmanism and Buddhism knowledge is the essence of religion, and knowledge of divine things was elaborated by Buddhism into a system of religious philosophy.

On the other hand, the view has also been held that religion is essentially a matter of feeling, an affair of the heart, a state of the soul in which thought and will are in abeyance. The principal feelings that lie at the root of religion have been variously recognised as the feeling of fear, the feeling of dependence, the feeling of creatureness, and finally love. The most celebrated type of religion rooted in love is that of the mystics who cleave to God with a love passing the love of women, and whose love is crowned by union with the heavenly spouse in the bonds and the joys of spiritual marriage.

Finally, there is the view that religion is nothing else but moral action and that the attitude of mind by which it is approached is that of volition. The questions, such as the character of God and His relation to man and human destiny, are of no concern to religion. Religion, in fact, on this view is independent of intellectual propositions. What religion brings to man is ethical conduct and goodness, and this it can do without inculcating any belief in a good and omnipotent Creator, and in a personal God who is the ground of goodness.

This is the position characteristic of many of the intelligentsia of our days, who hold that questions of doctrine are matters of indifference to religion. Religion, it is maintained, is a certain attitude of the spirit, an emotional mood which is compatible with every sort of belief or unbelief. Faith in morality, in goodness, is the sole content of religion according to this school of thought, and in holding to this faith the exponents of this view consider themselves to be religious men. This is but one of the many and varied types of what may be comprised under the general term ' religion of humanity ', which includes among its most noted modern exponents the late Professor John Dewey of the Columbia University in America, and Julian Huxley in this country; and Mordecai Kaplan, of the New York Theological Seminary, in his work *Judaism as a Civilisation*[3] has given us a Jewish version of this type of religion.

The deficiencies of an ethical system not based on a belief in God have already been pointed out in a previous chapter, and nothing need be added for our purpose to what has been said.

Similarly, there is no doubt that the religion which concentrates on the intellectual attitude at the expense of the other attitudes cannot in the long run fulfil its true function. The serious defect of a religion which has purely an intellectual purpose is that the standard it sets is much too high and exclusive. Religion, after all, is not for philosophers only, but also for the common man; but the knowledge demanded by the intellectual type of religion presupposes no little intellectual labour, and no mean intellectual power, beyond the reach of the average man and woman. The result of this is seen in Brahmanism, which ceased to be bound up with any distinctive doctrine of God, and a Brahman, provided he obeys the customs of his people, can choose any doctrine he likes. He can be a Theist, or an Atheist, just as he fancies.

Nor is the religion which concentrates mainly on the emotional attitude in any better way. Undoubtedly, a religion that makes mystical experiences its principal content must also be exclusive and beyond the reach of the average man. But, apart from this consideration, the energy spent in achieving mystical experience cannot but encroach upon the claims of society. The love that fixes the affections on a divine object has no room for the love of fellow-man. This is illustrated by a number of incidents in the lives of the saints in the Orient of which the following (cited by W. P. Paterson, *The Nature of Religion*) is a typical example:

One day, Fudayl (a Sufi Saint) had in his lap a child four years old, and chanced to give it a kiss as is the way of fathers. The child said, ' Father, do you love me ? ' ' Yes,' said Fudayl. ' Do you love God ? ' 'Yes.' 'How many hearts have you?' 'One.' 'Then,' asked the child, ' how can you love two with one heart ? ' Fudayl perceived that the child's words were a divine admonition. In his zeal for God he began to beat his head and he repented of his love for the child and gave his heart wholly to God.[4]

But leaving aside these exalted mystic souls and

turning to ordinary mortals, we may say that religion of mere feeling can possess no moral quality. Pure feeling is non-moral, and so is religion from which the cognitive or intellectual element has been eliminated non-moral. What makes our love for a true friend, for example, such a noble thing is the recognition by our mind of the character of our friend. So it is with religion. What imparts to religion its peculiarly ennobling moral quality is the knowledge it communicates to us of the character of God and His goodness. Once, however, you empty religion of its intellectual content, you deprive it of the source from which it draws its original and positive moral force.

It is the glory of the Jewish religion that in it we have a balance unique in its kind of the three attitudes, intellect, feeling and the will being unified and blended therein into one singularly harmonious whole. This claim on behalf of Judaism has already been emphasised by Judah Halevi, the celebrated twelfth-century Jewish Poet-Philosopher in his *Kuzari*. His presentation of this thesis is the best we have on the subject, so that no apology is required for quoting here at some length some of the relevant passages.

This book, it might be mentioned, is written in the form of a dialogue between the King of the Khazars and a Rabbi, designated as *Haber*.

In reply to the question put to the *Haber* by his royal interlocutor, Alkhazari, as to the doings of the pious man among the Jews, the *Haber* is made to reply: ' The pious man (*Hasid*) is nothing but a prince who is obeyed by his senses and by his mental as well as physical faculties. . . . He subdues his passions, keeping them in bonds, but giving them their share in order to satisfy them as regards food, drink, cleanliness, etc. He further subdues the desire for power, except for the purpose of instruction and reproof . . . He allows the senses their share, according as he requires them for the use of his hands, feet and tongue, as necessity or desire arises. The same is the case with hearing, seeing . . . and imagination, conception, thought, memory, will-power which command all these senses, but are in turn subservient to the rule of the intellect. . . .'[5] And so Halevi proceeds to show in detail how Jewish religious life is so organised as to evoke that three-fold response of the intellect, emotion and will; and significantly enough he ascribes this unity of intellect, emotion and will not to the man in the street, but to the *Hasid*, the saint.

This statement, it is to be noted, is but in conformity with the supreme command of Judaism, to love God with all heart, soul and might (Deuteronomy, vi. 5). The heart, in Hebrew Scriptures is, as is known, considered the seat of the intellect, as the soul is expressive of emotion and feeling. The Hebrew phrase, *be-kol meodeka*, usually rendered, ' with all thy might ' is taken by the Sages of the Talmud to mean ' with all thy money,' ' thy wealth '[6]—money and wealth spent in service to fellowmen. Thus, in this command, the Jew is enjoined to unify in his religious life and conduct the dictates of the intellect with the impulse of the emotions and the driving force of the will. These three aspects of human personality, made one in the service of God, correspond in turn with the three great principles on which, according to Jewish teaching,[7] the world is founded: Torah (study), *Abodah* (divine worship), and *Gemiluth Hasadim*, practice of goodly deeds—service to fellow-man. Whilst Torah involves an activity of intellect, *Abodah* is the expression of our emotions, and *Gemiluth Hasadim* a product of the will.

It is significant that these three attitudes of mind are subsumed in this command under the Law of Love: ' And thou shalt love the Lord thy God with all thy heart—the intellect—with all thy soul—the emotions— and with all thy wealth—the will.' The love of God which is enjoined upon a Jew is thus not an affective love—a love, the content and aim of which are exhausted and fulfilled by the very experience and emotion of the lover. It is a love in which all powers of common life come into play and enter into full action. In other words, the command to love God is not an appeal to the senses, nor does such love denote union to God through the emptying of the mind of all thought, like that which is pictured by the mystics.[8] The love of God is an active love. Here the centre of gravity is placed in the action of man. Man loves God best when he acts best. The love of God must be rooted in knowledge, and gains its full ripeness in action. In every case, in the Bible, the command to love God is followed by the injunction to observe His laws, and to seek His righteousness in a life of service and loyal devotion to duty.[9]

This active love, which constitutes the love of God in Judaism, distinguishes it from the love of non-Jewish mystics with whom love is purely feeling, to the exclusion of all other activities of the mind.[10] The spiritual love of the mystics, as described particularly

68

by Christian mystics, is a romance with all the familiar features of earthly marriage between a man and a woman.

The surrender of the soul to the source of all love has frequently been represented by Christian mystics under the symbolism of human love and marriage. James H. Leuba in dealing with Christian mystics and the expressions used by them, says: ' Whoever has read the mystics must have been struck and perhaps scandalised by the erotic character of their language and their images. . . . The communion of God with man is, by the mystics, put entirely in terms of profane love. The terms " lover " and " spouse " designate by turn Jesus and sometimes God, who is often confused with His son. The virgin is the " incomparable love," " the daughter of delight," " the unique dove." In the course of one page Ruysbrock [the Dutch mystic (1293-1381)], accumulates the following terms: " amorous embracements," " bonds of love," " ecstatic beatitude," " amorous immersion." '[11]

The great illustration is the experience of St. Theresa, who has given an extremely minute and vivid account of her mystical experiences. In the spiritual castle, she distinguishes seven mansions of the soul. The sixth is described as the place of complete union and ecstasies, accompanied by the vision of the humanity of Christ, the pangs of desire, and the wounds of love. Thence the soul passes to the highest mansion in which the heavenly marriage is celebrated.[12]

These extravagant and erotical features, so charac-teristic of Christian mysticism, are alien to Jewish mystic thought. While it is true that the tender rela-

69

tions between God and Israel have, from the earliest days of the Prophets onwards, particularly in the Song of Songs, been described and celebrated in the affectionate terms of bride and bridegroom, no prophet was so presumptuous as to describe the relations between himself and God in the marital terms of husband and wife, or to call his individual soul by the name of the wooer or the bride of God. The love of the Old Testament saint had an element of filial affection, as is illustrated in the words of the Psalmist, ' He will call me, thou art my Father, my God and Rock of my salvation, and also I will set him as first-born ' (Psalm lxxxix. 27). Similarly, in mediaeval Jewish mystical literature, the relation between the individual soul and God finds its most tender accents in those of a daughter to her Father—the soul is the daughter of God[13]—very rarely in those of a beloved to her lover. But as the essence of filial piety is honour and obedience and duty, the sense of divine sonship carries with it more of reverence and obedience and duty than of emotional tenderness and self-intoxication with love.

Thus it is that Judah Halevi, as we have seen, was able to choose as representative type of the Jew who secures the full harmony and co-operation of intellect, emotion and feeling, the *Hasid*, whose sensitive soul is capable of entering upon a mystical experience achieved by attaching himself to what Halevi calls the ' Divine Thing ' (*ha-inyan ha-Elohi*),[14] which is central to his system and interpretation of the contribution which Judaism has made to religious thought.

It is thanks to this unity of intellect, emotion and

will, so fundamental to the Jewish religion, that Jewish mystics throughout the ages were essentially practical men and men of the world. While they could approach more or less closely the fascinated and inebriated love of non-Jewish mystics, they never set great store on the ecstatic tumult of the soul, nor did they seek mystical experience as an end in itself. It was always related to the needs of humanity. The all-absorbing passion of the Jewish mystics was not the salvation of self, but the Messianic redemption of mankind through the establishment of the Kingdom of God on earth—*Tikkun Olam be-Malkut Shaddai*. Thus it was from the Jewish mystics that emanated the first mighty impulses that gave rise to the Jewish National Movement, culminating in the rise of the State of Israel in our own days. One need only read the works of Rabbi J. L. Maimon (Fishman) and of his son-in-law, Isaac Rafael (Werfel), and Israel Halperin,[15] to realise what an important and vital part was played by the mystics of the Luria School in the sixteenth century, and later in the eighteenth century by the mystics of the school of Besht, in the establishment and growth of the *Yishub*. And so, throughout the ages, Jewish mystics were essentially practical men of the world, men of action. While it is true that these saintly men followed a certain monastic type of conduct, yet they were normal, hard-headed, shrewd men of affairs. Unlike the dismal and neurotic babblers and fantasy-ridden ranters of the mediaeval and later Church monasticism, the Jewish mystics were logical expounders of Jewish religion and ethics, in whose personality intellect, emotion and will formed a har-

monious symphony dedicated to the loving service of
God and man.

This practical significance of the love of God in
Judaism, and the conduct it inspires, determine the
place assigned to faith in the religious life of the Jews.
While Judaism is based on certain definite doctrines
which give it significance and value, it attaches no
importance to beliefs as beliefs. Faith was never
regarded by Judaism as something meritorious in
itself. Faith is considered of value only in so far as it
leads to right action. In Judaism all beliefs are submitted to the practical test: Do they serve as a means
of fostering righteous conduct and moral life ? This
accounts for the comparative absence in Judaism of a
systematisation of doctrine, such as is to be found in
other religions. Whilst insisting on the acceptance of
certain doctrines which supply it with its real positive
and inspiring force, Judaism refuses to ascribe to faith
in itself any particular mystical power, assuring man
of divine grace, as does Christianity. Faith in God is
indeed meaningless unless translated into righteous
action. To profess belief in God and act as if He did
not exist is considered by Judaism to be of no value
whatsoever. Readers may still recall the criticism
aroused by Mr. de Valera's condolences to the German
Government on the death of Hitler. In his defence, a
correspondent in *The Catholic Herald* wrote: ' Not only
was Mr. de Valera logically and technically correct, but
as head of a Christian State he behaved in a perfectly
Christian—one might say Christ-like—way.' ' He is
not likely,' he continued, ' to be deterred by the thought
of what millions of muddle-headed morons might

think of his action.' Then follow the significant words:
' Hitler was a very wicked and misguided man, but he
was not anti-Christ.'[16]   This means that having had
faith in the Christian sense, whatever his depravity,
Hitler is a saved man and must not be condemned.
This is an attitude totally inadmissible in Judaism. On
the contrary, from the Jewish standpoint, to know God
and act in rebellion to His will is worse than to deny
His existence altogether. Nimrod, who, in the Bible,
is described as a mighty hunter before the Lord
(Genesis x. 9), is regarded by the Rabbis of the Talmud
as representing the type of the brazenly wicked man,
who knows his Master, and yet of set purpose rebels
against Him.[17]

By relating faith to action, Judaism has been able to
maintain and develop its unique way of life in which
religion is not, as elsewhere, limited to a particular
sphere of human activity, but is the synthesis of all.
It is this integration of the religious and secular which
forms, as Macmurray has shown, the distinctive
characteristic of the Hebrew religious consciousness,
and which has made Jewish culture *integral* in a sense
in which no other can claim to be.[18]

But this is not all. During the first World War,
when Christian nations were slaughtering one another,
there arose a general outcry that Christianity had
failed. G. K. Chesterton, a master of epigram, thereupon came out with his famous rejoinder, ' No,
Christianity has not failed, it has never been tried.'
This rejoinder has now become stock-in-trade with
all apologists for Christianity, when confronted by the
challenge—how it is that 2,000 years of Christian

THE FAITH OF JUDAISM

teaching have not been able to eradicate from Christian peoples those bestial instincts of murder and hate that have laid waste the world twice within a generation ? Whilst the saying ' Christianity has not been tried' may be witty as a rejoinder, the obvious question which will occur to anyone who reflects further on the matter is, why has it not been tried ? How is it that Christianity with all its rich resources—moral, spiritual and material—has been able so little to impress itself upon its adherents as to make them at least try it out and live in amity according to its gospel of love ? If it has not been tried would not the reason lie somehow within Christianity itself ?[19] The fact is that Christianity, with all the excellencies of its ethical code, has failed to provide a solution to the most difficult problem which has perplexed moralists of all ages: how to make human impulses keep pace with the finest products of ethical teaching ? This is a problem with which all moral and religious systems, including Christianity, have sought to grapple, but in vain. The only religion which has shown how this can be solved is the Jewish religion. The Torah, with its system of religious observances, to which Christianity opposes, with a sense of ' superiority ', the Pauline conception of Faith, is the only machinery ever devised to fortify man against the onrush of anti-moral and anti-social impulses that would sweep away the mud-embankment of all his best intentions, whilst at the same time training him to a good and righteous life.[19a]

Thanks, too, to the Torah the Jewish people, notwithstanding its thousands of years of persecution and unparalleled martyrdom, has not ceased to strive to be true to ethical and religious ideals—even on behalf of its very tormentors. Even those Jews who have broken away from the religious bond that has held the Jewish people together for millenia have not been able to escape altogether the humanising and elevating influence of the Torah, deeply engrained in their consciousness by a religious loyalty of hundreds of generations. To-day, as ever, the Jew—even the non-religious—is distinguished for his benevolence, his compassion, his strong family affections, his hatred of violence, his aversion to cruelty, even to animals, such as that which is associated with hunting for sport. ' When a Jew says,' remarked Walter Rathenau to Albert Einstein, ' that he is going hunting to amuse himself, he lies.'[20] It is true that some Jews have in recent years resorted to violence, but other nations did not have to wait for 6,000,000 of their kith and kin to be massacred and slaughtered in order to be driven, in desperation, to robbery, murder and plunder. ' Our fathers ', wrote Josephus, the Jewish historian, about two thousand years ago, ' did not betake themselves, as did some others, to robbery; nor did they, in order to gain more wealth, fall into foreign wars, although our country contained many ten thousands of men of courage for this purpose.'[21]

And what is true of the Jew in the remote past has been true of the Jew throughout the intervening centuries to the present day. To-day, as ever, the Jew is passionately attached to the ideals of social justice, and continues to dream of the coming of a kingdom of righteousness, with the rule of the good and true on earth. With this devotion to these ideals, he combines

75

an indomitable faith in their final triumph. It is this incurable optimism of the Jew, which is rooted in his religious heritage, that has endowed him with a peculiar vitality and toughness of fibre, enabling him to survive where others would have long since perished. The attitude of the Jew to the evils that beset his existence is that of the front-line soldier, who is fully conscious of the dangers of the battle, but is sustained by the righteousness of the cause for which he is fighting, and by the full realisation of his own responsibility to contribute to ultimate victory. For the Jews, to live is a collective duty imposed upon them by God, within the framework of the great unceasing struggle of the good with the evil, for the establishment of His Kingdom. To this duty, Israel has through an unbroken procession of centuries dedicated titanic energies; and it is in fulfilment of this duty that the Jewish people will continue the struggle, with a loyalty that is undying, and a determination that is unbending, ever sustained by the unquenchable and all-triumphant faith and conviction that, after all, ' the Kingdom belongs to the Eternal God ' (Psalm, xxii. 29).

NOTES

[1] Whilst this classification is generally speaking correct, it must not be overlooked that no pursuit of science is possible without great discipline and application, whilst much emotional satisfaction can be derived from scientific discovery. Similarly, art must not be so devoid of the intellectual as to offend reality; nor can any action be considered truly moral if it is performed without sympathy and understanding. See Cyril H. Valentine, *What we mean by God?* (1929), pp. 51ff. Cf. also B.T. Sotah, 21b, for description of a

' foolish saint ': ' For example, a woman is drowning in the river, and he says, " It is improper for me to look upon her and rescue her ".'

[2] G. W. F. Hegel, *Philosophy of Religion* (E.T. by E. B. Speirs, 1895), I, p. 19.

[3] See M. Kaplan, *Judaism as a Civilisation* (1934). The rise of ' religion of humanity ' is associated with the name of Auguste Comte (1798-1857), and its essential view is the entire elimination of the supernatural from religion. This attitude is fundamental to all pragmatism and humanism of the nineteenth and twentieth centuries, in whatever form they may appear. This too is the trend of Kaplan's *Judaism as a Civilisation*, and as such his conception of Judaism must be regarded as a travesty of the Jewish religion.

[4] Cited by W. P. Paterson, *The Nature of Religion* (2nd ed. 1928), p. 298, a work on which I have largely drawn in these pages.

[5] See *Kuzari*, III, 2.

[6] See Mishna, Berakot, IX, 9.

[7] See *Ethics of the Fathers*, I, 2.

[8] The idea of union with God, which is basic to the mystery religions, is totally alien to Judaism, where the distinction between the creature and the Creator is never lost. Man, in the view of Judaism, can never become God, but ever more man in the image of God. See A. Schweitzer, *The Mysticism of Paul the Apostle* (E.T., W. Montgomery [1931]), p. 37.

[9] See Sifre on Deuteronomy, vi. 5: ' Because it says, " Thou shalt love [God] ", and I do not know how to love [Him], therefore it teaches " And these words shall be upon thy heart " [as if to say], set these words upon thy heart and thereby you will recognise Him who said and the world came into being, and cleave in His ways.'

לפי שהוא אומר ואהבת את ד׳ אלקיך בכל לבבך איני יודע באיזה צד אוהבים את הקב״ה ת״ל והיו הדברים האלה וכו׳ תן הדברים האלה על לבבך שמתוך כך אתה מכיר את הקב״ה ומדבק בדרכיו. ' "And thou shalt love the Lord thy God "—[that is] make Him beloved of human creatures as did thy father Abraham.' ואהבת את ד׳ אלקיך — אהבהו על הבריות כאברהם אביך.

[10] Bahya ben Asher ben Halawa (d. 1340) in his Commentary on the Pentateuch, Deuteronomy vi. 5, explains that the reason why

77

the Torah uses in connection with the command to love God, the term ואהבת instead of וחשקת, which is expressive of greater intensity of devotion, is because the latter is all-exclusive in its connotation, and would not allow room for any other love beside the love of God.

[11] Quoted by M. H. Farbridge, *Life—A Symbol* (1931), pp. 240ff.

[12] W. P. Paterson, *op. cit.*, p. 294.

[13] See *Zohar*, on Exodus xxi. 9. See also G. Scholem, *Major Trends in Jewish Mysticism* (ed. 1946), pp. 226ff. and 403. See also S. A. Horodezky, *Torat ha-Kabbalah shel R. Moshe Cordovero* (1924), p. 201. הנשמות בנים למקום ('The souls are the children of the Omnipresent.')

[14] See *infra*, p. 140.

[15] See Isaac Werfel, *ha-Hasidut we-Eretz Yisrael* (1940) and Israel Halperin *ha-Aliyot ha-Rishonot shel ha-Hasidim* (1946).

[16] See *Catholic Herald*, June 1, 1945. The view expressed by this correspondent, and allowed to pass without editorial comment, is but the product of Paul's attitude in opposing belief in God through Christ, which he calls ' Faith ', to obedience to the Law, which he calls ' Works.' This opposition, as has been shown, gave rise to the antinomian antithesis, expressed in the following tabular form:

| The Jewish faith produces obedience to God. | The Christian faith emancipates men from all restraints and requirements. |

That is to say, that whilst the Jew who believes must live in accordance with God's revealed will, the Christian, so long as he has faith in the risen Christ, is at liberty to indulge in all licence with impunity. Orthodox theologians have been at pains to prove that such a conception of faith was far from Paul's mind, [see e.g. W. D. Davies, *Paul and Rabbinic Judaism* (1947), pp. 221-2] but ' however much they may have dismissed the fact, it is at the expense of Paul's logic '; see S. Baring-Gould, *A Study of Paul* (1897), p. 334-6. Here we have the answer to the question whether there are dogmas in Judaism, a question regarding which there is quite a considerable literature (see Bibliography, *Jewish Encyclopaedia*, *s.v.* ' Articles of Faith.'): there are dogmas in Judaism, in so far as Judaism insists on definite religious beliefs, which form the content of its faith, yet these cannot be strictly regarded as dogmas, seeing that they are stressed not for their own sake, but because they are directly related to human conduct. For a fuller exposition of this point of view, see I. Epstein, *Judaism*, ch. 6. See also Martin Buber, *Two Types of Faith* (E.T., Norman P. Goldhawk, 1951), p. 33, where he describes Christian faith as ' believing that ', and faith for Judaism as trust in God, as personal and present. Whilst Buber's comparison of the Jewish and Christian conceptions of faith is correct, it is incomplete without the added differentiation in the relation of each to human conduct. For an historical treatment of dogmas in Judaism, see D. Neumark, *Toldot ha-Ikkarim be-Yisrael* (1913) and *The Principles of Judaism, an Historical Outline*, in his *Essays in Jewish Philosophy* (1929), pp. 101-44.

[17] יודע רבונו ומתכווין למרוד בו Sifra on Leviticus, xxvi. 14.

[18] See J. Macmurray, *op. cit.*, p. 28. Macmurray remarks that ' one might tend to refer to the mediaeval culture as another case where all the departments of culture are synthesised in religion '; but, he points out, the very struggle between the temporal and the spiritual power in the mediæval world ' defines a fundamental failure in integration.' *Op. cit.*, p. 29.

[19] This failure of Christianity is admitted by so devout a Christian as S. L. Frank, a Russian priest and a great theologian, in his work, *God with Us* (E.T., T. N. Duddington, 1946), p. 210: ' How many crimes, inhumanities, indescribable, shameful sins, have been, and are being committed by mankind, enlightened by the lofty and saving truth of Christianity ! Sometimes those crimes have been committed in spite of the peoples' faith, and often—which is still worse—in the name of it. How much blood has been shed by men who acknowledge the supreme commandment of love ! How much pride, greed, hatred, love of power, cruelty has been shown by men who know the righteousness of humility, disinterestedness, mercy, and self-sacrifice ' (p. 210). See also M. Hay, *Foot of Pride* (1950), and Charles Singer, *The Failure of Christianity* (1943).

[19a] This is discussed at greater length in chapter xiv.

[20] See A. Einstein, *The World as I see it* (1935), p. 95.

[21] See Josephus, *Against Apion*, I, 12.

CHAPTER V

THE TWO SOURCES OF THE JEWISH RELIGION

WE have seen in the last Chapter that in Judaism, knowledge, love of God and moral action are inextricably bound up together. Knowledge has to lead to love of God and morality, and these should be based on knowledge. The kind of knowledge which serves this purpose is knowledge of the teachings of the Jewish religion, and it is to a more particular examination of these that the remaining chapters will be devoted.

First and foremost among the teachings of the Jewish religion are its affirmations about God and His relation to man. It is these affirmations which have always evoked in the Jew his deepest religious feelings, and inspired him to moral action.

Despite all assertions to the contrary, a sound instinct tells us that religion and moral life are indissolubly connected with what we think of God. The religious Jew may indeed well do without a complete systematisation of his knowledge of God, but some such knowledge he must certainly possess. As we have seen, there must be a cognitive content to his religion, and it is their connection with the cognitive side that imparts to the emotional and volitional sides of the Jewish religion their particular dynamic and moral quality.

How then do we obtain this knowledge of God which is so necessary to sturdy faith ? What is the source of

80

For notes on this chapter, see pp. 93-98.

this cognitive content which is vital for the devout faith of the Jew?

The human mind in its search for God has invariably followed two distinct paths—the one taken by philosophical theology, with reason as its weapon; the other by the philosophy of religion, with revelation as its basis.

The method of the philosophical theology has been to direct attention to the manifestations of beauty and order that pervade the world-process and that point to a spiritual principle sustaining and controlling the whole. The contemplation of the majestic grandeur of the starry heavens and the mysterious workings of Nature reveals the handiwork of a great Author of infinite power and glory, the essential truths concerning whom, it is claimed, can be apprehended by the unaided faculty of the human intellect and by the mere exercise of reason.

Opposed to this is the religious philosophy that entirely distrusts reason and, so far as it philosophises, ' proposes to erect religious faith on philosophical scepticism.' The underlying assumption of this philosophy is that human intelligence is debarred by its own limitations from penetrating into the ultimate heart of things, and that unaided reason serves only to discover that God is unknown and unknowable.

This method of approach relies in its religious quest on historical and experiential data, which bear witness to a close relationship between man and the Divine, and falls back on revelation—the experience of an individual or a people—for all knowledge about God and human destiny.[1]

Whether religion is a matter of the intellect or other-wise has thus been a subject of endless discussion among philosophers of all ages; and it is a problem fundamental to religious philosophy—Jewish and non-Jewish. Modern philosophers continue to debate this formidable point with the same keenness as did those philosophers from whom they are separated in time by many centuries. Bergson, for instance, tells us that some other faculty besides reason is necessary to apprehend reality.[2] This other faculty he calls ' intuition '. And what is the Bergsonian intuition other than an echo of Judah Halevi's ' inner eye,'[3] the prophetic perception which he regards as the sole means whereby man can apprehend God ? While in Maimonides' definition of faith as ' that which is apprehended by the mind,'[4] we seem to anticipate in simpler words Hegel's declaration that ' all religion is thinking.'[5]

The problem is, however, older than philosophy. In early Judaic literary sources we already meet what would at first appear to be the clashings and crossings of these two attitudes. In Deuteronomy (iv. 32-5) it is the historical and experiential data—the Exodus and the Revelation at Sinai—that invariably supply the source whence all knowledge of God comes. ' For ask now of the days of the past, which were before thee, since the day that God created man upon the earth, and from one end of heaven unto the other, whether there hath been any such things as this great thing is, or hath been heard like it ? Did ever a people hear the voice of God speaking out of the midst of the fire as thou hast heard, and live ? Or hath God essayed to go and take unto Him a nation from the midst of another nation, by trials, by signs, and by wonders, and by war and by a mighty hand, and by an outstretched arm, and by great terrors, according to all that the Lord your God did for you in Egypt before thine eyes? Unto thee it was shown that thou mightest know that the Lord He is God; there is no one else beside Him.' Here the emphasis is unmistakable. The knowledge of God is grounded in the national experiences of Israel. Different is the position assumed by prophet and psalmist. ' Looking through Nature up to Nature's God,' they summon the external world of phenomena to give witness to the One and Only God. ' The heavens declare the glory of God, and the firmament showeth His handiwork ' (Psalm xix. 2). ' Lift up your eyes on high and see: Who hath created these ? ' (Isaiah xl. 26). ' Seek Him that made the Pleiades and Orion . . . The Lord of Hosts is His name ' (Amos v. 8). ' He that planteth the ear, shall He not hear ? He that formeth the eye, shall He not see ? ' (Psalm xciv. 9).[6] And these arguments are for prophet and psalmist most convincing. It is true there are to be found here and there some who say ' There is no God.' But these are mere fools—knaves. ' The *nabal* (knave) said in his heart: " there is no God" ' (Psalm xiv. 1). His atheism, that is to say, is not due to the head, and a result of deep thinking, but springs from a base and depraved heart, overheated by the flames of passion that master the head and destroy all rationalism, corrupting, and making him indulge in ' abominable works.'[7]

Religious thought has thus for long been haunted by the distinction between revelation and reason, as the starting points of two markedly distinct methods of approach to religion. Both Jewish and non-Jewish theology of the Middle Ages spent much thought upon the relation of revelation and the power of unaided reason. The first mediaeval Jewish philosopher to grapple with the problem was Gaon Saadia in the tenth century.[7a] He sought to explain the relation by the following simile.[8] A man weighs his money and finds that he has a thousand pieces. He gives different sums to a number of people, and then, wishing to show them quickly how much he has left, he says that he has five hundred pieces, and offers to prove it by weighing the money. When he weighs the money, which takes little time, and finds that it amounts to five hundred pieces, they are bound to believe what he told them. But there may be among them a cautious man who wants to find out the amount left over by the method of calculation, that is by adding together the various amounts distributed and subtracting the sum from the original amount. Revelation according to Saadia is a weighing process which gives us the truth at once by a direct method. Reason corresponds to calculation. A cautious man with plenty of time may use it to establish a truth which has been proved to him by the short and certain method of weighing. But obviously calculation cannot change the result which weighing has already given. This is Saadia's theory of the relation of reason to revelation. He is convinced that the teachings of Judaism cannot be against reason. Yet revelation is a short and more direct road to truth. It saves man groping in the dark for long. It illumines his path and points to him the way to right conduct and life eternal.

This may appear, on first approach, a blind irrational attitude to religious truth. Yet on some reflection we find that it is neither blind nor irrational. The fact is that we all order our life on the basis of beliefs, the acceptance of which saves us from many troubles, and prevents us from wasting our time and endangering our lives by walking down blind dangerous paths. If we insisted, for example, on testing for ourselves the value of medicine prescribed to us by the medical man before taking it, we might cut off all chances of recovery and of coming to any opinion about anything at all. Premature death would preclude any further speculation about life and its problems.[9] We accept our medicine on trust, and leave it to the testimony of the expert.

Looked at from this point of view, the attitude of Saadia to the problem emerges in a clearer light. Accepting revelation as a fact, and that revelation must correspond to the ultimate nature of things which is rational, Saadia holds that all the teachings of the Jewish religion, as revealed, answer the test of reason, when examined by the mind of a perfectly intelligent being.

It should further be observed that Saadia recognises another function in revelation. It conveys the religious truths which can be discovered by reason, to those who from lack of faculty or opportunity would not otherwise have known them, as weighing would help those who cannot do their sums,[10] a conception practically identical with that enunciated by Joseph Butler (1692-1752), when he stated that a part of the office of revelation is to be ' a republication of natural religion.'[11]

G

This method of dealing with the problem of the relation of reason to revelation was adopted and further developed by Maimonides in the 34th chapter of his *Guide*, Book I. In this chapter, Maimonides conceives revelation as fulfilling a five-fold function in supporting or supplementing the knowledge won by unassisted human efforts.[12] These five functions, as Jacob Guttmann[13] has shown, were taken over *in toto* by Thomas Aquinas in his *Quaestiones*, where he deals with the differentiation between natural and revealed religion, a differentiation which has ever since been followed by the theologians of the scholastic tradition, and which is still commonly accepted to-day.

Summing up the situation in the light of Saadia's and Maimonides' treatment of the problem, we may say that these two religious thinkers far from seeing reason and revelation in opposition to one another, regard them as separate but co-ordinate sources of divine knowledge. With their common source in God, reason and revelation are but different methods of apprehending reality. The apparent discord between the two kinds of truth is to be traced to the limitation of the human intelligence and the deficiencies in man's reasoning power rather than to a lack of unity between the truths themselves.

There still, however, remains the problem how to deal with such an apparent contradiction between reason and revelation whenever it does make its appearance. On this question no precise answer is to be found among Jewish philosophers. A case in point is Saadia Gaon, whose attitude to this question is differently interpreted by Malter in his work on Saadia

Gaon,[14] and David Neumark in his essay on Saadia's philosophy.[15] According to Malter[16] ' Saadia was indeed the first Jewish philosopher fully conscious of the basic difference between the Jewish and the philosophic conceptions of truth, and he gave special emphasis to the fact that Judaism is primarily and essentially a religion based on historical experience, philosophic experience being required only for the purpose of furnishing secondary evidence for the genuineness and truth of its manifold teachings.' Opposed to this is the view of Neumark, who categorically declares,[17] ' Not only does Saadia not say that Scripture is the primary, and reason the secondary source of truth (as Malter would maintain), but he means to say the *very opposite* of this: Reason is primary, Scripture and revelation secondary *in rank* as sources of truth.'

Both Malter and Neumark appeal in support of their respective views to different passages in Saadia's *Emunot we-Deot*—passages which on the first approach seem conflicting. But in reality both Malter and Neumark have missed the point in Saadia's thesis. What Saadia intends to convey in the passages to which Neumark appeals in support of his view,[18] was that where reason and revelation appeared in conflict, revelation had to be adapted to reason by means of interpretation where this is possible. But at the same time Saadia agreed, as is indicated in those passages which Malter quotes,[19] that in the last resort there was something inherently deficient in human reasoning so that it could not be made the final test of truth, and that the statements of revelation had accordingly to be accepted, even in cases where they could not be accommodated with reason.[20]

This, too, was the view held by Maimonides, though expressed by him more clearly. The limitations of the human intellect for apprehending certain truths is the theme to which Maimonides devotes the whole of chapter 31 in the first book of his *Guide*, and which recurs throughout his works;[21] and by his declaration in Book II, chapter 25, that no demonstrative proof in the world would make him accept the eternity of the universe, as taught by Aristotle, because it would involve the total collapse of the Torah,[22] is sufficient evidence that for Maimonides, the great rationalist, revelation, not reason, is the final arbiter of the truth or falsity of any religious teaching, notwithstanding the assertion to the contrary by a number of modern Hebrew writers, including Ahad Ha-Am in his essay *Shilton ha-Sekel* (' Supremacy of Reason ').[23]

Evidence in support of this supremacy of faith in the Jewish view is afforded on first approach by the story of the *Akedah* (the Binding of Isaac). Abraham's readiness to sacrifice his only son, Isaac, has always been regarded throughout the generations as a classic model of true faith. Yet, if we consider the situation, it would appear that this faith involved the suspension of both reason and ethics. It involved the suspension of reason because what Abraham believed was absurd—that God would contradict Himself, that after having promised him that ' in Isaac shall thy seed be called ' (Genesis xxi. 12), He should command him to slay him; and it involved the suspension of ethics, because judged by ethical standards the demand made on Abraham and accepted by his faith was that he should commit murder. Yet Abraham, because he believed in God, believed that both reason and right were under God's absolute decision, and subordinate to faith. Is there any more striking evidence of the absolute sovereignty of faith, even at the expense of reason and morality ?[24]

This absolute sovereignty of faith affirmed by Maimonides, and confirmed by the story of the *Akedah*, calls for an interpretation of the relation of revelation to reason different to the one given by Saadia and Maimonides. If revelation has after all the last word, what are we to make of the distinction between revelation as a weighing process and reason as a counting process ? One solution, of course, is *not* to give revelation the last word. This was the attitude adopted by Moses Mendelssohn in dealing with the question; and a brief discussion of it might be of advantage at this point.

Mendelssohn's treatment of the problem constitutes a departure from the Saadia and Maimonides tradition. As a son of the period of ' Enlightenment ' that gave the supreme place to reason and that would admit no proposition which relegated reason to a secondary position, Mendelssohn could not accept the views of those philosophers who would allow in religion truths which could not be discovered by the unaided human intellect. ' I acknowledge,' declared Mendelssohn, ' no immutable truths but such as are not only conceivable to human understanding but also admit of being demonstrated and warranted by human faculties ';[25] much less would he admit the possibility of subordinating reason to religion. For Mendelssohn, the only articles of religion which admit of such direct proof as should command the universal assent that is yielded to postulates of mathematics, are three: (1) The existence of God ; (2) Providence; (3) Immortality.   These three articles constitute, according to Mendelssohn, the common principles of all religion. But unlike other religions that had superimposed upon the body of ' common-sense ' teachings a system of creeds indispensable to individual salvation, Judaism, according to Mendelssohn, boasts of no exclusive revelation of immutable truths.   It is not revealed religion. It is revealed law. At Sinai the Divine Voice issued commandments—commandments consisting of deeds not beliefs. Judaism does not say, ' You shall believe,' but, ' You shall do.'[26]

This declaration of Mendelssohn has proved a fascinating playground for the mental gymnastics of modern Jewish theologians, some of whom went so far as to maintain that according to Mendelssohn, it mattered not what a Jew believed provided he conformed to a certain norm of law and conduct.   The absurdity of this view—' the great dogma of dogmalessness '[27] as Schechter called it—is patent to anyone who is not blinded by the desire to get rid of all positive beliefs in Judaism.   Mendelssohn's conception of revelation, though it be merely of the Law, implied of course definite religious beliefs.   The giving of the Law presupposes the idea of a Supreme Lawgiver, Whom the Jew is commanded to trust, and in Whom he must believe.   It is clear that what Mendelssohn meant to convey by his dictum was that the final and directive source and repository of the truths common to all religions was not to be found in revelation, but in reason and common sense, thus making the human mind the final arbiter of religious truth. For he held that you cannot make a man believe nor persuade him into a belief, unless you can convince him by logical arguments. And as the Sinaitic Revelation with all its stupendous setting could only awe, not convince, it could not be made the source and basis of religious truth. The people accordingly, so Mendelssohn assumed, before they could be summoned to the foot of the Mount Sinai to receive the Law, had to be initiated in the teachings of Natural Religion, in the belief in God, Providence and Immortality. Equipped with this knowledge, they became fit to be the recipients of the Divine Legislation, which served to strengthen the religious and national bond of the Jews, to inculcate religion, and to stimulate the early searchers after truth to seek further instruction on the fundamental things of life.

It may be assumed that Mendelssohn's views on the place of dogma in Judaism, as laid down in his *Jerusalem*, are highly what the Germans would call *tendenziös*. They must not be divorced from his main thesis which among other things was a plea for religious toleration. And it was only by indicating that Judaism was not wedded to any particular dogma that he felt he could secure a measure of toleration for his brethren. Nevertheless, in limiting Judaism to a Religion of the Law, he not only ran counter, as Hermann Cohen well remarks,[28] to the whole trend of the history of the Jewish religion, but he has torn out the very heart of Judaism, with lamentable results.

It is true, Mendelssohn is not alone among Jewish

philosophers in maintaining that the human intellect is capable of discovering all knowledge of God and the world and the human soul. Saadia also was of the same opinion. But he was the first to uphold the self-and-all-inclusive sufficiency of ' common sense ' to arrive at this higher knowledge, denying to revelation any share in guiding man along his quest for the Divine. In other words, he is alone among Jewish religious philosophers in substituting philosophy for faith, and in making Reason the mistress instead of the handmaid of Religion. This, indeed, was a principle fraught with danger. He himself might have been ever so confident in the self-sufficiency of common sense to build up with mathematical certainty a system of ' Natural Religion ' commanding universal assent. But at the same time one dare not ignore the fact that Reason, like Conscience, can be an accomplice as well as a guide. It all depends on what reason sets itself out to prove. Moreover, with all the competence of reason to produce irrefutable arguments and proofs in support of religious truths, it can never grip the human conscience with the same sense of certitude as comes from Revelation. For human judgment is, in the best of circumstances, liable to err, but Revelation is to the believer an infallible guide. Mendelssohn himself, who extols reason above all, nevertheless does not hesitate to express his scepticism in its regard, and advises the true philosopher ' always to be diffident of his convictions, and not to cease to bear in mind that they are only his own convictions, and that other rational beings, who have started from other points and have followed different cues, arrive at quite opposite conclusions.'[29] (The very argument which Saadia[30] used in support for his insistence on the need of revelation.) And although Mendelssohn would not regard atheists as rational beings, endowed with common sense, yet it will be agreed that this was merely his own conviction, about which, as a true philosopher, he would logically have to be diffident, thereby indirectly undermining the very principles of religion to which he had dedicated his life.

This was the impasse into which Mendelssohn was led by his rationalism that discarded the revelation of religion, and it was this attitude of his which was, undoubtedly, responsible for much of the apostasy that ran through his family and his disciples, despite his ' common-sense ' religion, and the conception of the revelation of the Law which he propagated.

It will be evident from this brief historical sketch that Jewish thought considers both reason and revelation necessary vehicles for the attainment of the knowledge of God on which all faith must be founded. Yet, since it has been shown that, in the last resort, as Maimonides asserts, and the story of the *Akedah* corroborates, the final arbiter is revelation, the definition of the relation of revelation to reason as given by Saadia and Maimonides will appear inadequate. Such a definition must consequently be sought elsewhere and this is the quest which must next engage our attention.

NOTES

[1] See W. P. Paterson, *The Nature of Religion* (2nd ed. 1928), pp. 13-20.

[2] See Henri Bergson, *L'Evolution créatrice* (1907) and *Introduction to Metaphysics* (1903); See *infra*, p. 107.

[3] עין נסתרת, *Kuzari*, IV, 3.

[4] *Guide for the Perplexed*, I, 50: ההאמנה היא ענין המצויר בנפש (in Alharizi's version) האמונה. The Arabic word is *itikad* which David Kaufmann, *Attributenlehre* (1877), pp. 369ff., renders *Glaube* (' Faith '). According to Jehudah I. Kaufmann, in his Hebrew edition of the *Guide* (1948) *a.l.*, it denotes ' conviction '. See also J. Albo, *Ikkarim*, III, 25. ' Anything that is subject to belief must be conceivable by the mind '; cf. also *op. cit.*, I, 19.

[5] *Philosophie der Religion*, ed. Bolland (1907), I, p. 17. The latest exponent of the view that the knowledge of God is exclusively based on revelation is Karl Barth, one of the most famous of Christian Protestant theologians. In his Gifford Lectures on *The Knowledge of God and the Service of God* (1938) he explicitly declares himself an avowed opponent of all natural theology based on reasoning. ' God,' he writes, ' is one and the only one, and proves himself to be such by his being both the author of his own being and the source of all knowledge of himself. In both these respects he differs from everything in the world. A god who would be known otherwise than through himself, i.e., otherwise than through his revelation of himself would have already betrayed *eo ipso* that he was not the one and the only one, and so was not God. . . . The knowledge of the one and only God is based on the fact that the one and only God makes himself known . . . otherwise he cannot be known at all ' (p. 19). This view expressed with the dialectic characteristic of Barth would seem to have been anticipated and expressed more simply by Judah Halevi in his declaration that ' for a man to grasp the true nature of God would imply a defect in Him ' (*Kuzari* V, 21). אלו היו משיגים אמיתתו היה זה חסרון בו. Judah Halevi, however, as it will be noted later, does not reject altogether the evidence of Nature, and in so far cannot be said to share the extreme view of Barth, who allows no room for natural theology in his scheme of thought. Barth was of course greatly influenced by Kierkegaard, who violently opposed any attempt to prove by means of reason the existence of God, declaring that ' to prove the existence of a person who is

actually in existence is the most shameless affront one can offer him, being an attempt to make him ridiculous; but the misfortune is that people have no inkling of this, that they seriously regard this as a pious undertaking.' See *Concluding Unscientific Postscript*, by 'Johannes Climacus' (S. Kierkegaard), from Walter Lowrie's *Kierkegaard* (1938), p. 336. . . . The nearest approximation in Jewish religious literature to the attitude of Barth and Kierkegaard seems to be (*a*) the statement in the *Sefer Ha-Yashar*, viii, that 'the fact that our reason cannot prove His existence is the best proof that He exists.' כי העדר ידיעת מציאותו יתחייב להיות נמצא; (*b*) the dictum of Rabbi Nahman of Bratzlaw (1772-1810) that 'it is a mark of wisdom to be as a beast before God' שהוא חכמה לעשות עצמו כבהמה and who declared that the greater the difficulty to justify the ways of God, the greater is the proof of His inscrutability. (See S. A. Horodezky, *Torat Rabbi Nahman mi-Bratzlaw* (1923), pp. 74 and 84.)

[6] See also Job, xxxviii-xli, where the ordering of Nature is made to testify the transcendent greatness and wisdom of God, cf. also Wordsworth's 'Ode to Duty' the stern daughter of the Voice of God, to whom is ascribed the power which sustains the stars in their courses:

' Thou dost preserve the stars from wrong,
And the most ancient heavens through thee are fresh and strong.'

[7] See *supra*, p. 26.

[7a] On Philo's treatment of the problem, see H. A. Wolfson *Philo*, (1947), Vol. I, pp. 143ff.

[8] See *Emunot we-Deot, Introduction*, Slucki ed. p. 13; Rosenblatt, E.T., p. 32.

[9] See *Kuzari*, V, 2, quoting in this connection the saying: ' Life is short and work is much ': החיים קצרים, והמלאכה מרובה

[10] See *Emunot we-Deot, loc. cit.*

[11] Joseph Butler, *Analogy*, II, 4-7.

[12] The five functions of Revelation, according to Maimonides, summarised, are as follows: (1) The subject matter of revealed

religion is difficult, subtle and profound, so that few can discover it by unaided reason. (2) Human intelligence is insufficient and limited. (3) The preliminary studies involved are many and of long duration, and thus liable to prove wearisome to those who would by their own researches seek to reach the desired goal. (4) The defects in man's physical constitution and his inner disposition are often a bar to moral and consequent intellectual perfection. (5) Man's preoccupations with his material wants cannot but interfere with his proper application to study. Cf. Bahya ibn Pakuda, *Hobot ha-Lebabot* III, 3. See also Julius Guttmann, *Zur Kritik der Offenbarungsreligion in der islamischen und jüdischen Philosophie*, in *M.G.W.J.*, 78 (1934), pp. 456-464.

[13] Jacob Guttmann, *Das Verhältniss des Thomas von Aquino zum Judenthum und zur jüdischen Literatur* (1891), p. 37.

[14] Henry Malter, *Saadia Gaon—His Life and Works* (1921).

[15] David Neumark, *Essays in Jewish Philosophy* (1929), pp. 145-218.

[16] H. Malter, *op. cit.*, p. 175.

[17] D. Neumark, *op. cit.*, p. 168.

[18] (a) ' In general, I say, any description of God or of His actions occurring in the Scriptures, or in the words of others among us, Monotheists, which is found to contradict what is dismissed by sound reasoning is undoubtedly a figure of speech ' (*Emunot we-Deot*, II, 3, ed. Slucki, p. 44; Rosenblatt, E.T., p. 100): וכלל אני אומר
כל מה שימצא בספרים ובדברינו המיחדים מלשון בוראנו וממעשיו וחולק
על מה שמחייבו העיון האמתי בלי ספק שהוא דרך העברה מהלשון.
(b) ' Any interpretation that agrees with reason must be correct, whereas any that leads to what is contrary must be unsound and fallacious ' (*Emunot we-Deot*, IX, 3, ed. Slucki, p. 133; Rosenblatt, E.T., p. 333): וכל פירוש מסכים למה שיש בשכל הוא האמת ,וכל מה
שמביא אל מה שהוא חולק בשכל הוא הבטל. See also *op. cit.*, VII, 2; Rosenblatt, E.T., p. 265-6. The Seventh Treatise of Saadia's *Emunot we-Deot*, dealing with the Resurrection of the Dead, has come down to us in two Arabic versions, and the one used by Ibn Tibbon for his Hebrew translation varies considerably from the one

published by S. Landauer (Leyden 1880) from which Rosenblatt's English translation is made.

[19] Malter does not specify where Saadia actually declares that revelation is primary. He merely writes, ' This is clearly stated by Saadia in his Introduction to the *Kitab Al-Amanat* [the Arabic title of Saadia's work], pp. 22-6 (Heb. Slucki, pp. 11-13).' This vagueness of reference led to Neumark's criticism. The statement, however, that ' God has given us the assurance that it is not possible for deniers to have any sound objections to raise against our Torah, nor for doubters [to adduce] any proofs to invalidate our faith ' (*Amanat*, p. 22, Slucki ed. p. 11; see also *supra*, p. 19): והבטיחנו כי לא יתכן שיהיה לכופרים טענה בתורתנו, ולא ראיה למספקים באמונתנו warrants Malter's inference regarding Saadia's view on the primacy of revelation.

[20] See also *Emunot we-Deot*, II, Slucki, p. 41; Rosenblatt, E.T., pp. 92ff., the gist of Saadia's argument being that what is infinite cannot be embraced by the finite human mind.

[21] This too is the view expressed by Philo, who holds philosophy to be subordinate to Scripture, because human knowledge is limited, and philosophy, based as it is upon human knowledge, is accordingly unable to solve many problems; see H. A. Wolfson, *Philo* (1947), I, pp. 152-4.

[22] This subject is discussed more fully in chapter IX.

[23] See *Ten Essays on Zionism and Judaism*, by Ahad Ha-Am, translated by Leon Simon (1922), pp. 162-222. Hebrew: *Al Parashat Derakim* (Berlin, 1921), IV, pp. 13ff.

[24] The faith of Abraham as exemplified in the *Akedah* forms the theme of S. Kierkegaard's remarkable book *Fear and Trembling* (E.T. by Robert Payne, 1939), in which he sets forth his conception of faith as a spiritual, inward relationship, which has to do just with the hardness, the impossibility, even the absurdity of faith.

[25] See Moses Mendelssohn, *Jerusalem* (E.T. by M. Samuels, 1834), pp. 89ff.

[26] For the pages which follow, see I. Epstein *Judaism of Tradition* (1931), pp. 147ff.

[27] See *J.Q.R.* (1895), I, p. 9.

[28] Hermann Cohen, *Religion der Vernunft aus den Quellen des Judenthums* (ed. 1919), p. 421.

[29] See M. Samuels, *Memoirs of Moses Mendelssohn* (1827), p. 100.

[30] See *Emunot we-Deot, Introduction;* ed. Slucki, p. 2; Rosenblatt, E.T., p. 4.

[See Excursus I, pp. 360-367.]

CHAPTER VI

THE RELATION OF REVELATION TO REASON

TO determine whether reason or revelation is the root of religion, we must first take note of the fundamental implications of religion. Religion, as has been observed, is concerned to assert the personal factor in an apparently impersonal world, which science attempts to describe but cannot explain. Its object, that is to say, is not to teach the existence of a Supreme Being, a Creator, a Providence. This is a task that might well be left to science, philosophy and metaphysics, each of which has sufficient arguments, drawn from the general character of the scheme of things, to make out a case for the truth of God's existence which, despite Kant's criticism and that of others, cannot but impress the mind with its strength.[1] But however irrefutable and irresistible the arguments may appear, they do not present an unambiguous vision of a definite personal relation to God which constitutes the original and positive content of the Jewish, as well as that of its daughter religions. The essential nature of the religious belief that marks it off sharply from the mere theism arrived at by philosophy (in which we may include science) is the assumption of a personal relationship between man and God. ' Thou shalt call and the Lord will answer: thou shalt cry and He will say " Here I am." ' (Isaiah lviii. 9). This close relationship which religion, with varying force and clearness, has ever

99

For notes on this chapter, see pp. 111-118.

sought to affirm, is, as already stated,[2] the true secret of religion's overwhelming hold over the human heart in all ages.

Philosophy may prove the existence of some mysterious power, force or energy, in Nature and beyond, to whom we owe our life, but such a power is a mere metaphysical phantom, too abstract to satisfy the deepest longings of the human heart. Philosophy may indeed have a good deal to say about what God is not, but very little to say about what He is. And even after having done its best in describing Him, the attributes that reveal the personal character of God are, as far as philosophy is concerned, left undefined. He remains the Great Unknown, towards whom men might occasionally feel attracted as they might feel attracted to any other ideal, but never turn in prayer and worship, much less expect a response. The God reached by philosophy may, moreover, be conceived as the prototype of perfection, and in proportion as he is thus idealised the contemplation of him may determine in man the sense of duty and morality, but he is too impersonal to have the power of transmuting human character and personality, so as to produce ' the precious from the vile ' (Jeremiah xv. 19). It is only religion, whose centre of gravity is to be found in the relationship between man and God, that does for us what philosophy cannot do. It speaks to us of an eternal Being with whom man can enter into the closest relationship, and in that relationship find the satisfaction of his fuller life.

But that is not all. Apart from the comforting and sustaining message of religion—a message which calls

forth the whole of man's reverence and love—its
affirmation of relationship between man and the Divine
raises the individual to a plane of excellence and value,
beyond the reach of all philosophy. By its root-declaration that man has been fashioned in the image of God,
the individual is dowered with infinite powers and
energies that enable him to grow increasingly in likeness
to Him by the understanding and knowledge of Him.
This emphasis on the value of the individual reveals
the practical insight and directive energy of religion
from which there have proceeded at all times the highest
human spiritual and moral achievements, and which
have produced in men and women of all ages an
enthusiastic response to the Divine summons. ' Ye
shall be holy, for I the Lord am holy ' (Leviticus xix. 2).
But this inspiring thought of religion can flow only
from a personal relationship entered into by God with
a human soul—a relationship whereby God's essential
character in His dealings with men is revealed: even as
it is only through a personal relationship that we come
to know the character of our fellow-man. A chemical
analysis of our friend, John Smith, may tell us that he
is compounded of so much fat, sugar and lime, and
other substances,[3] but all this description will not help
us to determine his character, the morality or immorality
of the man. For the knowledge of this we must rely on
a personal experience of him, which enables us to know
him as he is, his personality. So it is with the human
knowledge of God. The contemplation of God's work
in Nature may enable us to perceive His glory, wisdom
and might. But it is to His self-revealing and self-
disclosing work, through patriarch, prophet and people,

H

that we must go for the knowledge of His character which constitutes the main content of religion.

This conception of the distinction between the knowledge of God that comes to us by way of philosophy (and science), and that which religion communicates, has been worked out at length by Judah Halevi in his *Kuzari*, where he also shows that this distinction is indicated in the two names of God: *Elohim* and YHWH (the Tetragammaton). The term *Elohim*, which describes God as the total of all forces controlling the universe, the unifying principle of existence, denotes God of the philosophers, the God discovered by investigation and scientific study of the external phenomena. The Tetragammaton, on the other hand, is the Divine proper name,[4] and denotes the personal character of God as disclosed through His revelation. In short, *Elohim* is the God of Nature (i.e., of Philosophy); YHWH, the God of Revelation (i.e. of Religion).

To quote the *Kuzari*:

' Said the Rabbi: . . . the meaning of *Elohim* can be grasped by way of speculation; for reason indicates that the world has a Guide and a Controller . . . but the meaning of YHWH cannot be apprehended by speculation, only by prophetic vision. . . .'

' Said the *Kuzari:* Now I understand the difference between *Elohim* and YHWH, and I see how far removed is the God of Abraham from the God of Aristotle.[5] Man yearns for YHWH as a matter of feeling and conviction, whilst attachment to *Elohim* is the result of speculation. A feeling of the former kind invites him who possesses it to sacrifice his life for

Him and to love Him even unto death. Speculation, however, makes veneration a necessity only as long as it entails no harm; and it will endure no pain for its sake.'[6]

Religion is thus revealed, or it is no religion. Mere philosophy and speculation will evolve a deism or theism, and one might even maintain that theistic conceptions will continue to command the assent of rational thought in the future, as it has on the whole— taking a long view of intellectual history—done in the past. The appeal of the prophet as he pointed to the stars to tell the idol worshippers of the mighty power of the One God has not lost, with the lapse of millennia and the advance of knowledge, any of its force. The modern discoveries of science in every department of knowledge have brought along with them a fuller realisation of the incomparable wonders of God's work, and, far from having weakened the significance of the prophet's message, have rather added to a deeper comprehension of the grandeur of its meaning. But whilst such consideration will provide the theoretical framework for religion, it will not lead to a practical, living, soul-sustaining religion, flowing through divine worship into all activities of human culture. For the personal ' touch ' that is fundamental to religion—and, in fact, its unique and distinguishing feature—can be born only from experience, but no philosophy can act for experience, can supersede experience. It is the recognition of the distinct value of religion, whose depths and vastness escape all the confines of philo-sophical concepts, that has led to the association of non-rational elements with the content of religious consciousness. From Schleiermacher, who has defined religion as a ' feeling of dependence,'[7] onwards, hosts of writers have emphasised the fact that religion is rooted beneath and beyond the intellect in primary emotional states, inexpressible and incommunicable, because irreducible to any other states.

The nature of the instincts and emotions that enter the constitution of religion varies with almost every writer on the subject. Fear, admiration, subjection, reverence, all have been respectively regarded at one time or another as elemental factors in our religious ideas.[8] It will not be necessary to add to the list. Mention might, however, be made in this connection of the *numinous* feeling (from the Latin *numen*, divinity), which is claimed by the coiner of this happy phrase, Rudolf Otto in his fine work, *Das Heilige* (' The Idea of the Holy '), as expressing a mental attitude peculiar to religious experience, which he further describes, as already mentioned on a previous occasion, as ' creature-consciousness.'[9] It is the creature-feeling of self-abasement into nothingness before an over-powering, absolute might of some kind that arises in the presence of the *numen*. The Divine impresses himself upon man as the unapproachable, overwhelming in his majesty, terrible in his going forth, wrapped in mystery; and in the presence of this, what Otto called, *mysterium tremendum*,[10] the creature abhors himself and counts himself dust and ashes. Thus under the overwhelming impression of the unlimited power and the impenetrable mystery of God, Job exclaimed ' I have heard thee by the hearing of the ear, but now mine eye seeth thee, wherefore I abhor myself

and repent in dust and ashes ' (Job xlii. 5-6). And
Isaiah confronted with the vision of the Lord arising
' to shake mightily the earth ' feels the nothingness of
the human race: ' Cease ye from man whose breath is
in his nostrils, for wherein is he to be accounted for '
(Isaiah ii. 22).[11]

Together with this self-abasement, reverence and
awe, which this mystery of the Divine imposes, there
goes a feeling of attraction and fascination. Whilst
man seeks to hide himself and flee from the presence
of the awful Divine Majesty, he is at the same time
fascinated by it. These two aspects of the human
attitude to the Divine are already reflected in the story
of Jacob wrestling, where the Patriarch is pictured as
striving with God, and being smitten as an enemy,
while yet he clave to him as his friend and would not
let him go until he blessed him. ' I will not let thee go,
except thou bless me ' (Genesis xxxii, 27).[12] But, however unshakable Otto's central position may appear,
and however incontrovertible is the existence of what
are called ' non-rational ' factors that lead to the apprehension of the Divine, there is something lacking in all
pathological accounts of religion. They are all tainted,
like philosophy, with a subjectivity which, while it
may not in all cases invalidate, offers in no case a guarantee of the objective truth proclaimed by religion. Even
the ' numinous ', which Otto claims to be felt as
objective and outside self, cannot escape this charge.
Granting that the feelings aroused by the manifestation
of the numinous point to an objective reality, and
involve an experience on the same level with the
cognitive, yet this objectivity is valid only in so far as

the human side of the relationship (already described) is concerned. There is revealed the existence of a mysterious power, towards which man feels attracted, and which affects the human mind with fear, fascination, and awe:

> ' A presence that disturbs me with the joy
> Of elevated thoughts; a sense sublime
> Of something far more deeply interfused,
> Whose dwelling is the light of setting suns,
> And the round ocean and the living air,
> And the blue sky, and in the mind of man—
> A motion and a spirit, that impels
> All thinking things, all objects of all thought,
> And rolls through all things.'[13]

But there is a second side to the relationship—the side Divine. It is not enough to recognise and perceive the human reaction to the Divine presence. The spirit of man will not be satisfied without the assurance that this Divine presence is more than a fascinating blind vital force, that it is One whom it can love and trust, and who is ever ready to respond to the human claims made upon Him. In other words, what matters to the religious mind is not so much what man feels and thinks about God, as what God thinks about man. Does He hearken to our prayers and supplications? Does He pay heed to our worship and our conduct in life? Is He really concerned about our fate and destiny? But such questions cannot be answered either by philosophy or psychology, but by God himself, through a revelation—a revelation which is not merely the result of an historical process, and evolved out of man's inner consciousness, but an intrusion from above, beyond the peradventure of man's objective moral tendencies, sentiments and beliefs, leaving no doubt in the mind of the recipient that the Lord had spoken.

We can now see somewhat more clearly the distinction between philosophy and religion, reason and revelation. The distinction is not one of method but one of content, and corresponds to the distinction between the indirect knowledge *about* and direct knowledge *of* —a distinction which forms the starting point of Bergson's theory of intuition. In the former we know the object from *without*, by *analysis*, by ' the operation which reduces the object to elements already known, that is, to elements common to both it and other objects.' In the latter we know the object, as it were, from *within*. We know it by *intuition*, which is that ' kind of intellectual sympathy by which one places oneself within an object in order to coincide with what is unique in it and, consequently, inexpressible.'[14] Applying this account of the knowledge of God, we recognise reason as providing an indirect knowledge *about* God, derived from the study and investigation of our physical environment, from His revelation in Nature; whilst Revelation carries with it a direct knowledge *of* God that comes from a personal experience wherein God reveals Himself to the soul of man.

We have thus seen that for imparting the religious idea of God reason requires to be supplemented by revelation. If this is so, the question may be asked, cannot reason be dispensed with altogether? One does not need to reason out the existence of a father whose presence and love is experienced, or of a friend, whose companionship is enjoyed. This indeed, would be the case if the revelation of religion involved an experience like that of mysticism of the Indian type, in which the human mind, in its desire to escape from the evanescent and temporal, is emptied of all conscious-ness and becomes identical with the eternal order into which it is merged and absorbed. In this experience the tendency to self-immolation is never absent, result-ing in the reduction of the stature of man to the level of Nature, where neither reason nor morality need be sought. But while this may be the case with mystic or Nature religions, it is quite otherwise with the religion of the Bible.[15]

Unlike mysticism, Biblical revelation does not imply an escape from the temporal into the eternal order of things, but on the contrary, the unveiling of the eternal purpose and will underlying the temporal. In mysti-cism, man figuratively ascends to Heaven; in Biblical revelation, it is the Eternal who, so to speak, descends to earth. ' And YHWH (the Eternal) came down upon Mount Sinai ' (Exodus xix. 20), making Himself and His will known in the social-historical world. But in the social-historical world, human reason plays no mean part and, consequently, Biblical religion must recognise the significant place of reason in the temporal order in which the Eternal is revealed.[16]

These two types of revelation, the strictly individual-personal, which is that of the mystic and Nature reli-gions, and the historical-social, which is that of the Bible, correspond (like the philosophic and religious conceptions of God mentioned above, but in a different way) to the two names of God, *Elohim*, which denotes the manifestation of the Divine in Nature, and YHWH, which expresses God's personal character, as revealed in the historical experiences of the nation. This distinction will also explain the difficulty which has been raised in the previous chapter by the story of 'The binding of Isaac'. The difficulty disappears when it is reflected that the command to Abraham to sacrifice his son came to him, as the Biblical text tells us, from ELOHIM: 'And *Elohim* tried Abraham' (Genesis xxii. 1). In other words, it was the outcome of a purely individual-personal experience, involving a flight from the social-historical into timeless intercourse with God, in which reason and morality do not come into play. But whatever the validity of such a revelation, it is not the revelation of the Bible, the revelation in which God manifests himself as YHWH in the context of the historical and social process, in which the claims neither of reason nor of morality may be ignored.[17] It was the experience of this YHWH revelation which, we are told in the Bible, subsequently came to Abraham and made him desist from the sacrificing of his son. 'And Abraham called the name of that place, *YHWH Yireh* ('The Eternal seeth') (Genesis xxii. 14); for where God reveals Himself in His personal character as YHWH, there is no place for human sacrifices, or for any action which does violence to the dictates of reason or claims of morality.

Thus the relation between reason and revelation becomes clear. The content of revelation, consisting of knowledge derived from experience, is not reducible to logical concepts. The personal touch which it pro-

vides is one which no amount of philosophy or speculation can discover for itself, as little or no amount of
reasoning or speculation can ascertain the real character
of John Smith, with whom we have had no personal
contact or experience. But, nevertheless, since the
' personal touch ' concerns the social-historical world,
it must fit in with the general character of its context,
which is both rational and moral. Thus it is that,
while what may be described as the impersonal framework of religion must be rational and conform to reason,
the ' personal ' content, which is its distinguishing
quality, cannot be so constricted, but must be allowed
a freedom of expression, even to overflow, as can be
drawn from the rich inexhaustible fount of experience
of the individual and the people.

The relation of reason to revelation can thus be said
to be analogous to the relation of the body to the soul;
and revelation is richer in content than reason, even
as the soul is richer in energies and resources than the
body. Yet, both are closely interlinked; and even as
the soul which escapes the body can have no existence
in the context of earthly life, so can revelation which
overthrows reason have no existence in the context
of the social and historical world, in which revelation
fulfils itself. In brief, while Revelation need not
necessarily be confined within the limited framework
of reason, it can do no violence to reason. This is the
test to which the teachings of Judaism, as revealed,
may be readily submitted; and in submitting them to
this test it will be found, in the words of Bahya ibn
Pakuda, that though ' reason may not enjoin them all,
it nevertheless does not reject any of them.'[18]

NOTES

[1] Notwithstanding the speculative difficulties against the argument from design which Kant raises, he confesses that ' This argument always deserves to be mentioned with respect. It is the oldest, the clearest and the most in conformity with human reason . . . and it would be utterly hopeless to attempt to rob this argument of the authority it has always enjoyed ' (*Critique of Pure Reason, Transcendental Dialectic*, II, ch. iii, section 7, E.T., J. M. D. Meiklejohn, 1924), p. 383. Even Darwin was so deeply impressed by the argument of design that he is led to write with regard to it: ' I am conscious that I am in an utterly hopeless muddle (about it) . . . Again I say, I am and shall ever remain in a hopeless muddle ' (*Life and Letters*, Vol. II, p. 353).

[2] See *supra*, p. 53.

[3] See *infra*, p. 186.

[4] See *Kuzari*, IV, iff. On the Tetragrammaton, as a proper name see B.T. Sanhedrin 38b and Nissim b. Reuben (b. *c.* 1340), *Shenem Asar Derashot*, iv.

[5] כבר התבאר לי ההפרש בין אלוקים ויי, והביגותי מה בין אלוהי אברהם ואלוהי ארסטו.

[6] *Kuzari*, IV, 15-6. Judah Halevi's interpretation of the two Divine Names is already implied in the Rabbinic exegesis which associates *Elohim* with the attribute of justice (*Din*), and YHWH with that of mercy (*Rahamim*) (See J.T. Taanit, II, 1; Midrash Genesis Rabbah, xii, 15 and xxxiii, 4), Divine mercy or goodness being the special mark of the divine governance of the universe as affirmed by religion. Philo reverses the significance of the two Names, and according to A. Marmorstein, *The Old Rabbinic Doctrine of God* (1927), pp. 43ff., Philo was following here an earlier Palestinian tradition. See also A. H. Wolfson, *Philo*, I, p. 224, particularly n. 39, where all the recent literature on the subject is listed. The texts, however, which Marmorstein adduces in support are far from conclusive. All they show is that the Name YHWH in a particular construction (אני יהוה) is used in connection with judgment, and the expression (אלי), my God, (not *Elohim*) in

connection with mercy; but no Rabbinic text is available proving that these two Names in themselves have the reversed significance attached to them by Philo. More correct is the view expressed by G. F. Moore, *op. cit.*, III, p. 121, that ' Philo, who read the Bible in Greek, was led by the substitution of Κύριος for YHWH to connect it with the idea of sovereignty in its traditional aspect, and Θεός [*Elohim*] conversely with the beneficent power.' But however it may be, Judah Halevi, in his interpretation of these two divine Names, propounds a view which at long last is beginning to gain wide acceptance, namely, that the use of the Names YHWH and *Elohim* does not rest upon a difference of documents, as has been maintained for well over fifty years, but, in the words of Professor I. Engnell, of Uppsala, one of the foremost Biblical scholars of our times, ' upon something which is bound up with the fact that the different divine names have different ideological associations and therewith different import. Thus, YHWH is readily used when it is a question of Israel's national God, indicated as such over against foreign gods, and where the history of the fathers is concerned, etc., while on the other hand, *Elohim*, " God ", gives more expression to a " theological " and abstract-cosmic picture of God, and is therefore used in larger and more moving contexts . . .' (Quoted by C. R. North, *Pentateuchal Criticism*, in *The Old Testament and Modern Study*, ed. by H. H. Rowley [1951], pp. 66f.). The documentary theory resting principally on the change of the divine Names has indeed been subject to considerable attack within recent years from many quarters, and among Jewish scholars who have delivered crushing blows against it may be mentioned B. Jacob, *Das Erste Buch der Tora, Genesis* (1934), U. Cassutto, *La Questione della Genesis* (1934), and M. Z. Segal, in *Tarbiz*, Vol. IX (1938), pp. 123ff. The effect of all these attacks has been, to use again the words of Engnell, to bring ' chaos within the well-ordered, but entirely fictitious and anachronistic construction which constitutes the Wellhausenian fabric of learning.' (Quoted by C. R. North, *op. cit.*, p. 65). It might be added that one need only read that essay by C. R. North to be struck by the confusion that exists in the ' Higher Critical ' schools, and to realise that ' Higher Criticism ' can no longer be considered an exact science, and that there is nothing in its still so-called 'assured results' to upset the traditional acceptance of the unity and Mosaic authorship of the Pentateuch.

The greatest single factor in undermining the structure of Biblical criticism is undoubtedly archaeology, which proves that the basic moral and religious doctrines which constitute the faith of Israel belong to the earliest period of its history and are not, as a critical school assumes, a product of a later age. As an example may be cited the discovery of the Hammurabi Code which clearly controverts the fundamental assumption of the critical school that the Law could not have preceded the Prophets. See further my article, 'Judaism', *Encyclopaedia Britannica* (1955 printing).

[7] See *supra*, p. 48.

[8] For a good account of the various instincts with which religion has been associated, see W. P. Paterson, *op. cit.*, pp. 74-104.

[9] See *supra*, p. 49. In explanation of the term Otto writes: '*Omen* has given us "ominous", and there is no reason why from *numen* we should not similarly form a word "numinous"' (*Op. cit.*, p. 7).

[10] Otto, *op. cit.* The numinous denotes, 'a quite specific kind of emotional response, wholly distinct from that of being afraid' (*op. cit.*, p. 13), approximating to the English 'awe' in its deepest and most special sense (see *op. cit.*, p. 14). Attempting to describe it, Otto writes, 'the feeling of it may at times come sweeping like a gentle tide, pervading the mind with the tranquil mood of deepest worship' (*op. cit.*, p. 12); and in illustration of this 'numinous' as reflected in the liturgy he cites the service of *Yom Kippur*, the great Jewish 'Day of Atonement', which is 'unusually rich in numinous hymns and prayers, including prayers as wonderful as the *u-beken ten pachdeka* [see *A.P.B.*, p. 239]:

"So then let Thy fear, O Lord our God, come over all Thy creatures and the reverent dread of Thee upon all that Thou hast made, that all Thy creatures may fear Thee, and every being bow before Thee, and that all become banded together to do Thy will with a perfect heart"' (*op. cit.*, p. 190).

Otto in fact is said to have conceived his notion of the numinous, as a central factor in religion, while participating in a Day of Atone-

ment service in a simple North African Synagogue; see I. Heinemann, *Das Ideal der Heiligkeit im hellenistischen und rabbinischen
Judenthum*, in *Jeshurun*, VIII (1921), p. 118. See also G. Scholem
op. cit., pp. 56-7, with reference to the ' *Hechalot* books ' (esoteric
tracts describing the heavenly halls of the mystics' visions) in which
' we have, as it were, a full treasure-house of such numinous hymns.'
What is of particular significance in the numinous feeling, as conceived in the prayer cited from the Day of Atonement—and it is a
point overlooked by Otto—is that far from inducing quietism, it
becomes a motive of action, the doing of the divine will ' with a
perfect heart.' This in itself sharply marks off the numinous from
ordinary fear, which, whilst it will impel a man to activity so as to
ward off harm or avert danger, is never able to stir him to the
fulfilment of duty ' with a perfect heart.' This in turn imparts to
the numinous, in the Jewish conception, a new content which makes
it akin to love, and in fact the product of love. The recognition of
a religious emotion such as the numinous denotes is common in
Jewish religious thought, which distinguishes between *Yirat ha-
Onesh*, the fear of punishment, and the much loftier *Yirat ha-Rome-
mut*, the fear of the Exaltation, or as Abraham ibn Daud (*Emunah
Ramah*, ed. Weil, p. 100) designates it, *Yirat ha-Gedulah*, the fear
of the Greatness, which Joseph Albo, *Ikkarim* III, 32, describes as
' the highest quality ', תכונה אחרונה, in religion: ' For when a man
reflects and considers that God sees his open as well as hidden
acts, and compares his imperfection and poverty of understanding
with the greatness and exalted character of God, he will stand in
awe before Him, and will be ashamed to transgress His commandments and not to do His will, as a person is ashamed to do an
unbecoming thing in the presence of an honourable prince, a
respected and wise elder, who has a reputation for learning, character
and dignity. Though he may not contemplate that any harm will
come to him from a violation of his command, nevertheless he will
without doubt feel ashamed and abashed and will hesitate very
much to offend his honour in his presence ' (*Ibid*). Now Maimonides
dealing with this nobler type of fear makes it clear that it is grounded
in the love of God: ' Which is the way to love and fear Him ? At
a time when man reflects on His works and His wonderful and

stupendous creatures, and perceives from them His wisdom which is incomparable and infinite, he immediately loves, praises, glorifies and yearns with a great longing to know the " Great Name," as David said, " My soul thirsteth for God, for the living God " (Psalm xlii. 3). And when he reflects upon these very things, he immediately starts back, and is struck with fear and dread, and is conscious that he is a creature, insignificant and lowly, benighted, standing with only slight and scanty knowledge before the One who is perfect in knowledge; as David said, " When I consider Thy heavens, the work of Thy fingers . . . what is man that Thou art mindful of him ? " (Psalm viii. 4f.) '—*Yad ha-Hazakah, Yesode ha-Torah*, II, 2. In short: the religious man's progress in relation to God is (*i*) fear of punishment; (*ii*) love of God; (*iii*) fear of the Exaltation. Thus is preserved the distinction between the Creator and the creature, who can never become ' a being deified '; see *supra*, p. 77, n. 8.

[11] See R. Otto, *op. cit.*, pp. 38-9.

[12] See *op. cit.*, pp. 220-1.

[13] William Wordsworth, *Tintern Abbey*.

[14] H. Bergson, *Introduction to Metaphysics* (E.T., T. H. Hulme, 1913), p. 6.

[15] On these two types of revelation, see N. Söderblom, *The Nature of Revelation* (E.T., F. E. Pamp, 1933), p. 178; and R. Niebuhr, *The Nature and Destiny of Man*, (1943), I, pp. 135-6. See also Julius Guttmann, *Die Philosophie des Judenthums* (1933), pp. 37-8.

[16] See J. Maritain, *Science and Wisdom* (' *Science et Sagesse* '), E.T., Bernard Wall (1940). Dealing with the essential character of the wisdom of the East, he writes that ' it is first of all and above all an *ascensus*, a *movement upwards*, whereby man endeavours to pass into superhuman conditions and enter into divine liberty. From this point of view, we can see the full significance of the athleticism of mortification, the strained asceticism, and the plethora of means and recipes and methods of perfection and contemplation which can be observed in the Orient ' (p. 9). On the other hand, speaking of

the wisdom of the Old Testament, he writes, ' It is differentiated by
the fact that man does not achieve it by his own efforts. *Quis
ascendit in caelum* ? " Who will ascend heaven and look for it ? "
The heart of Israel knew that no effort of asceticism and mysticism
could *force* that wisdom. Wisdom must give itself, must itself open
the gates and descend from heaven ' (p. 14).

[16] In the Rabbinic Literature Abraham's first religious experience is said to have come to him from his reaction to the wonders of
the external world of phenomena; see *supra*, p. 80, and B.T.
Nedarim 32a.

[17] Even Judah Halevi, whose attitude to Greek philosophy is
expressed in his lines:

' Let not Greek wisdom entice thee,
    Which has no fruits, but only blossoms.' (*Diwan*, ed. Luzzatto
    fol. 41).

ואל תשיאך חכמת יונית
אשר אין לה כי אם פרחים

yet recognises the rightful claim of reason, and insists that the
Torah could not include anything which contradicted reason (see
Kuzari, I, 67, and I, 89). Reason for Judah Halevi is indeed no
mean rung in the ladder leading up to God (*ibid.*, III, 19), as is
evidenced by the primacy of place it occupies in our daily supplications. See I. Epstein, *Judah Halevi as a Philosopher*, *J.Q.R.*, *New
Series* (1935), pp. 211-12.

[18] *Hobot ha-Lebabot*, *Introduction*, אין השכל מחייב בהם, ולא דוחה
אותם Similarly, Judah Halevi, *Kuzari*, I, 67: חלילה לאל שתבא
התורה במה שידחה השכל ' Heaven forbid that the Torah should admit
aught which proof or demonstration rejects.' See also *ibid.* 89.
This attitude is well summed up by Joseph ben Shem-Tob
(d. 1480), who draws a distinction between what is *above* human
reason, and that which is *counter* to reason. ' There is a difference
whether we say that prophecy is *above* human reason, or whether
we say that it contradicts reason. For these two statements, though
denoting for simpletons one and the same thing, show on reflection
not a little difference in meaning. When we say that prophecy
is *above* reason, we mean that there are many things which

can become known only through prophecy, and not by means of demonstrative proof; not that things which demonstrative proof obliges us to accept should be contradicted by prophecy, for prophecy cannot deny that the whole is greater than a part, or the first axioms and their derivatives ' (Introduction to his Commentary on Profiat Duran's Epistle, *Al-Tehi ka-Aboteka* (' Be not like Thy fathers '), quoted in Moses Alashkar's *Responsa*, 117). This corresponds somewhat to the distinction drawn by Coleridge between reason and understanding. The understanding he regards as concerned only with the world of senses, and so dealing with conditional judgments; where it strayed into the field of spiritual realities it became often a mere faculty of unreason, though it was useful as a negative canon in rejecting what was altogether inadmissible. But reason was in accord with the moral and spiritual nature of man, and was a faculty of intuition in regard to universal and necessary truths (quoted by P. Gardner, *Modernism in the English Church* [1926], p. 70). Applied to the doctrines of Judaism, we can say that though they may not all be in accord with understanding they are all in accord alike with reason and the established truths of scientific teaching. Contrast with this the Tertullian dicta: ' *Credo quia absurdum* ', ' *Credibile quia ineptum* ', ' *Certum est quia impossibile est* ' (' I believe because it is absurd ', ' To be believed because it is foolish ', ' It is certain because it is impossible '), making incredibility the test of credibility; see Tertullian, *On the Flesh of Christ*, V. Judaism, on the other hand, whilst having too much respect for human intelligence to subscribe to any proposition involving the total surrender of human reason, nevertheless rightly recognises the limitations of the human faculties and senses and may well proclaim as an act of revealed faith, ' *Credibile quia non intellectum est* ' (' To be believed because it is beyond the understanding ')—quite a tenable and rational position which would be unscientific to assail or deny *a priori*. This limitation of the human intellect applies not only to the spiritual realities, but to reality as a whole. ' In our endeavour to understand reality we are somewhat like a man trying to understand the mechanism of a closed watch. He sees the face and the moving hands, even hears it ticking, but he has no way of opening the case. If he is

I

ingenious he may form some picture of a mechanism which could be responsible for all things he observes, but he may never be quite sure his picture is the only one which could explain his observations. He will never be able to compare his picture with the real mechanism, and he cannot even imagine the possibility or the meaning of such a comparison.'—A. Einstein and L. Infield, *The Evolution of Physics* (1938), p. 33.

CHAPTER VII

REVELATION AND PROPHECY

IT will have become evident that whilst reason and revelation are both constituents of religion, revelation is the distinctive one. Religion is essentially concerned to assert the existence of a personal relationship between man and God, and this, it has been shown, can be attested only by a personal experience for which no philosophy could act as substitute.

Revelation thus becomes the foundation of all vital religion. If this is true of religion in general, it is at least equally true of the religion of Israel, out of which all higher religions have proceeded. Indeed, the authority of all the affirmations of Judaism rests on the fact that it is a revealed religion. Judaism teaches that from the beginning all knowledge of the will of God was derived from a progressive series of personal revelations. Genesis teaches that God commanded Noah a number of precepts which came to be recognised as the foundation of religious and social life, for all men and people. Abraham was favoured with personal communications, whereby he learned to know the Lord as God of all the earth, and His way to do righteousness and justice. The Torah itself, which was to become the supreme guide in the individual and collective life of the people, was given to Israel through the mediation of Moses whom ' the Lord knew face to face ' (Deuteronomy xxxiv. 10). Also to the people of Israel itself was vouchsafed the experience of a

119

For notes on this chapter, see pp. 129-133.

revelation at the foot of Sinai which enabled it to apprehend the Divine in a unique manner. The purpose of the Sinaitic revelation to the Israelites was to confirm before their eyes the divine character of the mission of Moses, whose teachings they were to accept henceforth on trust. ' Lo, I come unto thee in a thick cloud, that the people may hear when I speak with thee, and believe thee for ever '[1] (Exodus xix. 9). True it is that following Moses there was a long line of prophets who, under the impact of the Divine Spirit, were able to interpret the happenings of the day in the light of God's moral purpose, and the spirit of God continued to speak to the people through a long succession of scribes and teachers of the Oral Law.[2] But it was the Mosaic revelation that invested the words of the teachers and prophets of Israel with authority; and it was only in so far as they took their stand on ' The Torah which Moses set before the children of Israel ' (Deuteronomy iv. 44) that their teachings were recognised as genuine and authentic.[2a]

Revelation as a psychological experience implies the inter-penetration of the infinite mind of God and the mind of man. Postulate a personal God, and it must be possible for His thoughts to find entrance into finite minds; and it is, moreover, reasonable to assert that in the early childhood of the human race, when the mind of man could not rise unaided to the loftiest spiritual heights, there were necessarily displays of power in the supra-natural realm, and divine manifestations that did not need to recur.

Like all the deepest experiences of the human mind, that of revelation must remain a mystery. Yet it by

no means denotes an interference in the natural course
of things. Given a mind at the living heart of existence,
all creation is but a revelation of the creative activity
of the Mind of the universe; and all activities of the
human spirit, as expressed in science, art or literature,
are in a sense a revelation of that Supreme Mind. It
is in virtue of some such idea that Judaism bids us, on
seeing a sage, whether Jew or non-Jew, to praise God
for having ' given of His wisdom to flesh and blood '.
And it is precisely in accordance with this attitude that
Judaism, whilst it makes the Sinaitic revelation the
basis of its teaching, alike in the domain of religion and
morals, does not deny the possibility of other revelations and of other men outside Israel coming under the
impact of the Divine Spirit.[3] Is not Balaam acknowledged by the Talmudic authorities as a prophet among
the nations of the world ? ' " There arose not in Israel
a prophet like Moses "—(Deuteronomy xxxiv. 10)—but
among the nations of the world one did arise, namely
Balaam.'[4] This, however, affords no sufficient reason
for accepting without considerable circumspection and
suspicion the claim made by any individual of having
experienced a revelation. There is always an admixture
of subjective elements such as feelings, moral tendencies, inherited prejudices, and environmental influences, which cannot but give rise to the doubt whether
the assertion made by any particular teacher or sage,
saint or even mystic, that God had revealed Himself to
him may not after all be grounded on self-deception.
' Not a few,' in the words of Judah Halevi, who was
evidently alluding to Mahomet and the Founder of
Christianity, ' have conceived out of their own inner

consciousness a religion and framed laws and said in all honesty that the laws emanated from God.'⁵ But if an individual, however exalted and perfect, might be the victim of delusions and hallucinations, and believe that God had spoken to him, it is another thing to say that the collective consciousness of a whole people should fall a victim to the same self-delusion and hallucination.

This consideration in itself raises the Sinaitic Revelation above all other experiences of the human spirit in communion with God. Not to an individual alone did the Voice at Sinai speak, but to the myriad souls of Israel assembled at its base. Nor is it to the point to argue that we have no right to assert that one nation should have been favoured more than other nations by God with such an exclusive communion. The fact remains that the revelation of God through the human spirit is not evenly distributed among individuals. Moses, Isaiah, and the other peerless Jewish prophets— those supreme religious geniuses—stand on a plane totally different from that on which other seekers after God find themselves. And what applies to individuals is equally true of peoples. That the Jewish people has been distinguished throughout the ages for its peculiar apprehension of spiritual values, and gifted to an extraordinary degree with the religious sense, cannot be contested; nor can it be denied that certain experiences in the life of the nation, such as those that followed the passing of the Egyptian tyranny, could only have served to enhance and intensify the spiritual receptive powers of the Jewish people to an extent unsurpassed since. How national experience can affect the genius of a nation is illustrated by the heights to which English literature rose in the soul-stirring days of the first Elizabethan age. Similar in its effects was the experience of Israel at the foot of Sinai. The passing of the Egyptian tyranny with the miraculous deliverance that ensued was productive among Israel of an amazing outburst of spiritual power which has never been equalled since and which, in the words of the Talmudic Sages, ' enabled the maidservant to perceive what even the prophets in their prophetic ecstasy could not attain.'[6]

As to the character of the Sinaitic Revelation, the statement of R. Ishmael (a second-century Palestinian teacher), with reference to the first two Commandments, is most illuminating: ' [The words] " I " and " There shall not be unto thee " have been heard from the mouth of the Omnipotent.'[7]

This simplifies considerably the whole conception of the Revelation at Sinai (*Maamad-har-Sinai*). According to Rabbi Ishmael, only the first two commandments did Israel hear from God, whereas the other commands the people received from Moses. This is another way of saying that that national mystical experience at Sinai which enabled Israel to apprehend in a unique manner the divine was limited, as far as the people themselves were concerned, to God's special dealings with Israel (as proclaimed in the first commandment), and to His Oneness (as affirmed in the second commandment.)[8] The other commandments the people accepted on trust at the hands of Moses, whose divine mission they had seen confirmed before their eyes.

It will, of course, be argued that granted that such a national spiritual experience as that represented by the Sinaitic revelation is possible, what proof is there that it did ever occur in the life of Israel? In other words, what evidence is there that the Biblical record of the revelation at Sinai is historical, and does not belong altogether to the realm of myth and fiction? Here, an impartial judgment cannot be in doubt about the answer. Apart from the impossibility of accounting for such a notion arising and passing unchallenged unless it had substance in fact,[9] the history of Israel is one of the most impressive evidences in favour of this claim. The wonderful and amazing story of our people is bound to confirm any candid and unbiased student of religion in the belief that there has been a real covenant between God and Israel—a unique spiritual experience — a revelation in the life of our people, that was productive of the most momentous results in history and that transformed a people which for generations had been brick-making helots into the most tremendous dynamic moral and spiritual force the world has ever seen. Indeed, so all-compelling is the character of this historical evidence that it has been acknowledged by writers and thinkers of many different schools of philosophy and thought. To give one example where many could be quoted, let the words of the late Nicolas Berdyaev, the well-known Russian philosopher, suffice: ' The Jews ', he writes in his book *The Meaning of History*, ' have played an all-important rôle in history. They are pre-eminently an historical people and their destiny reflects the indestructibility of the divine decrees. Their destiny is too imbued with the " metaphysical " to be explained either in material or positive-historical terms. . . . I remember how the materialist interpretation of history, when I attempted in my youth to verify it by applying it to the destinies of peoples, broke down on the case of the Jews, whose destiny seemed absolutely inexplicable from the materialistic standpoint. And, indeed, according to the materialistic and positive criterion, this people ought long ago to have perished. Its survival is a mysterious and wonderful phenomenon demonstrating that the life of this people is governed by a special predetermination, transcending the process of adaptation expounded by the materialistic interpretation of history. The survival of the Jews, their resistance to destruction, their endurance under absolutely peculiar conditions and the fateful rôle played by them in history—all these point to the particular and mysterious foundation of their destiny.'[10]

Turning from the Sinaitic Revelation to that of the prophets of Israel, we are afforded a similar legitimation of their claim, which is shared by no other religion. ' One of the best proofs that the prophets were not victims of self-illusion,' declares Judah Halevi, ' is provided by the harmony and agreement among all the prophets in regard to themselves and their mission.'[11] This idea is further developed by W. Sanday in his work *Inspiration*. ' If one prophet here, and another prophet there,' he writes: ' had been supposed to be sent by God and to have words put in their mouths by Him, it would not be so surprising; but as it is we find the whole line of prophets stretching from Moses, from Amos, from Nathan, from Samuel to Malachi, all make the same assumption. The formulae which they use are the same—" Thus saith the Lord ".

" The word of the Lord came," " Hear ye the word of the Lord." Such an identity of language implies an identity of psychological fact behind it; but if an individual may be subject to delusions, it is another thing to say that a class so long extended could be subject to them—and to delusions with so much method about them.'[12]

Furthermore, if we examine many of the utterances of the prophets we note that they are acutely conscious of the contrast between their own feelings and ideas on the one hand and, on the other, the purpose and mind of God who constrains them. This is vividly presented in the prophets' resistance to the divine call and their reluctance to answer it as well as in the conversations they hold with God, their arguments, their contentions with Him, reflecting their own feelings, questions and complaints. Such instances recur constantly in the writings of the prophets. One has only to think in this connection of Isaiah, Amos, Jeremiah, how they all pleaded with God not to be burdened with His mission. The prophets are thus clearly conscious of two distinct currents or forces within them, the current of their own feelings and the over-mastering pressure of God who possesses them, making His mind and will articulate to them and through them.[12a]

The prophets, because they are conscious of being even violently dealt with and possessed, belong to a class entirely by themselves. Their communications are not essays in self-expression like those of the poet and sculptor, musician and painter. They are *inspired* in the real sense of the word. They had something breathed in them from without, something that carried with it that sure sense of *givenness*,[13] whereby the human spirit responds to the self-manifesting spirit instructing man in his laws and his ways.

Psychologically considered, the individual upon whom the spirit of God has come remains, like revelation itself, a mystery. In much of what the prophets said or did, we must go beyond them and recognise that they were wrought upon by some mysterious force lying beyond the veil of phenomena. The nearest approach to the gift of prophecy is that of genius, and like genius prophecy defies every attempt to explain it on natural grounds. As Shakespeare was inspired above all other poets and Beethoven above all other musicians, so were the Hebrew prophets inspired above all other religious teachers. By some power, of which we have no knowledge, they were able to burst through the bonds of their natural environment, and perceive things not perceived by others and see things not seen by others. And just as genius can defy the limitations of circumstance and environment, so can the prophets, for genius is not a quality of the mind, but a quality of the soul.

A certain school of psychologists, of which the late Dr. William Brown of Oxford was the most noted representative in this country, are wont to make a distinction between what they call the empiric ego, the ego of the mind, and the pure ego, the ego of the soul. While the former is within the province of psychology, the latter is beyond its domain. For psychology, it is maintained, is not the science of the soul, but the science of the mind, the mental processes in time. Psychology deals with the structure of the mind, shows how it develops in course of time, how the young child starts with his ego partly organised and to a certain extent inherited. The child inherits aptitudes and interests from ancestors, just as it inherits the organisation of physical body. It inherits talent, which is characteristic of the empiric ego, the ego which is the result of experience, of the inter-relation of man with his environment. But there is one thing that the child cannot inherit. It cannot inherit genius. For genius is the product of pure ego. It does not come from heredity or environment. If we consider, say, Shakespeare, we find no evidence of supreme literary gift in any of his ancestors or in the history of his race. Such powers as genius exhibits have their source, not in the empiric ego, the mind which psychologists can analyse, but in the pure ego, the soul.[14] And it was the peculiar quality of the soul of the prophets that made them the supreme religious geniuses of history.

Like genius, their prophetic gift was essentially creative. Genius produces new things which have never before existed. It is not always easy to say wherein the originality lies, but the quality of creating something which may be called new is the distinction between genius and talent. Talent can be helped along by rules and patterns. Genius gives rise to new rules which are afterwards established by analysis. ' First comes *creation*—revelation, beauty of character, the building up of society, a work of art. Then comes *theory*—theology, ethics, political science, theory of art. It is just the same as in God's created world—first, the flower, then the science of flowers, botany. Genius

appears as a part of the Almighty's continuous creation.'[15]   Existence is difficult to understand and often
seems to be bitterly void of meaning.   Then genius
appears, and by its activity and creation it often helps
us to grasp the meaning of existence.   Viewed in this
light, the prophets of Israel, from Moses onwards,
were the greatest creative geniuses in history.   In considering their teachings, which were in violent conflict
with all the tendencies of their environment and the
trends of their age, and the effect of their teachings on
the widest and most permanent field, it is impossible
not to feel that they exhibit a unique power that was
creative of new values, which show them to have been
in closer touch with reality than other men.[16]   These
values constitute the quintessence of Judaism; and an
examination and discussion of them forms the subject
of the chapters which follow.

NOTES

[1] See Maimonides, *Yad ha-Hazakah*, *Yesode ha-Torah*, 8, 1.

[2] The Oral Law (of which the Talmud is now the repository) is
that body of Jewish traditional teaching which in its origin goes
back in an unbroken chain of continuity to the Men of the Great
Assembly, and from them to the Prophets, and through the Prophets
and the Elders to Joshua, and finally to Moses who received it from
God Himself.   Its function is twofold.   In the first place it interprets
the ordinances of the Written Law, explaining their contents and
defining their scope.   As such, the Oral Law forms an integral and
indispensable part of the Written Law, for without the Oral Law
it would be impossible to observe the Written Law.   How for example
could the Biblical Sabbath laws be observed, if there were no Oral
Law to define the term ' work ' ?   In the second place, the Oral
Law adapts and modifies the ordinances of the Written Law to

changes in conditions and circumstances—social, domestic and economic. As such the Oral Law serves to transform the Torah from a mere written document liable to become obsolete into a continuous revelation keeping pace with the ages. Hillel's *Prozbul*, designed to overcome the operation of the year of Release in regard to the cancellation of debts, is an example of a Biblical Law (Deuteronomy xv. 15ff.) modified to meet altered conditions. Included in the Oral Law with all the authority it commands are the numerous measures and enactments introduced by the recognised religious leaders either as a ' hedge round the Law ' (e.g. the prohibition of handling a working implement on the Day of Rest) or as an expression of religious devotion and loyalty (e.g. the kindling of lights on Chanukah). T. H. Huxley, *Science and the Hebrew Tradition* (1893), p. 363ff, dealing with the ' hedge round the Law ' writes, ' The world being what it was, it is to be doubted whether Israel would have preserved intact the pure ore of religion which the Prophets had extracted for the use of mankind as for the nation, had not the leaders been zealous even to death for the dross of the law in which it was embedded. Of all the strange ironies in history, perhaps the strangest is that Pharisee is current as a term of reproach among theological descendants of that sect of Nazareans who without the martyr spirit of those primitive Puritans would have never come into existence. They, like their historical successors, our own Puritans, have shared the general fate of the poor wise men who saved cities.' In an article, entitled *The Rabbinic Tradition*, contributed to a volume of essays, *The Jewish Heritage*, which is in course of publication, I have shown that the Oral Law is characterised by its progressiveness, permanence and authoritativeness, as well as by its fundamental conception of the unity of religion and life, which has made Judaism into a way of life, deeply devotional and spiritual, without being unworldly and unpractical.

[2a] That the Prophets were in no sense innovators but simply revivers of the Mosaic religion, is shown by W. F. Albright *From the Stone Age to Christianity* (1946), pp. 86, 230ff.

[3] Seder Olam Rabbah, 1: ' Eber (the son of Shem) was a great prophet.' נביא גדול היה עבר also 21: ' These (Shem and Eber) are the prophets that arose to the nations of the world before

Abraham.' אלו נביאים שעמדו לעולם עד שלא בא אברהם אבינו לעולם
Similarly in Midrash Genesis Rabbah, LII, 11. See also *Tanna de-be Eliyyahu*, IX: ' I call to witness heaven and earth, that on all human beings whether gentile or Israelite, man or woman, according to their deeds so does the Holy Spirit rest upon them." מעיד אני עלי
את השמים ואת הארץ בין גוי ובין ישראל, בין איש ובין אשה, בין עבד ובין
שפחה, הכל לפי מעשה שעושה כך רוח הקודש שורה עליו. In Midrash Ruth Rabbah, II, 1, it is stated that the Holy spirit rested on Rahab.

[4] Sifre on Deuternonomy xxxiv. 10. See also Midrash Numbers Rabbah XX, 21. In Baba Bathra, 15b, seven are said to have arisen as prophets among the nations: Balaam and his father, Job, Eliphaz the Temanite, Bildad the Shuhite, Zophar the Naamathite, and Elihu the son of Berachel, the Buzite. See also Midrash Leviticus Rabbah, II, 9.

[5] *Kuzari*, I, 87: ואפשר שיתדמה לו . . . כאיש שמדבר עמו ושומע
דבריו בנפשו . . . ובמחשבתו ואז יאמר כי הבורא דבר בו. See also Jacob Anatoli (1199-1256), *Malmad ha-Talmidim*, p. 192: ' For the nations do not boast of any of their saints or prophets having performed signs or wonders openly in the sight of their friends or enemies. All the miracles of which they boast are but hidden and secret things, for they say that in such and such a place, in a certain cave or mountain or forest, such and such a thing happened and there the prophet performed the miracles.' כי אלו האומות
לא התפארו באחד מקדושיהם או נביאיהם שעשה אותות או מופתים גלוים לעיני
האוהבים והאויבים רק כל מופתיהם אשר יתפארו בם הם דברי מטמוניות
וסתרים כי אמרו במקום פלוני, במערה אחת או בהר אחד, או ביער אחד אירע
כך וכך ושם עשה הנביא מופתים. Even the Resurrection which is central to Christianity was witnessed only by three women, among them Mary Magdalene, ' from whom seven demons had gone out,' and the disciples who saw Jesus after the crucifixion were very few indeed; see J. Klausner, *From Jesus to Paul* (E.T. by William E. Stinespring, 1942), pp. 255-6 and 439.

[6] See Mechilta on Exodus, xv. 2.

[7] B.T. Horayot, 5a: אנכי ולא יהיה לך מפי הגבורה שמענו

[8] See Maimonides, *Guide*, II, 33. Cf. Baruch ben Abraham, the ' Maggid ' of Kosow (18th Century), *Yesod ha-Avodah*, Introduction,

31: ' Moses did not hear a voice of words from God at all, but apprehended the whole Torah with his intellectual and spiritual faculties, when he prepared himself for that wonderful prophecy which was vouchsafed to him.' משה לא שמע קול דברים מפי הקב״ה כלל ועקר רק השיג בשכלו כל התורה בהשגה רוחנית ושכלית כשהכין עצמו לנבואתו הנפלאה.

⁹ The fact that no other religion ventured to make such a claim is the best guarantee of the validity of Israel's claim regarding the Sinaitic revelation; Cf. Saadia, *Emunot we-Deot*, Introduction, Slucki ed., p. 12. Rosenblatt, E.T., p. 29.

¹⁰ Nicolas Berdyaev, *The Meaning of History* (1936), pp. 86-87. See also Bahya ibn Pakuda, *Hobot ha-Lebabot*, II, 5: ' If anyone seeks evidence at the present (for the wonders of the Exodus and for the Sinaitic Revelation), let him look with candid eyes at our position among the nations since the Exile began, and our settled condition in their midst, notwithstanding that we do not agree with them in belief and practice, of which disagreement they are aware . . . This is even as our Creator promised us, "And yet for all that when they are in the land of their enemies I will not reject them, neither will I abhor them utterly to destroy them, to break my covenant with them . . ." (Leviticus xxvi. 44) . . . " If it had not been for the Lord who was for us, let Israel say now . . . when men rose up against us, then they would have swallowed us up alive, etc. . . ." (Psalm cxxiv. 1ff.).' Eloquent too are the words of Jacob Emden (1697-1776) giving expression to the same thought in his *Siddur* (Warsaw ed. p. 8): ' We are the exiled nation, the scattered sheep, after all the troubles and vicissitudes we have passed through during thousands of years, nor is there any nation in the world which is being persecuted as we are. How many have been our oppressors, how mighty those who rose against us from our youth, in order to destroy and uproot us; to the utmost have they afflicted us because of their hatred, of which jealousy is the cause, yet they have not prevailed against us. . . . Of all ancient and mighty nations the memory is lost, their expectations gone, their shadow departed, but we who cleave unto the Eternal, are all alive to this day. . . . What can the sharp-witted philosopher say to this ? Hath the hand of chance wrought all this ? By my life !

When I reflect on all these wonders, they appear to me greater than all the miracles and wondrous acts which God performed for our ancestors in Egypt and in the wilderness, and in the Land of Israel. The longer the exile lasts, the more confirmed does this miracle become, and all the acts of His power and might '.

[11] *Kuzari*, iv 3: והראיה הגדולה על אמתתם הסכמת כל המין ההוא על הצורות ההן

[12] W. Sanday, *Inspiration* (1893), p. 149.

[12a] See Ch. Gore, *Belief in God* (Pelican Book, 1939), pp. 8off.

[13] See F. Von Hügel, *Essays and Addresses on the Philosophy of Religion* (1921), pp. 56ff.

[14] See W. Brown, *Personality and Religion* (1946), pp. 157-8. A genius is also not subject to the limitations of time. Mozart in speaking of one of his compositions tells us that he had it in his head before he wrote it down. He heard all the notes *together-zusammen*. That was a wonderful experience, he said, the like of which he never heard again. See W. Brown, *op. cit.* p. 149. ' Mozart describes thus the manner of his composing: First bits and crumbs come, and gradually join together in his mind, then the soul getting warmed to the work, the thing grows more and more, " And I spread it out broader and clearer, and at last it gets almost finished in my head, even when it is a long piece, so that I can see the whole of it at a single glance in my mind, as if it were a beautiful painting or a handsome human being; in which way, I do not hear it in my imagination at all as a succession—the way it must come later—but all at once as it were. It is a rare feast! All the inventing and making goes on in me as in a beautiful strong dream. But the best of all, is *the hearing of it all at once."* ' Quoted by William James, *Principles of Psychology*, I (1890), p. 255. Cf. *Kuzari*, IV, 5, where the Prophets are said to be able to perceive a variety of things all at once, ברגע אחד.

[15] See N. Söderblom, *The Living God* (1933), p. 356.

[16] The former tendency among modern scholars to regard the Prophets merely as ecstatics has now given way to a more sober appreciation of their intellectual gifts and religious genius; see Th. J. Meek, *Hebrew Origins* (1950), pp. 176ff.

K

CHAPTER VIII

THE CONCEPTION OF GOD

THE prophets to whom, as already stated, we owe the ideals of true religion and true morality, were neither theoreticians nor philosophers. They were essentially practical men, with little or no interest in pure speculation, but concerned more with facts of daily life. As practical men, their whole teaching was given for practical and not for speculative purposes. While it is true that many of their propositions belong to the domain of the intellectual, their insistence upon the acceptance of these propositions was because of their practical implications.

In this spirit did the prophets indicate to us the attitude of Judaism to the whole body of truths about God and man, constituting the faith of Israel. While Judaism is based on certain fundamental doctrines which give it significance and value, it attaches, as mentioned previously,[1a] no importance to beliefs as beliefs. Faith was never regarded by Judaism as a consecrated act on which salvation depends, and it is considered of value only in so far as it leads to right action. Faith, indeed, in Judaism is meaningless unless translated into right action. There is thus no place in Judaism for the Pauline doctrine of justification by faith, which forms the corner-stone of the Christian religion, in any of its interpretations. The mere act of faith neither wins for the sinner any forgiveness, nor bestows on the believer some unnatural power to

134

realise a goodness of which he is naturally incapable.

Faith in Judaism is not a theological concept, but a purely human act, expressed in a certain norm of conduct, and is of the same category as the faith that governs human relations. We constantly live by faith, and in our common intercourse with our fellows we daily exercise this function. On the whole, we trust our fellow-men and act on this trust; on the whole, we assume our fellow to be one on whose word we may rely, and we act on this assumption. This is the kind of faith, distinguishable only by its unyielding and unflinching character, by its moral intensity and its special object, on which stress is laid in the Jewish religion. It means firm reliance upon God and trust in Him, and the kind of conduct that proceeds from this reliance and trust. A man who has firm confidence in the justice of God will himself be just. A man who has absolute reliance in the righteousness of God will himself be righteous. This close connection between human conduct and faith is expressed by the Hebrew term *Emunah*, which denotes both faith and faithfulness, i.e. trustworthiness. The man of faithfulness is an *Ish Emunah* or *Emunim;* and the man of faith is a *Baal Emunah*. For it is the man of the highest faith in God who is a man of the greatest faithfulness, and it is only the man of faithfulness who can be truly considered a man of faith.[1]

Judaism thus fixes the centre of gravity for faith in man himself. His firm faith in God makes him a man in whom there is trusting, whom God, so to speak, trusts. Abraham was a classical example of such a man.

Of him it is said, ' And thou didst find his heart trust-worthy before thee' (Nehemiah ix. 8).   The godless man is not so much the man who has no faith in God, but the man in whom there is no faithfulness.   He belongs to those of whom it is said ' They are children in whom there is no trusting ' (Deuteronomy xxxii. 20). Whilst the righteous man, as the prophet Habakkuk tells us (ii. 4), is one who lives by his faithfulness,[2] a faithfulness which is the fruit of his faith.   In the Pauline conception, on the other hand, the whole centre of gravity is placed in God.   With the Fall as the pivot of his system, Paul denied man any merit whatsoever, and he consequently had to transform the whole conception of faith into something purely theological and mystical, charged with supernatural qualities and powers to save man from divine wrath, to redeem him from the pangs of sin and death, brought about by the disobedience of Adam, the first man.[3]

Bearing in mind this attitude of Judaism in regard to faith, we may now proceed to set forth and examine the various doctrinal affirmations of the Jewish religion. The whole Jewish religion revolves around the accept-ance of the existence of a ' personal ' God.   By this is meant the affirmation that what controls our life is not a blind force of which we know little, or nothing, but a supreme Being which, although beyond our imagining, is yet possessed of intelligence, purpose, will and other excellent qualities which we are wont to associate with the term ' personality '.   Of course, we may say—nay, we must say—that the term ' per-sonality ' is totally inadequate to describe God.   It is a term too much limited by its human associations to be applied to God. We nevertheless use it of God, because the word ' personality ' expresses the ' most glorious ' form of existence with which we are acquainted;[4] and, when we speak of God as a person, we mean that God is not an impersonal force. He is not a mere force or law, not an It, but a He.

This must be insisted upon, as we could not, as persons, have any relationship, such as that which constitutes the essence of all religious belief, with an impersonal force. An impersonal God must remain impervious to human prayers and supplications, and cannot be possessed of any of those higher values we strive to realise in our lives. It was in order to awaken and to safeguard this sense of personal relation with God that the Bible did not hesitate to resort to anthropomorphic descriptions of God, ascribing to Him attributes of a Person.[5] The very word ' personality,' however, explain it as you will, is suggestive of limitations and imperfections. To obviate these religiously dangerous implications, Judaism emphasises the incorporeality of God, as all limitations and imperfections in human personality are imposed in a large measure by the body that envelops it; and forbids the making of any image of God.[6] God is thus affirmed to be Pure Spirit. It is, of course, impossible for us to envisage a spirit, as our experience does not reach out to something which cannot be seen, touched or felt; but neither can the human spirit, the soul, the life that fills the human body, as well as everything around us, be seen.

' " Bring me a fruit from that tree." " Here it is, venerable Sir." " Cut it open." " It is cut open,

venerable Sir." " What seest thou in it ? " " Very
small seeds, venerable Sir." " Cut open one of them."
" It is cut open, venerable Sir." " What seest thou
in it ? " " Nothing, venerable Sir." Then spake he,
" That hidden thing which thou seest not, O gentle
youth, from that hidden thing verily has this mighty
tree grown." [7]

Indeed, He whom we see not is the source and life
of all being. In fact the human soul provides the Sages
of the Talmud with the nearest analogy after which
God is best conceived.

' As the soul fills the body, so God fills the world;
as the soul sustains the body, so God sustains the world;
as the soul sees but is not seen, so God sees but is not
seen.' [8]

It will be noted that the analogy between God and
the soul, as applied by the Talmudic Sages, goes
beyond the mere idea of God as the invisible source of
existence. It also serves to illustrate the conception of
the immanence of God, that is, His omnipresence,[9]
which has ever been recognised as fundamental to
Jewish doctrine: ' As the soul fills the human body,
so God fills the world.' The immanence of God is a
dominant tenet of Jewish religious faith. Already in
the Bible we find this truth affirmed over and over
again in no uncertain terms. ' Can any man hide
himself in secret places that I should not see him?
saith the Lord, Do I not fill Heaven and earth? '
(Jeremiah xxiii. 24). ' The fullness of the whole
earth is His glory ' (Isaiah vi. 3)—His glory (*Kabod*)
denoting here the manifestation of the Divine presence.[10] Or, as the Psalmist so beautifully expresses it,

' Whither shall I go from Thy spirit ?
Or whither shall I flee from Thy presence ?
If I ascend up to Heaven, Thou art there,
If I make my bed in the nether-world, behold, Thou
  art there.
If I take the wings of the morning,
And dwell in the uttermost parts of the sea,
Even there would Thy hand lead me,
And Thy right hand would hold me '

(Psalm cxxxix. 7-10).

The teaching of the Bible is equally the doctrine of
Rabbinic Judaism. So deeply conscious were the
Rabbis of the all-pervading presence of God, that they
coined a special term to describe it. This term is
Shechinah,' which means literally, ' Indwelling '.[11]
' The *Shechinah* is everywhere,'[12] ' there is no place
devoid of the *Shechinah* '[13]—are some of the dicta by
which they sought to give expression to this overwhelming sense which they had of God's omnipresence. The thought of divine immanence also
suffuses the whole of the Jewish mystic literature.
Among the most impressive utterances in this connection may be quoted the one in the ' Song of Unity '.[14]

' Everything is in Thee, and Thou art everything.
Thou fillest everything and dost encompass it.
When everything was created, Thou wast everything,
Before everything was created, Thou wast every-
  thing.'[15]

The doctrine that God is in everything does not
mean that He is revealed in equal fullness, say, in a clod

139

of earth and in a man; this would be indistinguishable from pantheism.[16] What it does mean is that everything reveals His activity at least in some measure and degree —all according to the character of the medium through which it is made manifest. In a sense God is present even in the smallest particle of matter, the recent discoveries of the miracles of matter, its atoms, its ions, its electrons, only serving to testify to the divine activity which energises it. In a higher degree He is present in a plant, for a plant is alive; higher still in an animal, for the animal is truly animate; still higher in human personality, for man is made in the image of God, and still higher in the godlike man. The doctrine of the different degrees of divine immanence forms the basic theme of Judah Halevi's *Kuzari*. His conception of the *al-amr al-ilahi*, (in Hebrew: *ha-inyan ha-elohi*),[17] the ' Divine Thing ',[18] is an attempt to define this doctrine within the context of Jewish religious thought. With this conception, Judah Halevi seeks to counter the arguments of the naturalism that would limit divine activity in the universe. All that occurs in Nature is ultimately the work of God. There is no clear-cut distinction between the natural and the supernatural. All is conceived as being in one continuous order. There is nothing absolutely natural. The whole creation is embraced by the unceasing and unfailing, ever-active ever-sustaining Divine Thing. Nor is there anything absolutely supernatural. It is only a question of the degree of the intractability in the informed medium within which the Divine activity manifests itself. Just as the rays of the sun are reflected in varying intensity and character according to the nature of the bodies receiving its light, so is the extent of the manifestation of the Divine Thing dependent upon the nature of the medium in which it is expressed.[19]

Reverting to the Rabbinic comparison of God and the soul, whilst keeping steadily before our mind the necessary inadequacy of the analogy, we may pursue it a little further and apply it to the conception of the transcendence of God, that is, His otherness and independence. It is true that the soul fills and sustains the body, but only in so far as it animates the body and endows it with life and energy. But in no way, at least in Jewish teaching, is the soul identical with the body or dependent upon it. It transcends the body, and has an existence apart from man's physical frame.[20] So it is with God and the world. God is present everywhere in the world; but that does not mean that He is identical with the world, or limited by it. Nor does it follow, because the world is dependent upon Him, that He is dependent on the world. He is present and active in His universe, not because He is organically one with it, but because He is master of it, the whole universe being pervaded, enveloped and sustained by the mystery of His will.

The transcendence of God lies at the foundation of the Jewish religion. Already on the first appearance of God to Moses in the burning bush He revealed Himself under the name *Ehyeh Asher Ehyeh*, ' I Am that I Am,'[21] which involves the idea of God as the absolute self-existent being, the only ' I Am ', a claim which no mere form of existence can make. As the ' I Am ', God is pure being, unique, unqualified and ineffable. He is *Kadosh*, the Holy One, that means, He is wholly other, *sui generis*, incomparable.[22] ' To whom will ye liken Me, that I should be equal, saith the Holy One ' (Isaiah xl. 25). He is exalted and sublime, transcending every phenomenon, unconditioned by any mode of manifestation or existence, and independent of all beside Himself. ' Thus saith the High and Holy One that inhabiteth eternity, Whose name is Holy. I dwell in the high and holy places ' (Isaiah lvii. 15).

These two concepts of immanence and transcendence, as it has been well remarked, although tending in opposite directions, never existed in Jewish religious thought separately, but always intermingled so as to form the unitive Jewish doctrine of God.[23] Unmistakably clear, in this connection, is Jeremiah's declaration, ' Am I a God near at hand, saith the Lord, and not a God afar off ' (Jeremiah xxiii. 24). Sufficiently explicit too, is Isaiah's song of the *Seraphs:* ' Holy, Holy, Holy is the Lord of Hosts, the fullness of the whole earth is His glory ' (Isaiah vi. 3), in which we hear the proclamation both of God's transcendence (His Holiness), and His immanence (the fullness of the earth which constitutes His glory).[24]

What is true of the Bible is equally true of the teaching of the Rabbis. Maintaining and deepening, in homily, parable and wise saying, the Biblical doctrine of God, they gave formal expression to it in the classical phrase, ' He is the place of the world, but the world is not His place.'[25]

The God of Jewish teaching is thus both immanent and transcendent. He is immanent in the sense that there is no element or phase of existence that does not reflect His presence and activity; and He is transcendent in the sense that He is completely other than, and entirely independent of, all aspects and manifestations of His nature and being. Both aspects of God are stressed in Jewish doctrine.[26] For a God of absolute transcendence would be too far away to be relevant to our lives; whilst a God of pure immanence would be too much immersed in our being to be of any real help to us.[27]

The precise relation of these two elements of transcendence and immanence is admittedly hard to define, but the Rabbinic analogy between God and the soul affords, as we have seen, some model on which this relationship is to be conceived.

Much is heard to-day of the age-old reluctance to attribute personality to God. Modern writers prefer to speak of God as impersonal; the assumption being that by this usage a higher plane of thought is reached than that common to the highest religions, which are stigmatised as anthropomorphic in that they make God in the image of man. A typical representative of this attitude is Julian Huxley, who in his book, *Religion without Revelation*, pleads for the ' liberation of the idea of God from the shackles of personality,'[28] and expresses his conviction that ' religion of the highest and fullest character can co-exist with a complete absence of belief in revelation in any straightforward sense of the word, and in that kernel of revealed religion, namely a personal God.'[29]

What exactly he means by God, after denying to Him His attributes of personality, Huxley does not attempt to explain. The best he can say on the subject is that ' God is one name for the Universe as it impinges on our lives.'[30]   Neither does he adduce any reason for retaining belief in a God who is non-personal, and with whom one cannot enter into personal relationship. Huxley is apparently not unaware of the difficulty, and he seeks to fill the void thus created by affirming the existence of a spiritual Universe possessed of spiritual values, such as truth, beauty, goodness, which should call forth our love and reverence. He does not, however, seem to realise that to speak of a spiritual Universe that is non-personal, involves a contradiction in terms. Spiritual values are, after all, centred in personality, and it is meaningless to talk of spiritual values without the association of a living personality. Intelligence, ethical concepts or values are perceptible only in personalities, and can emanate from, and be expressed only by, personalities. And so is an impersonal deity a contradiction in terms. It may be a materialistic deity, but not one of ' high religious maturity.' Once he is deprived of will, purpose, and other such attributes that constitute personality, he becomes like the idols of the heathens of old that have ears and hear not, eyes and see not. Nor will any amount of refinement or sublimation of his essence endow him with a spiritual quality. He will remain a material being, mechanical in his behaviour and with reactions not different to that of electricity or gravitation.

It will have become evident that religion has no meaning without the postulate of a ' personal ' God. Nor has a spiritual Universe any significance without the recognition of a personality behind the scheme of things.

The mistake of these moderns who recoil from the

thought of ascribing personality to God, is to confuse
' personality ' and ' corporeality.' In fact the two are
quite separate and distinct. ' Corporeality ' is restric-
tive; ' personality ' is expansive. ' Corporeality ' is
quantitative; 'personality' is qualitative. ' Corp-
poreality ' is instrumental; ' personality ' is functional.
What imparts to a mind personality is not the hands,
the eyes, the brain, but the power to organise, direct
and unify the various component parts of the body
into one single purpose and goal. Personality is mind
become autonomous—mind become emancipated from
bondage to the body. If the Universe has a mind, that
mind would then be more, rather than less, personal
than our own. For it would have more, rather than less,
unity and organicity.[31]

Now that the ultimate reality is to be conceived in
terms of mind is a postulate which the recent study of
Nature has compelled many a modern scientist to
adopt. Physicists, as well as psychologists, have as a
result of their researches come to the conclusion that the
emergence of mental and psychical characteristics in
certain things is inexplicable, unless we attribute such
mental and psychical powers and propensities to the
universe as a whole and to the elemental units which
constitute the substratum of things. They refuse,
therefore, to translate reality into bare materialistic
terms. The most distinguished of these scientists,
Whitehead, finds it impossible to complete an account
of the natural order without assuming the existence of
that which is ' beyond the flux of things.'[32] Given a
mind as the ultimate reality, how else are we to describe
it than at least in terms of personality, at the same time

of course not failing to recognise that it immeasurably surpasses and transcends all that we know of personality in its human form ?

As W. R. Matthews remarks, ' All thought must, after all, be conditioned by the experience and nature of the thinker. To try to find concepts which are not in some sense human, is like to attempt to jump out of one's skin. We cannot use categories which we do not possess, nor measure the world with any instrument but our own intelligence.'[33] A divine being can, therefore, be described by man only in those terms with which he is most familiar, namely, those terms in which he describes his own being. ' I address my prayers to a personal God ', writes Tolstoy in his Diary, ' not because God is personal (I know that He is illimitable), but because I myself am personal and limited. If I wear green spectacles I see everything green, although I know perfectly well that the world is not green.'[34]

The materialist who describes the world as a machine, does not escape this limitation. ' In a sense,' says James Ward, ' we are always anthropomorphic, since we can never divest ourselves of our consciousness; hence not only spiritualistic intuition but the very mechanical interpretation of the Universe, which in the last analysis derives its concepts from our human experience, is of an anthropomorphic nature.'[35] Indeed, if theism is anthropomorphism, materialism is what B. H. Streeter calls ' mechanomorphism '—an attempt to fashion the infinite in the image of a machine. A machine is after all something made by man for the attainment of certain ends. Hence to use the term

' Mechanism ' at all for the description of natural phenomena is to be guilty of a double anthropomorphism. The anthropomorphism of religion interprets the Universe in terms of human personality—that is to say, in terms of the most remarkable natural product of the Universe. But mechanism is a conception doubly anthropomorphic, for it is derived from artificial constructions devised by human personality for its own private uses.[36]

This has always been the view of Judaism, and is not something which has been forced upon it by modern thought. Whilst the Torah, as already mentioned, found it necessary to resort to anthropomorphistic terms and expressions with reference to God, the Rabbis have, at the same time, always insisted that all anthropomorphic expressions in the Torah were simply due to the inadequacy of human speech and are not to be taken literally. ' We describe Him by comparing Him to His creatures in order to make intelligible to the human ear as much as it can understand.'[37]

We have seen that the concept of divine personality is the life-breath of religion, without which there could exist no possibility of personal relations with the supreme reality—a relation which religion is concerned to maintain. But there is another implication in the concept of personality which makes it basic to the Jewish doctrine of God. Personality connotes on the one hand freedom and on the other hand individuality or distinctiveness. Thus we come to the heart of Hebrew theism which distinguishes it from all pantheistic religions, ancient and modern. In pantheism,

God is One, not merely in the sense that there is one God only, but in the sense that nothing truly exists save God. He is infinite, not merely in the sense that he possesses all perfection, but in the sense that all which exists is embraced within the divine Being, and all that occurs is a mode of divine life and activity. In the pantheistic scheme of thought, according to Spinoza, its most prominent exponent, besides God no substance can be granted or conceived, because God is the in-dwelling not transcendent—that is, external—cause of all things. God in pantheism is thus no longer a personal Being with will and purpose, but an underlying reality which in-dwells or inheres equally in all things, good or bad, ordinary or extra-ordinary.

But that is not all. Pantheism, in identifying the universe with God, is not distinguishable from atheism. Schopenhauer described it ' a polite form of atheism.'[38] In fact, it is not different in principle from polytheism, except that whereas polytheism worships Nature, pantheism compounds God with Nature. But to identify God with all, or the sum of things, is to deny alike God's freedom and distinctiveness, and thus to abandon the chief elements in monotheism.[39] For there is a great difference between the assertion that all reality depends upon God, or even as Jewish mysticism, through the voice of Moses Cordovero (1522-1570) expresses it, ' God is all reality,' and the assertion that ' all reality *is* God.'[40]

Here, too, as in all matters of Jewish doctrine, the test applied is practical. Morally, pantheism is bereft of all content. Once identify God with the actual world, and moral distinctions vanish into the universal vacuum and disappear altogether. Since evil exists, as well as good, God must be sinful as well as holy, cruel as well as merciful, unjust as well as just.

The more thorough-going pantheists admit this. Hegel, for example, says, ' What kind of an absolute Being is that which has not all actuality and more particularly evil within itself ? '[41] The pantheist may speak of cosmic perfection, but this has no moral connotation. The non-moral character of pantheism has been well expressed by William James, when he writes, ' Visible nature is all plasticity and indifference —a moral multiverse, as one might call it, and not a moral universe. To such a harlot we owe no allegiance. With her as whole we can establish no moral communion; and we are free in our dealings with her several parts to obey or destroy, and to follow no law but that of prudence in coming to terms with such of her particular features as will help us to our private ends. If there be a divine Spirit of the Universe, Nature such as we know her cannot be its *ultimate word* to man. Either there is no Spirit revealed in Nature, or else it is inadequately revealed there, and (as all the higher religions have assumed) what we call visible Nature, or *this* world, must be but a veil and surface-show whose full meaning resides in a supplementary or *other* world.'[42]

So much for the moral character of pantheism. Nor can the pantheistic doctrine meet the requirements of the religious criterion. It appeals, indeed, to the sense of obligation, and disposes the soul to utter resignation; but it provokes the moral nature in man to

L

protest and revolt, since most people find it impossible
to pay reverence to a Being who is equally at home in
the soul of the saint and of the libertine. Nor does it
adequately meet the aspirations of the heart. It is true
that pantheistic mysticism is associated with the love
of God which can become a veritable intoxication of
the soul; but the general mass of mankind have found
it beyond their power to love a God who, being
impersonal, cannot know, love or care. Indeed, Spinoza,
who has been described by Novalis as a ' God-intoxi-
cated man ' (*ein Gottbetrunkenner mensch*), derived his
intellectual love of God, as has been shown by
students of Spinoza (A. E. Taylor, among others)[43],
not from his own philosophy but from his Jewish
traditional background. Nor can pantheism even
satisfy the religious demand for the knowledge of
God. Its strength, it is openly claimed, lies on the
intellectual side and, as a fact, the pantheistic idea has
been the core of some of the great philosophical systems. But whatever the merits of pantheism on the
theoretical side, it fails to provide that conception of
God which is demanded by the religious mind. For
by negating the personality of God and the doctrines
which are governed by this conception, pantheism has
reduced God to a notion of a process of thought, or of
a series of volitions, without a Being to whom it
belongs or to whom it can be related and who, for all
practical purposes, is non-existent.

Similar failure to answer the practical criteria
attaches to all other attempts made in recent times to
resolve the deity into pantheistic creativity. Whether
divinity is to be conceived as an *élan vital*,[44] an uncon-

scious force striving after perpetual re-creation as
Bergson contends, or as a deity in the process of
becoming, never continuing in one stay, but always to
be, as Samuel Alexander[45] suggests, God in these
systems is virtually non-existent and for all practical
purposes is no God.

For all these reasons, Judaism must reject all these
pantheistic doctrines, however attractively they may be
dished up as religion. Without repudiating the rightful
place of philosophy, it yet affirms that not the blind
undifferentiated life of monism is God, but the God
revealed to Israel, and proclaimed by the prophets of
Israel. The God who is in this world and yet beyond
it, who conditions the Universe, and is yet not conditioned by it. The God who is both immanent and
transcendent, near and afar off. The God whom the
myriads of Israel address in the loving accents of Jewish
traditional piety as *Abinu She-ba-Shamayim*, ' Our
Father Which art in Heaven '[46]—a father ever near at
hand to his children on earth, though His Being is, so
to speak, afar off in heaven.

The immanent-transcendent God of Israel is the
One and Only God, the essence and principle of *all*
existence. Here we come to the distinctive doctrine
of Hebrew monotheism, which asserts that there is one
God only, the sole creator and ruler of the universe.[47]

The idea of the one and only God, however, does
not exhaust the content of Hebrew monotheism. The
passage from polytheism to Hebrew monotheism, it
has often been remarked, is an irreversible step which
affects the whole quality of the religion. The constant
and relentless struggle between polytheism and mono-

theism which the early history of Israel reveals did not
resolve itself merely into a question of numbers—the
one God against the many gods. Belief in one God only,
as some students of comparative religion will tell us,
may be the result merely of a poor imagination. In its
struggle with polytheism, Judaism had to deal not only
with the idea of plurality. It was faced also with the
necessity of supplying a new conception of the Divine
character, radically different from that of polytheism.
Polytheism, being deeply rooted in the gratification of
the senses and worship of natural forces, has essentially no moral, no spiritual quality. There is no moral
attribute attachable, say, to a thunder-clap, a tree, the
sea, the sun, the sky and its constellations, which were
the objects of polytheistic cults, since all moral attributes are necessarily connected with personality.
Worlds asunder is Hebrew monotheism. It emphasises
what Hermann Cohen[48] described as the ' Einzigheit ',
as well as the ' Einheit ' of God; that is God's uniqueness, His unique moral character, no less than His
absolute Unity—in the mathematical sense. Its one
and only God is the God of Holiness—a qualitative
rather than a quantitative concept.

Whilst Divine holiness, from the conceptual standpoint, denotes, as we have seen, God's transcendence
and independence of all beside Himself,[49] there also
radiates from it, at the same time, in the words of
G. A. Smith, ' heaven's own breadth of meaning,'[50]
which makes it the fittest expression for all moral
attributes of God. For once we proclaim God as Holy,
in the sense that He is independent of all manifestations
of life and existence, we affirm Him to be an absolute

Free Personality, and thus open the way for attributing to Him all moral qualities with which the term ' Holiness ' came to be associated.

The fullest disclosure of the moral character of God, which constitutes His Holiness, was made, we are told, by means of a special theophany to Moses, in which God revealed Himself as a merciful being, gracious, slow to anger, abundant in lovingkindness and truth, keeping lovingkindness to a thousand generations, forgiving iniquity, transgression and sin, but who will by no means clear the guilty (see Exodus xxxiv. 6-7).

These attributes, generally known as the Thirteen Divine Attributes, resolve themselves into two main groups: Retributive Justice (*Din*), and Mercy (*Rahamin*).[51] Mercy includes among its derivatives, compassionate, slow to anger, and—the greatest of all—abundant in lovingkindness. The Hebrew term, *Hesed*, rendered lovingkindness, is one of the most pregnant words of the Hebrew language, the full meaning of which no one English word can carry. It is a word related to tenderness and love and thus may be translated ' tenderlove ': God is full of tenderlove.[52] One of the principal marks of His tenderlove is the forgiving of sin. Retributive justice is expressed in the punishment of the impenitent and guilty. This, too, is an integral feature of Divine holiness, for it is a mark of God's holiness that He is intolerant of evil. A God who is all tenderlove, overlooking sin and iniquity, so that it makes no difference to Him whether a man is a saint or a sinner, is not a God to be worshipped and scarcely a God to be exalted. ' Thou wast a God that forgavest them, and Thou takest vengeance of their doings; therefore: Exalt ye the Lord our God and worship at His holy hill. For the Lord our God is Holy ' (Psalm xcix. 8-9).

The idea of a one and only God, possessed of all moral attributes, and first proclaimed by Judaism, made its appearance at a later age also in Greece, among many of its philosophers and poets. Xenophanes, Anaxagoras, Euripides and Plato, among others, bore witness to a lofty conception of the deity which has many points of affinity with Hebrew Monotheism.[53] But whereas in Greece this idea was arrived at by way of philosophy and speculation, by reflecting on the need for a unifying metaphysical principle behind the scheme of things, in Judaism it was apprehended by means of a revelation, a direct experience of God, who had made Himself known to the Jewish people by His wondrous acts of judgment, deliverance and salvation, and who had communicated to them His will, character and purpose.[54] This difference in the origin of the monotheistic idea among the Jews and the Greeks determined their respective doctrines of God. To the Jews, God was essentially ' personal '; to the Greeks He remained impersonal. To the Jews He was the self-revealing God; to the Greeks He was the unknown God. Fundamental to the Jewish monotheistic doctrine is the great Deuteronomic utterance, known as the *Shema*, from the Hebrew word with which it begins: ' Hear, O Israel: The Lord Our God, the Lord is One ' (Deuteronomy vi. 4)—' One ' in the sense that He alone is God, and no other.[55] ' And thou shalt know this day and lay it to thine heart, that the Lord, He alone is God in Heaven and upon the

earth beneath, there is none else ' (Deuteronomy iv. 39).
' I, even I, am the Lord; and beside Me there is no
saviour ' (Isaiah xliii. 11). ' I am the Lord, that is My
name and My glory to another will I not give ' (Isaiah
xlii. 8). The negations are as emphatic and insistent as
the affirmations. They negate all embodiments and
notions of the deity which, however refined and sub-
limated, veil the one and only God of Israel more
than they reveal Him.[56]

Judaism has, as yet, made the only unfaltering
testimony to the one and only God; and until all other
religions are rescued from their worship of idols,
physical and metaphysical, the Jewish people must
preserve all that has made their individual and national
witness to the one and only God effective. Thus only
can the time be hastened when, as foreshown by the
prophet, ' The Lord shall be King over all the earth,
in that day shall the Lord be One, and His Name,
One ' (Zechariah xiv. 9).

NOTES

[1a] See *supra*, p. 72.

[1] See I. Epstein, *The Talmud, Seder Zera'im*, Vol. 1, *Introduction.*
(Soncino edition, 1948), pp. xv-xvi.

[2] See Elijah ben Moses di Vidas (d. 1518), *Reshit Hokmah, Massa
u-Mattan.* ' Anyone who deals faithfully has it accounted for him
as if he would have fulfilled all the 613 precepts; for we learn in
Tractate Makkot, " Habakkuk came and reduced them (the 613
precepts) to one (principle), as it is said, But the righteous shall
live by his faith." ' The reference is to B.T. Makkot 24a, on which
see S. Schechter, *Studies in Judaism* (1896), pp. 283ff. For parallels

to the Makkot passage, see Tanhuma (ed. Buber) § 10, and numerous others cited by G. F. Moore, *Judaism*, Vol. II, p. 84.

³ See J. Klausner, *From Jesus to Paul* (English translation by William F. Stinespring, 1947), pp. 517-520. See also *supra*, p. 78, n. 16.

⁴ So Joseph Irgas (1655-1730), *Shomer Emunim*, 39 (Amsterdam ed., 1736): הצורה המפוארה שבצורות

⁵ ' All are agreed that necessity forced us to ascribe corporeal attributes to God, and to describe Him by attributes properly belonging to His creatures, so as to obtain some conception by which the thought of God's existence should be fixed in the mind of men.' כי הדחק הביאנו להגשים הבורא יתעלה ולספר אותו במידה הבוראים כדי לשער ענין זה שיקוים מציאות הבורא יתברך בנפשות (Bahya Ibn Pakuda, *Hobot ha-Lebabot*, 1, 10). It is for this reason that Judah Halevi looks favourably on the anthropomorphic descriptions of the deity in the mystical work, *Shiur Komah* (' The Measures of the Divine Stature '), because he considers it of inestimable value as a road along which the simple, devout mind can travel from superstition to rational ideas; see *Kuzari*, iv, 3. As against Halevi's attitude stands the unqualified condemnation of the work by Maimonides who declares that that work ought to be destroyed because a ' substance which has a (physical) stature is certainly a strange god ' (see Maimonides, *Responsa*, 373, ed. A. Freimann). G. Scholem (*Major Trends in Jewish Mysticism*, p. 66) suggests that ' its authors had not in mind the substance of the divinity but merely the measurements of its appearance.' In other words, the work does not purport to describe an objective reality, but merely a subjective feeling in the mind. This, too, it is well to note, was how the strong ' anti-intellectualist' Moses ben Hisdai Taku (13th century), though questioning the authenticity of the *Shiur Komah* (see *Ketab Tamim*, in *Ozar Nechmad*, iii, Vienna, 1860, p. 62), interpreted the manifestation of the Divine in the form of a man such as is described in Ezekiel i. 26, and Daniel vii. 9 (see *op. cit.*, p. 80). He opposes his interpretation to that of Saadia (*Emunot we-Deot* ii. 10), Judah Halevi (*Kuzari*, iv. 3), and Maimonides (*Guide*, I, 5, 10, 18, 19, 21), who understood these Biblical passages as

referring to some objective reality in the form of a person, created from an ethereal light, or fire, or as Saadia designates it, ' a second air ' (*awir sheni*). On Saadia's theory see M. Ventura, *La Philosophie de Saadia Gaon* (1934), p. 190, and A. Altmann, *Saadia's Theory of Revelation* in *Saadia Studies* (ed. E. Rosenthal, 1943), pp. 22-4. Such an opinion Taku regards as idolatrous, and he subjects it to unsparing criticism. Viewed in this light, Taku was far from being an anthropomorphist, and there is accordingly little justification for the attacks against him on this score by Jewish historians; e.g. I. H. Weiss, *Dor Dor we-Dorshaw* (1924), v. pp. 23-5; H. Graetz, *Geschichte* (4th edition), vii, pp. 153ff.; S. W. Baron, *A Social and Religious History of the Jews* (1937), ii, pp. 132, 134.

[6] This is already emphasised over and over again in the Bible. ' The prophets already warned us to be on our guard against the conception that God has any form or likeness, as it is said, " Take ye therefore good heed unto yourselves . . . for ye saw no manner of form " (Deuteronomy iv. 15). " But ye saw no form; only a voice " (*ibid*. iv, 12). This means, Guard your minds and thoughts so as not to represent the Creator under a form, or conceive Him under the likeness of anything real or imaginary, since your eyes never perceived any form or likeness when He spoke to you. And it is said, " To whom will ye liken God ? What likeness will you compare unto Him? " (Isaiah xl. 18). " To whom will ye liken me that I should be equal, saith the Holy One " (*ibid*. xl. 25) . . . and there are several other passages of similar import.' (Bahya ibn Pakuda, *Hobot ha-Lebabot*, i, 10). Whether the Scripture teaches the idea of the incorporeality of God, with all its philosophic implications of distinction between matter and form, may be a moot point (see E. Kaufman, *Toldot ha-Emunah ha-Yisraelit*, II, 1938. pp. 231ff., and H. A. Wolfson, *Philo*, II, pp. 95f.), but there is no question that its insistence on the unlikeness of God carries with it the teaching of His spirituality, at least in the sense that He is free of all weaknesses and limitations of the flesh, with which the spirit is contrasted in Scripture, as in Isaiah xxxi. 3; Psalm lxxxiv. 3; Job xiv. 22. Cf. E. König, *Theologie des Alten Testaments* (1922), p. 141: ' The spirituality of God belongs to the oldest principles of the religion of the Old Testament.'

[7] From the Chandogya Upanishad, quoted in A. Huxley, *Perennial Philosophy* (1947), p. 9.

[8] Midrash Rabbah, Leviticus, iv. 8.

הנפש הזאת ממלאה את הגוף והקב״ה מלא את עולמו . . ;
הנפש הזאת סובלת את הגוף והקב״ה סובל את עולמו . . ;
הנפש הזאת רואה ואינה נראה והקב״ה רואה ואינו נראה.

Cf. also Midrash Rabbah, Deuteronomy ii. 37, and the fuller passage in Midrash Tehillim, on Psalm cii. 1, for the interpretation of which see Joseph Irgas (1655-1730) *Shomer Emunim* 31d (Amsterdam ed. 1736) and the photographic ed. (Berlin, 1927); and also B.T. Berakot 10a. See also Judah Halevi, *Kuzari*, IV, 3 : ' God is the spirit of the world, its soul, intellect and life, as He is called " the life of the Universe." ' האלהים הוא רוח העולם ונפשו ושכלו וחיותו כאשר נקרא חי העולם: ' There also exists in the universe a certain force which controls the whole . . . it is the source of the existence of the Universe, and all its parts. That force is God, blessed be His Name. It is on account of this force that man is called a microcosm, for he likewise possesses a certain principle which governs all the forces of his body ; and on account of these comparisons, God is called the " Life of the Universe " ; comp. Daniel xii. 7, " And he swore by the life of the universe " ' (Maimonides, *Guide*, I, 72). See also *ibid.* I, 69. The phrase ' Life of the Universe ' is also found in the Prayer Book. See *A.P.B.*, p. 36, and the notes in the *Seder ha-Tefillah*, pp. 89 and 123 and S. Baer, *Siddur*, p. 568 ; also A. Marmorstein, *Shibbalim*, in Ludwig Blau's Jubilee Volume, *We-Zot Li-Yehudah* (Budapest, 1926), p. 212, and *The Old Rabbinic Doctrine of God*, Vol. I (1927), p. 85. See further Midrash Tehillim on Psalm xix. 8, and Tosafot B.T. Shabbat 31a, in the name of the Yerushalmi : ' The order Zeraim is designated by the term *Emunah*, Faith, because man believes in the " Life of the Universe " and sows.' See I. Epstein, *Seder Zera'im*, Introduction (Soncino ed. 1949), pp. 16-7.

It ought to be noted that there is no suggestion here that God is to be conceived as the mind ($\nu o \hat{v}_s$) of the world, or the soul ($\psi v \chi \acute{\eta}$) of the world like the Stoic Logos. The soul is used by the Rabbis merely as a figure of speech, and not as a description of God. For an account of the various Greek theories of God as the mind and the soul of the world, see Harry A. Wolfson, *Philo*, Vol. 1, pp. 323ff. For further literature, see E. C. Dewick, *The Indwelling God* (1938), pp. 71-80, and W. D. Davies, *Paul and Rabbinic Judaism* (1948), pp. 178f., and bibliography quoted in the notes.

[9] ' The term immanence is used in modern theology to denote the presence of God in the world.' Hastings' *Encyclopaedia of Religion and Ethics*, Vol. 7, p. 167a, *s.v.* ' Immanence.' It is derived from the Latin *immanere* (' remaining in ').

[10] See Maimonides, *Guide*, I, 64, and Crescas, *Or Adon.* I, 3; for a full discussion of the various interpretations given to the term *Kabod*, see H. A. Wolfson, *Crescas' Critique of Aristotle* (1929), pp. 459-462. See also I. Abrahams, *The Glory of God* (1925), pp. 17.

[11] *Shechinah* and *Kabod* are often interchangeable terms. See Saadia *Emunot we-Deot*, II, 10 and also I. Efros, *Some Aspects of Yehuda ha-Levi's Mysticism*, *Proceedings of the American Academy for Jewish Research*, Vol. XI, 1949, pp. 39-40.

[12] B.T. Baba Bathra, 25a: שכינה בכל מקום

[13] Midrash Exodus Rabbah, II, 9: אין מקום פנוי בלא שכינה See also Sanhedrin 39b. Striking is the simile in Midrash Canticles Rabbah, III, 15: ' The tabernacle was like a cave, adjoining the sea. The sea came rushing in and flooded the cave, but the sea was not in the least diminished. So the tabernacle was filled with the radiance of the Divine Presence, but the world lost nothing of this presence.' See parallel passages, with slight variations, Pesikta de-Rab Kahana, ed. Buber, 26. An extremely valuable contribution to the idea of Divine Immanence in Rabbinic teaching is J. Abelson, *Immanence of God in Rabbinical Literature* (1912).

[14] The Unity Hymn, *Shir ha-Yihud*, was composed by members of the inner circle round R. Judah ha-Chassid (d. 1217).

[15] כולם בך ואתה בכולם, סובב את הכל ומלא את הכל.
בהיות הכל אתה בכל, ולפני הכל כל היית.
ובהיות הכל את כל מלאת.

—from the version found in Moses Taku's *Ketab Tamim*, in *Ozar*

Nechmad, III, p. 8. This version varies from the one in the printed editions of the ' Hymn for the Third Day.'

[16] See *supra*, pp. 147ff.

[17] A term coined by Judah ibn Tibbon (1120, d. *circa* 1200), the Hebrew translator of Judah Halevi's philosophic work, written in Arabic under the title *Kitab al Khazari*.

[18] The Arabic term *amr* (' Word ') has been generally understood to correspond somewhat to the notion of the hypostatic *logos;* see H. Hirschfeld, *Judah Hallewi's Kitab al Khazari*, Introduction, p. 9, and I. Heinemann, *Tenuat ha-Historia shel R. Yehudah Hallevi*, in *Zion*, IX (1944), pp. 168ff. H. A. Wolfson, however, in *Hallevi and Maimonides on Prophecy*, *J.Q.R.* (*N.S.*) XXXII (1942), p. 370 shows that whilst there is occasionally an attempt in the *Kuzari* to personify the *amr ilahiyy*, this is to be understood only in a figurative sense, as denoting divine command, power, wisdom, will, etc.

[19] See I. Epstein, *Judah Halevi as a Philosopher*, in *J.Q.R.* (*N.S.*), XXV (1935), p. 201ff. Cf. D. Neumark, *Essays in Jewish Philosophy*, p. 231ff.

[20] See *infra*, pp. 341f.

[21] See Joseph Albo (1380-1440), *Ikkarim*, II, 27 : ' " I am that I am " that is, the Existent, whose existence depends on His own essence, and not upon another . . . the expression " That I am " is in the first person, as if to say, because *I* am, not because another than *I* is. My existence and power are not dependent upon another at all, as is the case in the other existents. None of the existents could say of himself " I am that (because) I am." They would have to say, " I am that (because) He is . . . " that is, I am in existence because another than I is in existence, namely, the First Cause, upon whose existence that of all other beings depends. But God's existence depends on Himself and not upon another cause. Therefore, to Him alone of all existing things is applicable the name " I am that I am " '. Hermann Cohen, *Die Religion der Vernunft aus den Quellen des Judentums* (ed. 1919), p. 49, renders the phrase, *Ich bin der Ich bin* (' I am the I am '), in the same sense as Albo. Somewhat different is the emphasis in Maimonides' interpretation of the phrase, as

denoting God's absolute existence, including the idea of the eternity of His existence. God is ' the existing Being which is the existing Being ' (*Guide*, I, 63). This rendering has been adopted by Aquinas (see Jacob Guttmann, *op, cit*., p. 41). Judah Halevi takes the phrase as an assurance of the Divine Ever-presence with His people: ' " I am that I am," the one who is present, present with you whenever you seek me ' (*Kuzari*, IV, 3). Similarly, M. Buber, *Das Kommende* (1932), p. 84, translates the Name as ' *Der Daseiende* ', which he amplifies thus, ' I will be there with you, my nation, my folk.' This makes the phrase to denote not so much Existence as Relation ship. There are many other renderings varying with these two concepts: ' I am wont to be that which I am wont to be ', that is unchangeable; ' I will become what I will become ', implying that no words can adequately sum up what God *will become* to His chosen people, so that He may just as well remain nameless; as well as several others, for which see Peter Munz, ' *Sum Qui Sum* ' in the *Hibbert Journal*, L (1952), p. 146. But there is no doubt that whatever the exact significance, we have in the name ' *Ehyeh asher Ehyeh* ' an affirmation—explicit or implicit—of the attributes of God's transcendence—His eternity, self-existence and independence; see E. König, *Theologie des Alten Testaments* (ed. 1922), p. 155.' For the ancient Hebrews, God and the world were always distinct. God was not involved in the processes of nature. These processes were caused by God, but He was distinct from them.'—A. B. Davidson, in *Hastings' Dictionary of the Bible*, II, p. 196, *s.v.* ' God (in O.T.) '. The entire independence of God, as taught by Judaism, denies the postulate that the world is necessary for the being of God, even as God is necessary for the being of the world. Compare the assertion of Hegel that ' God without the world is not God,' or of Whitehead, that ' God is completed by the individual, fluent satisfactions of finite fact '—(See E. L. Mascall, *He who is*. [1943] p. 97). As against these views, Judaism stresses the entire independence of God: ' Thou wast the same ere the world was created, Thou hast been the same since the world was created ', *A.P.B.*, p. 8. Cf. Midrash Yalkut Shimeoni Deuteronomy, 836, and the Jerusalem Talmud Berakot, IX, 1. This doctrine of the independence of God has been well expressed by William Temple, *Nature, Man and God* (1934), p. 435, in his two quasi-mathematical equations:

$$\text{God} \; - \; \text{the World} \; = \; \text{God}$$
$$\text{The World} \; - \; \text{God} \; = \; \text{O}$$

The name EHYEH is the form of the Divine Name YHWH, when used by God Himself. Various etymologies have been proposed for the Divine Name but the Biblical derivation from the verb *hawah* (' to be '), the form being the third singular of the simple imperf. indicating God's existence or His relation to Israel, remains the most satisfactory. More obscure is the origin of the name. The latest attempts to connect it with the alleged YW of the Ras Shamra tablets has found little acceptance. A tradition that the worship of YHWH ante-dates Moses is preserved in Genesis iv. 26, as well as in many subsequent passages (e.g. xii. 8; xv. 8), which claims that the name was known to the patriarchs. Historical criticism would therefore assign these Genesis passages to a different author (J), but as the context clearly indicates, the revelation to Moses did not concern the name itself, but its significance as denoting that God was ever present in history and with His people. W. F. Albright, *From the Stone Age to Christianity* 1946, p. 197, makes the name YHWH to be a causative imperf. with a meaning: ' He who causes to be ', for which he finds an old Egyptian parallel. Should this be so, the suggestion could be hazarded that the patriarchs understood the Divine Name to denote God's creative activity, and that the revelation to Moses consisted in its new significance as meaning: ' the God who is with His people.' It may further be suggested that the new significance of YHWH as revealed to Moses did not replace its older significance with which in fact it is indissolubly connected. As such the Name represents the imperfect of the causative as well as of simple form, which explains why it is left unvocalised. The hypothesis that YHWH was a Kenite deity, a storm god, first suggested by R. Ghillany (von der Alm) in 1862, no longer enjoys the vogue it once did, as it is realised that Moses could hardly have succeeded in inducing the people to entrust their fate to a foreign deity of whom they had no knowledge and upon whom they could not look but with distrust ; see my article in *Encyclopaedia Britannica* (1955 printing), *s.v.* ' Judaism.'

[22] The term *kadosh* is variously derived from an Arabic root meaning ' to be separate, distinct ', or a Babylonian, meaning ' to

be bright ', ' clear ', that is ' free from defect '. See Norman H. Snaith, *The Distinctive Ideas of the Old Testament* (1944), pp. 24ff, and Helmer Ringgren, *The Prophetical Conception of Holiness* (1948), pp. 3ff. See also Isaac Efros, *Holiness and Glory in the Bible*, in *J.Q.R. (N.S.)*, XLI (1951), pp. 363ff. where he discusses the funda-mental concepts of transcendence and immanence, as reflected respectively in the terms *kadosh* and *kabod*.

[23] See I. Efros, *ibid.*, p. 363.

[24] See Crescas, *Or Adon.* I, 2, who explains this verse of Isaiah to mean ' though God is holy and separated . . . still the earth is full of His glory. כי אם היותו קודש ונבדל . . . הנה מלא כל הארץ כבודו

[25] See Midrash Tehillim on Psalm xc., i., and Midrash Genesis Rabbah, LXVIII, 9. הוא מקומו של עולם ואין העולם מקומו. A variant of this phrase is found in Midrash Exodus Rabbah, XLV, 6: אתרי טפלה לי ואין אני טפל לאתרי Cf. Tanhuma *Tissa*, XXVII. The significance of the term ' Place ', as applied to God is explained by Philo who states that God is designated ' Place ' because He contains the world and is not contained by the world (*De Fuga et Inventione*, XIV, 75). For a full discussion of this term as understood by Philo, see H. A. Wolfson, *Philo*, I, p. 247-251. See particularly p. 248, note 44, where he accepts the view that ' this term is undoubtedly of native Jewish origin ', as maintained by A. Marmorstein, in *The Old Rabbinic Doctrine of God*, I (1927), pp. 92-3.

[26] Classical in this connection is the passage in B.T. Megillah, 31a ' Rabbi Johanan said, Wherever you find in the Scriptures the greatness (Transcendence) of the Holy One Blessed be He, there you also find His humility (Accessibility, or Immanence). ' This is written in the Torah (Pentateuch), repeated in the Prophets and again in the Hagiographa.' (The Scriptural quotations are Deu-teronomy x. 17-18 ; Isaiah lvii. 15 ; Psalm lxviii. 5-6 ; I Kings viii. 57 ; Deuteronomy iv. 4 ; Isaiah li. 3 ; xlii. 21. See the passage in the *A.P.B.*, p. 214). This too is the underlying idea of the formula, common to all benedictions in which the invocation of God first in the second person is followed by another in the third person : ' Blessed art Thou O Lord, our God, who has, etc. . . .', The

relation of man to God is thus an I-$\left\{{\text{Thou} \atop \text{He}}\right.$ relation; see Solomon
ben Adreth (1235-1310) quoted by Jacob ben Solomon ibn Habib
(c. 1460-1516) in his notes on the *En Jaacob*, Berakot 40b; see also
David ben Joseph Abudraham's *Commentary on the Prayer Book*
(Warsaw 1877 ed.), p. 24, and Ch. L. Ehrenreich's edition (Cluj
1927), p. 143, note 13. God, that is to say, is near, still He remains
far. See J.T. Berakot, IX, 1, הקב״ה נראה רחוק ואין קרוב ממנו
and Yalkut Shimeoni, *Deuteronomy* 825: הקב״ה רחוק וקרוב cf. also
Sefer Ha-Yashar, iii (towards the end), see also J. Abelson, *Immanence of God*, pp. 286ff.

[27] The doctrine of transcendence in its extreme form results in
the view that God has no real concern with the Universe. This
according to Maimonides was the view of the early idolators, see
Yad ha-Hazakah, *Abodah Zara*, I, 1. Cf. A. N. Whitehead, *Adventure of Ideas* (1933), p. 157, ' God made His appearance in religion
under the frigid title of the " First Cause " '. On the other hand
the doctrine of pure immanence in its logical conclusion becomes
indistinguishable from pantheism.

[28] Julian Huxley, *Religion without Revelation* (1927), p. 12.

[29] *Ibid.*, p. 23.

[30] *Ibid.*, p. 15.

[31] See Bernard Heller, *God in Jewish Literature and Life*, *Central
Conference of American Rabbis* (1943), pp. 260-2.

[32] A. N. Whitehead, *Science in the Modern World*, Pelican Book
(1938), p. 222.

[33] A. W. R. Matthews, *Studies in Christian Philosophy* (2nd ed.
1928), p. 193.

[34] Quoted by Kenneth Walker, *Meaning and Purpose* (1944),
p. 105, n. 1.

[35] Quoted by J. Needham, *Mechanistic Biology and the Religious
Consciousness*, in *Science Religion and Reality* (1926), pp. 249f.

[36] See B. H. Streeter, *Reality: a new Co-relation of Science and
Religion* (1927), pp. 11-12.

[37] Mechilta on Exodus xix. 18. See A. Marmorstein, *The Old Rabbinic Doctrine of God*, Vol. II (1937), pp. 121ff.

[38] ' Pantheism is only a polite form of atheism . . . the maxim of the pantheist, " God and the world are one " is merely a polite way of giving the Lord His *congé*,' quoted by Ernst Haeckel, *The Riddle of the Universe* (E.T., J. McCabe Watts, 1913), p. 238.

[39] The Psalmist finds in this the distinction between God and the deities of the pagan world, ' But our God is in Heaven, He does whatsoever He pleases ' (Psalm cxv. 3).

[40] האלוה כל נמצא. ואין כל נמצא אלוה, quoted in G. Scholem, *Major Trends in Jewish Mysticism* (1946), p. 409 n. 19. S. H. Bergmann, *ha-Rav Kook*, in *Etudes Orientales à la Mémoire de Paul Hirschler*, ed. by O. Komlós (1950), p. 2, designates this attitude by the term ' Panentheismus ' (*Pan-en-theo*) to distinguish it from Spinoza's pantheism.

[41] ' *Welches absolute Wesen ist dies, das alle Wirklichkeit und besonders das Böse nicht an ihm hat.*'—Hegel, *Geschichte der Philosophie*, *Werke* XV (1836), p. 302.

[42] See William James, *The Will to Believe* (1897), p. 43-4.

[43] A. E. Taylor, *The Faith of a Moralist* (1930), I, p. 9. See also L. I. Akselrod, *Spinoza and Materialism* in *Spinoza in Soviet Philosophy*, ed. G. L. Kline (1952), p. 65.

[44] See Henri Bergson, *L'Evolution créatrice* (1907) (E.T., 1911).

[45] See Samuel Alexander, *Space, Time and Deity* (1927).

[46] ' Father ' as an appellation of God is a characteristic of the Hebrew Bible. See e.g. Deuteronomy xxxii. 6; Jeremiah iii. 4 and Malachi ii. 10. Frequent too is the phrase ' God in Heaven ' e.g. Genesis xxiv. 3, 7. The combined expression ' Our Father in Heaven ' is traceable to Isaiah lxiii 15-6. See A. Marmorstein, *op. cit.*, Vol. I, p. 56ff. The earliest use of ' Our Father ' as an invocation in prayer is 1 Chronicles xxix. 10. See G. F. Moore, *Judaism*, III, p. 190.

[47] It is this all-exclusive claim of the Hebrew monotheism which distinguishes it from other monotheistic faiths or tendencies known

M

as ' henotheism '—a term coined by Max Müller—or more commonly, ' monolatry ', which, while recognising a supreme God, does not deny the reality of other lesser or minor gods, and their influence and powers in the affairs of men. This conception of Hebrew montheism, it has been rightly pointed out, is a correlate of the Hebrew insistence on the unconditioned nature of God. Only a God who transcends every phenomenon, and who is not conditioned by any mode of manifestation, only an unqualified God, can be the one and only ground of all existence; see *Before Philosophy*, by H. Frankfort and Others (Pelican Books 1949), p. 243.

[48] Hermann Cohen, *Die Religion der Vernunft aus den Quellen des Judentums* (1919), pp. 41ff.

[49] See *supra*, p. 141.

[50] G. A. Smith, *Isaiah* (1927), I, p. 63.

[51] On the Thirteen Divine Attributes, see G. F. Moore, *Judaism*, I, pp. 387ff., and I. Epstein, *Jewish Way of Life* (1946), pp. 132ff. See also B.T. Rosh Hashanah 17b, particularly Tosafoth, *s.v.* שלש These Thirteen Attributes describing God's dealings with man are known as ' Attributes of Action ', as distinct from the ' Essential Attributes ', which are concerned to describe His essence—His Unity, Eternity, Omnipresence, Omnipotence, Omniscience, Incorporeality. ' The Attributes of Action ' have according to Rabbinic teaching, been communicated as norms of conduct to man: ' As He is merciful, so be thou merciful; as He is compassionate so be thou compassionate, etc.' (B.T. Sotah, and Yalkut Shimeoni, Deuteronomy, 975). See, however, I. Epstein, *op. cit.*, pp. 138ff, where it is shown that the same applies in a sense to the ' Essential Attributes ' which also provide guiding principles of human conduct.

[52] The American Revised Standard Version of the Bible (1952) renders the term, ' steadfast love.' The recurring use of this term is a refutation of the fallacy that God is represented in the Old Testament as God of Judgment, while in the N.T. He is seen as the God of Love.

[53] See J. Adam, *The Religious Teachers of Greece* (1908), pp. 297ff.

and 362ff. See also Gilbert Murray, *Five Stages of Greek Religion* (1925), p. 92.

[54] For the implication of this Jewish apprehension of God, see *supra*, pp. 124f. and *infra*, pp. 278f.

[55] See Commentary of RaShBaM (Solomon ben Meir, 1085-1174) and Abraham Ibn Ezra, (1093-1167) *a.l.* and this is undoubtedly the way in which the Hebrew word *Ehad*, rendered ' One,' is to be understood. See G. A Smith, *Isaiah* (1927), II, p. 38. There is no assertion or implication of the unity of God in the metaphysical sense. The idea of God as pure, simple, and not composite being belongs to the realm of philosophy, rather than that of prophecy. What it does insist on is that there *is* but one God. See G. F. Moore, *Judaism*, I, pp. 291, 361, and III, p. 115, n. 108. The view, commonly associated with the name of Wellhausen, and long in vogue, that Hebrew monotheism began with the eighth-century prophets, and became explicit with ' Deutero-Isaiah ', has now given way to a more conservative attitude, and no less a scholar than W. F. Albright has shown that monotheism had been established in Israel since the days of Moses; see W. F. Albright, *From the Stone Age to Christianity* pp. 196ff, 2nd ed. 1946. See also E. Kaufman, *Toldot ha-Emunah ha-Yisraelit*, II, (1938), pp. 15ff. For a general survey of the latest literature on the subject, see H. H. Rowley, *The Antiquity of Israelite Monotheism*, in *Expository Times*, LXI, 1949-50, pp. 333-8; see also G. W. Anderson, *The Hebrew Religion in The Old Testament and Modern Study*, ed. H. H. Rowley (1951), pp. 289ff. Mention should also be made of the considerable body of opinion which postulates an initial monotheism in religious development (Andrew Lang, W. Schmidt, among others); and that polytheism arose from an original ' monotheism ' and not *vice versa* is in the view of I. Engnell of Uppsala ' the ultimate fact which confronts the inquirer into the beginnings of religion ' (G. W. Anderson, *op. cit.* p. 287). Cf. Maimonides, *Yad*, *Abodah Zarah* I, 1. where he attempts to trace how idolatry came into the world and corrupted the fair faith of mankind. On the distinctive characteristics of Hebrew Monotheism that mark it off sharply from any other forms of ' monotheism ', see my article in *Encyclopaedia Britannica*, *loc, cit.*

[56] Thus is excluded not only the multiplicity of gods in the various polytheistic creeds still extant to-day, but also the Trinity of the Christians, which, however much it may be explained away so as to make it compatible with the idea of the *One* God in the metaphysical sense, remains a direct denial of the *Only* God—the God who revealed Himself in the national experiences of the Jewish people. It is this implication of the Deuteronomic declaration that has led the Church to make the rejection of the Jewish people by God the very corner-stone of its theology, and which also accounts for Paul's antagonism to the Law, which is bound up with God's special dealings with the people of Israel (see *infra*, pp. 291ff). Cf. Joseph Albo, *Ikkarim*, III, 25 and Levi ben Abraham Hayyim, *Liwyat Hen*, in *Ginse Nistarot* (ed. J. Kobak, III, 1872), pp. 130-4, and Bahya ben Asher (*c*. 1255-1340), Commentary on Deuteronomy vi. 4.

CHAPTER IX

GOD—THE CREATOR

WE have seen that in Jewish teaching God is both immanent and transcendent. His presence and activity in Nature and in the human mind carries with it the idea of His immanence; whilst His unconditional spirituality involves the idea of His transcendence. Thus, though immanent and present in all things, He is yet absolutely distinct from them all. Implicated in no conditions of time and space, He is lifted into distinctiveness and transcendence. But because God is not bound to the Universe, because He transcends the world, He is a full personality both free and distinct. He is possessed of a freedom which is exercised in His mastery over life and Nature, and first made manifest in creation.

The Biblical doctrine of Creation cannot be understood without a preliminary consideration of the problem of the relation of God to the world. The relation has been presented in many ways, of which the most important are Emanation and Creation. Emanation theories have taken various forms, but the essence of all of them is that the world proceeds from God by a kind of necessity, as, say, the rays of the sun proceed from the heat of the sun. It is the nature of the divine to overflow. The idea of Creation is distinguished from that of Emanation in that it does not conceive the world as following by necessity from the divine nature, but as being produced by an act of will.

169

For notes on this chapter, see pp. 185-193.

In brief, Emanation teaches that God *had* to create; Creation, that He *willed* to create.

In considering the problem of the relation of God to the world, it is between these two theories that Jewish religious thought has to choose to-day as it did in the past—whether the world has come into existence by necessity or as the result of an act of free will of a Creator.

That this, indeed, is the great point at issue will become evident when we turn to Maimonides' treatment of the problem. Like all other Jewish thinkers that preceded and followed him, Maimonides considered the question of the origin of things one of the root problems of religious philosophy. Readers will probably recall the words of Ephraim Jackson in Oliver Goldsmith's ' Vicar of Wakefield,' who said that the ' cosmogony or creation of the world has puzzled the philosophers of all ages.' But to the religious philosopher the problem was more than a mere matter of speculative interest. It was of the utmost importance, for upon the satisfactory solution of it depended his religious faith. The difficulties involved were complicated and varied. Ever since the days of Philo, the literal Scriptural account of the Creation, representing God as creating the world in time and *ex nihilo*[1] (out of nothing), appeared at variance with the philosophers' conception of God. His activity as eternal cause implied an eternal creation. Then again the whole problem had to be considered with reference to the belief in divine interference with the natural laws of cause and effect—a belief inculcated by Biblical history and by which religious faith stood or fell.

Thus the question of harmonising the conceptions of philosophy with the Genesis narrative resolved itself into the larger and by far more important question of reconciling the fundamental teachings of the religion of the Bible with the teachings of philosophy.

To this twofold problem Maimonides applied his gigantic intellect, and in his solution of the problem we are afforded a large measure of light and guidance to meet the challenge of our own days.

The relevance to our times of Maimonides' treatment of the problem cannot be appreciated without some reference to the philosophical concepts or theories with which mediaeval Jewish philosophers had to contend. There was, on the one hand, the Aristotelian theory which taught the eternity of the Universe as being the result of the working of cause and effect, and which subjected everything to the inexorable laws of Nature to the entire exclusion of any freedom of the Divine to deviate from the existing scheme of things.[2] On the other hand, there was the Platonic theory which represented God as an artist, a designer, working on some pre-existent formless matter.[3] This theory, whilst also upholding the eternity of the Universe, did not deny the element of divine will coming into activity at creation. The world existed from eternity because the divine artist always willed to create. The admission of the element of will at creation allowed for the intervention of God in the organic process of Nature.

From these introductory observations we can proceed to consider somewhat more closely Maimonides' treatment of this important problem.

Maimonides, in dealing in his *Guide* with the problem of creation, after meeting the Aristotelian—the Peripatetics'—arguments in support of eternity and showing in II, 18 that they are not conclusive, devotes the subsequent chapters (19-24) to arguments in favour of non-eternity. He does not, however, claim that his arguments are of a demonstrative character. They are merely *ex absurdo*. He builds up his case, that is to say, by showing the absurdities involved in the theory of eternity—absurdities which render the theory more difficult of acceptance than that of non-eternity. Now it is usually held that these arguments *ex absurdo* are adduced by him in order to *prove* non-eternity.[4] This view, however, is hardly tenable. Maimonides never intended to produce any kind of proof—not even *ex absurdo*—in favour of non-eternity. All he was anxious to maintain was that the world is a product of free will, and as such its non-eternity becomes as possible as its eternity. Once this is admitted, the teaching of the Bible can easily be accepted without any fear of running counter to the undoubted and well-established truths of philosophy.

That this is as far as Maimonides would appeal to logical reasoning is evident from the following. After stating that those ' modern philosophers '[5] who maintain that God produced the universe by His will, but that it had always to be so and will always be so, though they have clearly abandoned the term ' necessary result,' yet have retained the conception of it— perhaps in order to avoid an objectionable expression[6] —he proceeds to this effect: There is no difference between Aristotle's view that the world is a necessary result and our own, that it is by will. *We mean just the same.*[7] The difference resolves itself merely into a question of relation. Whilst, according to Aristotle the relation between God and the world is that of causality, and everything besides Him is the necessary result emanating from God; in our view, the relation is that of an agent and its product, and the whole Universe is the result of God's design and will. All of which makes it palpably clear that Maimonides' intention was not to establish non-eternity, but that the nature of the relation between God and creation was not that of cause and effect, but of free will, admitting temporal no less than eternal creation.

This interpretation of Maimonides helps to throw light on his summing up of the problem in II. 25: We do not reject, he declares, the Eternity of the Universe because certain passages in the Scriptures affirm the Creation, for these could somehow be explained in conformity with the theory. For two reasons, however, have we not done so. Firstly, because the theory has not been proved, and thus there is not sufficient reason to explain away figuratively the literal meaning of the Biblical text. Secondly, because the acceptance of the theory would necessarily lead to the rejection of the whole Torah, and be in opposition to the fundamentals of our religion.[8] This reasoning of Maimonides as usually understood is by no means free from difficulty. According to the first reason, the rejection of the theory is only provisional, that is, subject to the absence of any demonstrative proof. Whilst according to the second the theory is entirely debarred from all consideration, as it would undermine the whole structure of the religion. And the question which will naturally suggest itself is: Having regard to reason 2, wherefore did Maimonides consider it necessary to introduce reason 1, thereby allowing for the possibility of the acceptance of that totally subversive theory ?

The interpretation of Maimonides offered above, however, removes the difficulty. The term ' Eternity of the Universe '[9] employed by Maimonides has a two-fold signification. It may be taken in the first instance in the Aristotelian sense, that the world has been produced as a necessary result, a view which Maimonides has shown from arguments *ex absurdo* to be untenable; or again it may mean that the world had been created from eternity by an eternal will, a possibility against which Maimonides has no objections to offer, based on purely philosophical grounds. The only ground for his rejection of the latter is the one given in reason 1. Since there is no demonstrative proof in support of the theory of the Eternity of the Universe, i.e. *by Will*, there is no warrant for departing from the plain literal interpretation of the Bible. Should, however, eventually some cogent proof be forthcoming in favour of the theory, the Bible would present no insuperable barrier, and the theory could be accepted, since it still makes Will the determining factor in the ' Eternity,' and thus allows for the miraculous and supernatural element in the religion. So far the purpose of the first reason. The second reason on the other hand deals, as Maimonides expressly states, with the Eternity of the Universe, in the Aristotelian sense, in virtue of which ' everything in the Universe is the result of fixed laws, Nature does not change, and there

is nothing supernatural.'[10] This theory in contradistinction to the first, is, in the view of Maimonides, in
opposition to the foundations of our religion . . . and
the whole teaching of our Torah would fall with it,
and hence it must be rejected.

To sum up then Maimonides' position. For Maimonides, the question of eternity or non-eternity of the
Universe is of no religious significance; all that matters
for religion is whether the world is the product of cause
and effect, or the result of the free activity of a creator.
The former view, which is the Aristotelian, is totally
incompatible with the religious attitude, as it denies
the possibility of the intervention of God in the natural
or historical process. The latter view, which is associated with the name of Plato, has in itself nothing
objectionable from the religious standpoint, since it
admits the element of divine will in creation. The only
exception that may be taken to it is that it does not
agree with the literal sense of the Genesis narrative.
This, however, Maimonides states is no serious
objection, as there would be no difficulty in explaining
away the Biblical story of the creation in the same way
as the anthropomorphic expressions in the Bible have
been explained. They are not to be taken literally, but
as conveying in popular phraseology high and important religious truths. The only reason for rejecting
this theory is because it cannot be proved. On the
other hand, the Aristotelian theory, he declares, cannot
be considered at all and this for two reasons: firstly
because there are overwhelming reasons against it,
and secondly because, were it to be accepted, it would
lead necessarily to the rejection of the whole Torah

and is thus in opposition to the fundamentals of our religion.

Interesting in this connection is the remark of A. E. Taylor that Aquinas had caused something of a scandal in the thirteenth century by maintaining that it is impossible to prove by reason alone that the world had a beginning in time, removing thereby what hitherto had been regarded as the strongest argument for establishing the existence of God.[11] Evidently, he did not know that here, too, as in other things, Aquinas took over from Maimonides, who devotes a considerable part of the second book of his *Guide* to this theme; although it might be mentioned that in this Maimonides had already been anticipated by Judah Halevi, in his brief declaration that, apart from the teachings of Revelation, all arguments in this connection are unconvincing, the problem of the beginning of things belonging to the realm of the unknowable: ' The question of eternity and creation is baffling and the arguments on both sides are evenly balanced.'[12]

This exposition of Maimonides' attitude to the doctrine of ' creation in time ' can help us to clarify his views on the related doctrine of ' *creatio ex nihilo* '. On the face of it, these two doctrines seem to be so interlinked as to suggest that the rejection of the former must, of necessity, involve the rejection of the latter; and if that be so, then the fact that Maimonides, as we have seen, was prepared to compromise, at the bidding of reason, on ' creation in time,' would warrant the assumption that he would likewise surrender the doctrine of *creatio ex nihilo*, once the theory of pre-existent matter had been demonstratively proven.

This indeed is how all the commentators and students of Maimonides have understood his position. Joseph Albo, for example, in his *Ikkarim*, I, 2, declares in effect that for Maimonides, *creatio ex nihilo* is not a fundamental principle of the Torah, and might thus be discarded, should the theory of a pre-existent eternal matter be established, notwithstanding the plain literal sense of the Genesis account to the contrary. Similarly H. A. Wolfson asserts that, according to Maimonides, the Platonic theory of the creation of the world out of pre-existent matter, ' eternal, unborn and unmade ', is compatible with the Scriptural story of the creation.[13] This presentation of the view of Maimonides, however, stands refuted by his categorical statement in his *Guide*, II, 13 (*First Theory*), that *creatio ex nihilo* is a fundamental principle of the Torah, ' second in importance only to the Unity of God,'[14] because any other theory than that of *creatio ex nihilo* implies the existence of another uncreated being beside God—a notion totally inadmissible in Jewish teaching.

The misinterpretation of Maimonides' attitude to this problem arises from a false antinomy that opposes the doctrine of *creatio ex nihilo* to the theory of pre-existent matter. In reality it all depends on what we mean in speaking of pre-existent matter. Wolfson himself has already drawn attention to the two distinct views held regarding the significance of pre-existent matter. Some there are who conceive it to be (*i*) eternal and (*ii*) uncreated; whilst others understand it as matter created by God, and pre-existent only in so far as it was called into being by Him before the creation

of the world.[15] It is only if pre-existent matter is taken
to be eternal and uncreated that it must be considered
the direct opposite to *creatio ex nihilo*. Once, however,
the term is interpreted simply in the sense of matter
created by God prior to the creation of the world, the
theory becomes quite compatible with the doctrine of
creatio ex nihilo, which in this case would be applicable
to the pre-existent matter out of which the world was
finally created.

The principal objection to the idea of an eternal and
uncreated matter is that it postulates the existence of
another eternal and uncreated being beside God. This
objection is generally met by the answer that though
the matter is eternal and uncreated like God, it is not
of the same order of existence as God, as it depends
upon God to give it shape and form.[16] Maimonides
who quotes this answer is left unimpressed by it, and
still insists that to assume that something else beside
God existed before the universe is an infringement of
the Unity of God.[17]

As to Maimonides' own position on the question,
in the light of his attitude to the theory of the eternity
of the universe as set forth above, all that might be
maintained is that he would find no objection to the
theory of an eternal matter, provided that the free
eternal will of God is made its determining factor. It
might be argued that this proviso might be essential
in regard to the theory of the eternity of the universe,
in order to safeguard the fundamental doctrine of·
God's governance of His world, but that it could be
waived in treating of the theory of eternal matter, in
which God would still be regarded as the ' Author and

Lord of all things '. This argument, however, as we have seen, does not appeal to Maimonides. Hence whilst Maimonides would not rule out altogether the idea of the eternity of matter as long as its very existence is attributed to the free activity of the Divine will, he would not countenance any departure from the doctrine of *creatio ex nihilo*, in favour of a notion of a pre-existent matter, that would imply the existence of some other eternal and uncreated being, in independence of God.[18]

Maimonides' treatment of this problem has been discussed at some length for two reasons. First, it should serve to dispose of the fallacy sedulously fostered by a number of modern Jewish writers, to mention only Ahad Ha-Am, that Maimonides was an outright rationalist, who was prepared to overthrow the teachings of the Torah at the bidding of reason.[19] His attitude to the Aristotelian theory, as well as his insistence on *creatio ex nihilo* (as defined), is the best refutation of this assertion. Secondly, because it indicates to us the very method we are to employ in considering the problem of the origin of things in the light of the new scientific conceptions of our days. The problem as it presented itself in the days of Maimonides was, as we have seen, of a twofold character. On the one hand, there was the question of the Genesis narrative. On the other hand, there was the problem of the very foundations of religious faith. And the same twofold problem presents itself to-day. The question of the hypothetical hylic matter which exercised the mind of Jewish philosophers in the Middle Ages is of little interest nowadays, but the question of the generation of the world in time and how it came into existence is still a matter of endless debate among us. Has the world been created in time, or has it existed from infinity ? Has it come into existence suddenly by divine fiat, or as the result of a long process spread over millions of years, known as evolution ? And were its existence from infinite time and the evolutionary process to be proved, how would this affect the Bible and the whole of the theistic position ? Now, as to the narrative in Genesis, Maimonides has already shown that this presents no insuperable obstacle to any scientifically proven hypothesis, seeing that the story in the Bible is not so much concerned to give scientific facts as to establish certain religious truths. These truths, however, must stand unshaken, and it is in the light of these truths that all scientific theories have to be examined.

Proceeding from these two principles, let us just consider how Maimonides would deal with the modern scientific theories regarding the origin of things. First as to the question whether the world had a beginning in time, Maimonides would say that this is a thing beyond the competence of science to determine. T. H. Huxley has well expressed the sober scientific attitude to this question when he wrote in his *Science and the Hebrew Tradition:* ' It appears to me that the scientific investigator is wholly incompetent to say anything about the first origin of the material universe. The whole power of his organon vanishes when he has to step beyond the chain of natural causes and effects. No form of nebular hypothesis that I know of is necessarily connected with any view of the origination of the nebular substance.'[20]   On the other hand, Maimonides might have well adduced some of the modern arguments based on contemporary physical theory which led Sir James Jeans to declare: ' Everything points with overwhelming force to a definite event or series of events of creation at some time or times, not infinitely remote.   The Universe cannot have originated by chance out of its present ingredients and neither can it always have been the same as now.'[21]

But after showing that the question of the origin of the world in time cannot be answered by science, Maimonides would proceed to argue that the religious concept of creation has nothing to do with the question whether the world had a beginning in time. All it seeks to affirm is that the world and all it contains is a free act of God, without Whom nothing could at any moment exist. The same attitude Maimonides would adopt with regard to the theory of evolution. He might well have echoed the statement of Huxley, the militant champion of agnosticism, which, owing to its general importance, is quoted here almost in full: ' There is a good deal of talk, and not a little lamentation, about the so-called religious difficulties which physical science has created. In theological science, as a matter of fact, it has created none. Not a solitary problem presents itself to the philosophical Theist at the present day which has not existed from the time that philosophers began to think out the logical grounds and logical consequences of Theism. . . . In respect of the great problem of philosophy, the post-Darwinian generation is in one sense exactly where the pre-Darwinian generations were. The doctrine of evolution is neither anti-theistic nor theistic. It simply has no more to do with theism than the first Book of Euclid has.'[22]

Evolution is, after all, a process and a means of activity, not to be confused with the act of creation itself. In other words, it is not concerned with the question of *who* created the world, but *how* it was created. All that the doctrine of creation insists on is that the world and all it contains is the product not of necessity, but of the free will of God, and that it is completely dependent on His will—whether it came into existence as the result of an eternal creative activity, or through the slow process of millions of years, or, as the Biblical narrative presents it, in six days. Here too, as in all matters of Jewish belief, the doctrine of creation is emphasised not because of the doctrine itself, but because of its tremendous practical consequences. A rejection of the doctrine of creation would only lead to the rejection of the whole Torah. Firstly, the doctrine preserves the transcendence and freedom of God, the practical import of which has already been the subject of discussion.[23] Secondly, the doctrine carries with it as its corollary God's preservation of the world. Both—creation and preservation— are aspects of the divine creative activity. The same divine activity which brought the world into existence preserves the world from collapsing into non-being. This relationship of God to the World, both as its Creator and Preserver lays, as it will be seen,[24] the foundations for the Biblical emphasis upon the meaningfulness of human history and human life, and pro-

vides the only ground upon which the whole super-
structure of religious and moral life and action can be
erected and maintained, and without which in the
words of Maimonides: 'the whole Torah would
collapse.'

Turning to the problem presented by the Genesis
narrative, here, too, Maimonides would have maintained that whatever may be the popular notion,
Judaism is not tied down in its exposition of the
Genesis narrative to the letter of the text, and can
rightly accept the view of modern Biblical scholars
that the Bible is not a text-book of physical science, but
a store-house of spiritual wealth. Its object is not to
teach the human race scientific facts, but the ways of
God and the knowledge of the Lord.

This treatment of the Bible, it might be noted, does
not imply a retreat forced upon Judaism by modern
scientific knowledge, nor a departure from the true
spirit of Jewish tradition, but rather a reversion to the
best traditions of the past. It was not the scientific
outlook that made the Aggadist of the third century
Rabbi Isaac, quoted by Rashi on Genesis i. 1, question
the relevancy of introducing the Bible with the story
of creation.[25] Conceiving the Torah primarily as a
Book of the Law, setting forth the laws and regulations
governing the life of the Jew, the Sage felt that some
explanation was needed for embodying therein the
story of how the world came into existence. And the
greatest of our Rabbis knew quite well that the use of
precise and correct expressions by the Scriptures
would not always be productive of the best results; on
this is based the well-known Talmudic dictum to the

effect that the Torah in communicating its truth often employed human phraseology and popular language, not always technically accurate, but possessing the immense advantage of being understood by all. It was his recognition of this method of exegesis that enabled Maimonides—whose Orthodoxy no one at the present day will venture to impugn—to declare that the Biblical text was no insuperable bar to the acceptance of the Platonic theory of the Eternity of the Universe once its proof was *positively* demonstrated; and that the intention of the Torah is not to teach us physical knowledge, but ways of life and living action, is a principle clearly enunciated in a number of writings by acknowledged teachers in Israel of old. Typical in this connection is the declaration of Joseph Solomon Delmedigo (1591-1655): ' Know that the prophecies have not come to teach sciences, for their main object is action for the fulfilment of precepts. Consequently, one cannot bring proof from the words of the Torah regarding the science of Nature, for the Torah has spoken in human speech.'[26] In other words, the object of the Torah is not to disclose the knowledge of natural phenomena and natural processes, which man is capable of discovering for himself, but rather to convey in sublime picture-language, understood by all men of all ages, heavenly messages concerning God and His relation to man. It is these messages with which we are mainly concerned; and that these messages have lost nothing, but, on the contrary, have gained in grandeur and significance, from the advance in science and progress in knowledge, is a truth which a close study of Judaism can only serve to confirm.[27]

NOTES

¹ The first chapter of Genesis is generally held to promulgate both creation in time and *ex nihilo*. Whilst ' creation in time ' is clearly taught in the initial word *Bereshit* (' In the beginning '), creation out of nothing is evident on a plain reading of the narrative, in which God is represented as bringing about the work of the six days of creation by nothing more than a series of uttered commands: ' God said, Let there be light, and there was light ', and so on. Here in stark contrast with the general run of the other creation stories in the ancient world, ' there is no manipulation, no emission of substance, no medium between God and the world, nothing but the omnipotent fiat by which the creatures received their very existence together with their natures ' (E. L. Mascall, *Existence and Analogy* [1949], p. 146). The idea that God created the world out of nothing was thus always considered from the earliest times so self-evident in the scheme of Biblical religion that it called for no special affirmation by the Synagogue. Greek philosophers, however, from the days of Empedocles (b. *c.* 460 B.C.E.) onwards, propounded the theory of a pre-existent eternal matter, out of which all things came into being; but all this excited little interest in Jewish circles, and creation *ex nihilo* continued to maintain itself unchallenged as the established Jewish doctrine on the subject. The only definite deviation from this position is to be found in the Jewish-Hellenistic work, *The Wisdom of Solomon*, composed during the first century before the Common Era, where it is said that God created the world ' out of formless matter ' (Wisdom of Solomon, XI, 17). On the other hand, another contemporary Jewish-Hellenistic writer, the author of *The Second Book of Maccabees*, avows the ancient Jewish teaching, when he declares that God made heaven and earth and all that is therein ' out of things non-existent ' (2 Maccabees, VII, 28). (H. A. Wolfson's suggestion in his *Philo* I, p. 303, that he might have meant ' relatively non-existent ' does not appear tenable.) As to Philo's attitude, H. A. Wolfson, *op. cit.*, pp. 301ff., in opposition to a number of scholars, D. Neumark, among others, shows conclusively that Philo held to the belief in *creatio ex nihilo*. When we come down to later Talmudic times, we still see this belief accepted without questioning, only a heathen philosopher venturing

to shock his Jewish hearers by expressing an opinion to the contrary (see *infra*, n. 3). It is also significant that throughout the whole wide extent of Talmudic and Midrashic literature there is not (except for a doubtful passage, for which see *infra*, n. 3) the slightest indication that *creatio ex nihilo* was taken for otherwise than granted in the Jewish schools. Mediaeval Jewish philosophers, however, called upon to face the growing challenge of Greek philosophy, sought to find *explicitly* in the text what had hitherto been accepted as *implicit*, their idea being that a direct Biblical enunciation of the doctrine of *creatio ex nihilo* would serve to restrain the faithful from embracing a theory which they considered irreconcilable with the fundamental Jewish doctrine of the entire independence of God (see *supra*, p. 160, n. 21). Some claimed the notion of *creatio ex nihilo* in the Hebrew verb *bara* ('created'), a term which is used exclusively of divine activity, and which they held to denote a *creatio ex nihilo*. So Saadia (*Commentary on Isaiah*, quoted by M. Ventura, *La Philosophie de Saadia Gaon* [1934], p. 110), Maimonides (*Guide*, III, 10), Nahmanides (*Commentary*, Genesis I, 1), Bahya ben Asher (*Commentary*, Genesis I, 1), among others. The employment, however, in many instances of the term *bara* where no *creatio ex nihilo* is involved (see Abraham ibn Ezra, Genesis I, 1), led others to look for the source of this doctrine elsewhere, and Elijah ben Solomon, the Gaon of Vilna (1720-97), in his *Addereth Eliyyahu* (Genesis I, 1) finds it in the expression *bereshit* which, if taken to refer to the primeval chaos described in verse 2, affirms *creatio ex nihilo*. This assumes that *bereshit* is used here in the 'absolute state,' which normally should take the definite article; but its absence is explained by the Vilna Gaon on the significant ground that time itself formed part of the 'work of the beginning.' (Cf. Maimonides, *Guide*, II, 13: 'because time belongs to things created, it cannot be said that God produced the universe in a temporal beginning'.) Modern Biblical scholarship, discussing the implications of the terms *bara* and *bereshit*, merely repeats what has been said before, without advancing substantially the matter any further. See John Skinner, *Genesis*, in the *International Critical Commentary* (1910), pp. 12-14, and particularly A. Heidel, *The Babylonian Genesis* (ed. 1951), pp. 89ff., where the recent literature on the subject is given. This absence of any definitive Biblical teaching on the question has opened the door for the accommodation of the Genesis account of the creation to the various theories propounded by Greek philosophers on the problem of creation, so long as this could be achieved without doing violence to the fundamental Jewish doctrine of God (see *infra*, n. 18).

2 Aristotle's views on the subject are not clear. He himself declares that there is no demonstrative proof available for the problem. See *Topics*, I, c. 11. The eternity of the Universe has been ascribed to Aristotle only by his commentators. See Maimonides, *Guide*, II, 15 and S. Munk's remarks *a.l.* See also E. Zeller, *Die Philosphie der Griechen* (1921), II, 2, p. 431-4.

3 This view is found in Plato in his *Timaeus*, 29 and 53; see *Dialogues of Plato* (translated by Benjamin Jowett) 2nd edition, Oxford (1875), III, pp. 613-5 and pp. 657-658. Whether Plato also taught the eternity of the universe is a matter of controversy both among the ancient and modern philosophers. See Munk's French Version of the *Guide*, II, p. 111, note and Zeller *op. cit.*, II, 1, 727, notes 2-4, where the extensive literature on the controversy is listed, as well as Ueberweg-Prächter, *Grundniss der Geschichte der Philosophie*, I, *Das Altertum* (1926), p. 315. To this is to be added the illuminating note in A. E. Taylor's *Commentary on Plato's Timaeus* (1928), pp. 71ff. The Platonic view gave rise to a number of theories as to the process whereby this pre-existent formless matter had become moulded into a well-ordered and harmonious universe. Proceeding from the law of causality that ' like produces like,' it could not be admitted that God, the simple cause, immaterial and incorporeal, could operate immediately upon composite matter, or directly produce the myriad forms of nature. Thus there arose the Neo-platonic theories of emanation that ascribed creative powers to inferior causes, and that taught that the world was the result of a succession of causes and effects till there arose the lower realms of body and matter. There is an allusion to the Platonic theory of pre-existent matter in the Midrash, Genesis Rabbah, I, 9, where we read that a philosopher said to Rabban Gamaliel II (*fl. c.* 90-110): ' Your God is a great artist, He found good material which assisted

Him in making the world '—a remark which Rabban Gamaliel
greeted with an imprecation. Maimonides, *Guide*, II, 26, also traces
the Platonic theory in a passage which he quotes from *Pirke de-Rabbi
Eliezer*, chapter 3 (a work attributed to Rabbi Eliezer ben Hyrcanus
[40 ?-117], but now generally regarded as dating from about the
ninth century) and which he considers very strange. Maimonides'
interpretation of the passage has been, however, disputed by a
number of mediaeval Jewish writers, to mention only Isaac Arama
(d. 1494) in his *Akedat Yitzhak* Genesis, Portal II. See D. H. Joel,
Die Religionsphilosophie des Sohar (1849), p. 320ff.

⁴ See, for example, Munk, *op. cit.*, II, p. 144, note 2, and S. Eisler,
Vorlesungen üeber die jüedische Philosophie des Mittelalters, III, p. 69,
A. Rohner, *Das Schöpfungsproblem bei Maimonides, Albertus Magnus
und Thomas von Aquin*, p. 85.

⁵ Behmenyar, a disciple of Avicenna, is representative of these
' modern philosophers ' (אלפלאספ"ה אלקאילין); see De Boer,
Philosophie des Islam, p. 147.

⁶ See Maimonides, *Guide*, II, 21: שנו מלת החיוב והשאירו ענינו,
אולי שהם כוונו ליפות המליצה או להסיר ההרחקה

⁷ *Ibidem*: כלנו אל התחלה אחת נכוין (כלנא נחו מבדא ואחד)

⁸ *Ibidem*: הנה היא סותרת לדת . . . תפול התורה בכללה

⁹ (קדם אלעאלם) קדמות העולם

¹⁰ It is only in connection with the second reason, סבה שנית that
Maimonides introduces the Aristotelian theory אבל אמונת הקדמות
ע"צ אשר יראה אותו אריסטו שהוא ע"צ החיוב ולא ישתנה טבע כלל
אלו התאמת להם מופת על Also towards the end ולא יצא דבר ממנהגו
דעת אריסטו תפול התורה בכללה, whereas in connection with the first
reason הסבה] האחת] the phrase ' eternity of the universe ' is used in
general terms. This exposition of Maimonides' attitude has been
made the subject of an article by me in the *M.G.W.J.*, Vol.
75 (1931), pp. 335-348, entitled *Das Problem des göttlichen Willens
in der Schöpfung nach Maimonides, Gersonides und Crescas*. In view
of the clear distinction made by Maimonides between the Aristotelian and the Platonic theory of the eternity of the universe, it is
strange that Judah Alfacar of Toledo (d. 1235), in his letter to

David Kimhi (1160-1235), in connection with the anti-Maimonidean controversy, should have criticised Maimonides for his readiness to accept the Aristotelian theory of the eternity of the universe: ועוד שיש בו לענין הקדמות שאלו נמצא עליה מופת ברור לאריסטו בחוק ההגיון ומשפטו היה יכול להוציא מעשה בראשית מידי פשוטו. See *Iggerot* in *Kobez Teshubot Ha-Rambam* (Leipzig ed. 1859), III, p. 1 c. See also Graetz, *History of the Jews* (Hebrew ed.) V, p. 60. The same error is made by H. A. Wolfson, *The Platonic, Aristotelian and Stoic Theory in Hallevi and Maimonides*, in *Essays presented to J. H. Hertz* (ed. by I. Epstein, E. Levine, C. Roth), pp. 438-9.

[11] See A. E. Taylor, *St. Thomas Aquinas as a Philosopher*, in *St. Thomas Aquinas*, Papers read at the celebration of the sixth centenary of the canonisation of St. Thomas Aquinas (1925), pp. 42-3.

[12] *Kuzari*, I, 67.

[13] See H. A. Wolfson, *op. cit.*, p. 430.

[14] והוא שנית ליסוד היחוד

[15] See H. A. Wolfson, *loc. cit.*

[16] See H. A. Wolfson, *op. cit.*, p. 431.

[17] See Maimonides, *Guide*, II, 13 (*First Theory*), anticipating the argument mentioned by Maimonides in the *Second Theory*, in answer to the objection. Wolfson's assumption that Maimonides was expressing his own views in the *Second Theory* is difficult to follow.

[18] The view of Maimonides as resulting from the present exposition may be expressed in the following tabular form:

Theory	Compatible with Scripture	Incompatible with Scripture
Eternity of Creation	Platonic	Aristotelian
Pre-existent matter	Created	Uncreated

This too seems to have been the attitude of Judah Halevi, who states in his *Kuzari*, I, 67: ' If a believer in the Torah finds himself obliged to acknowledge and admit pre-existent matter and the existence of many worlds prior to this one, he would not impair his belief that this world was created at some particular time.' The juxtaposition of the two concepts of pre-existent matter and of a succession of worlds indicates that the pre-existent matter Halevi had in mind was one which had been created by God, even as were the successive worlds. On the theory of successive worlds, see *infra*. The use by Judah Halevi of the term ' eternal ' (קדימ״ה) to describe the pre-existent matter to which he refers provides no proof that he meant ' eternal, unborn and unmade,' as Wolfson asserts (*op. cit.*, p. 430). Maimonides too, uses this very term with reference to his interpretation of the Platonic theory of the eternity of the Universe. The only difference between Maimonides and Halevi seems to resolve itself into the question whether the theory of the eternity of *this* universe can be considered compatible with Scripture; whilst Maimonides does not regard the theory *per se* as irreconcilable with the Genesis account, Halevi would reject it altogether. On the other hand, the same juxtaposition referred to in Halevi's statement warrants the assumption that the successive worlds he had in mind followed in succession to the pre-existent eternal matter proceeding from the free act of God (cf. however, H. A. Wolfson, *op. cit.*, p. 430). The theory of successive worlds, which originated with the Stoics, finds support in Talmudic passages quoted already by Maimonides, *Guide*, II, 30: ' Scripture says, " one day "—Rabbi Judah ben Simon says, Hence you learn that the order of times existed before the creation of the world. Rabbi Abbahu said, Hence we learn that God built worlds and destroyed them '. (Midrash Genesis Rabbah, III, 7.) (For all the relevant Rabbinic literature on the subject, see M. Kasher, *Torah Shelemah* [1927] I, pp. 84-89). In all this we have the germinal idea of eternal creation which appeals most to the modern mind and which has found its latest advocate in Fred Hoyle, *The Nature of the Universe* (1950), pp. 104-6. Provided this eternal creation is conceived as a free action of the Creator, there is nothing in it to make it unacceptable to a ' believer in the Torah.' Quite the reverse of the Maimonidean view is that of Gersonides who, whilst accepting the theory of an eternal and uncreated pre-existent matter (*Milhamot Adon.* VI, 1-16), insists on the doctrine of creation in time (*op. cit.*, V, 1-9). As against Gersonides and Maimonides is the view of Crescas, who considers even the Aristotelian view of the eternity of the universe compatible with the fundamentals of Judaism, provided creation, though a necessary act, is regarded as emanating not from Nature, but from the divine will (*Or Adon.* III, 1). For a full discussion of the views of Maimonides, Gersonides and Crescas and their relation to one another, see my article in the *M.G.W.J.* cited above n. 10. Still more thoroughgoing in adopting the Aristotelian theory is Isaac Albalag (middle of the fourteenth century) on whom see Julius Guttmann in *Louis Ginzberg's Jubilee Volume, Hebrew Section* (1946), pp. 76ff. A general survey of the various views of mediæval Jewish philosophers on *creatio ex nihilo* is given by A. Schmiedl, *Studien über jüdische, inbesonders jüdisch-arabische Religionsphilosophie* (1896), pp. 91-128.

[19] A. Ginzberg, *Parashat Derachim*, Essay, *Shilton ha-Sekel*, (' Supremacy of Reason '), Vol. IV, p. 14, Berlin (1921).

[20] T. H. Huxley, *Science and the Hebrew Tradition* (1893), p. 187. Similarly Ernst Haeckel, *History of Creation* (English translation, London, 1925), I, 8, writes, ' The process of creation as the coming into existence of matter is completely beyond human comprehension, and can therefore never be a subject of scientific enquiry '.

[21] James Jeans, *Eos* (1928), p. 95. Similarly, Lincoln Barnett, *The Universe and Dr. Einstein* (1949), p. 93: ' Most of the clues . . . that have been discovered at the inner and outer frontiers of scientific cognition suggest a definite time of creation.' The argument commonly advanced by modern physical science in favour of creation in time rests upon the so-called principle of entropy, the term meaning diffusion (of energy). Briefly the argument is that the interchange of energy between material systems results in a progressive evening out of the heterogeneity of the Universe, all change, variety and life becoming lost in one dreary monotone. Now if the Universe had existed from infinite time, this dismal consequence should have already occurred, so that the Universe would have been by now entirely homogeneous. But the fact is that it is not in this state; therefore it cannot have existed from an infinite time; see A. S. Eddington, *The Nature of the Physical World* (1929), p. 64ff. Eddington's attitude to the entropological argument is reserved, and after discussing possible solutions, he leaves the whole question undetermined. (See Eddington, *New Pathways in Science* [1935],

quoted in E. L. Mascall, *op. cit.*, p. 99, n. 1—exactly the attitude adopted by Maimonides in his day). Another argument is based on the mathematical calculation of the distance between any two galaxies and of their speed of recession, which indicates that at some definite time in the past they were crowded together in some small region. See E. Whittaker, *Space and Spirit* (1946), pp. 116-7. See also Fred Hoyle, *op. cit.*, p. 100, who argues from the fact that the Universe still consists almost entirely of hydrogen, which is steadily being converted into helium, and other elements throughout the Universe, that it cannot be infinitely old. Similarly, C. F. von Weizsäcker, Head of the department at the Max Planck Institute and Professor of Theoretical Physics at Göttingen University, in an address on the Third Programme of the B.B.C. on the theme ' The New Picture of the Universe ', expressed the view that the evidence regarding the age of the earth, of the sun, of the Milky Way and of the spiral nebulae all converges to indicate that all began about the same time. ' All these various calculations of age ', he says, ' produce the same result. And if a large number of calculations that are quite independent of one another as regards the conceptual aids they employ each produce the same result, this is precisely the kind of accumulation of probability which, in the sciences, encourages us to suppose that we are dealing with something real, in this case the real " age of the Universe." ' (*Listener*, Jan. 8, 1953.)

[22] F. Darwin, *Life and Letters of Charles Darwin* (1888), II, p. 203.

[23] See *supra*, pp. 147ff.

[24] See *infra*, pp. 229ff.

[25] See Yalkut Shimeoni, Exodus, 187. See also Nissim b. Reuben (1340-80), *Commentary on Genesis*, Jews' College, MS. Hirschfeld Catalogue No. 20 (Halberstam, No. 137): ר׳ מדברי נתבאר וכבר יצחק שאין כוונת התורה להעמידנו על חכמות הנמצאות כמו שחשבו המתפתים בעצמם ללא דבר הנמשכים אחר היוני. ' It is evident from the words of Rabbi Isaac that it is not the intention of the Torah to instruct us in the sciences of existing things, as have thought those who allow themselves to be seduced to things that are nought, and are attracted after the Greek (philosophers).'

[26] See, *Mazref le-Hokmah* (Basel ed.), p. 29ᵃ, לא שהנבואות וידעת
באו ללמד חכמות שעיקר תכליתם אל המעשה ר״ל לקיום המצות ולכן אין
להביא ראיי׳ מדברי תורה על חכמת הטבע כי דברה תורה בלשון בני אדם.
A. Geiger and others are certainly correct in maintaining that the
phrase, ' The Torah has spoken in human speech ' (or more literally:
' according to the language of man '), wherever it occurs in the
Talmud refers solely to Halachic dicta and rulings, and that its
application to Biblical anthropomorphisms is of post-Talmudic
origin. Nevertheless, there is much force in Marmorstein's conten-
tion (*The Old Rabbinic Doctrine of God*, II [1937], p. 120) that it is
more than a mere coincidence that the phrase is mainly used by
teachers who sought to remove in their expositions the implications
of the anthropomorphic forms and expressions in the Bible.

[27] See Letters of Rabbi A. I. Kook, *Iggerot Rayah*, (1943), pp. 105-6.
' It is known that the account of the work of the Beginning belongs
to the mysteries of the Torah, but if all the words were to be understood simply in the literal sense, what mystery would there be here ?
Already the Midrash declares, " It is impossible to give a full
account to man of the creation, therefore, Scripture simply tells us,
in the beginning God created the heaven and the earth " (Yemen
Midrash on Genesis I, 1. See Maimonides, *Guide, Introduction*)
. . . the principal thing which matters is knowledge which follows
from the narrative—the knowledge of God and of true moral life
. . . but in no way can there be any contradiction between the
words of the Torah and scientific teaching.'

CHAPTER X

EVOLUTION AND GENESIS

IN dealing with the conception of God as Creator, we have seen that the question whether the world had a beginning in time was, according to Judaism, of no fundamental importance to the doctrine of creation. All that Judaism insisted on in its doctrine was that the world and all it contained was the product, not of necessity, but of the free will of God. From this point of view, it was concluded that provided this essential content of the Jewish doctrine of creation remained inviolate, there was nothing in the evolutionary theory that need be regarded as hostile or opposed to the spirit of the Torah. This conclusion may well be felt to call for a fuller elaboration, and it is to this task that this chapter is devoted.

For the sake of argument we will assume that the most extravagant claims made by scientists in regard to the evolutionary process are correct, and that the fact of an unbroken evolution from the nebula to man is established beyond doubt. Even then it will be seen that the theistic position would be little affected. Nay more, if it could indeed be proved that the Universe has passed through this orderly and progressive development like the acorn that becomes the giant oak, the religious claim, so far from losing its force, would but receive additional strength. The more vast and complicated the design, the more intricate the interdependence of things great and small, the more impressive becomes the evidence of a divine wisdom behind

194

the scheme of things, evoking in us, in admiration, the psalmist's paean of praise: ' How manifold are Thy works, O Lord! in wisdom hast Thou made them all: the earth is full of Thy possessions.' (Psalm civ. 24).

Here, too, Maimonides is our best guide. It will be recalled that Maimonides was quite prepared to accept the Platonic theory of the eternity of the Universe, once it were indubitably demonstrated, because it was compatible with the belief that creation was the product of the Divine Will, and not of necessity.[1] A similar view, although not so unqualified as that of Maimonides, is also expressed by Judah Halevi, when he writes in his *Kuzari* 1, 67: ' If after all a believer in the Torah finds himself compelled to admit and acknowledge an eternally hylic (primordial) matter and the existence of many worlds prior to this world, this would not impair his belief that this world was created at a certain time in the past, and that Adam and Eve were (in this world) the first human beings.'[2] Applying this view, expressed by Halevi, to the theory of Evolution, we can likewise say that should a believer be compelled to admit Evolution, there would be no harm done to his faith, provided that he still maintains that all things, visible and invisible, did not come into being by some self-working process, but that they are the creation of God.

This, after all, as has been shown, is all that the Jewish doctrine of Creation is concerned to affirm; and this truth is not affected by the theory of Evolution. For Evolution, as is now recognised by eminent leaders in science, is not a cause but rather a means of creative activity. Behind the evolution of the Universe there is a cause at once controlling and permeating the process. Allowing for all evidences in favour of interpreting existence in terms of the evolutionary system, there still remain facts—tremendous facts—to be explained: the origin of life, mind, conscience, human personality, for each of which we must look back to the creative Omnipotence of the Eternal Spirit. Granting then, for instance, that man's descent is to be traced, as some scientists are generally fond of stressing, to the ape, or even to cabbages, as was not long ago suggested, it does not follow that man is an ape, because he is descended from apes, any more that man is a cabbage, despite the assertion that one is descended from the other. We may further analyse Man, as some American scientists with a flair for statistics have done, and discover that an average man 5 ft. 10 in. tall, and weighing 150 lbs., contains enough fat to make seven bars of soap, enough iron to make a nail of medium size, enough sugar to fill a shaker, enough lime to whitewash a chicken coop, enough phosphorus to make 2,200 match-tips, enough magnesium for a dose of magnesia, enough potassium to explode a toy cannon, together with a little sulphur. And we may reckon that these chemical elements at current market rates are worth, as we are told by these same scientists, about 98 cents. Accepting all this analysis and description, there has still to be explained the amazing mystery that all this 98 cents worth of chemical compounds should have produced saints, seers and sages.

The same limitations of the scientific evolutionary hypothesis are noticeable when applied to the history of thought and religion and morals. Even if religion could be shown to have evolved from barbarous beliefs and savage superstitions, and morals to have their origin in a combination of primary instincts, impulses and complexes, science would still have to explain the faith of a Job, who exclaimed: ' Though He slay me, yet I will wait for Him ' (Job xiii. 15)—to explain how it arose from mere animism and fetishism; to account for the conscience, the inner urge, of the martyr who sacrifices everything for the sake of moral or religious ideals—a sacrifice that raises the deed far above the mere Behaviourism of the New Psychology. Naturalism may meet the attack under the cover of a devout *belief* in a nebulous ' potentiality,' whereby later developments are explained away on the assumption that they were potentially present at the beginning. Religious philosophy, however, armed with the sound Aristotelian canon that the ' nature ' of a thing must be sought in its final form, returns to the charge with the rejoinder that a potentiality productive of high ethical and spiritual results essentially implies the existence of ethical and spiritual purpose from the beginning.[3] And the conclusion must be that evolution is conceivable only as the expression of a creative mind, deliberately producing by means of its physical and biological laws that wonderful organism which has reached its climax in Man, as we know him to-day, endowed with rational and intellectual power and energy, capable of appreciating the higher values of life, and the highest ethical and spiritual achievements; in other words, of a Supreme Universal Intelligence that visualised far back in the recesses of time the great ultimate goal of the works of the beginning.

o

Moreover, since the process culminates in the human organism, with its rational and creative intelligence, capable of the appreciation of the higher values of life, such as goodness, beauty and truth, its ultimate cause must be a mind transcending all human aspirations and endeavours, the ultimate reality in which all consists and through which all subsists, the Divine Infinite personality whom men call God. As Professor J. A. Thomson rightly remarks, ' Only a system with order and progress in the heart of it could elaborate itself so perfectly and so intricately, and so there is assuredly much to incline us to assert eternal providence, and justify the ways of God to Man.'[4] It is clear to all, save to the conservative scientist who cannot rid himself of the philosophical materialism of two generations ago, or to the professional or eccentric atheist, to whom the thought of a Supreme Being is too oppressive, that evolution and mechanism are irreconcilable concepts, and that science must still fall back upon a ' faith ' to fill in the gaps in any account of the Universe it may give.

> ' A firemist and a planet,
>   A crystal and a cell,
> A jelly-fish and a saurian,
>   And caves where cave-men dwell;
> Then a sense of law and beauty,
>   And a face turned from the clod—
> Some call it Evolution,
>   Others call it God.'[5]

' Some call it Evolution, and others call it God '—
Evolution *versus* God is thus no longer an issue between

science and religion, but is merely a modern formulation of the difference in the attitude to life which, from the earliest days of human thought, has distinguished the non-religious from the religious—'the fool, who saith in his heart, "There is no God," ' from the man of faithful heart.

This ages-long difference of attitude to life has been well summarised by Judah Halevi in his *Kuzari*.

' Said the Kuzari: " All that I can see is that they (the philosophers) have misled us by these names, and caused us to place another being on a par with God, if we say that Nature is wise and active. Speaking in their sense, we might say that Nature is a Creator."

' Replied the Rabbi: " Certainly, but the elements, the sun, the moon and the stars have powers such as warming, cooling, moistening, drying, etc., yet they do not merit that wisdom should be ascribed to them, or to be reckoned more than a function; while forming, measuring, producing, and all that shows an intention, can only be ascribed to the All-wise and All-mighty. There is no harm in calling the force which arranges matter by means of heat and cold ' Nature ', provided one refuses to ascribe to it wisdom. For instance, the faculty of creating the embryo must be denied to man and woman, because they but aid the matter in receiving the form of man from the wise moulder. . . . *And this is the root of faith and the root of disobedience."* '6

Had Judah Halevi to deal with the modern situation, he would have formulated the arguments in this dialogue somewhat on the following lines:

' Said the Kuzari: " All that I can see is that the materialistic scientists have misled us by the term

Evolution and caused us by this term to place another principle on a par with God, if we say that Evolution is possessed of wisdom and is self-acting. Speaking in this way, we might say that Evolution is God."

'Replied the Rabbi: "Certainly, but the living cells have the powers of adaptation, variation, and mutation, yet they do not merit that wisdom should be ascribed to them, or to be reckoned more than a function; whilst organising, directing and evolving and all that which shows an intention, can only be ascribed to one who is All-wise and All-mighty. There is no harm in calling the force which organises the living cell by means of adaptation, variation and selection, Evolution, provided we refuse to ascribe to it wisdom. . . . And this is the root of faith and the root of disobedience."'

Evolution, it will thus have been seen, is no longer in opposition to Creation, but a mere process by which all observed things have come into being. Looking at it in this way, there is nothing in the evolutionary theory which is inimical to the fundamentals of Jewish religious teaching and which must necessarily be rejected by him who is convinced of the truth thereof. On the contrary, the evolutionary idea answers wonderfully to the Jewish conception of creation as a process moving towards the development of life at ever higher levels of existence, and towards the consummation, as we shall see, of an earthly goal that is supremely good and perfect. In the words of the late Rabbi Kook: 'There is nothing old under the sun; everything rises, everything ascends, higher and higher; everything brings more and more light and life.'[7] Far, therefore,

from seeing in the doctrine of Evolution its arch-
enemy, the Jewish religion can welcome it as the
nearest approach to an ally to which it can point anywhere in the history of human thought.

There remains, however, to be explained the Biblical
account, which is generally considered to stand in
direct opposition to Evolution. A closer scrutiny of the
Genesis narrative should soon dispose of this view.
While this is not the place to examine to what extent
the details of the Bible story coincide with the order of
events as taught in our latest modern scientific text-
books, we may point to two remarkable and amazing
features in the Biblical account of the Creation, by
which no unbiased reader can fail to be impressed:
(1) Its insistence that the creative process was a
progression proceeding in slow advance by a series of
stages from the lower to the higher, each of which rests
on the preceding, with man at the apex; (2) that the
order of the Bible follows in its broad outline a chrono-
logical sequence which concurs with that taught by
science.[8] In going through the Biblical narrative, we
find on examination at least eleven great events set
forth in the same sequence as that adopted, or, at least,
not contradicted by modern science. Bearing these
two points in mind, what fundamental antagonism is
there between the inspirational and the scientific
account? Surely none, except that in the Bible the
whole process is dramatically regarded as if it occurred
quickly in six days, whereas science insists that it came
into existence through millions of years of constant
travail, struggle and development. In both accounts
the element of time and the succession of events are

limited. Nor need the term ' day ' mean a day in the
literal sense, as little as the recurring words ' God said '
are to be taken literally, for there was no one for God
to speak to.   The words must be understood as they
were by Saadia, Maimonides and Elijah ben Solomon
of Vilna (1720-97), among others, in the sense
that God willed;[9] and we have no more reason to
insist that the days are literal days than we have the
right to suppose that God literally spoke.   What we are
to understand in the phrase ' God said ' is that the
Almighty, for Whom nothing is hard, created all
things in such a way as might to man be represented
by a simple word of command.   Similarly what we
may understand by the term ' day ' is that God, the
Eternal One, to whom a thousand years, nay, a million
years are but as yesterday, created all things in such
periods of time as might to man be best represented
by six days.   Vast as the Universe is, man was to
regard it as being to God no more than a week's
work to himself.   In short, the time of Creation, however long in itself, was utterly insignificant to the
Eternal.

This, it may be added, is not purely a modern theory
advanced in order to reconcile the narrative of Genesis
with Science.   Surely no such considerations could
have entered the mind of the old Midrashist when he
explained the phrase, ' One day ', as meaning, ' a
thousand years which are but one day to the Holy One,
blessed be He.'[10]   More precise in this connection is
Levi Gersonides (1288-1344), who knew nothing of
geology and paleontology, and yet refused to regard
the days in Genesis as being literal, or as representing

any definite periods of time. God's creation is for Him timeless, and the six days indicate but the natural order and rank in existing things, proceeding from cause to effect, and from the lower to the higher.[11]

Believing that this approach does no violence to the Biblical text we mention it here as showing a marvellous harmony between the narrative in the Bible and the generally accepted scientific theories. The stately procession is the same, no matter whether you mean a day of twenty-four hours or a long period running into millions of years. Nor does the slowness of the process lessen the mystery. One does not make things plainer by substituting millions of years for six days. As G. K. Chesterton writes humorously in his *Everlasting Man*, ' An event is not any more intrinsically intelligible or unintelligible because of the pace at which it moves. For a man who does not believe in a miracle, a slow miracle would be just as incredible as a swift one. The Greek witch may have turned a sailor into a swine with a stroke of the wand. But to see a naval gentleman of our acquaintance looking a little more like a pig every day till he ended with four trotters and a curly tail, would not be any more soothing. It might be rather more creepy and uncanny. The mediaeval wizard may have flown through the air from the top of a tower, but to see an old gentleman walking through the air in a leisurely and lounging manner would still call for some explanation. Yet, there runs through all the rationalistic treatment of history this curious and confused idea that difficulty is avoided, or even mystery eliminated, by dwelling on mere delay, or on something dilatory in the process of things.'[12] The mystery remains. The mystery how anything exists. The mystery which bridged the gulf between living and non-living matter, between the vegetable and animal kingdom, between invertebrates and vertebrates, between the marine animals and the amphibians, between amphibians and reptiles, between reptiles and mammals, between mammals and the human body, and finally the mystery how the gulf was bridged between the soulless simians and human personality. Surely this mystery is not lessened by substituting the dust of animal species for the dust of the earth out of which the Bible tells us God formed man! Granted that all these advances have been made by the process known as Evolution, we must still ask, whence originate these internal inexhaustible forces capable of crossing these impossible gulfs? Science cannot answer. 'There is not a single fact,' writes du Noüy (the first scientist to apply mathematics successfully to biological problems) in his *Human Destiny*, 'or a single hypothesis to-day which gives an explanation of the birth of life or of natural evolution.'[13] And unless Science is satisfied to rank with the philosophers of Laputa who sought to make books by throwing letters at random, it too can only murmur with the Bible the words, 'In the beginning God made,' and for every advance from one stage to another in the process, echo 'God said.' All of which only serves to strengthen the conviction that as science comes more and more into the full possession of the truth as to the manner in which God worked in those days of the beginning, the unity of the Bible and science, of Torah and natural knowledge will be more discernible and complete.[14]

NOTES

[1] See *supra*, pp. 172ff.

[2] *Kuzari*, I, 67. ואם היה מצטרך בעל תורה להאמין ולהודות בחומר
קדמון ועולמים רבים קודם העולם [הזה] לא היה בזה פגם באמונתו כי העולם
הזה חדש. The original Arabic text has ילזא, which signifies ' compelled ' by logical means, for the Hebrew מצטרך, see D. Neumark,
Essays in Jewish Philosophy, p. 241, n. 18. On the difference
between Judah Halevi and Maimonides, see *supra*, p. 189, n. 18.

[3] ' Those who suppose . . . that perfect beauty and goodness do
not exist in the beginning . . . are mistaken in their views. For
the seed comes from prior creatures which are perfect, and that
which is first is not the seed but the perfect creature. E.g., one might
say that prior to the seed is the man—not he who is produced from
the seed, but another man from whom the seed comes.' *Metaphysics*
XII, 7. (E.T., Hugh Tredennick, Loeb Classical Library, ed. [1935],
p. 151.)

[4] Quoted by W. R. Inge in ' Conclusion ' to *Science, Religion and
Reality*, edited by J. Needham (1926), p. 367.

[5] Quoted by J. W. N. Sullivan, *The Limitations of Science* (1933),
p. 237.

[6] *Kuzari*, I, 75-77.

[7] See A. I. Kook, *Orot ha-Kodesh* (1938), II, p. 484: אין כל ישן
תחת השמש הכל פורח, הכל מתעלה, הכל מוסיף תמיד אור וחיים.

[8] See L. T. More, *The Dogma of Evolution* (1925), p. 88: ' The
order of appearance of living and non-living things in the first
Chapter of Genesis corresponds in a most remarkable degree with
the order of appearances as they are postulated by modern astronomy,
and also by modern geology and modern biology. . . . In the days
when the first chapter of Genesis was written, geology was an
unknown science. . . . The possibility that the author of Genesis
would manage to get the order correct merely by working with the
knowledge of those sciences or from guessing would be a hundred to
one against. Surely, we may see in the remarkable correspondence
between the order in Genesis and the order in nature the marks of

Divine revelation.'   Given in their sequence, the eleven events referred to are as follows: (1) The formless waste and void; (2) Darkness upon the face of the deep; (3) Light appears; (4) a clearing expanse of firmament; (5) the formation of seas; (6) Grass and herbs appear; (7) the sun, moon and stars appear; (8) Marine animals; (9) Winged-fowls; (10) Land-mammals; (11) Man.   Striking too is the mention of the creation of light on the first day before the formation of the sun. The sun being for long regarded as the source of light, the order was for long thought a difficulty. Talmudic teachers accordingly held that the sun was created on the first day, but it was only on the fourth day that it became visible as a distinct object.   See B.T. Hagigah 12a: הן הן מאורות שנבראו ביום ראשון ולא נתלו עד יום רביעי. and cf. Rashi on Genesis i. 18.   On the latest scientific view, however, light does not come from the sun but from ' outer space.'   But whatever may have been the source of the light stated in the Bible to have been created on the first day, the mere mention of this is indeed one of the most striking things in this striking narrative. See also G. J. Romanes, in *Nature*, 11th August, 1881 : ' The order in which the flora and the fauna are said by the Mosaic account to have appeared on earth, corresponds with that which the theory of Evolution requires and the evidence of Geology proves.'

⁹ ' The phrase, " And He said ", occurring in the account of creation, signifies " He willed " or " He desired ". This has already been stated by other authors, and is well known. A proof for this is . . . that a command can only be given to a being which exists and is capable of receiving the command ' (Maimonides, *Guide*, I, 65).   The reference to ' other authors ', as Moses of Narbonne (d. after 1362) points out in his commentary to the *Guide*, *a.l.*, is to Saadia, who renders the phrase ' God said ' in Genesis i. 3-26, ושא אללה, (' God willed '), and to Jonah Ibn Janach (990-1050). See Derenbourg's ed. of *Saadia's commentary on the Bible, a.l.* (1846), p. 5. n. 3. This is also how it was understood by Elijah b. Solomon (the Vilna Gaon), who notwithstanding his opposition to what he described as ' the accursed philosophy ' הפילוסופיא הארורה which misled, in his view, Maimonides (see the Gaon's *Glosses to Yoreh Deah*, 193, 13), nevertheless explained the phrase to mean

' He willed ' and was not to be taken literally. ‏ומלת ויאמר באורו הוא‏
‏הרצון‏ See also Nahmanides, Genesis i. 3. The adjective ' accursed '
with reference to ' philosophy ', did not emanate, in the opinion of
some, from the Gaon, but was inserted by another hand; see S.
Mirsky, *Bein Shekiah le-Mizrah* (1951), p. 347, n. 24.

[10] See Midrash Genesis Rabbati (ed. Ch. Albek, 1940), p. 10.
‏יום אחד אלו אלף שנים שהם יום אחד של הקב״ה, שנאמר כי אלף שנים‏
‏בעיניך וגו׳‏ See also M. Kasher, *Torah Shelemah* (1937), I. p. 94,
n. 448.

[11] Levi ben Gerson, *Milhamot Adon.* VI, 2, 8. ‏שמה שיוחס בהוי׳‏
‏הזאת שתהיה נשלמה בששת ימים אינו באופן שיהי׳ האחד לשני יום אחד‏
‏דרך משל, אבל אמרו זאת להורות על הקדימה שיש לקצת הנמצאות על קצתן.‏
See also Meir Leibush Malbim (1809-1879), *Commentary*, Genesis
i. 25. ' Creation stepped forward from stage to stage, and man is
the last stage.' ‏הבריאה צעדה ממדרגה למדרגה, והאדם הוא המדרגה‏
‏האחרונה.‏

[12] G. K. Chesterton, *The Everlasting Man* (1927), pp. 25-6.

[13] Lecomte du Noüy, *Human Destiny* (1947): ' As far as the origin
of life is concerned,' he continues, ' we are obliged to admit the idea
of a transcendent intervention . . . or to recognise that we know
nothing of these questions outside of a small number of mechanisms.
. . . This is not an act of faith, but an undisputed scientific statement. . . . It is not we but the convinced materialist who shows a
powerful, even though a negative, faith, when he ostentatiously
continues to believe without any proof that the beginning of life,
evolution, man's brain, and the birth of the moral ideas will some
day be scientifically accounted for.   He forgets that this would
necessitate the complete transformation of modern science, and that
consequently his conviction is based on purely sentimental reasons '
(pp. 134-5). Even Sir Arthur Keith, a Darwinist of the first order,
is compelled to confess: ' Biologists do not know as yet when or
how life began; they have no explanation to offer of its inner significance and ultimate meaning. Therein lies the weakness of their
case.' (*Westminster Gazette*, June 7, 1928). The absurd position into
which materialistic evolution is forced has been well expressed by
R. P. Phillips, quoted by Vera Barclay, *Challenge to the Darwinians*

(1951), p. 242: ' According to materialistic evolution matter destitute
of life, of its own power produces it (life); living matter destitute
of sentience brings it forth (sentience); and sentient life having no
intellect evolves this (mind) from itself. In each case the greater
being produced by the less, something is caused by nothing '.
Reviewing Miss Barclay's book, in the *Hibbert Journal* (L.) April,
1952, p. 296, R. F. Rattray, who describes himself as an ' Evolu-
tionist ', remarks with reference to Phillips' statement, that it is
indeed a paradox that up-to-date materialistic evolution should
believe in creation out of nothing. ' The present age ', he further
remarks, ' regards itself as enlightened. Posterity will marvel at
its gods '.

[14] The view that the Genesis account is derived from the
Babylonian Creation Epic, *Enuma elish* (' When above ') does not
stand the test of an objective comparison of the two accounts.
Apart from some cosmological notions that were common to the
Semitic world, ' there is nothing to link the Babylonian narrative
with that of Genesis ' (F. Kenyon, *Archæology of the Bible* [1940]
p. 47). Nor is it correct to maintain as does Harry M. Orlinsky,
Ancient Israel (1954), p. 25, that ' both accounts speak of light
before the creation of the sun ' (see *supra*, n. 8). The fact is that no
creation of the sun is mentioned in the Babylonian story, as Marduk
himself is the sun god. There is certainly no reference to a creation
in six days followed by a day of rest. Even those features which
bear the closest resemblance to Genesis, ' have no more similarity
than a mud hut to a palace ' (P. J. Wiseman, *Creation Revealed in
Six Days* [1948] p. 59). See also B. Jacob, *Genesis* (1934) pp. 69ff.

[See Additional Note, pp. 376-378.]

CHAPTER XI

MAN

THE striking correspondence that exists, as we have seen, between the Genesis narrative and the account which science gives us of the origin of things, warrants the claim that in reading the Bible we stand on holy ground, on which we may tread only with measured steps, reverence and humility[1a]; and it is with this spirit that the Biblical story of the creation of man must be approached.

It is noteworthy that in the Biblical account no special day is allotted to man. He is represented as originating, so to speak, in the evening of the same day on which the land animals, the mammals, originated. This presentation implies that the act of creation which produced man did not consist in giving him his form. In fact, as far as his body is concerned, man bears such resemblance to the highest types of mammals that he might have emerged from the soil like the other animals. Does not the Midrash itself comment on the Biblical verse ' Let the earth bring forth a living soul ' (Genesis i. 24)—this is the breath of the life of the first man ?[1]

The special distinction given man lies in the divine image impressed upon his animal body. It is this divine image that imparted to man his superiority and intelligence and infused his organism with infinite possibilities. It made man into a being with vast potentialities, rising above those of the animal kingdom, with a sense of conscious freedom, self-determination

For notes on this chapter, see pp. 223-228.

and self-control, as the recipient of faculties and powers which made him rank only a little less than divine. Herein lies the essential point and truth of the Biblical message that man bears the image of God. This is clearly stated in the text: ' Let us make man in our image and after our likeness, that they may have dominion over the fowl of the air, and over the cattle and over all the earth, and over creeping things that creep upon the earth ' (Genesis i. 26). And the next verses (27-8) that follow amplify the idea underlying the conception of the divine image: ' And God created man in His image . . . and He said to them, Be fruitful and multiply and replenish the earth and subdue it, and have dominion over the fish of the sea. . . .'

In the words of Shabbatai Donnolo (b. 913) in his work *Perush Naase Adam be-Tzalmenu*, ' This image and likeness, of which the Blessed One spoke, is not the form of the appearance of the countenance, but the form of the work of God and His activity in the Universe. As God is supreme and rules over man and over all the world, beneath and above, so is man; as God knows and discerns things that happened and foresees things to come, so man, whom God has granted wisdom to know; and as God supplies and gives food to all flesh, so does man sustain all the members of his household, his attendants, and his animals; and as the Creator built the world and laid the foundations of the earth, stretched the heavens and gathered the waters together, so man is able to build, to found, and to call and gather together, to sow, to make grow, to plant and to do . . . and in most things man is likened in

small measure to God, in accordance with the limitations of the strength and the short span of the life which
God has given him.' Here we have set forth the true
significance of the Biblical teaching, that man has been
made in the image of God;² and this truth is not
affected by the substitution of the dust of an animal
species for the dust of the earth.

Granted then that the body of the first man was
produced by normal generation from a species of non-
human ancestors, the divine breath that animated the
body brought into existence something new which
now for the first time entered into the sum of existing
reality. Here was a being which could think and will
and have dominion. Here was a being new, not in
degree, but in kind, transcending in inner perfection
all other existing beings. It was the first subsisting
intelligence, and its novelty could come only from the
original source whence the Universe had come—from
God.

It is true that we find some rudiments of intelligence
low down in the animal creation, to the extent of
planning and contriving, mating, laying snares, storing
food for the future, migration according to season—all
of which connotes a degree of consciousness. Among
the higher animals which have become domesticated
we can even trace some human characteristics, notably
a recognition of men as higher beings, and a kind of
affection for them, which may be dignified with the
name of love, culminating in an attitude which is not
different from what we call worship. This is conspicu-
ous particularly in a dog's relation to his master, leading
even to a sense of wrong-doing which may perhaps

figuratively be described as a sense of sin, and followed by a sort of repentance or at least expectation of punishment.

Yet with all the mental affinities between man and animals, his superiority, in the words of Julian Huxley, ' to the impersonality and irrationality of the rest of the Universe '[3] marks him as a distinct being, different in kind from all animals in creation. This superiority lies in man's faculty of reason, or the power of deducing new truths from those which he already knows, of passing from the known to the unknown. Man adds to the quality of *Hokmah* (Wisdom) that of *Binah* (Understanding), defined by the Rabbis as the capacity to understand one thing from another;[4] whilst in the lower creation we seek in vain traces of *Binah*. The sluggard is well counselled by the wise king to go to the ant and get himself wisdom (Proverbs vi. 6); but he would not be bidden to mark the ways of the ant and gain understanding. It is only man with his faculty of reason who possesses understanding, enabling him to contrive, to design, to discover, to invent, always producing new and elaborate machinery, tools, and techniques. The lower animals, on the other hand, even the most intelligent, are confined always within the same circle of action, unable to discover something new, to design something new. Even where their work shows design, the designing is not due to a conscious effort on the part of the animal, implying forethought, but merely the workings of instinct, which, divorced from full consciousness, is recognised as but a semi-automatic adjustment to environment. Thus it is that the instincts of the animals are practically the same, always and everywhere. They are not more advanced in some countries than in others, or in some individuals than in others. They are not even more advanced as time goes on. Birds make their nests now as they have always made them, in the same shape and with similar materials. Even the most sagacious of animals, such as the horse and the dog, which have been in contact with man for centuries, exhibit not the slightest progress, and are always held in the same groove from which they cannot be extracted. They are, generally speaking, non-educable. They can never reach the level of education to which deaf and dumb children can be brought. All this is because they lack the faculty of reason, because they are irrational. Man alone is progressive. Man alone is inventive. Man alone is able to design *consciously* things new and old, because he alone is rational. Man alone is able to apply himself to an infinity of subjects and pass from one occupation to another. He may begin life as a labourer and end as an artist. The lower animals are pinned down to one set of actions. A bird will never hollow out an hexagonal cell, nor will a bee with all its mathematical genius build a simple bird's nest of leaves and branches. The characteristic of the work of man, on the other hand, as Shabbatai Donnolo already emphasises in the passage quoted, is diversity. Because man alone of all creation is given the power of reason; because he alone of all creatures has been created in the image of God.

It is this rational principle of man with all the potentialities and power it implies that constitutes man's glory and honour, of which no scientific account of his origin can rob him. Science may, with the voice of

P

Sir Arthur Keith, express ' the conviction that man's brain has been evolved from an anthropoid ape, and that in the process no new structure has been introduced, and no strange faculties interpolated.'[5] This, however, does not in the least minimise the real difference in *kind* between man and his animal ancestors, which lies not in the bodily form, where it is admittedly small, but in the mental faculties, where it is enormous and immense. Nor does this explain away man's greatness and his ultimate triumph in the race for supremacy, or the fact that while the gorilla and chimpanzee were satisfied to ' rest on their laurels ' and ceased striving towards higher attainments beyond the mere muscular and physical, the proto-human stock resisted all these temptations and applied themselves with singleness of heart to develop an intelligence that was both rational and creative.

Reason is not the only faculty that distinguishes man from animals. In addition to his reason, or rather rooted in his reason, is the freedom of will which none but man possesses.[5a] Of course there are limits to human freedom, even as animals are not entirely bereft of a measure of free will. But whereas in the case of animals the will is determined from without, in the case of man it is determined by man himself. A hunting dog, for example, will deliberate and come to a decision as to which of two trails it is to follow. He is in doubt which of the two is the stronger, and will after some deliberation make his choice. But this choice is determined by his discovery. As soon as he discovers the stronger trail, he will follow it of necessity and be unable to resist it even if he would. Man, on the other hand, even after discovering what is of greater advantage to him, may still determine to follow at pleasure (in spite of what Behaviourism may tell us) that which is of less advantage. Again, whereas the choice of the dog is a sensuous choice, determined by his instincts, the choice of human free will is intellectual and determined by reason.[6]

Man is thus free, even as he is rational. In both these attributes, which distinguish him from the rest of creation, he shares something of the nature of God —of His wisdom and freedom.[7]

But that is not all. Flowing from his reason and freedom of will is man's moral character, that is, his capacity to acquire moral worth. For just consider human character at its best. The goodness that men and women have attained. Their self-consuming zeal for justice, their wonderful capacity for self-effacing love.[8] These noble qualities, for which we look in vain elsewhere in creation, did not come into existence with the appearance of man, but are the eternal realities of the very being of God. They are but the faint shadows of the attributes that exist in God, in whose image man was made. Man's moral character is but a reflection of the perfect moral character of his Creator, surpassing anything within human power to conceive. Man's capacity for goodness is a reflection of the goodness of his Creator, who made him; and man's love is a reflection of the love of the heavenly father who has begotten him. The idea that human goodness derives from the goodness of God is well expressed in the *Sefer ha-Yashar* of Zechariah ha-Yewani (thirteenth century):

' The good deeds which we perform point to the goodness of the Creator, just as smoke points to fire.'[9]

It is also a recurring thought in later Chassidic literature from which the following passages, where many could be adduced, may serve as examples:

Nahum of Czernobel (1730-1798), in his *Meor Enayim*, writes:

' It is clear to us that human love is but an offshoot of the divine love, for without that divine love no love could be aroused within our heart.'[10]

And similarly, the founder of the Chassidic movement, Israel Baal Shem-Tob (1700-1760), declared:

' It behoves every man to reflect, Whence is the source which evokes in me feelings of love, if not the love of God for His creation ? '[11]

It is because man is a free and moral being, even as he is a rational and creative being, that it is perfectly true to say, even after granting to science all its claims regarding man's biological evolution, that he was created in the image of God, since the special attributes which separate man from all else on this planet are precisely attributes of God Himself.[12] Yet, despite man's pre-eminence and unique position in the creative process, no special day is assigned to him in the Biblical narrative, but he is made to appear on the same day as the land animals. For whereas in regard to his physical nature, which he derives from the same earthly elements as the animals, man may be said to have been fully created from the first, the same cannot be said about his spiritual nature. Here creation was but the incipient stage of a spiritual development which had now become possible. The implanting of the divine image gave man reason and freedom, but it depended on man's use of these gifts whether they would lead to his realisation of this spiritual nature, or bring about his undoing. And, indeed, looking at the lowly average of mankind to-day, after the long laborious process through great tracts of time, one cannot but confess that man is still only at the beginning of his spiritual growth, and has yet a long way to travel ere the divine creative activity of the sixth day shall find its fulfilment in the emergence of the perfect man after the image and likeness of God.[13]

We will now turn to a closer examination of the Genesis account, following the two Maimonidean principles which, as has already been indicated, are to govern our treatment of Biblical texts: (1) that the words of Scripture are to be taken in their obvious sense until necessity arises of seeking a different interpretation; (2) that in the last analysis the criterion to be applied is the practical: how would the departure from the literal sense affect religious life and conduct? The same principle must be applied when considering the Biblical narrative relating to the history of the first man. After all, the historical narratives in the Bible are recorded not for the sake of the events themselves, but for the sake of their religious meaning and significance, and it is for these inner meanings and significances that we must search behind the dramatic Biblical account. In the words of the Jewish mystics, the stories of the Torah form but the external *lebush* (vestment) within which there lies a soul.[14] And it is this soul that we must try to discover and analyse.

Moses Cordovero (b. 1525) in his work *Elimah* speaks of the errors of many scholars of his day who ' believing in the literal sense of the text of the Torah, reject all true premises to the contrary . . . because it appears to them that were they to deny this they would be deniers of the Torah . . . and on account of this it is dangerous even to discuss the matter in their presence, because they take the texts of the Torah in their literal sense and consider fundamental faith whatever they had been accustomed to from their childhood.'[15] Cordovero was, it is true, referring to the inner significance of the Torah as conceived by the Esoteric Lore, the *Kaballah*, but his criticism of those who insist on taking literally in every case the Biblical texts has a wider application.

Let us now, in the light of these observations, examine the Genesis stories. We are all aware of the two different creation accounts in the Bible.[16] In the first account, male and female are both explicitly described as having been created by God: ' And God created man in his own image, in the image of God created He them; male and female created He them ' (Genesis i. 27). In the second account, woman is described as having been built from the rib of man. This divergence has already been noted by the Talmudic Sages, and among the various explanations they offered is one that Adam was bi-sexual at creation,[17] and only at a later stage was the female created out of him. The idea of the bi-sexuality of original man is already found in the *Symposium* of Plato,[18] who in turn, may have derived it, as has been suggested, from Babylonian sources.[19] But however that may be, the notion that the first

218

human ancestor was bi-sexual may contain some truth, which has its counterpart in the teaching of science that we vertebrates begin our embryonic lives not as male, nor as female, but as both; and the interpretation by the Talmudic Sages of the Biblical story in conformity with this notion only serves to show that there is much to incline us to the view that the two Biblical accounts regarding the creation of man may represent two stages in man's development. Nor can science raise any valid objection against the Scriptural teaching of the descent of the human race from one couple. Every evidence goes to indicate the unity of mankind.[20] The fact that all men all the world over, even the least civilised, have the gift of speech and power to grasp intellectual and moral truths, tends to show that we are all of the same family. This argument is moreover confirmed by the world-wide similarities in ancient traditions and folk-lore. Furthermore, as the study of philology advances, the kinship between the languages of all men is being gradually established. The unity of mankind is conclusively shown by the fact that all races inter-breed.

Yet while there is no valid reason for rejecting the Biblical account of the origin of man, there is every indication, as Joseph Albo, in his *Ikkarim*, I, 11, has already pointed out, that the story of the experiences of the first human couple in the first four chapters of Genesis was never intended to be taken literally, and that real Biblical history begins with Chapter v. What comes before reads rather like a description of primordial human nature, and an account of man's spiritual growth and development.[21] In other words, instead of being concerned to relate a factual series of events from the remote past, the narrative in the first four chapters presents a spiritual analysis of man's intrinsic nature, and traces before us some of those movements in man's spiritual evolution common to all manhood. It shows how man rose to freedom and lapsed into disobedience and sin, and describes the penalty he had to pay for this.

Here is not the place to deal with the spiritual significance of the story. It has been the subject of endless treatises and commentaries. But, whatever the significance may be, Judaism is not bound to the literal acceptance of the story of Adam's sin. All that the story is concerned to teach, in the words of the late Rabbi A. I. Kook, ' is that man, though he might attain the highest stage of perfection, and thus prove worthy of all glory and bliss, can forfeit all if he corrupts his ways, bringing thereby untold evil upon himself and upon the many generations that come after him.'[22] Thus it is that Judaism contains none of those doctrines such as the Fall, the Original Sin,[23] and Redemption by Faith, which are of central importance to Christianity, and it need not accordingly have the least anxiety lest the rejection of the literal sense of the story would affect any of the tenets or practices of the Jewish religion. Unlike Christianity, Judaism does not emphasise the fact that we all sprang from Adam in order to teach that we all sinned in him, because he was our parent, and that, having inherited his sin, we have need of Redemption. The purpose of the Jewish emphasis on our descent from Adam is rather social and ethical. It is to teach the unity of mankind; and

significantly enough this teaching is derived not from
any of the verses in the first four chapters, but from the
first verse in chapter 5, where, as already mentioned,
history in the form of chronology and genealogy begins:
' " This is the book of the generations of Adam "
(Genesis v. 1)—this is a comprehensive principle in
the Torah ',[24] implying that all men have a common
origin from an historical ancestor.

Nor need the antiquity of the human species, as
taught by science on the evidence of paleontology,
create any difficulty. The opinion that there have
existed many worlds before the present world has
considerable warrant in Jewish religious thought and
teaching,[25] even as the idea that there existed some
other species of human beings who had become
extinct before the creation of Adam is not unknown in
Judaic sources.[26] Admittedly, the abnormal longevity of
the antediluvian patriarchs does not yield, in our state
of knowledge, to an easy explanation. But the story
of their lives lies too far in the remote past to afford to
any one basing himself on the data of science, any
a priori ground to prove the impossibility of their
having enjoyed such longevity. Besides, whether taken
in its literal sense,[27] or understood as representing some
system the significance of which is altogether unascer-
tainable by us,[28] the chronology of these Biblical
personages is not of the slightest consequence to
Jewish faith and practice. All that the Bible intended
in including this genealogy is to link Creation with that
forward-moving sequence of events which forms the
warp and woof of Biblical history, and through which
the divine purpose for the individual, the nation and

the human race was to unfold itself. But this relationship between creation and the divine purpose, which
the Bible here seeks to affirm, is not affected by the
actual number of years lived by these Biblical figures
of old.

This attitude, if one feels obliged to adopt it in
regard to the Genesis chronology, would not at all be
inconsistent with true Jewish religious thought, which
recognises the value of the Biblical narratives to lie in
the teachings they enshrine, rather than in the narratives
themselves. As the late Rabbi Kook wrote in a striking
passage: ' It behoves every one who thinks aright to
know that . . . we are not obliged, in any way, to
deny or to oppose the views of modern scientists which
are generally held to be contrary to literal accounts of
the Torah, because it is not at all the object of the Torah
to tell us simple stories and events that have come to
pass. The main thing is the inner content and meaning
enshrined; and this stands out all the more whenever
we are confronted by some opposing force, which only
serves to rouse us to greater exertions and efforts [in
the discovery of the true significance of the Biblical
text]. . . . Once we appreciate this truth we shall
find it no longer necessary to contend against the
theories which are in vogue among modern scientists;
and no longer being concerned in the matter, we shall
be able to consider scientific facts objectively, always
being guided by the light of the Torah in the interpretation of these facts.'[29] Indeed, a little thinking, and
courageous independent thinking, is always very
wholesome, particularly in approaching these ancient
and sacred documents, which, as we have seen, bear

eloquent testimony to a divine origin. And to every challenging voice of critics and sceptics of our age, our reply to-day must be, as ever, ' Moses is true and his Torah is true, and they are liars.'[30]

NOTES

[1a] Even Ernst Haeckel could not withhold his admiration of the Genesis cosmology because of its remarkable correspondence with science. ' Two great fundamental ideas common also to the non-miraculous theory of development meet us in the Mosaic hypothesis of creation with surprising clearness and simplicity—the idea of separation or *differentiation*, and the idea of progressive development or perfection. . . . We can therefore bestow our just and sincere admiration on the Jewish lawgiver's grand insight into Nature and his simple and natural hypothesis of creation without discovering in it a so-called " divine revelation " '. (*History of Creation* [E.T., E. Ray Lankester] second edition, 1876, p. 38.) But how this ' grand insight ' came to the Jewish lawgiver without a divine revelation, Haeckel makes no attempt to explain.

[1] Midrash Genesis Rabbah, VII, 7: תוצא הארץ נפש חיה זה רוחו
של אדם הראשון

[2] *Op. cit.*, ed. Jellinek, p. 8. Cf. also *Zohar Hadash, Bereshit*, V: ' Rabbi Johanan said, Why was man created in the image of God ? A parable: A king ruled over a city and built palaces therein, and provided it with all the necessities, and all the people were subjected to him. One day, he summoned all the people of the city and appointed over them one of his governors, and said to them, Hitherto I concerned myself with all the requirements of the city and its buildings, towers and palaces, henceforth this one shall be like me. Similarly, [God said to man], I have put thee in charge of all the world, and all that is therein. As I ruled over it, and constructed it according to My will, so shall you build and perform the work of the world. . . . Therefore God made man in His image, . . . so that he should attend to all affairs of the world and its requirements

223

as He did at first.' That the term ' Image ' (*Zelem*) used in the context can by no means be taken in the physical sense, as has been suggested by Gunkel and others, see B. Jacob, *Genesis* (1934), p. 58, and E. König, *Kommentar zu Genesis* (1919), p. 151. The terms ' Image ' (*Zelem*) and ' Likeness ' (*Demuth*), are not, as is generally assumed, synonymous, but distinct. ' Image ' has an objective sense, and denotes God's nature and being (as explained *infra*). ' Likeness ', on the other hand, is subjective in meaning and denotes God's character as it impresses itself upon His creatures, through His activity in the Universe. In brief, ' Image ' expresses the divine ' attributes of essence ', ' Likeness ', the ' attributes of action '. (See *supra*, p. 166, n. 51.) Cf. Obadiah Sforno (1475-1550), on Genesis i. 27.

[3] J. Huxley, *The Uniqueness of Man* (1941), p. 31.

[4] See Sifre on Deuteronomy i. 13.

[5] Sir Arthur Keith, Presidential Address, British Association, Leeds Meeting, 1927, quoted by Vera Barclay, *Challenge to the Darwinians* (1951), p. 263.

[5a] The reconciliation of the doctrine of freewill with that of divine omniscience is one of the perennial problems of the Jewish religion as well as of the other religions derived from it. The well-known Talmudic maxim: ' All is foreseen, but free choice is given ' (*Ethics of the Fathers*, III, 15), is an affirmation of both doctrines without being an attempt at a solution of the contradiction involved. Jewish religious philosophy sought to solve the problem by the formula that God's knowledge is not causative, and this is best explained by Moses ben Baruch Almosnino (1510-1580), quoted by Samuel ben David of Uceda (sixteenth century) in his *Midrash Shemuel* (a commentary on the *Ethics of the Fathers*) a.l., that God's knowledge of the future is not like human knowledge, in that being outside the time process, God does not know the future *as* future, but in the same way as He knows the past and the present. Cf. Alan W. Watts, *The Supreme Identity* (1949), p. 54: ' From the standpoint of eternity, every moment of time, past, present, or future, is absolutely *now*, see also the diagram *ibid.* on p. 55, clarifying this concept.

[6] See M. Sheean, *Apologetics and Catholic Doctrine* (1943), pp. 54-55.

[7] Connected with man's rational faculty is his faculty of language. ' On the whole, man's development and control over language is unquestionably the greatest single achievement which his intelligence has compassed, and whether one thinks of it as cause or effect, its presence, more than any other factor, is responsible for his enormous superiority to his animal neighbours.' Quoted by R. A. Wilson in *The Miraculous Birth of Language* (1946), p. 77. See also Targum Onkelos on Genesis ii. 7: ' And man became a living soul,' which it renders ' And man became a speaking soul ' (רוח ממללא). See also Nahmanides, *Commentary*, a.l. It is for this reason that medieval Jewish philosophers designate man as distinct from other creatures as ' *medabber* ', that is, ' endowed with speech.'

[8] Man's capacity for goodness and love has been described by Martin Heidegger as his quality of ' self-transcendence ', denoting, namely, to quote his words, ' that man is something which reaches beyond itself—that he is more than a rational creature.' See R. Niebuhr, *The Nature and Destiny of Man*, I (1943), p. 173, particularly his quotation from Max Scheler.

[9] *Sefer ha-Yashar*, I,: נקח ראיה ממעשה הישר אשר אנו עושים על מעשה הבורא . . . כאשר נקח ראיה מן העשן על האש.

[10] *Meor Enayim*, on *Parashat Pinehas :* האהבה היא בבחינת נובלות מן האהבה העליונה שמבלעדי זאת לא יתעורר בנו מדה ההיא.

[11] *Tsawaat ha-RiBaSH* ראוי לחשוב באותו דבר שאני . . . אוהב אותה מהיכן בא . . . האהבה הלא הכל ממנו יתברך.

[12] For a fine illustration of this truth in English literature, see Robert Browning's poem ' Saul ', where the shepherd boy, David, after trying in vain all the resources of his genius to minister to the diseased mind of the poor old king, finds at last the true solace for him in the remembrance of God's love. If David cared so much for Saul, how infinitely more must God care.

> ' Do I find love so full in my nature, God's ultimate gift,
> That I doubt His own love can compete with it ?
> Here, the parts shift ?

Here, the creature surpass the Creator—the end what began ?
Would I fain in my impotent yearning to do all for this man,
And dare doubt He alone shall not help him, who yet alone can ? '
See G. Dawes Hicks, *Human Personality and Future Life* (1934),
p. 39.

[13] See Oliver Lodge, *Evolution and Creation* (1926), p. 131.
See also, Tobias Katz (1652-1729), *Maase Tobiah*: ' Authors have
questioned wherefore did not God assign a special day for the
creation of man . . . and they answered that it is because man is
not man in the true sense at the time when he is created, for his
perfection is not to be found with him at the time of the creation
as is the case with other creatures who achieve their end by their
very existence; and all this is part of the divine wisdom, to teach
man . . . that his perfection depends on himself insofar as he
strives to achieve it ' (*Maaseh Tobiah*, I, 1, Gloss by the son of the
author).

[14] *Pardes Rimmonim*, XXXI, 6, quoted by S. A. Horodezky in his
Torat ha-Kabbalah shel Moshe Cordovero (1924), p. 24: כי כמו
שהנשמה נתלבשה לבוש גופני כן התורה נתלבשה לבוש גופני.

[15] *Elimah Rabbati*, IX, quoted by S. A. Horodezky, *loc. cit*:
להאמין הענין כפשוטו והרחיקו כל ההקדמות האמיתיות המרחיקות ענינים
אלו . . . מפני שיתדמה אליהם שאם יכחישו זה יהיו כופרי התורה . . . ולזה
הענין זה מסוכן אפילו לדבר בו בפניהם מפני שיחשבו פשוטי התורה כפשטיותם,
ויחשבוהו עיקר האמונה לפי מה שהתנהגו בזה מילדותם.

[16] For an explanation of the apparent discrepancies of the two
accounts, see W. Möller, *Die Einheit und Echtheit der 5 Bücher Mosis*
(1931), pp. 220ff.; B. Jacob, *Genesis* (1934), pp. 71ff.; U. Cassutto,
La Questione della Genesi (1934), pp. 325ff., and *Torat ha-Teudot
we-Sidduram shel Sifre ha-Torah* (1942), pp. 68ff.; a popular summary
of the conservative standpoint on the subject is to be found in J. H.
Hertz, *Pentateuch and Haftaroth*, Genesis volume (1929), Additional
Note D, pp. 105ff.

[17] Genesis Rabbah, viii, 1. B.T. Erubin, 18a: אדם הראשון
אנדרוגינוס בראו

[18] Plato, *Symposium*, 189d-190a. See G. F. Moore, *Judaism* I,
p. 453 and III, p. 137, n. 81 and W. D. Davies, *Paul and Rabbinic*

Judaism, pp. 48 and 54. On the extensive literature on the subject
see L. Ginzberg, *Legends* (1909-38), V, p. 88, n. 42. It might be
mentioned that the idea also occurs in Philo (*De opificio mundi*), and
J. Freudenthal, *Hellenistische Studien* (1874), I, p. 69 states that
whilst it is not to be imagined that the Talmudic Sage had read
Plato's *Symposium*, he must have derived this idea from Philo or
some other Jewish Hellenist.

[19] See B. Jacob, *op. cit.*, p. 60.

[20] ' In no literature of antiquity is the unity of mankind so clearly
emphasised as in the Old Testament '—E. König, *Theologie des
Alten Testament* (1922 ed.), p. 51. This Monogenesis theory continues to enjoy the support of many noted scientists, as against the
Polygenesis theory which was strongly advocated during the second
part of the nineteenth century by racialists, such as Gobineau and
Pouchet in the interests of slavery, and which is still being embraced
in our days by Nazi theorists and their ilk (see B. Jacob, *op. cit.*,
p. 61). T. H. Huxley has well summarised Darwin's view on the
matter in the following words: ' The granting of the Polygenist
premises does not, in the slightest degree, necessitate the conclusion.
Admit that Negroes and Australians, Negritos and Mongols are
distinct species, or distinct genera, if you will, and you may yet,
with perfect consistency, be the strictest of Monogenists, and even
believe that in Adam and Eve are the primeval parents of all mankind.' (Quoted in S. Goldman, *The Book of Human Destiny* [1949],
II, p. 742.)

[21] ' It says, " This is the book of the generations of Adam," as if
to say that here is the beginning of the book, all that has come before
being the introduction stating the principles upon which the book
is based, but not forming part of the book itself.' ואמר זה ספר
תולדות אדם, כאלו אמר שמכאן הוא התחלת הספר, כי כל מה שכתב עד הנה
אינו אלא סדור התחלות הספר שאינו מן הספר.

[22] See A. I. Kook, *Iggerot Rayah*, (1943), p. 163. אנו צריכים רק לדעת
שהאדם אפילו יתעלה במעלה גדולה ויהי׳ מוכן לכל כבוד ועונג, אם ישחית
דרכיו יוכל לאבד כל אשר לו ויוכל להרע לעצמו ולתולדותיו עד דורות
רבים מאוד וזה הלימוד היוצא לנו מהעובדא של מציאות אדם בגן עדן
וחטאו וגירושו.

[23] While it is true that Rabbinic theology does recognise that the sin of Adam had brought death on all mankind (see e.g. B.T. Baba Bathra, 17a), the reference throughout is to physical death only, and is thus not to be confused with the Christian doctrine of ' Original Sin', which involves the condemnation of the whole human race to a death that is eternal, and from which none can be saved, except by faith in the Risen Christ.

[24] Midrash Genesis Rabbah, xxiv. 7: זה ספר תולדות אדם, זה כלל גדול בתורה

[25] See *supra*, p. 190, n. 18.

[26] See Midrash Tehillim on Psalm xc. 5 (Buber ed. 1891), p. 392: זרמתם שנה אלו תתקע״ד דורות שהיו קודם לבריאת העולם ונשטפו כהרף עין מפני שהיו רעים. Cf. however, parallel passage, B.T. Hagigah, 13b. See also M. M. Kasher, *Torah Shelemah*, I, pp. 86ff., quoting all the relevant passages from the Rabbinic and Kabbalistic literature. See especially Israel Lüpschitz (1782-1860), *Tiferet Yisrael*, V, Section *Derush Or ha-Hayyim*, pp. 561ff. See also A. I. Kook, *Iggeroth Rayah* (1943), p. 105.

[27] See Josephus, *Antiquities*, I, 3, 9; Maimonides, *Guide*, II, 37; Gersonides, Commentary on Genesis; and among moderns, E. König, *Die Genesis* (1919), pp. 320ff; and W. Möller, *op. cit.*, p. 277.

[28] See e.g. B. Jacob, *op. cit.*, p. 158, and M. D. [U.] Cassutto, in *Louis Ginzberg's Jubilee Volume*, Hebrew Section (1945), pp. 381-90.

[29] See A. I. Kook, *op. cit.*, pp. 163ff.

[30] B.T. Baba Bathra, 74a: משה ותורתו אמת והן בדאין

CHAPTER XII

DIVINE PURPOSE IN CREATION

JUDAISM, as we have seen, emphasises its particular doctrine of creation, not because of the doctrine itself, but because of its tremendous practical consequences. The doctrine of creation as taught by Judaism preserves, as has been shown, alike the freedom and the transcendence of God, the denial of which would involve the rejection of the whole Torah.

But there is another practical consequence which makes this doctrine fundamental to Judaism. In the Jewish doctrine of creation, as already stated,[1a] there is no real distinction between God's creation of the world and His preservation of it. Both are aspects of His creative activity. The same divine activity which brought the world into existence preserves it from collapsing into non-being. God's concern with the world is not to be thought of as relating merely to the provision of the world with its initial impulse to come into being, but as an incessant and intimate care for the beings to which God has given all they have and all they are. This is the truth which the Bible is never tired of asserting. 'I have graven thee upon the palms of my hands' (Isaiah xlix. 16). 'He hangeth the earth upon nothing' (Job xxvi. 7), and it is a truth which forms the theme of that grand Nature Hymn, the 104th Psalm. This universal teaching of the Bible is equally confirmed by the Talmudic Sages: 'God created and He provides; He made and He sustains ';[1] and the Jew affirms this, his faith in God's sustenance

229

and maintenance of existence, daily in his prayers, in the words: ' He reneweth daily the work of the Beginning.'[2a]   Were God for a single moment to withdraw His providence the whole of existence would collapse into non-being. ' Thou hidest Thy face, they are confounded ' (Psalm civ. 29).   Thus are excluded not only all pantheistic doctrines that would seek to confuse God with Nature, but also the notion of an absentee God, so fashionable in a past age, under the name of Deism—a notion which would conceive God's relation to the world as that of a watchmaker to a watch which he has constructed and which, having been set going, continues to function for some time, at any rate without any need for the continued presence or attention of its maker.

This belief in God's preservation of the world is a natural corollary to the Jewish doctrine of creation. The idea of ' creation out of nothing ' (as explained) carries with it inevitably the idea that the world depends on God's immediate will and power for its existence. This close connection between the two notions has been well brought out by Rabbi Shneur Zalman Ladier (1747-1812), the famous Chassidic teacher and leader, in his classic work, ' Tanya.' There he points out the error of those who would compare the work of God, the maker of heaven and earth, to the doings of man, and imagine ' that just as a vessel emerging from the smith does not require any more the attention of its maker, but is able to retain its shape and form even after he withdraws his hand from it, so, these fools think, it is with the work of God. But their eyes are shut and they are unable to see the great difference which exists between the work of man, who merely makes something out of something else (as for example when a smith makes from a bar of silver the form of a vessel), and the creative act of God, which brought something into being out of nothing . . . and that consequently the withdrawal of the power of the Creator can only result in the creature relapsing into nothing. Thus must the power of the Creator remain indispensable for the continued existence and being of the creation.'[2]

The relationship between God and the world, both as its Creator and Preserver, lays the foundation for the Biblical emphasis upon the significance of human existence and human life. Contrary to the notion that human life is meaningless, because it is shaped by blind forces, and that man is a puny and helpless creature because he is dependent entirely upon a physical organism, Judaism affirms the creative and life-giving action of an Eternal Spirit, Who is ever at work in His Universe, guiding the whole of human existence towards the fulfilment of a purpose that has been with Him from the very beginning, for the individual, the nation and the human race.

The conception of divine purpose constitutes the essential nature of the religion which Israel gave to the world. Affirming the existence of a Divine Sovereign behind the scheme of things, it discerns in the events of the day the unfolding of a divine process directed towards a goal. The full scope of the divine purpose has never been claimed to be comprehensible to our state of human knowledge;[3] but that such a purpose exists and that it is being worked out through

the domain of human existence has ever been a fundamental principle of Judaism.

' Of all things the Holy One, blessed be He, created
in His world, He did not create a single thing for no
purpose,' declared our Rabbis.[4] Similarly Maimonides
in his *Guide* writes, ' No intelligent person can assume
that any action of God can be in vain and purposeless.
. . .' ' According to our view,' he continues, ' and
the view of all that follow the Torah, all actions of God
are exceedingly good: " And God saw everything that
he had made, and behold, it was very good." '
(Genesis i. 31).[5]

Elsewhere in chapter 13 of the same book, Maimonides quotes the verse from the Proverbs xvi. 4:
' " Everything that the Lord made is for Himself "—
that is, for His purpose.'[6]

That the Universe must have some meaning and
purpose is a proposition which in our hearts we know
to be true, however little we may be capable of understanding them. It is impossible for us to believe that
a Universe that has no goal to give it meaning can be
intelligible and make any sense. ' [A world] in which
there is no finality in the sense of an increasing
purpose ', writes Wilbur Urban, in his *Intelligible
World*, ' no purpose in the sense of an imperishable
goal, would be an *intolerable* world, and to this extent
wholly unintelligible.'[7] If the Universe is really not
going anywhere but is only going, if it is not a movement towards ends that are good, then it is ' a tale
told by an idiot, full of sound and fury, signifying
nothing.'

True it is that some philosophers would deprive

the Universe of all value and meaning. Bertrand Russell, for instance, would have us believe that ' man is the product of causes which have no pre-vision of the end they were achieving . . . his origin, his growth, his hopes and fears, his loves and beliefs, are but the outcome of accidental collocations of atoms . . .'[8] ' Blind to good use, reckless of destruction, omnipotent matter rolls on.'[9] Russell, however, realises the anomaly which he has produced by his attitude, for elsewhere he points out that it is a strange mystery that man can judge a work of his ' unthinking Mother ' —Nature. ' It is a strange mystery,' he writes, ' that Nature, omnipotent but blind in the revolutions of her secular hurryings through the abysses of space, has brought forth at last a child subject still to her power, but gifted with sight, and with knowledge of good and evil, with the capacity of judging all the works of his unthinking Mother.'[10]

Strange indeed, strange indeed, that unthinking Mother Nature, without intelligence, will and purpose, should produce a thinking child, possessed of intelligence, will and purpose. The fact that the human mind cannot imagine the character of the purpose of God does not militate against this argument. ' The whole structure of this mysterious Universe and the conditions of man's physical life in it, as presented by modern science,' declares J. H. Morrison, ' must be accounted incredible. Is it not incredible that the terrific forces and velocities of the atoms should be fitted together to make the quiet beauty of the countryside, or that we ourselves compounded of these same forces and velocities should so peaceably live and work

and sleep ? In such an incredible world as this, and
with the limited knowledge we possess, it is folly to
reject any experience simply because it seems incredible.
Rather we may have courage to believe that as the
present world would have been counted incredible if
it had not been experienced, so there may be realms
of reality yet to be disclosed surpassing all human
imagination.'[11]

Similarly, Maimonides, in his *Guide*, writes: ' The
difficulties which lead to confusion in the question
" What is the purpose of the Universe ? " derive from
two causes. First, man has an erroneous idea of himself
and thinks that the whole world exists only for his sake.
Second (and here Maimonides anticipates Morrison's
argument), he is ignorant both about the nature of the
sublunary world and about the Creator's intention to
give existence to all beings whose existence is possible,
because existence is undoubtedly good.'[12]

This ignorance of which Maimonides speaks is,
however, emotional, rather than intellectual. It is
what Aldous Huxley calls ' Vincible Ignorance ', that
is, an ignorance which can be overcome by will-power.
' We don't know ', writes Aldous Huxley in dealing
with the problem of the purpose of life, ' because we
don't want to know. . . . Those who detect no meaning in the world generally do so because, for one reason
or another, it suits their books that the world should
be meaningless.'[13] Referring to his own attitude on the
question in his early days, when like so many of his
contemporaries he took it for granted that there was
no meaning in life, Huxley emphasises that it was not
entirely due to intellectual reasons. He had motives

for not wanting the world to have a meaning and, consequently, assumed that it had no motive. ' For myself, as no doubt for most of my contemporaries, the philosophy of meaninglessness was essentially an instrument of liberation. The liberation we desired was . . . liberation from a certain system of morality. We objected to the morality because it interfered with our sexual freedom. . . . The supporters of [that system] acclaimed that in some way [it] embodied the meaning of the world. There was one admirably simple method of confuting these people and, at the same time, justifying ourselves in our . . . erotic revolt: We could deny that the world had any meaning whatsoever.'[14]

Reverting to Morrison's statement, we are justified in saying not only that ' there *may* be realms of mind and spirit not yet disclosed to us,' but that there *must* be realms of mind and spirit to make intelligible what we have experienced and verified. The moment we admit the possibility of areas of inanity in the world system, we must give up all hope of understanding any part of the Universe and question even our own intelligence. This is the very argument employed by the psalmist in Psalm xciv. verses 8-9: ' Consider, ye brutish among the people, and ye fools, when will you understand ? He that planted the ear, shall He not hear ? He that formed the eye, shall He not see ? ' This verse was declared by John Stuart Mill to contain the strongest argument for the existence of God, the argument being that He who gave others the power to hear and see can surely Himself hear and see.[15] Applying this argument to the human mind, we can similarly say that surely no unintelligent force could produce a creature endowed with intelligence; nor could a purposeless Universe evolve a creature moved by purpose. To maintain, as does a materialistic philosophy, that man's mind is the product of an unintelligent Universe, without even attempting to indicate how this came about, is indeed to make absurd demands upon human credulity, and is itself the most irrational of all philosophies. It condemns as brutish those who hold it out of their own mouths. As Whitehead well remarks: ' Scientists animated by the purpose of proving that they are purposeless constitute an interesting subject for study.'[16]   For how and whence can they have obtained intelligence if the Universe is unintelligent at heart ?   Human intelligence is thus proof of the intelligence behind the scheme of things, and inescapably points to purpose and meaning in creation and in life, though we may not be capable of comprehending what these are.

But although the knowledge of the full significance of the divine purpose has not been given to man, we can discern part of this purpose in studying man. Made in the image of God, man, as we have seen, is possessed of unique attributes that are divine—reason, freedom, creativeness and moral goodness. And these attributes were not bestowed on man in vain, but in order to enable him to participate in the work of God. Thus it is that Judaism conceives the relation of man to God as that of a *Shuttaf* (a co-worker), co-operating with God in the fulfilment of His purpose.

The beginning of this co-operation is clearly indicated in Genesis. There we see God's creative power calling the world and man into existence under the figure of a brooding bird seeking to bring into being the promise of life beneath its wings. But the creative process does not end when the world and man have been created. That which had been created had to be maintained, developed and fostered. ' God established the earth, He created it not in vain, He formed it to be inhabited ' (Isaiah xlv. 18).

This task was entrusted to man. Adam, the first man, is described as a self-active, labouring and creative being, charged by the Divine Creator to develop the resources and the potential wealth of the earth which had come to him as a gift from God. In the words of the *Zohar Hadash*, ' God said to Adam, Hitherto I alone was engaged in the work; henceforth you (also) must work.'[17] And so every man, in his own way, must work, must create. Made in the image of God, he must make God's standards his own; and because God creates, he, too, must work and co-operate with Him in developing the world which has been committed to his care. ' A man ', declared our Sages, ' is in duty bound to love work and occupy himself with work, which God calls His own, as it is said, God rested from all His work which He did.'[18] If man fails to exercise these creative powers, the wrath of God manifests itself against him by causing him to lose them. In the physical organism, neglect of functions results in decline and final atrophy, and the same law operates in the world order over which man has been placed in charge. To refuse to work is to forfeit the blessing of God. ' For the Lord has blessed thee in all the work of thy hands ' (Deuteronomy ii. 7)—' If man does work', comments the Midrash, ' he receives the Divine blessing; if not he loses it.'[19]   Significant in this connection is the Midrashic passage: ' When Abraham was travelling through Aram Naharaim and Aram Nahor, he saw its inhabitants eating and drinking and revelling, and he exclaimed: " May my portion not be in this country."   But when he reached the promontory of Tyre and saw them engaged in weeding and hoeing at the proper seasons, he exclaimed: " Would that my portion might be in this country." '[20] Still more significant is the passage in the Jerusalem Talmud: ' Great is work, for the generation of the Flood was destroyed only because of robbery, whereas a workman may perform work and is exempt from the law of robbery '[21]—an allusion to the Biblical law which permits the labourer to eat of the produce on which he happens to be engaged (Deuteronomy xxiii. 25-6).

The implication of this passage is that the nation or society which destroys the principle of creativeness or productivity brings about its own dissolution and destruction.

God's attribute of creativeness is allied to His attribute of goodness.   His creative activity springs from His character of goodness, of which His tender-love, grace (*hesed*), is the highest expression.   God, as the Torah describes Him (Exodus xxxiv. 6 ; Numbers xiv. 18), is ' full of tenderlove ' (*rab hesed.*)   The world, in Jewish thought, was created in response to divine tenderlove: ' *Olam hesed yibbaneh.*'[22]   The tender-love of the Lord, according to the Psalmist, fills the earth (Psalm xxxiii. 5); and it is this divine tenderlove with which, in the words of the Jew's thrice-repeated daily prayers, ' God sustains the living.' Here, too, the attributes of God are to serve as a pattern for man. True human creativeness, like the creativeness of God, must be allied to goodness, otherwise creativeness ends in destruction, of which the atomic bomb is the latest manifestation. It is this conformity with the character of the creative activity of God, this obedience to Him, which lies at the basis of man's creative co-operation with Him. Without obedience to God, the human creative effort is bound to end in frustration and failure. This lesson too is already taught in Genesis. By reason of disobedience to God, Adam, we read, is cast out of the Garden, to toil by the sweat of his brow to subdue a thankless soil, which often rewarded him with nothing but thorns and thistles. But this is only the beginning of the sad story of human misery. Disobedience and sin that parted man from God end in parting man from man. Adam disobeyed the command of God, and his son, under the sway of a grasping and domineering spirit, disregards his brother's rights and kills him. The same story is repeated in the generations that follow. Human arrogance erects high towers for the glorification of self and in defiance of God, and the design fails, with disastrous effects. Society is torn asunder by discord, dissension and strife, and human unity is broken up into a number of diverse and warring classes and nations speaking different languages and thinking different thoughts.

Coming down to our own times, we have witnessed the repetition of the same old story, but on a larger and more tragic scale. Modern trade and industry, in pursuit of material wealth and power, have been dominated too much by selfish interests to be concerned with principles of right and wrong. Thus has human creative activity been perverted from the divine purpose which was to inspire it, and become the source of universal discord, ruin and death.[22a]

Creativeness and goodness are thus essential elements in the divine purpose, which is dependent for its fulfilment on man's co-operation; and Man, selected by God to be His agent, is called upon to co-operate with Him in the work of creative goodness.

This truth, already, as we have seen, suggested in a number of ways in the Bible itself, is also emphasised in the whole vast extent of post-Biblical literature. Among the many passages that could be drawn from Talmudic and other Rabbinic works, the following might be mentioned:

' In connection with the Work of the Beginning, it is written " [for therein He rested from all His work] which God had created to make ". It is not written, " which God had created." Did God create at the outset loaves ? Rather He created wheat, and man makes them into loaves. Thus God said: " As thou dost co-operate with me in the work of the beginning, so do thou co-operate with me with thy very self."[23]

' Every judge who performs justice in perfect truth, even for one single moment, is regarded as if he were a *Shuttaf* with the Holy One, blessed be He, in the work of His creation.'[24]

' When Israel do the will of the Omnipresent, they give increased strength to the One Above.'[25]

' A heavenly voice will in the future reverberate throughout the tents of the righteous, declaring: " He who collaborated with God, let him come and receive his reward." '[26]

'. . . When the mass of men are righteous and observe the commands of the Torah, the earth becomes invigorated and a fulness of joy pervades it, because the *Shechinah* rests upon the earth and there is gladness above as well as below. But when mankind corrupt their way and do not observe the commands of the Torah, and sin before their Master, they, as it were, thrust the *Shechinah* out of the world, and the earth is thus left in a corrupt state. . . . It is in this sense that we say that " Israel gives strength unto God ", that is, to the *Shechinah*, and thereby makes the world more secure.'[27]

' The existence of the world and the course of its development are in the hands of man, and depend on the creature conforming to [the character of] his Creator.'[28]

This principle of co-operation has its parallel in the world of nature. The seed produces fruit only when it falls into good ground, that is, into ground which has been prepared, and so is receptive and able to contribute its own dynamic quality to the creative end which is the purpose of the union. Here we see the soil is as important as the seed. Neither is complete without the other. The preparation of the ground is thus the essential contribution which human effort must make towards the fruitfulness of the seed. In the same way, it is man's active co-operation which conditions the fulfilment of God's purpose of creative goodness in His work.[29]

This idea of the need of human co-operation for the realisation of divine purpose in terms of creative goodness has much bearing on the problem of evil. When we consider the age-long process of creation as disclosed by modern science, we may well shrink back in horror. The Creator who made the world so beautiful has not made it good. There is indeed goodness among men, but it is always imperfect and, side by side with it, there is evil without end—lust, cruelty, selfishness, greed and treachery. Is then God who made the world so beautiful careless of the happiness of His creatures and regardless of the sin and crime which darkens human lives ? If not, why is the world so full of evil ?

The conception of the need of human co-operation helps us to answer the question briefly in this way. God made the world beautiful, because He loves the beautiful and can produce it without the intervention and co-operation of man. He has not made the world wholly good because goodness can only come about through the co-operation of men with one another and with God. Goodness cannot be produced by compulsion. It must be the free offering of the will, recognising the laws of goodness and yielding to it. Goodness throughout the Universe is impossible, apart from the willing denial of selfish inclinations on the part of the individuals who form its social content. It takes man as well as God to make the world good. To have the world uniformly good would have meant to deprive man of his free will, which is his glory and distinction. The freedom to choose good involves the freedom to do evil. This freedom meant the coming into existence of a countless multitude of individuals in competition with one another, each striving towards the realisation of its own potentialities, and thus common life became inevitably a struggle with pain, disappointment and slaughter. The struggle for existence, the sacrifice of one another—all became inevitable.[30] Yet these elements became the means of an upward movement towards higher forms of life and therefore towards the full realisation of the purpose of God. While we are no nearer comprehending why this should be the nature of existence, there is no longer any initial contradiction between divine power and divine goodness. If the world waits upon man's co-operation for its perfection, the evil we see in it is all due to the absence of man's share in this co-operative work with God; and the question why God did not make the world uniformly good becomes as little perplexing as the question why He did not make loaves to grow out of the earth, and why He did not equip the world with engines, motor-cars and wireless-sets. It is all a question of co-operation, which is basic to all creative activity, whether in the domain of physical nature or of moral endeavour. And it is only when every individual being in the Universe will participate in this co-operation, with all it implies of willing self-denial and self-surrender, that the world will become good as it is beautiful.

At the basis of the co-operation in creative goodness is the harmony which must exist between God and man and between man and his fellow-man, as partners in this co-operative work. Harmony involves the perfect co-ordination of the parts which together make up the whole. Failure in such co-ordination in the physical world means friction, jarring and ultimate breakdown; in the spiritual world it means discord, strife and destruction. Harmony is therefore an essential element in that process of fulfilment in which man has been charged to co-operate.

The supreme principle assuring order and harmony is Justice. Details of this law of Justice have, according to Jewish tradition, been communicated to mankind through Noah under the seven commandments, viz., abstention from: (*i*) Idolatry; (*ii*) Blasphemy; (*iii*) Incest; (*iv*) Murder; (*v*) Theft; (*vi*) Not to eat flesh cut from a living animal, and (*vii*) The command for the administration of Justice.[31] These seven duties do not, however, exhaust the laws guaranteeing the harmony essential to the co-operation between man and God. Whilst constituting for humanity the universal law of Justice, they are, as the Talmud points out, mainly negative in character.[32] They are thus regulative, not creative. As such, they stand only at the beginning of the work of man's creative co-operation with God. Creativeness alike in man and in the divine enter into full activity only when prompted by Righteousness. Whilst Justice, which seeks to safeguard human rights, guarantees the world-order against lapsing into chaos, Righteousness, by insisting on duties to others, is a dynamic principle in the co-operative activity towards the fulfilment of creation. Justice and Righteousness are thus the fundamental conditions of man's co-operation with God in the fulfilment of creation. These conditions are not beyond the power of man to satisfy. Man's spiritual affinity with the Divine, in whose image he has been made, endows him with a personality capable of approaching the divine pattern set before him. Man, however, from his earliest days failed in this divine charge committed to him. The story of this failure is writ large across the face of human history, and never on a wider and more tragic scale than in our times. But God will not be thwarted in His purpose.

'The Lord of Hosts hath spoken, who shall annul it?' (Isaiah xiv. 27). Human beings must at all costs learn to co-operate with one another and with God. If human obduracy of heart and obstinacy of will bar the way, there are divine judgments that now and then are made manifest in the form of visitations of diverse sorts, from wars to social upheavals, to teach mankind the lessons of co-operation and righteousness. 'For when thy judgments are on earth, the inhabitants of the world learn righteousness' (Isaiah xxvi. 9). And these visitations will recur over and over again until mankind shall have at long last taken well this lesson to heart. If, after six years of 'blood, sweat and tears,' which this generation has passed through, mankind still refuses to co-operate with God's righteous purpose and the world continues to be torn, distracted, and bewildered, with passions of hatred and cruelty raging unchecked in so many places—what else is mankind to expect, but another manifestation of divine judgment, in the form of a much more cruel and more devastating war, upon their apostasy from Him? Yet, the world

R

is safe in the hands of God, who, as Creator, will not allow it to drift to shipwreck and irremediable ruin; and, no matter how much it might ' zigzag ', God will surely bring it home at last in fulfilment of His righteous purpose for His creation.

NOTES

[1a] *Supra*, p. 182.

[1] Tanhuma, *wa-Yera* (ed. Buber), 24. הוא בורא והוא מפרנס,
הוא עושה והוא סובל

[2a] *A.P.B.*, p. 39.

[2] Sh. Z. Ladier, Tanya, *Likkute Amarim*, II, 2. Cf. Descartes, *Meditations*, III, ' The conservation of a substance in each moment of its duration requires the same power and act that would be necessary to create it, supposing it were not yet in existence.'

[3] See Maimonides, *Guide*, III, 13: ' Just as we do not ask what is the purpose of God's existence, so we do not ask what was the object of His will which is the cause of the existence of all things that exist.' כשם שלא נבקש תכלית מציאותו יתברך כן לא נבקש תכלית
רצונו אשר בעבורו נתחדש כל מה שנתחדש.

[4] B.T. Shabbat, 77b: כל מה שברא הקב״ה בעולמו לא ברא דבר אחד
לבטלה.

[5] *Guide*, III, 25.

[6] *Op. cit.* III, 13.

[7] Wilbur M. Urban, *The Intelligible World* (1929), p. 343.

[8] Bertrand Russell, *Philosophical Essays* (1910), p. 60.

[9] *Op. cit.*, p. 70.

[10] Bertrand Russell, *Mysticism and Logic* (1918), p. 48. Similarly Darwin propounds the question: ' Can the mind of man which has, as I fully *believe* (italics mine), been developed from a mind as low as that possessed by the lowest animals, be trusted when it draws such grand conclusions [in denial of a First Intelligent Cause] ? . . . Would anyone trust in the conviction of a monkey's mind if there

are any convictions in such a mind ? ' (*Letters*, I, 313). See also Joseph Needham, *Mechanistic Biology and the Religious Consciousness* in *Science, Religion and Reality* (1926), p. 247; '. . . if man had been evolved in the struggle for existence as the evolutionists said, then his mind must also be conceived of as the produce of such a struggle, and could therefore hardly be fitted for the grasping of absolute truth. " The forceps of our mind are crude," said Bergson . . ., " and they crush the delicacy of reality when we attempt to hold it." '

[11] J. H. Morrison, *Christian Faith and Science To-day* (1936), p. 72.

[12] *Guide*, III, 25.

[13] Aldous Huxley, *Ends and Means* (1937), p. 270.

[14] *Op. cit.*, p. 273.

[15] See T. Witton Davies, *Psalms* (In *Century Bible*) *a.l.*

[16] A. N. Whitehead. The passage might be quoted in full: ' Many a scientist has patiently designed experiments for the purpose of substantiating his belief that animal operations are motivated by no *purposes*. He has spent his spare time in writing articles to prove that human beings are as other animals so that " purpose " is a category irrelevant for the explanation of their bodily activities, his own activity included. Scientists animated by the purpose of proving that they are purposeless constitute an interesting subject of study '. (Quoted by R. A. Wilson, the *Miraculous Birth of Language* (1946 ed.) p. 103.) See also C. E. M. Joad, *Guide to Philosophy* (1936), pp. 534ff. on the self-contradiction of Materialism, which while denying reality to any thought beyond the condition of the brain that happens to have produced it, at the same time claims to be able to give an objective account of the world as a whole.

[17] *Zohar Hadash*, Genesis, v. אמר לו הקב״ה לו [לאדם] עד כאן הייתי אני משתדל במלאכה מכאן ואיליך אתה תשתדל בה.

[18] *Aboth de Rabbi Nathan*, XXI., חייב אדם להיות אוהב את המלאכה ועוסק במלאכה ,הקב״ה קורא אותה מלאכתו שנאמר מלאכתו אשר עשה.

[19] Midrash Tehillim, on xxiii. כי ד׳ אלוהיך ברכך בכל מעשה ידיך,
אם עשה הרי הוא מתברך ואם לאו אינו מתברך

[20] Midrash Genesis Rabbah, xxxix. 9. בשעה שהיה אברהם מהלך
בארם נהרים ובארם נחור ראה אותם אוכלים ושותים ופוחזים אמר הלואי לא
יהא לי חלק בארץ הזאת, וכיון שהגיע לסולמה של צור ראה אותן עסוקין
בניכוש בשעת הניכוש, בעידור בשעת העידור, אמר הלואי יהא חלקי בארץ
הזאת.

[21] J.T. Maaserot, II, 6. גדולה מלאכה שלא חרב דור המבול אלא
מפני הגזל, ופועל עושה מלאכה ופטור מן הגזל.

[22] This is the Rabbinic rendering of Psalm lxxxix. 2 (English
version: ' Mercy shall be built up for ever '): see B.T. Sanhedrin,
58b, taking *Olam* in the later Hebrew sense, denoting ' World '.

[22a] See A. R. Osborn, *Christian Ethics*, (1940), 13ff; 294-6.

[23] Midrash Bereshit Rabbati (ed. Albek), p. 73. אשר ברא אין כתיב
כאן אלא לעשות, שמא ברא תחלה גלוסקאות אלא חטין והן עושין גלוסקאות,
כך אמר אלוהים כשם שאתה משתתף עמי במעשה בראשית השתתף עמי בעצמך.

[24] B.T. Shabbat, 10a: כל דיין שדן דין אמת לאמתו אפי׳ שעה אחת
מעלה עליו הכתוב כאלו נעשה שותף להקב״ה במעשה בראשית.

[25] Midrash Lamentations Rabbati, i. 35: בזמן שישראל עושין רצונו
של מקום מוסיפין כח בפמליא של מעלה.

[26] J.T. Shabbat, VI, 2. עתידה בת קול להיות מפוצצת באהלי צדיקים
ואומרת כל מי שפעל עם אל יבא ויטול שכרו.

[27] Zohar, *Noah* (Soncino English Edition), I, p. 198.

[28] *Maareket ha-Elokut*, ascribed to R. Peretz of Barcelona (thirteenth century), VIII: קיום העולם וסבתו הוא ביד מין האדם, אם ידמה
הצורה ליוצרה

[29] This idea of co-operation between man and God explains the
significance of prayer. Apart from the dependence on God and the
sense of reverence and worship of God's wisdom, power and holiness
which it expresses, prayer is a method of co-operation with God in
enabling man to meet a difficult situation. How God does His share
man cannot presume to tell; but it is to the extent that we surrender
ourselves in prayer, and attune our spirit to the spirit of God, that
God responds to our calls upon Him, and meets us in our need—as

Joseph Albo (*Ikkarim*, IV, 18) puts it: '
come down upon the recipient when he
state of preparation to receive them. A
pare himself, he withholds the good fro
it has been determined from on high tha
prosper in a given year, and he neglec
that year, then God may bring the n
land, but his crops will not prosper, s
or sowed. He withheld the good from himself because
prepare himself to receive it. . . . In this way it is clear that prayer
or right conduct helps to prepare a person to receive the good influence, or to nullify the evil that has been decreed concerning him '
(Translation, I. Husik). See also Joseph Irgas, *Shomer Emunim*, II,
77, quoting the Zohar on Genesis ii. 6: ' " And there went up a
mist from the earth "—from an activity below there is stimulated
a corresponding activity on high. Come and see: a mist ascends
from the earth and then a cloud is formed, one joining the other to
form a whole.'

[30] See Charles D'Arcy, *Science and Creation* (1925), pp. 106ff
Cf. also N. Berdyaev, *Freedom and the Spirit* (1935), p. 160: ' The
world that God has created is full of evil, it is true, but at its heart
there lies the greatest of all goods, namely, the freedom of the spirit,
which shows that man bears the divine image. Freedom is the only
answer to the problem of justifying God. The problem of evil is
the problem of liberty.' Similarly A. I. Kook, *Iggerot Rayah*, II,
p. 139 (paraphrased): ' Any good which is not the result of free choice
is not real good, for goodness is a quality which imparts to its bearer
a character all his own, in accordance with the measure he absorbs
of it within himself (which could not be the case were goodness
uniform).' כל טוב שאינו בחירי אינו טוב גמור מפני שאין העצמיות של
נושאו מתייחדת בכל מלואה עם טובו, וכל טוב הוא נמדד רק באותה המדה
שהמקבל סופג אותו אל תוכו.

[31] See Tosefta Abodah Zarah, VIII, 4; B.T. Sanhedrin 56b.
For details, see *Jewish Encyclopedia*, *s.v.* ' Laws, Noachian ' (VII,
p. 648). See also I. Epstein, *The Jewish Way of Life*, pp. 26ff. It
should be noted that these Noachian laws do not include an express
command to confess the one and only God. Provided there is no

which Judaism condemns not so much because it is a false as because it is a false morality, humanity as a whole is not ...ged to accept the pure and sublime conception of Hebrew ...onotheism; see I. Epstein, *Judaism* (1945 ed.), p. 17. See also J. Wohlgemuth, *Das jüdische Religionsgesetz in jüdischer Beleuchtung* (1919), pp. 84-6. An excellent work devoted to the discussion of the Noachian laws and all their implications is Elijah Benamozegh, *Israel et l'Humanité* (1914), ed. by A. Pallière (1875-1950), a proselyte and defender of Judaism. For a striking analogy between the Noachian laws and what Philo called ' Natural Laws ', see H. A. Wolfson, *Philo*, II, pp. 185ff.

32 See B.T. Sanhedrin, 58b.

[See Additional Note, pp. 379-382.]

CHAPTER XIII

GOD AS THE LORD OF HISTORY

THE attitude which Judaism bids us to adopt in regard to the vicissitudes of fortune, in the lives of nations no less than individuals, is a direct consequence of its fundamental conception of God, not only as Creator, but also as the Lord of History, directing and guiding the whole of the historical process towards a goal to be attained here on earth.

The idea of the appearance of God in the events and unfolding of history is not the least of the tremendous contributions of the Jewish religion to human thought and culture. The Jews were the first people to introduce into humanity the conception of the revelation of God in history. Everywhere except in the prophetic teaching, history is at the bottom meaningless, a mere repetition of sin and misery. The ancient Persians, for example, believed that what happens upon earth is due to two cosmic forces, Ormuzd and Ahriman,[1] the power of light and the power of darkness. Light and darkness are locked in perpetual struggle, and no decisive victory is ever won by either of them within history as we know it. The ancient Chinese, too, believed that there were two forces which were called Yin and Yang, one a destructive or male principle, which always comes in with a rush, with arms akimbo, or charges about like a bull in a china-shop, the other a female or upbuilding creative principle, with neither Yin nor Yang ever gaining mastery. To the ancient Greeks and Romans, history appeared as a series of

251

For notes on this chapter, see pp. 272-277.

cycles or circles of recurring events or periods. Far
back in the dim past there was a golden age which, as
man moved through the cycle, gave place to ages of
less worthy metals—the silver age, the bronze age, the
iron age. In the distant future, the golden age will
return, not, however, to abide, but to give way to an
unending repetition of the same cycle.

This cyclic theory is particularly associated with the
name of Plato, by whom life was viewed as having
moved through a cyclic upward phase of 72,000 solar
years as the result of the creative impulse, after which
there was a corresponding downward phase of equal
duration, which called for a renewal of the divine creative act to inaugurate once again a new cycle of the
same character.[2] Aristotle, too, thought that the arts
and sciences have been discovered and lost an infinite
number of times.[3] The Pythagoreans and Stoics even
believed that there would be an exact repetition of
events, and Marcus Aurelius, in his *Meditations*, went
even so far as to maintain that an intelligent man of
forty may be said to have seen all that has happened
or ever will happen.[4] The cyclic theory carries with it
a profound pessimism, which sees no meaning in history, no sign of purpose and progress in life. No wonder that the cycle theory is now being rejected by most
modern writers as terribly depressing. ' We should be,'
writes Arnold Toynbee in his *Study of History*, ' the
victims of an everlasting " cosmic joke." All human
endurance becomes the torment of a Tityos or an
Ixion[5] ' [the two mythical figures of whom the former
was perpetually consumed by vultures, and the latter
was attached to a perpetually revolving wheel].

With the seventeenth century, the cycle theory began to give way to the theory of continual progress. The guiding principle underlying the idea of progress is that of an immanent power operating in history and bringing chaos under the dominion of reason. Round this creed, which was brought into vogue by the French Encyclopaedists,[6] have grown up diverse philosophies, associated with the names of Kant, Fichte, Hegel and Schelling, among others. But fundamental to all these philosophies is the confidence in the inevitability of human progress. With the acceptance of the Darwinian theory of evolution, the idea of the inevitability of progress as applied to human nature was acclaimed with the fervour of a dogma. The finest exponent of the idea of progress towards moral perfection was Herbert Spencer. ' Progress ', he writes, ' is not an accident but a necessity. What we call evil and immorality must disappear. It is certain that man must become perfect.' ' Always towards perfection is the mighty movement, towards a complete development and more unmixed good.'[7]

Now in dealing with the idea of progress as giving meaning to history, it is necessary first to determine what is progress. But most of those who have dwelt on progress as something that is inherently characteristic of the movement of history have been very slow to offer us any definition of the term. If it merely means something different, there is no reason to regard it as progress. For progress we need a direction, a standard, a fixed standard by reference to which we may judge whether we are advancing or receding. Unless such a standard exists, we have no means of knowing what we mean by progress, or whether what we do is for the good of society. How can we hope to build a harmonious national community or a tolerable international order, unless the majority of people are in substantial agreement on the difference between right and wrong, good and evil, and what constitutes a satisfactory human existence ? Indeed, the most alarming symptom of our time is precisely the absence of agreement about values. Nothing illustrates our confusion of thought more plainly than the manner in which the Russian and Western statesmen use the term ' democracy ', with little, if any, common ground in regard to what democracy really means. On both sides democracy is equated with their own national interests, or, more philosophically, with a vague higher expediency. And what applies to the ideal of democracy is true of all other ideals, such as justice, freedom, good neighbourliness, to which widespread homage is being paid in these days of post-war world tension. But as long as higher expediency is the determining factor there is the danger of abandoning justice, democracy and good neighbourliness altogether. The higher expediency can justify some very dubious proceedings, and it is not difficult to imagine circumstances in which the general good might seem to require fraud and violence, even to the extent of liquidating whole sections of the community. And thus the question remains, what precisely is the goal towards which progress is striving ?

But even granted that there is general agreement as to the meaning of progress, the whole belief in the inevitability of progress is a superstition with no warrant from natural history. The theory of evolution to which Darwin and Spencer appealed in support of their belief in progress is of no avail. As Rabbi Kook well expresses it, ' Evolution, unless it is supported by an absolute guarantee of its continuation, is not free from the possibility that it might stop in the middle of its course and even go backwards.'[8] This indeed is a possibility envisaged by T. H. Huxley, when he declared that ' The theory of evolution encourages no millennial expectations. If for millions of years our globe has taken the upward road, yet sometime the summit will be reached, and the downward road will be commenced.'[9] Besides, Darwin himself has already emphasised the *a*moral content of evolution. All that evolution does is to make things more and more complex—for better or for worse. The doctrine that what is strongest must be right has no scientific justification. Evolution thus offers no guarantee of human perfectibility, nor a criterion by which to judge mankind's progress towards perfection. Furthermore, the assumption that all progress means advancement of the good ignores the fact, so tragically exemplified in our days, that every heightened potency of human existence may represent greater possibility of evil. Indeed, the greatest danger to which mankind is exposed to-day is the inability to control the means of evil-doing which progress in the development of material and intellectual resources has placed at the disposal of man.[10]

The danger to humanity arising from the enormous increase in man's power of destruction also knocks the bottom out of the Marxist interpretation of history. The belief in a dialectical process in history which

ensures progress and development through the conflict
of opposing forces—economic and political—is scarcely
tenable in an age in which the cosmic power in the
command of man has brought the complete disintegration of the social order within the realm of possibility.
Bertrand Russell, writing as far back as 1934, long
before the discovery of the atomic bomb, has pointed
out the erroneous character of the Marxist assumption
that the outcome of conflicts must always be the establishment of some more advanced system. That this is
not the case he shows to have been amply demonstrated in history, in which ' the examples of decay and
retrogression are at least as numerous and as important
. . . as the examples of development.' Nor is there
the slightest ground, he rightly argues, for the belief
that the conflict between Communism and Capitalism,
which according to Marxist analysis is fundamentally
inherent in modern civilisation, must necessarily in
the end lead to the establishment of Communism.
' We all know,' he writes, ' that modern war is a somewhat serious matter, and that in the next world war it
is likely that large populations will be virtually exter-
minated by poison gases and bacteria. Can it be
seriously supposed that after a war in which the great
centres of population and most important industrial
plant had been wiped out, the remaining population
would be in a mood to establish scientific communism ?
Is it not practically certain that the survivors would be
in a mood of gibbering and superstitious brutality,
fighting all against all for the last turnip or the last
mangel-wurzel ? '[11]

Nor is that all. There is always the intrusion of the

unpredictable, which determines the issue of the conflict at least to as great an extent as the workings of
the dialectical process in history. To quote Bertrand
Russell again:

'Admitting that the great forces are generated by
economic causes, it often depends on quite trivial and
fortuitous events which of the great forces gets the
victory. In reading Trotsky's account of the Russian
Revolution, it is difficult to believe that Lenin made no
difference, but it was touch and go whether the German
Government allowed him to get to Russia. If the
Minister concerned had happened to be suffering from
dyspepsia on a certain morning, he might have said
" No " when in fact he said " Yes," and I do not think
that it can be rationally maintained that without Lenin
the Russian Revolution would have achieved what it
did.'[12]

And so to come down to our own days: the crushing
defeat of Germany in the second World War, which led
to the emergence of Soviet Communism as a world
power, sufficiently formidable to challenge the whole
of Western civilisation, must be ascribed *inter alia* to
causes that lie altogether outside the range of operation
of the Dialectic. Amongst these must be included
what has been described as the ' Miracle of Dunkirk,'
which made it possible for Great Britain to rescue the
shattered remnants of her Expeditionary Force, and
thus gain a breathing-space for ultimately rallying
round her other nations in defence of civilisation. Had
the sea been less calm at this critical juncture in human
history, it is most likely that what is now the Soviet
Union would have formed part of the Hitler Reich,

leaving indeed little room for the rule and spread of Communism.

Considering the part played for good or evil by the unforeseen and fortuitous in the development of human destinies, and man's inability to control the heightened potency of his destructive powers, there is surely little ground for the belief in the inevitability of progress. It is precisely here that Jewish teaching has most to say to us. In its conception of history are to be found principles of permanent validity determining the meaning of progress. History in the Jewish conception is not a chaos leading to nowhere, but an overall progression with a definite goal which it derives from God who is above history, and who rules and controls history.[13] For God in Jewish teaching is not only the Lord of Nature, but also the Lord of History. History is the arena wherein God's activity on behalf of man is made manifest, and in which, and through which, His eternal purpose is being fulfilled. It is this which gives history its significance. All events in history are full of meaning, and it is in terms of that meaning that all historical happenings have to be interpreted.

The idea of the participation of God in the events of the day is the dominant note of Biblical history. No one reading the Bible can fail to be impressed with the plan and purpose its narratives unfold. The call to Abraham, the Egyptian bondage, the Exodus, the Revelation at Sinai, Israel's Election and entry into the Promised Land, are not isolated and unrelated episodes, but are all parts of a closely-knit drama, in which the end is already foreshadowed in the beginning; and it is this idea which is fundamental to prophetic teaching and the Jewish thought it inspired. The Exile, the Restoration, the subsequent destruction of the second Hebrew State and Temple, and the dispersion of the Jewish people among the nations, are not viewed as mere products of the contingent and unforeseen, but as parts of a divine plan, working towards the fulfilment of a purpose that was with Him from the beginning, for the individual, the nations and the human race. Empires may rise and fall, civilisations may flourish and decay, but everywhere there is the persistent activity of God, giving to all the movements of history, unity, direction and purpose.

It is this idea of the disclosure of the divine purpose in the lives and affairs of men and nations which distinguishes the prophets, and the spirits akin to them, from other saints and great men of religion. Characteristic of all saints is their claim to have sought and found God and entered into close communion with Him. But other great saints of religion have sought and experienced God by flying from history into timeless intercourse with God. The prophets communicate with God in history. They hear His voice in the happenings of the day. They discern His will in all the vicissitudes of fortune in the lives of nations and individuals. History thus gains unsuspected significance. All that happens therein is of fundamental importance. All is living, tangible drama unfolding itself and moving amid manifestations of divine judgment, goodness and grace towards the fulfilment of an eternal purpose.

This Jewish belief is not a product of a later age, born from a sense of disillusionment and despair,

seeking relief in the vague hope of better days to come.
It is a genuine tradition, based on the conviction that
this is God's world, chosen by Him to become the
scene of a divine order, fulfilling itself in and through
history, with the establishment of righteousness and
justice on earth.

It is this conviction which has proved the saving
strength of the Jewish people throughout the ages. The
Jews, it has been said, believed in hope against hope.
No people has suffered more cruelly from ' man's
inhumanity to man ' than have the Jews. Yet they
have refused to abandon the hope that somewhere and
somewhen justice will be done in this world, ' Shall
not the Judge of all the earth do judgment ? ' (Genesis
xviii. 25). Here is announced the indomitable Jewish
conviction that the world, to use the Rabbinic phrase,
is not *Hefker* (' ownerless '),[14] with no one to care for or
to be concerned about what is happening therein.
There is no human action that is allowed to go unre-
quited. There is no moment in human history over
and against which God does not stand as Judge. And
history has, to some extent, justified this indomitable
faith of the Jew. The late Dean Inge, none too friendly
to the Jewish people, writing in 1940, at the very height
of Hitler's triumphs, declared, ' The Jews have stood
by the graves of all their oppressors in turn. They may
yet say to their latest persecutors: " The feet of them
that buried Assyrians, Babylonians, Greeks, Romans,
and Spanish Inquisitors are at the door and shall carry
thee out." '[15]

The conception of the revelation of divine purpose in
history is universally admitted to be the greatest con-

tribution which Jews have made to religion. Professor John Macmurray has actually written a book on the subject, entitled *The Clue to History*,[16] and it is one of the most interesting and stimulating books that have appeared in recent years in this country. It is not surprising that he goes straight to the Old Testament in his search for a clue. Of all peoples, he shows, the children of Israel found meaning in history, and could explain every part of their pilgrimage as a nation by the overruling wisdom of God. The Old Testament, he points out, is of more value for the philosopher's quest than the New Testament, because its clear analysis of the meaning of this life is not complicated by the problem of a life beyond the grave in which the New Testament fixes its centre of gravity.[17]

The Hebrew people created a religious civilisation centred in the Law, and were satisfied that they could find the will of God in this life ; and what were the conclusions they reached on this basis ? As Macmurray says: ' Jewish reflection thinks history as the act of God. Where our historians say, " Caesar crossed the Rubicon ", or " Nelson won the Battle of Trafalgar ", the Jewish historian says " God brought His people up out of the Land of Egypt." '[18]

It would not be correct to say that the idea that historical events have a religious meaning originated with Israel. It is a very ancient belief, common among other nations of antiquity, that the good fortune of a nation or tribe depends on the favour of the gods. But Judaism introduced two revolutionary concepts of God that transformed the idea of the conditions of such divine favour and, with it, the whole conception of

S

historical events. The first is, as already shown, the moral character of the deity—a concept which is entirely absent from polytheism;[19] the second is that of God's universality. The one and only God is not only the God of Israel, but of all the peoples of the earth. ' Are ye not as children of Ethiopians unto Me, O children of Israel ? ' saith the Eternal. ' Have I not brought Israel out of the Land of Egypt and the Philistines from Caphtor and the Syrians from Kir ? ' (Amos ix. 7). These two revolutionary concepts transformed the whole idea of the conditions for securing the favour of God, as well as the conception of human history. As a moral God (a God of righteousness and justice), He demands moral conduct and righteous action as conditions of His favour. And all events in history must, therefore, be interpreted in terms of this divine call to morality and righteousness. His universality carries with it the idea that there is only one moral law for all men, and that His divine call to righteousness goes forth not only to Israel but to all the nations of the earth.

The relevance of these ideas to the Jewish conception of history is clear. It means that all events in the history of the nations, no less than those of the Jewish people, are to be interpreted as divine judgments, with the purpose of turning mankind to righteousness in life and action. The implications of the Jewish conception of history are, accordingly, twofold. Positively, the Jewish interpretation of history insists that only righteousness exalts a nation. Negatively, it asserts the awful consequences that flow from evil-doing. Violence and aggression may for some time make headway, but at last they must be broken, because they are in conflict with the unshakable purpose of a righteous God. ' Fret not thyself because of evil-doers . . . for they shall soon wither like the grass ' (Psalm xxxvii. 1-2). ' For the wicked shall perish; and the enemies of God shall be as the fat of lambs, they shall pass away in smoke, they shall pass away ' (*ibid.* 20). In this connection, it must be remembered that the mills of God grind slowly and that the consequences may be long-delayed. Some would treat this delay as the denial of justice, but Judaism interprets it as the long-suffering patience of divine judgment. For sin and disaster, as conceived by Judaism, though standing to each other in a relation of a cause and effect, are not linked in an automatic mechanical sequence. There is always the possibility of repentance which has the power to avert disaster. All the anticipations of disaster for evil-doing in the Bible, as our Rabbis point out over and again, are hypothetical judgments, and dependent on man, who, with repentance and change of heart, can avert their coming into operation.[20]

If sin and evil produce disaster, the evidence must be apparent in history. Now does the study of history confirm this ? The process of history is so complex that it is necessary to be careful not to read into it the interpretation we desire; but one of the convictions which grow upon the mind in the study of the past is that nations which have practised barbarism and cruelty have declined and even vanished from the field of history. ' One lesson, and only one ' (wrote Froude years ago in an address on *The Science of History*), ' history may be said to repeat with distinctness; that the world is built somehow on moral foundations; that, in the long run, it is well with the good; in the long run it is ill with the wicked.' ' But this,' he continues, ' is no science; it is no more than the old doctrine taught long ago by the Hebrew prophets.'²¹ Again he writes, ' [History] is a voice for ever sounding across the centuries the laws of right and wrong. Opinions alter, manners change, creeds rise and fall, but the moral law is written on the tablets of eternity. For every false word or unrighteous deed, for cruelty and oppression, for lust and vanity, the price has to be paid at last: not always by the chief offenders, but paid by someone. Justice and truth alone endure and live. Injustice and falsehood may be long-lived, but dooms-day comes at last to them, in French revolutions and other terrible ways.'²²

That is not to say that we can trace in history some rational or predictable consistency by virtue of which every criminal receives exactly the punishment he deserves. The *cri de coeur* of the prophets complaining to God about the prosperity of the wicked, oppressing nations, and the suffering of the just,²³ is sufficient to refute such an assertion. What the Bible does teach, and that for which Froude claims history in support, is that evil acquiesced in brings its penalty in the long run. Sooner or later, the price has to be paid in catastrophe and degradation, in revolutions or world wars, ' those terrible things ' in which, as the Psalmist (lxv. 6) says, ' God answers us in righteousness.' That there are chastisements in history is a truth which no one who has lived through the terrible experiences of our times will deny. The collapse of Germany, as anyone with a knowledge of history will affirm, is but the result of the disregard of the claims of morality in international relations which has characterised German politics for almost a century. For a time it paid and brought in rich dividends, making Prussia the nucleus of a united German nation and the leading military power of the old world. But a limit was ultimately set by the judgment of history to German injustice and aggressiveness, leading to the Nemesis that has overtaken the Hitler Reich in our days.

An earlier illustration of the judgment of history is afforded by the Spanish Inquisition. Historians show that the Inquisition for a time increased the power and prestige of Spain. Yet ultimately it contributed, as is generally recognised, to the decadence of that country, from which it has never recovered. It is not strange that a great modern historian, Arnold Toynbee, in his monumental *Study of History*, passing in review the rise and decline of the twenty-one civilisations, of which we have historical records,[24] should place on the title-page of the fourth volume the verse of Psalm cxxvii: ' Except the Lord build the house, their labour is but lost that build it.' The cause of break-down, as Toynbee traces it, is life blinded by anti-spiritual and unsocial self-interest, and shaken and shattered by what he calls ' an outbreak of internal discord.'[25] Similarly, in our own times, those who held fast to the Biblical tradition had no illusions as to the terrible judgment that would visit mankind as the result of the policy of fraternisation with evil which dominated the period between the two wars. At least the Jews who ' if ', as the Rabbis declare, ' are not prophets, are the children of prophets ',[26] had no doubt on that score. Our generation, at least, having passed through such fires of judgment, should listen to the prophetic voice which, as Froude says, ' forever sounds through history the laws of right and wrong.' And so to come down to our present post-war world, there is indeed much in contemporary events to support the view that history is the arena of divine judgment. In the words of Professor Herbert Butterfield, ' Looking at the spectacle which the world now [1950] presents to us, I think it not too much to say that if Germany is under judgment so are all of us—the whole of our existing order and the very fabric of our civilisation. . . . We to-day must feel ourselves to be living in one of those remarkable periods when judgment stalks generally through the world, and it becomes a question whether the orders and systems to which we have been so long attached can survive the day of reckoning.'[27]

But the source of all evil that calls for the judgment of God in the events of days, according to the Biblical tradition, lies in man's unwillingness to recognise and acknowledge the weakness of his position. In other words, the sin of man, in the Biblical view, consists in the vanity and pride through which he imagines himself and his nation, with its culture and civilisation, to be self-sufficient, and to be able to manage their own affairs independently of God. This sin of pride as the cause of all catastrophes in history is the recurring theme of the Bible. Isaiah traces the corruption and consequent downfall of Babylon to pride. Ezekiel castigates the pride and self-sufficiency of various princes and nations of the world, such as Tyre, Egypt

and others, in the same vein. And, likewise, the
Psalmist (Psalm xlix) sees the human problem in terms
of the same prophetic insight, inveighing against those
' who trust in their wealth and boast themselves in
the multitude of their riches.'[28]

The serious view which the Bible takes of the sin of
pride and its awful consequences for human history
receives striking confirmation from a modern writer
whose philosophy of life has constantly been opposed
to the Biblical. Bertrand Russell, in one of his recent
works, *History of Western Philosophy*, warns the world
against the danger arising from the sense of power in
human communities. ' Man, formerly too humble,
begins to think of himself almost as a god. . . . In all
this, I feel a great danger; the danger of what may be
called " cosmic impiety ". The concept of " truth "
as something dependent on facts largely outside human
control has been one of the ways in which philosophy
has hitherto inculcated the necessary element of
humility. When this check upon pride is removed, a
further step is taken on the road to a certain kind of
madness. I am persuaded (he continues) that this
intoxication is the greatest danger of our time and that
any philosophy which contributes to it is increasing
the danger of vast social disaster.'[29]

Divine judgment in history does not imply something
introduced from outside like the judgment of a capri-
cious tyrant whose will and law are arbitrary, bearing
no relation to the act of the person upon whom judgment is pronounced. The judgment of God is relevant
to the structure of the Universe. God has so created
the world that the pride of man must destroy itself in

vain rebellion against his Creator. Human nature has been recognised to be essentially self-destructive. Every human activity that is made in defiance of the will of God contains in itself the seeds of self-destruction. ' His own iniquities shall ensnare the wicked ' (Proverbs v. 22).

There was once a man who succeeded after seventeen years of patient fiddling in making a straw clock, but it caught fire by its own friction when it began to keep time.[30] This is a parable of the destructive nature of whatever originates from the will of man. A concrete example is afforded by the fate of freedom in modern society. Modern man has expended much treasure of blood, sweat and toil for the sake of freedom; and yet, having won it, he is ready to throw it away for the sake of security. This is noticeable in the drift to conform to the standards of various groups and collectives, and the readiness of men to surrender personal freedom to some social order which would control all individual activities.

The root of the trouble is the egoism that vitiates all struggles for freedom, the egoism of nation, class or group involved in the struggle. In all strivings for freedom the principal motives are political and economic, but when economic activity and political power are regarded as the chief end of human strivings, it is natural to prize these above freedom, and to go so far as to reject freedom when it clashes with the security which comes from the economic and political power. This is exactly what happened in Nazi Germany, and we see this in the case of Russia in which a visible political and economic dictatorship has been established, and which shows the same egoistic character in the commonwealth of nations as the avaricious capitalist does in the commonwealth of economics. This process is also gradually taking place in Western democracies, where personal freedom, though not despised, is no longer honoured as it was.

Here we have an example of the self-destructive nature of human activity that sets itself against the will of God, and the process by which this self-destruction comes to pass is precisely the divine judgment made manifest in history. It is the divine judgment on a humanity which imagines it can establish a stable society on the principle of egoism; a humanity that fails to realise that the only principle which can serve as a basis for constructive human relationships is to be found not in the self-seeking of individual class and group, but in service to all. Men with their creative and organising abilities must grasp the fact that they are part of one social organism and that the important thing is for them to exercise their gifts in the interests of all. But this idea of service, as distinct from egoism, as a principle of social relations, can find its life-giving force only in the service of God. Only through the service of God can man emancipate himself from his selfish cult of narrow interest, and free himself from the egoistic and self-seeking element in his nature. Only in the service of God can perfect freedom be found, and in His will our peace. This is the significance of the Rabbinic saying: ' There is no free man, but the one who occupies his mind with the Law of God.'[31] For the law of God serves to teach this truth and cultivate the spirit of freedom in service. And the ideal Messianic society in the Judaistic conception is, as Maimonides already points out, not one in which everything is subservient to economic factors, but where economic security serves as a basis for a freedom in which men and women have the fullest liberty to express their personality in every legitimate way.[32]

The judgment of God, however, is redemptive in character. Its object is to demonstrate the futility of all human attempts to establish a society on egoistic principles in defiance of His will, and thereby to lead men gradually on the road to progress, of which the fundamental characteristic, as outlined by John Fiske, is the ' continuous weakening of selfishness and continuous strengthening of sympathy.'[33] In this gradual human development through divine judgment, wars play an important part. Wars are, of course, the inevitable results of man's irrational passions, having their root in national pride. And just as God has so ordered the world that insanitary conditions should bring disease, so it is part of the divine moral world order that social evils must result in war. And it is just as foolish to rail against God for the one as it is for the other. ' The folly of man perverteth his way, and his heart fretteth against God ' (Proverbs xix. 3).[34] God will not interefere to take away the consequences of human evil, as he will not interfere to take away the consequences, say, of failing to take away dustbins. Yet through the forces of destruction let loose by man, God is ever watchful to secure general recognition of the essentially destructive character of human nature, and through it increased human co-operation in the fulfilment of His divine purpose for His redemption of humanity.

Thus does divine judgment, made manifest through wars, possess a redemptive quality. Wars indeed often bring forth results very different from the aims of those who first embarked upon them, not only in the sphere of politics and invention, but also in the moral domain. This is true of all wars, and particularly of the last World War. It is still too early to determine the ultimate consequences of the last war and the changes and developments that will occur as a result in religious and ethical thought. But we can perceive at least some faint glimpses of the part it is going to play in the slow evolution of humanity towards its destiny. It is gradually bringing about the recognition that humanity must march forward as one, with its corollary, that the material resources of mankind must be more justly distributed and more peaceably enjoyed. As a result of the second World War humanity—at least part of it—has come to realise itself as one being, growing and ascending from an infinite past with infinite powers in the future. This new realisation, still partial and fragmentary, has not yet been well digested into a new religion. There will still be further disillusionments and further crises to overcome. This cannot be otherwise. All human experiments in social engineering, whether Socialism or Communism, without reference to God, are bound to fail, no less than Feudalism or Capitalism have failed. It was a profound remark of the Russian novelist, Dostoevsky, in his *Brothers Karamazov*, that whilst Christianity missed the boat when, in bringing the message of eternal hope to humanity, it forgot man's need for bread, Marx's Socialism missed the boat when, in its zeal to assure bread to men, it forgot that man lives by more than bread alone. And he predicted that out of this extremism there would spring the opportunity for the enslaving Caesars to place the yoke again on the neck of mankind. But this failure of all human experiments is the very ground of hope. Nothing succeeds like failure. Man's inability to achieve Utopia, it has been said, feeds not the spirit of despair, but the radiant hope which outshines even the lurid glare of the atomic bomb. It may well be that the stage is now being set for the terrible calamity in which men, in the words of the prophet, ' will say to the mountains, " Cover us " and to the hills, " Fall on us " ' (Hosea x. 8), crying to them for protection against their own inventions. But if history, which is controlled and guided by God, does not lie, all these crises will be surmounted. Out of the crucible of suffering, humanity will yet learn to try again and do better, and thus ultimately come to the fullness of its heritage and march onwards to the destiny which the Lord of History has set for the children of men.

NOTES

[1] Ahura-mazda (' Wise Lord ') and Angro-maingu (' hostile spirit ').

[2] See J. B. Bury, *The Idea of Progress* (1920), p. 10.

[3] See *op. cit.*, p. 9, n. 2.

[4] ' The rational soul wanders round the whole world and through the encompassing void, and gazes into infinite time, and considers the periodic destruction and rebirths of the universe, and reflects

that our posterity will see nothing new and that our ancestors saw
nothing greater than we have seen. A man of forty years, possessing
the most moderate intelligence, may be said to have seen all that is
past and all that is to come, so uniform is the world ' (*Meditations*,
XI, 1), quoted by J. B. Bury, *op. cit.*, p. 13.

[5] Arnold Toynbee, *Study of History*, IV, p. 30ff, quoted by W.
R. Inge, *The Fall of the Idols* (1940), p. 26, n. 1. In our own times the
cyclic view of history has found its exponent in Oswald Spengler,
in his work, *Der Untergang des Abendlands* (E. T., by Ch. F. Atkin-
son, ' The Decline of the West,' 2 vols., 1926-8). For Spengler the
march of history is determined by biological necessity, and world
history is but the collective biography of a succession of cultural
organisms, each subjected to the same biological laws of growth and
decay as any other thing in the realm of nature, and existing only
to give birth to another culture in which the same process will be
repeated, without any meaning and purpose whatsoever, spiritual
ideals, moral principles, religious beliefs evinced by any particular
culture being mere epiphenomena, possessing no abiding significance
or value. Spengler's book ' has become the classic summary of the
now familiar pessimism of the twentieth century with regard to its
own historical future.'—H. Stuart Hughes, *Oswald Spengler* (1952),
p. 165.

[6] Name by which a group of French writers were known, of whom
the chief were Diderot and d'Alembert, all of whom contributed to
an extensive encyclopedia.

[7] See J. B. Bury, *op. cit.*, pp. 338-340.

[8] A. I. Kook, *Iggerot Rayah* (1943), p. 164.

[9] T. H. Huxley, *Evolution and Ethics* (1894), p. 85. Similarly N.
Berdyaev, *Freedom and the Spirit* (1935), p. 30: ' There is no universal law of development and progress. . . . The good is the result
of freedom, not of necessity. Various elements, principles, and
organisms, taken in isolation, develop and progress, but development
and progress are not an obligatory law for the life of the universe
as a whole.' See also J. Macmurray, *Clue to History* (1938), p. 114,
who points out that it is a complete confusion of thought to identify

progress with evolution, for whereas evolution is a natural process of development, and is therefore unintentional, progress depends upon taking thought, and involves an intentional co-operation of different individuals for the achievement of a common end.

[10] ' There is scarcely a good invention which is not put to a diabolical use as soon as it is invented. Modern means of communication have brought men closer to one another, but the individual has become more homeless.' Emil Brunner, *The Divine Imperative* (1937), p. 282 (E.T. of *Das Gebot und die Ordnungen*).

[11] Bertrand Russell, *Freedom and Organisation* (1934), p. 225.

[12] *Op. cit.*, p. 228.

[13] ' World history is revealed as a universal process of redemption fulfilling itself in fixed stages foreseen by God. As there were six days for the Creation, so there are six days of world history, the first four days of holy history during which the Temple stands are followed by the fifth and sixth days, bringing the ascendency of the world beasts, i.e. empires of the world, until the Sabbath of the world will restore the undisturbed harmony on earth.'—Fritz Baer, *Galuth* (1947), pp. 11-2. See passage of *Tanna de-be Eliyyahu* in B.T. Abodah Zarah 9a, which perceives in history a well-defined process, with Creation as its beginning, Revelation at Sinai its central point, and Messianism its goal.

[14] See Yalkut Shimeoni, Exodus, 396.

[15] W. R. Inge, *The Fall of the Idols*, p. 23.

[16] John Macmurray, *The Clue to History* (1938).

[17] *Op. cit.* p. 30.

[18] *Op. cit.*, p. 38.

[19] See *supra*, p. 152.

[20] See, e.g., Jeremiah xviii. 7, Ezekiel xviii. 21ff, and B.T. Rosh Hashanah 17b. The classical example is of course provided in the Book of Jonah. " They [the prophets] were not concerned in predicting events as such, but they were tremendously concerned in the present and its reformation. Hence what predictions they made

were seldom categorical, but usually conditional, intended as warnings to their audience of the inevitable consequences of their evildoings . . . in their labours, in contrast with the professional prophets, they were successful to the degree that their predictions did not come true." Th. J. Meek, *Hebrew Origins* (2nd ed. 1950) p. 176.

[21] J. Anthony Froude, *Short Studies in Great Subjects* (1915 ed.), I. p. 21.

[22] *Op. cit.*, p. 27. As against Froude's view may be set that expressed by H. A. L. Fisher in his preface to the *History of Europe* (1936): ' Men wiser and more learned than I,' he writes, ' have discerned in history a plot, a rhythm. a predetermined pattern. I can see only one emergency following upon another, as wave follows upon wave, only one great fact with respect to which, since it is unique, there can be no generalisation, only one safe rule for the historian: that he should recognise in the development of human destinies the play of the contingent and unforeseen ' (p.v.). While this may be ' the safe rule for the historian ', one cannot ignore the acute words of the Swedish historian, Harald Hjärne (quoted in N. Söderblom, *The Living God* [1933], p. 371-2): ' The laws of human development go their way undisturbed through the ages, with or against the will of acting persons and peoples. What are these laws? No one knows their innermost nature, but their effects are sometimes perceived more or less distinctly, when one listens attentively to the voices of the past. Sometimes in the very way in which events form their own connection, we catch a glimpse of something which resembles a human countenance, with a smile, that is at once both severe and mild at the nations, who believe themselves to be going their own ways, but constantly go where they have never wished to go. If this glimpse is an illusion, yet the suspicion arises that the inexorable laws of development are in reality not a system of dry rules, but utterances of a Personal will, against which no other can prevail.'

[23] E.g. Jeremiah xii. 1ff.; Habakkuk i. 2ff.; Psalm xciv. 3ff.

[24] I.e. the Egyptian, Andean, Sinic, Minoan, Sumerian, Mayan, Syriac, Indic, Hittite, Hellenic, Arabic, Iranian, Hindu, Mexican,

Yucatec, Babylonian, Orthodox Christian (in Russia), Orthodox Christian (outside Russia), Far Eastern (in Japan and Korea), Far Eastern (main body outside Japan), and our own Western Civilisation.

[25] A. J. Toynbee, *op. cit.*, IV, p. 120.

[26] B.T. Pesachim, 66b.

[27] H. Butterfield, *Christianity and History* (1950), p. 52.

[28] See R. Niebuhr, *The Nature and Destiny of Man*, I, pp. 221ff Similarly Butterfield, *op. cit.*, p. 60: ' Judgment in history falls heaviest on those who come to think themselves gods, who fly in the face of Providence and history, who put their trust in man-made systems, and worship the work of their own hands, and who say that the strength of their own right arm gave them victory . . . And, similarly, if men put their faith in science and make it the be-all and end-all of life, as though it were not to be subdued to any higher ethical end, there is something in the very composition of the universe that will make it execute judgment on itself, if only in the shape of the atomic bomb.'

[29] Bertrand Russell, *History of Western Philosophy* (1946), p. 856.

[30] See D. R. Davies, *Divine Judgment in History* (1943), p. 6.

[31] *Ethics of the Fathers*, VI, 2.

[32] See Maimonides, *Yad ha-Hazakah, Hilekot Melakim*, XII, 5. ' In that (Messianic) era there shall be neither famine nor war, neither jealousy nor strife. Blessings will be abundant, comforts within the reach of all. The one preoccupation of the whole world will be to know the Lord . . . as it is written: " For the earth shall be full of the knowledge of the Lord, as the waters cover the sea " (Isaiah xi. 9).

ובאותו הזמן לא יהיה שם לא רעב, ולא מלחמה, ולא קנאה ותחרות
שהטובה תהיה מושפעת הרבה, וכל המעדנים מצוין כעפר ולא יהיה עסק כל
העולם אלא לדעת את ד' בלבד . . . שנאמר כי מלאה הארץ דעה את ד'
כמים לים מכסים.

[33] John Fiske, *Outlines of Cosmic Philosophy*, II, p. 201, quoted in J. B. Bury, *op. cit.*, p. 372.

[34] Cf. Maimonides, *Guide*, III, 12: ' The numerous evils to which

individual persons are exposed are due to the defects existing in the
persons themselves. We complain and seek relief from our faults;
we suffer from the evils which we, by our own free will, inflict on
ourselves and ascribe them to God, who is far from being connected
with them.'   ורוב הרעות הנופלות באישיו הם מעצמם. ר״ל מאישי בני
אדם החסרים ומחסרונותינו נצעק ונבקש עוד ומהרעות נעשה אותם בעצמנו
בבחירתנו נכאב וניחסהו לשם. חלילה לו ממנו. Moses Cordovero
illustrates this truth by the following parable: ' A man found a
house properly equipped and well-ordered, and in the house there
was sufficient wood and fuel as required for cooking, and oil for
lighting, and an adequate amount of wick for his needs, but instead
of putting this to use little by little, as the necessities of life
demanded, he set fire to all the wood, the wick and the oil, with
the result that he burnt down the whole house and he himself did
not escape unscathed. He thereupon began complaining against
the owner of the house, when in reality he was to blame for mis-
using what was intended for his service.'   משל לאדם שמצא בית מסודר
בכל ובבית עצים הרבה ואש כדי צורך הבישול. ושמן להדליק להאיר לו.
ופתילה רבה כדי צורכו. ויהיה ענין זה להשתמש ממנו מעט מעט כדי צורך
הנאות לחייו והוא הבעיר העצים כולם ושרף הפתילה והשמן והעצים והאש,
וכמעט היה נשרף כל הבית ונשרף הוא, והתחיל הוא צווח על בעל הבית וכו׳
See S. A. Horodezky, *Torat ha-Kabbalah shel R. Moshe Cordovero*,
p. 371.

CHAPTER XIV

ISRAEL AS INSTRUMENT OF DIVINE PURPOSE

THE unfolding of divine purpose in history, which Judaism bids us to discern, is nowhere made so manifest as in the history of the Jewish people, the people whom God has chosen as the special instrument for the fulfilment of His purpose. The whole history of Israel is shot through with the presence of the Divine. ' Here,' in the words of Professor Peake, ' God who is never absent from history strikes into its stream with an intense energy.'[1] How else are we to account for the unique place this small nation has come to occupy in the history of mankind, and for the all-pervasive influence of its religious thought and moral teaching ? Among what other people do we find that intimacy with God, that knowledge of His character and insight into His purpose, which Israel derived from the succession of those peerless prophets who made known and justified the ways of God to man ? And what of the peculiar historical destiny of the Jewish people? Where in the annals of mankind are we to find a parallel to that amazing survival and miraculous emergence of the Jewish people into Statehood after two thousand years of exile, dispersion, martyrdom, and suffering ? How can we account for all this except by the fact that God has chosen Israel as the people to serve His eternal purpose, and that, in some unique sense, He is ever present in their wonderful history ?[2]

How the Jewish people came to be chosen to serve God's eternal purpose is told in the Bible.[3] The story

278

begins with the creation of the world by God, and the formation of man in the Creator's image. His affinity with the divine makes man a personal self-conscious and spiritual being designed for communion with his Maker, and endowed with faculties enabling him to fulfil a spiritual destiny. He is placed amid exquisite, idyllic scenes, surrounded by all that is good and beautiful. Man, however, by his conscious choice of what is antagonistic to the will of God introduces the first discordant note into this blissful harmony. Attracted by the seductive charms of the senses, he yields to temptation and thus has a taste of the fleeting and illusory pleasures of sin. He finds sin pleasing and gratifying for the moment. ' Stolen waters are sweet ' (Proverbs ix. 17). From that moment evil has invaded his soul and become for him a stark reality, opposing its rule to the hitherto undisputed rule of the good over the heart of man. But where evil is, there God cannot abide; and man is sent away from the Divine Presence to a life of conflict, discipline and sorrow. Thereupon begins the struggle between good and evil for the mastery of man. But divine tenderness does not leave man unaided. God Himself is concerned in the struggle, on the outcome of which the fulfilment of His purpose depends, and is there to help to win man back unto Himself, and restore to him his God-given destiny.

But the task is by no means easy. Evil has made man refractory. The first act of disobedience leads to murder; and murder leads, with the increase of knowledge, to the forging of instruments of destruction, and this again to the glorification of violence. One sinner makes many. The evil example of one is quickly fol-

lowed by others until ' the earth is filled with violence '
(Genesis vi. 11). But a world which is dead to the
negative demands of justice would be much less
responsive to *positive* claims of righteousness.[4] Wickedness at length reaches such a point that the just and
righteous God finds it necessary to destroy mankind.
But the Creator's patience is not at an end, nor His
hopes for the human race. Noah is a *righteous* man.
The Flood comes, but he is spared. With the new
generation, however, that springs from him, a new
type of sin appears on the scene—a sense of self-
sufficiency that would banish the Creator from the
Universe; and the old story bids fair to be repeated
again. The reason for this second failure of mankind
lay not so much in the absence of knowledge of what
is right, as in the weakness of the human will to act
upon that knowledge. The source of the social malady
was not in the head, but in the heart, its imaginings
and strivings, with their attendant greed, envy, lust,
jealousy and ill-will, that were productive of all evil.
' For the imagination of man's heart is evil from his
youth ' (Genesis viii. 21), or rather, as a result of the
unchecked tendencies which grow up with him from
his youth, and which he finds difficult to overcome.[5]
But God will not be thwarted in His purpose. The
human race must somehow be restored unto Him. If
it rejects one opportunity, He gives it another. He
raised from among the sons of men Abraham, a man
of spiritual majesty and moral grandeur, ' a man of
faithful heart ' (Nehemiah ix. 8). In him and his seed
all the nations of the earth are to be blessed. At the
divine behest, he leaves his native land for a country

selected to be the scene of historic revelation. With
him God makes a covenant claiming him and his
descendants for His instruments in shaping human
destiny. In preparation for this, their divinely assigned
rôle, his descendants would have to go through various
kinds of discipline, of which a centuries-long enslave-
ment and bondage would be the most severe and
effective. Abraham gladly submits to the divine call to
him to become the instrument of God's purpose.
Wherever he goes, he brings with him the knowledge
of the Lord and His ways—the practice of righteousness
and justice (Genesis xviii. 19). His work for God is
carried on after him by Isaac, and after Isaac by Jacob.
With Jacob's sons, God's long-laid plan begins to take
clearer shape. Through a combination of wondrous
events and circumstances, Joseph is set over the affairs
of the mightiest Empire of the time, and thus serves
the high ends of God. Driven by hunger, his family
joins him, and after years of sojourn in Egypt, Israel
is enslaved. Through the painful discipline of bondage, and the miraculous deliverance that follows, the
people—at least part of it—becomes conscious that it
is called to be a vehicle of divine knowledge to
the world, and an instrument for the fulfilment of
God's redemptive purpose for humanity.

How the slavery in Egypt was turned by Divine
Providence into a mighty creative instrument furthering
His redemptive purpose is one of the most instructive
chapters in social history.[6] In these early days, which
we have to view in their historical perspective, the
whole moral and social life of humanity was kept at a
low ebb under the pressure of the Egyptian regime

which strove for world-mastery and world-domination.
Slavery with racial and social repressions and discrimi-
nations was its method; animism with base superstitions its philosophy. Israel itself, forced to enter
Egypt under the duress of famine, and lured to stay
there by the laziness of decadent souls, was slowly
subjected to a slavery which, as time went on, became
not only increasingly degrading but also increasingly
senseless even from the slaveholders' point of view.
Whatever economic interest they might have had
erstwhile in keeping the slaves down became over-
shadowed by their fear of them. The relation between
the Egyptian taskmasters and the Israelite slaves thus
ceased to have any economic justification, and became
based on purely political considerations, with a corre-
spondingly increased trend towards destructive and
de-humanising brutality. At this stage, slavery for
Israel in Egypt became degrading beyond imagination,
and complete physical destruction threatened the whole
people, when the masters saw no more profit in the
further existence of their slaves.

This was the moment chosen by God to make Israel
His chosen people, to become His special instrument,
not only for bringing down the rotten edifice of
Egyptian tyranny, but also for the promotion of the
ideals of justice and righteousness, for the redemption
of mankind. What this selection implied was communicated to them in the call ' And ye shall be unto
me a kingdom of priests and a holy nation ' (Exodus
xix. 6).

Priesthood in Judaism is defined not by social status,
but by the functions involved: ' And they shall teach

my people the difference between holy and profane, and make known to them the difference between what is clean and unclean ' (Ezekiel xliv. 23).

What is true of the priests in Israel applies to the nation as a whole in its priestly mission. As a kingdom of priests, Israel's divinely appointed vocation was that of teaching. In teaching, however, there is no possibility of fulfilment without the readiness of the pupil to learn. But there are no better pupils than the teachers themselves, and there is no more profitable learning than from those whom you teach. ' Much have I learned from my teachers; more from my colleagues; and from my disciples more than from them all.'[7] The nation was thus to become priest, teacher and pupil at the same time, and what applied to the nation as a whole applied to every individual. Each was to give the other the best he possessed, each was to learn how to bring out from the other the best he possessed. The Kingdom of Priests where everybody is a priest, a teacher and a pupil at the same time, is the starting point for the achievement of that very ideal state of social harmony and co-operation which is the final aim of all righteous and holy endeavours on earth.

Israel were thus not chosen for themselves. The mission they received carried no distinction with it. It was part of God's design that they were to serve His righteous purpose. It is His work they were called upon to do in the whole world, transforming the darkest corners of God's earth. ' I the Lord have called thee in righteousness and have taken hold of thy hand and set thee for a covenant of the peoples, for a light of the nations ' (Isaiah xlii. 6). ' And I will give thee for a light unto the nations, that My salvation may be unto the end of the earth ' (*ibid*. xlix. 6).

God's selection of Israel does not imply any inequality or favouritism. In the selection of Israel, we have but a manifestation of the divine selective process at work in history, as we know it to be at work in Nature, though with a difference. The universe has been described as ' quite a shockingly selective place.'[8] Out of an apparently infinite space only a relatively tiny portion is occupied by matter of any kind. Of the stars, perhaps only one has planets. Of the planets, only one is at all likely to sustain organic life. Of the animals, only one species is rational. The same selective process appears also in operation in human history. The whole of human history would seem to show that God prefers one person before another. There are differences of mind, body, gifts. One man appears to be more favoured than his fellow, more clever, more beautiful, more prosperous. Yet the selectiveness as it appears in human history is not of the kind at work in Nature. The selection in Nature, with the appalling waste it involves, appears a horrible and unjust thing by human standards. But in history people who are selected are in a sense selected for a supreme honour, but it is also a supreme burden—a burden of service. Higher attainment means higher responsibility. So, this apparent inequality and favouritism which Israel's selection implied was but designed to afford them greater opportunity for service.

Viewed in this light, the selection of Israel is not unfair in the way it was first suspected, nor an anomaly to the exceptionless universal love of God for man;

because Israel, who had been selected for the great honour of being an *Am Segulah*, has been chosen for great tasks and services on behalf of the human race: they have been selected to do God's work in fulfilment of His purpose to mankind. The choosing of Israel has been God's universal choosing of mankind. His love for Israel is but the first step to the recognition of His love for all men, and it is precisely because the love of God is unending that He chose Israel to be one of the mediating factors in this universal love.

But in order to fit themselves for their universal priestly calling for which they had been chosen, Israel had to be a ' holy nation.' The significance of this charge is to be found in the root meaning of the Hebrew word for ' holy '—to be separate, distinct from.[9] Israel had to be a ' holy nation ', that is a nation set apart, separate and distinct from other nations, with its own peculiar way of life and conduct.

This separation was essential for Israel alike in the domain of religion and morals. The relentless struggle which the Jewish people, by virtue of their selection, were called upon, from their earliest days, to wage against idolatry was not only because it was a false religion, but also because it was a false morality. Idolatry, whatever its form, whether that of Canaanite Baal-worship, or Babylonian astral worship, was essentially immoral, degradingly immoral. For what was idolatry but the deification of the natural processes connected with fertility ? Whether it was the sun or any other natural power, the idol was served as a mysterious deity behind the natural forces. Idolatry was thus the worship of the sensual, and its beliefs were based on the notion of sympathetic magic, so that immorality was accepted as a means of increasing fertility in flocks and fields, and was regarded as a religious act. It is understandable that in a religion which makes the exaltation of the sensual its chief aim, ethics, as we understand them, have no place and receive no recognition. For this reason the Jews had to keep themselves separate from the idolatrous nations, alike in matters of worship and moral conduct.

With this end in view, the Jewish people were given the Torah. By means of the Torah, they were to develop a way of life which was to be distinct from the way of life of surrounding nations. Instead of a ritual which was debasing and degrading, the Torah was to offer them a system of religious observances which were conducive in a unique manner to their moralisation and perfection. Instead of a morality which was self-centred, the Torah was to provide them with an ethic which placed service to others at the centre of its system. In and through the Torah, Israel was thus to become a holy nation, distinct and separate, morally and religiously, from all other nations of the world.

How was the Torah designed to achieve this end? The Torah is distinguished from all other systems regulating human conduct both by its method and its scope. The cause of the human failure lay, as we have seen, in the heart rather than in the head. It was moral rather than intellectual. This problem how to make man's impulses keep pace with his ethical knowledge is one that has perplexed moralists of all ages: it is one thing to teach man what is right and good, but it is another to make him disposed and willing to obey and live up to the ideal.[10] As Lecky remarks, ' Simply to tell men what is virtue, and to extol its beauty, is insufficient. Something more must be done if the characters . . . are to be moulded, and the inveterate vices eradicated.'[11]

This moral problem which philosophy is incapable of meeting is taken over by religion. At this point both Judaism and Christianity step in, each with its distinct method of dealing with the human situation.

Proceeding from the notion that man is a fallen creature, Christianity has no faith in human nature. Man, in the eyes of Christian teaching, is hopeless and corrupt. His body and flesh are contaminated, his appetites are rooted in evil, and his whole natural being is opposed to the will of God and to all that is good and lovable. The only good in man is that which proceeds from the soul—and that only in so far as it is kept free from the taint of the body. Hence the Christian doctrine of the irreconcilable antagonism between the flesh and the spirit, the body and the soul, material pursuits and holiness of life, and its consequent commendation of asceticism as providing the only means of escaping the horrors of sinful matter, which are a bar to the fullness of moral and spiritual life.[12]

Judaism, in accord with Divine purpose, has faith in human nature, and turns with confidence to man, as once God turned with confidence to Israel, though they were corrupted by slavery in Egypt. Judaism embraces the highest and the lowest—the body and the soul—with the same solicitude, conferring upon them both the same rights and linking them both to a common purpose, in co-operation towards a higher plane.[13]

This harmony in Judaism between the claims of the body and the aspirations of the soul is achieved by means of the Torah. Extending to all details of life, the Torah becomes the means for establishing the supremacy of the will of God as the measure of all directions and strivings of the human heart. All the common ways of life, all political, social, cultural and domestic interests come under its rule. In marked contrast to the Christian discipline, whose influence, as we have been told by the late Archbishop Temple, is determined by the comparatively rare moments of worship in which the devotee is obliged to remember God,[13a] the Torah discipline penetrates every moment in the life of the Jew, to strengthen him not only in the service of God, but also to bring all human occupations into relation with the will of God. Given this accord, the will of God is no longer something other than, or opposed to, man's real nature, but *is* man's real nature. The Jew is thus able to attain moral and spiritual perfection without fleeing from the world, without sealing his senses hermetically to the beauties and blessings of existence. His spiritual victory involves no suppression of the rightful use of the body, but rather its cultivation with due self-restraint, resulting in a condition of mental adjustment in which ' all deeds ', in the word of the Sages, ' are performed for the sake of Heaven.'[14]

The Torah thus fulfils a twofold function. It not only indicates the ways of right conduct but also provides the means whereby this right conduct can be realized. For this purpose the Torah prescribes, side by side, two sets of commands, socio-moral and religious. It sets forth, in other words, precepts concerning the relation between man and God, and it also ordains rules governing the relations between man and man. Each category of commands, in its turn, is divided into two classes, negative and positive, corresponding to the laws of Justice (*mishpat*) and Righteousness (*zedakah*). The negative precepts in the sociomoral commands, such as those prohibiting murder, theft and unchastity, lying speech and slander, are part of the Law of Justice; the positive precepts in this set of commands, such as those exhorting love of fellow-man, including the stranger, and the exercise of mercy and practice of charity towards all men, are part of the Law of Righteousness. A division of like significance exists with regard to the religious laws. The negative precepts, in so far as they train in self-mastery and self-control and help in eradicating vice, provide restraints on evil-doing, and are related to the Law of Justice; whilst the positive precepts, with their inspiring ideals inculcating the love and fear of God, dependence on Him, and gratitude for His tender love and bounty, act as incentives to well-doing, and are related to the Law of Righteousness.[15]

From this relationship of the religious commands—ritual and ceremonial—to the Laws of Justice and Righteousness it follows that the observance by the individual of a religious precept is not a mere isolated act of devotion; because inasmuch as it is an aid to morality it is a social act. Likewise, the transgression of a religious command is no longer a matter of private concern only, for in so far as it weakens the individual's moral fibre and his spiritual power of resistance to evil, it is a social offence. Thus do the commands of the Torah—the religious and moral—combine in indissoluble harmony to constitute that way of life which is to mark off Israel as a ' holy nation,' separate from all other peoples of the earth.

This separation, so necessary in the far-off days of the past, when the Torah was given to Israel, still remains necessary if Judaism is to maintain its undiminished value in the face of the various forms of idolatry—physical and metaphysical—that persist to the present day. This being so, the need for the continuance of the Torah must be accepted, notwithstanding all the limitations and transformations which historic life has always worked outwardly and inwardly even on these apparently rigid forms. The Torah must remain a means of separation of Judaism from all other religions, faiths and systems; yet at the same time the quintessence of Judaism must be recognized as lying in its universalism. This means that the separation which the Torah is to effect is not to denote opposition to the world of culture. Israel's call to be a ' holy nation ' is directly related to its world-wide mission as a ' kingdom of priests.' Whilst primarily given to the Jew, the Torah has essentially a universal tendency, embracing all the sons of men. By means of Israel's testimony to God and to His righteousness, through the Torah, there is to be effected the moralization of all humanity, the hearts of all mankind turning to the worship of the One and Only God in purity and in truth, and to each other as brothers with one Heavenly Father.[16]

Separation, however, is not the only purpose of the Torah. There are in the innumerable forms and usages of the Torah, so many channels of communion and worship, with the positive power of inspiring and deepening the love of man for his creator, realising thereby for himself a true purpose which imparts true and absolute value to his being and existence. This is a fact which cannot be understood in all its depth by an outsider. Only he who has lived the life of the Torah knows what a heaven's ladder it is.

With the rise of Christianity a new conception was attached to the Torah, in order to discredit it. The opposition to the Torah, of which there are already indications in the teachings of Jesus, reached its full vehemence with Paul. To Paul, Torah, which, following the Greek mistranslation, he called ' *Nomos* ', the Law, was the most formidable enemy obstructing the dissemination and progress of the ' good news.'[17] He therefore relentlessly disparaged the Law as worthless and obsolete, contrasting the slavery of those who live under the Law with the freedom of those who believe in Jesus. All that the Law can do, according to Paul, is to make man conscious of sin. For if it had not been for the Law, he says, in effect, I should never have learnt what sin was. I should not have known what it was to covet if the Law had not said you must not covet (see Romans vii. 7-8). This strange argument led Paul to conclude that the Law was a curse, engendering sin and working wrath. It was given to man because of the sin of Adam, and from this curse there was only one way of escape: faith in Jesus. The argument was that just as the heathen cannot escape the wrath of

God owing to the horrible sin he is urged to commit by clinging to idols, so the Jew can as little escape by the Law the wrath of God. Instead of removing the germ of death brought to the world by Adam, the Law was given only to increase sin, to make all the greater the need of divine mercy, which was to come through faith in Christ, the new Adam.[18]

Paul's attitude to the Law was determined, of course, by his doctrine of salvation through Christ. He had committed himself to the belief that Jesus had died on the cross to atone for the sins of mankind. This was in opposition to the teachings of Judaism that atonement and consequent salvation are procured through observance of the Law; he thus had to disown the Law. For, as he correctly remarked, if righteousness came by the Law, then Christ is dead in vain (Galatians ii. 21).[19]

However this may be, Paul in his polemic is guilty of deliberate perversion of the significance of the Law. In the conception of Judaism the Law, far from being an instrument of sin, has been given as a means of conquering sin; or, as the Talmudic Sages express it, ' as an antidote to the Evil Urge.'[20] Nor was the Torah given as a mark of divine wrath. On the contrary, it was vouchsafed to Israel as a token of divine love, designed to train them in moral holiness, in order to make them all the more worthy in the eyes of the Holy One, Blessed be He. ' The Holy One, Blessed be He, was pleased to declare Israel righteous, He therefore gave them the Torah to study and many commandments to do, as it is said, " It pleased God, in order to justify him [Israel], to magnify the Torah and make it glorious " ' (Isaiah xlii. 21).[21] These words of Rabbi Hananiah ben Akashia, a Jewish teacher of the first century and probably a contemporary of Paul, were specifically directed against the perverted view of Paul. This is clear from the phrases, ' to declare righteous ', and ' to justify Israel ', the very phrases which Paul uses in describing the effects of faith in Jesus.[22] Not by faith in a sacrificed god is righteousness and justification secured, but by means of the Torah, the Law and its precepts.[23] And it is also in protest against the Pauline views that the words of Rabbi Joshua ben Levi (first half of the third century) were uttered, ' Woe unto the human creatures for the contempt of the Torah ', with the reflection that follows: ' None is free but he who occupies himself with the Torah.'[24] Paul and his followers after him may well have regarded the Torah as a sinister force of darkness and of slavery in contradistinction to the freedom under Christ, but to the Jew perfect freedom from all subversive trends and anti-moral inclinations is to be found only in the Torah.

The attack against the Law, begun with Christianity, has assumed a new form in modern times. It has become fashionable in certain quarters to look upon the ceremonial laws as mere empty formalism, of a barren and unprofitable character, and what is more, as subversive of the true religious spirit. In support of this view, appeal is made to the Prophets. Amos, for instance, declared, in the name of God, ' I hate, I despise your feasts, and I will take no delight in your solemn assemblies. . . Take thou away from me the noise of thy songs, and let me not hear the melody of thy psalteries ' (Amos v. 21-23). Nor was Isaiah less emphatic, when he exclaimed, 'For what purpose is the multitude of your sacrifices unto Me ? saith the Lord ' (Isaiah i. 11). And thus there has been evolved a theory of antagonism between prophet and priest justifying the rejection of the ceremonials of Israel, both in their positive and negative aspects. The prophets, it is contended, as exponents of an exalted religion, were animated by a deep contempt for the externalities of religion; and, being chiefly concerned with inward reality, character and disposition, they strenuously opposed the lower religion of priestliness with its insistence on ritual and ceremony.

The critical view, so sedulously fostered by modern theologians—Jewish and non-Jewish—ignores the fact that the prophets denounced not only sacrifices but also Sabbath and Temple attendance and prayers. This shows unmistakably their real attitude. We know of course Isaiah's scathing rebuke, ' Your new moons and your appointed feasts my soul hateth; they are a cumbrance unto me; I am weary to bear them. And when ye spread forth your hands, I will hide mine eyes from you; yea, when ye make many prayers, I will not hear; your hands are full of blood ' (Isaiah i. 14-15). And yet no one will maintain on that score that the Prophet aspired to abolish the Sabbath day, or advocated the discontinuance of prayers and public worship. To single out, therefore, the ceremonial laws for condemnation from other devotional practices still honoured in their observance by all religious people, is a mark of inconsistency, or of deficiency in the true critical faculty.

The fact is that, fundamentally, there is no quarrel

between prophet and priest, nor did any conflict of any sort ever exist. As servants of God, they both cherished common ideals. The task of the prophet was to enunciate moral and religious principles; the priest had charge of the ceremonial of devotion and worship. They thus both complemented each other. The prophet did much to deepen the ideas which the ritual conveyed; and the priest helped to intensify the people's religious consciousness. The prophet did not exalt the ethical at the expense of the ritual, nor did the priest exalt external observances at the expense of moral values. It was the divorcement of external observance from inner piety and moral integrity that aroused the prophets' scathing rebuke and indignation. With their passion for reality they insisted that devotional expression must be accompanied by inward sincerity and righteousness of life. Nor did the good and genuine priest—for there were false priests as there were false prophets—ever hold that one could shelter himself behind the carcass of a sacrifice from the judgment of heaven upon his moral turpitude and waywardness of conduct. To imagine priest and prophet continually at loggerheads, each one fighting for the presentation of his own exclusive religious outlook, is to betray a misunderstanding of the spirit that animated them both, and of the all-directive energy that moved them in their moral and spiritual strivings, and that has worked wonders in men and women of all ages, including our own.[25]

But there is another objection to meet. Granted it might be argued that the ceremonial laws possess the moral regenerative powers claimed on their behalf, does not, nevertheless, the careless and thoughtless manner in which they are generally performed deprive them of all merit and worth ? To argue thus is to overlook an important psychological law in virtue of which bodily conditions and movements powerfully affect the mind. As Professor Pratt in *The Religious Consciousness* rightly remaks, ' A process once perceived and attended to tends to be set up or imitated in the muscles of the percipient. . . . And so close is the relation between reaction and feeling, between bodily expression and inner state, that he who imitates another's act, posture or expression is likely to share, at least incipiently, in the mental attitude thus expressed.'[26] This tendency has already been recognised by the Talmudic Sages in the well-known dictum, ' Through work misapplied in purpose, the purpose is eventually achieved '[27]; and in the statement to the effect that the devotional attitude is non-indispensable in religious exercises.[28] While of course it is desirable—nay, important—that the conscious attention to the motive should be present while the religious act is being performed, the value of the mere mechanical performance should not be underrated. However loosely and perfunctorily one may address himself to the fulfilment of a ritual, the supreme thought of ' One above ' cannot be absent from his mind ; and the psychological effect of that thought multiplied and intensified by the daily fulfilment of the multifarious rites required in the life of the Jew can hardly be exaggerated. Such are the high fruits of religious practices which the average nonobservant Jew has no opportunity of enjoying. And as long as the Jews cling fast to their ceremonials, even if it be a mere matter of habit or convention, the destiny of our people in the world of morality and pure religion is assured, in accordance with the psychological process moulding them towards that end, as expressed in the well-known tag:

> ' Sow an action, reap a habit;
> Sow a habit, reap a character;
> Sow a character, reap a destiny.'[29]

One might be so bold as to say that morally and religiously the ceremonial precepts are more effective than mere prophetic preachments. But that is not all. The religious observances have a corporate-national significance of incalculable importance and value. The Jewish religious precepts have proved throughout the ages up to the present day the greatest preservative force of the Jewish religion and the Jewish people. For thousands of years they have served as a visible unifying bond, welding the Jews throughout the world into one community by means of common experiences, interests and ideals. The religious precepts were the links which prevented a break in the endless succession of generations. Thanks to them, the Jewish people is the only one which, in the four thousand years of its history, has never had to begin afresh. The unvarying character of the religious precepts, the undeviating form of the ritual observed and celebrated, down all the ages and all over the globe, by Jews of different shades of thought, loyalties and philosophies, constitute the outward evidence of a continuity of spirit unexampled in history. On the soil of this continuity the efforts of generations had time to come to fruition.

While thus connecting the present with the past, the observance of religious precepts affords the guarantee for the preservation of this continuity in the future.

It is therefore easy to understand why Judaism jealously mounts guard on the adherence to its religious precepts. There is, as we have seen, nothing exclusive in their aim and still less can they be given an aggressive character. They are, on the contrary, of a defensive nature. As history and experience have shown, wherever and whenever Jewish life has throbbed with ritual and ceremonial, there Judaism thrived and flourished, prosperity and adversity alike failing to overwhelm it. But as soon as these were discarded from the equipment of religious life, there followed disintegration and decay; categorical imperatives, ideals of universalism and social justice, proving no more powerful to stop the sweeping process of dissolution than Mrs. Partington's broom to stem the onrush of the waves.

The religious precepts served well in the past in safeguarding the Jewish people from being submerged, notwithstanding the successive storms that over-whelmed mankind. We see there is no dogmatism in the Jewish insistence on the ceremonial Law. The aim of Messianism itself is, in Jewish interpretation, to make precepts obsolete.[30] But they are not yet obsolete, because, alas, we are very far yet from the Messianic era. ' It is sheer self-deception to imagine that in our times of general disintegration and decay, the world has risen morally to that height that it can dispense with the spiritual aid which the practical observances provide.'[31] These words, written by Rabbi

298

Kook as far back as 1908, apply with even greater force to our own times, when the absence of any moral progress corresponding with the immense progress made in the discovery of natural processes is bringing mankind within sight of complete breakdown. Indeed, the terrific power of destruction now at the command of man leads a modern writer, Lewis Mumford, in his work *Programme for Survival*, to advocate a moral tightening by the introduction of all kinds of inhibitions, abstentions and renunciations, in order to train us in the habit of that vital self-restraint so essential to survival.[32]   But surely no humanly contrived restrictions and restraints can take the place of those divinely ordained in the Torah.[33]   There is therefore no reason for the Jews to alter their attitude towards these means which preserved Jewish continuity in the past, and which can prove an incalculably steadying factor in the preservation of human society.

The religious precepts thus fulfil a threefold function —religious-individual; corporate-national; ethical-universal.   These three functions are not unconnected; they are all intertwined, forming a complete unity. By offering the individual a foothold on which to stand and train himself for a religious, righteous and holy life, they make him a worthy member of his people, kept together as it is by the cement of the ceremonial law.   The heritage of Israel thus remains preserved, and its treasures contribute to the moral-ethical enrichment, and ultimate redemption, of the whole of humanity.

But for the universal redemption of humanity, the continuity of the united spiritual power of the Jewish people is necessary. The ancient Jewish State fell, but the Jewish people had to remain. It was otherwise with Greece. With the State disappeared the people. Their disappearance, however, did not involve the loss of the Greek spirit, which remained alive and continued fruitful in literary and artistic works, begetting new life in the culture of other peoples. The spirit of Israel needed other conditions for its expansion. While the Greek spirit could work its way through the different nations and cultures without opposition, the spirit of Israel, with its ideals of righteousness, required a continuous, forward-moving, dynamic force to over-come the resistance it would encounter in its course, and along its path of development. Such a force only that people could supply from whose loins the prophets have issued.

This universal rôle assigned to Israel finds striking expression in the famous fifty-third chapter of Isaiah. To this chapter the preceding one is an introduction, of which the first and tenth verses give the keynote.

' Arise, awake, put on thy garments, O Zion,
　　Put on thy beautiful garments, O Jerusalem, the holy city . . .
　　And all the ends of the earth shall see the salvation of the Lord.'

In the midst of this scene of universal salvation stands the Suffering Servant—Israel, the cynosure of the eyes of all the redeemed nations.[34] The nations at long last recognise their errors in judging him. Hitherto they had thought that he had suffered because God had forsaken him for his sins. Now they come to realise that he had all along been innocent, and had done no violence; that all his sorrows and sufferings were marks of their own wickedness and misdeeds. It was *they* who had sinned in crushing him; it was *they* who had committed violence in oppressing the innocent Servant of the Lord.

> ' Surely, our diseases did he bear and our pains did
>   he carry,
> Whereas we did esteem him stricken, smitten of
>   God and afflicted.
> But he was wounded because of our transgressions,
> He was crushed because of our iniquities.'

The Suffering Servant is the symbol of suffering mankind. The suffering of the Jewish people down all the ages is no mark of their guilt, but symptomatic of the moral structure of the outside world. Their miseries throw a grave reproach on other peoples. And so every injustice in history is an accusation against a civilisation that has not learnt its elementary duties towards the weak and helpless.

But if there were no healing power in humanity, life would end in complete tragedy. This would mean the end of Creation. Against such a despairing final view of human life, the prophet proclaims the redemptive quality in suffering. Out of the conflict of good and evil there comes not merely a restoration of harmony, but something even better than there was before—the salvation of the whole human race.

Israel is thus the Suffering Servant, whose world-historical mission is to share, by righteousness in knowledge and action, in the divine training and healing of the human race. His suffering is that of all who are willing to suffer for a great cause; the suffering of the scientist in his dangerous battle with disease, and of the heroic reformer in his struggle for social purity. In its nature it is therefore spiritual, dynamic, opposing evil with good. In suffering from the injustice of the nations, Israel has typified all those who suffer from injustice and cruelty; and by his endurance in faith and in obedience to the Torah, Israel is contributing to the spiritualisation of the social order, and to the final redemption of the whole of humanity.[35]

The appearance of this jubilant thought of world-redemption in Israel is indeed one of the marvels of the human spirit. How incomprehensible must appear the emergence of this idea inside a national conscious-ness which thought and felt that the choosing of Israel was an exclusive choice! It did arise; and the harmo-nisation of nationalism and world outlook thus became one of the basic problems of prophecy.

Among the prophets who contributed greatly to this harmonisation was Jeremiah. The universality of religion is one of the sublime apprehensions of the prophets, on which Jeremiah laid special emphasis in the grand messages he gave to the world. Jeremiah believed in the conversion of all peoples to the worship of the one and only true God, a self-conversion to be effected through the knowledge of the worthlessness of their idols. ' O Lord . . . unto Thee nations shall come from the ends of the earth, and shall say, Our fathers have inherited nought but lies, even vanity and things wherein there is no profit ' (Jeremiah xvii. 19). At the same time, he insisted that Israel would not lose its independent unity. For him it was ever the historic Israel which will build anew the chosen state for the extension of the true divine worship among all the peoples of the earth. ' Return, O backsliding children, saith the Lord, for I am a Lord unto you, and I will take you, one of a city and two of a family and will bring you to Zion, and I will give you shepherds according to my heart, who shall feed you with knowledge and understanding. . . At that time they shall call Jerusalem the throne of the Lord, and all the nations shall be gathered unto it, to the name of the Lord, to Jerusalem, neither shall they walk any more after the stubbornness of their evil heart ' (Jeremiah iii. 14-17). Here we see the interpenetration of the two ideas. The nations, while retaining each one its own separate individuality, are led by Israel in a universal Reconciliation to God.

A key to this universal Reconciliation is the knowledge of the Lord. The knowledge of the Lord draws its universal significance from the fact that it is not theoretical. It refers neither to God's existence nor to His laws. Jeremiah denounced those that handle the Torah, who certainly were not ignorant of God's existence or of His Laws, because they knew not God (ii. 8). The knowledge of God spoken of is not an *acquisition of new* facts, but an *impression* of *old* facts— an impression which masters man's thoughts, heart, mind and feelings, making him willing and disposed to do and obey the divine demands made upon him. It is a knowledge which by the awareness and the experiencing of the divine presence enables man to be possessed of a real understanding, and a spiritual insight

into the character of God and His delight in the workings of justice, righteousness and tender love (Jeremiah
ix. 23). Such a knowledge, unlike theoretical knowledge, is possible for all men. Given the experience,
it can go out to all peoples of every class and
distinction.

Despite the sufferings unparalleled and trials untold
which Israel has been called upon to endure throughout
the centuries, it never lost sight of the great world-
mission, assigned to it from the beginning of its history.
This is the faith that has given the Jewish people the
courage to face and battle with the storms and tribu-
lations of centuries, and that has moulded their attitude
towards the perilous circumstances that beset their
existence. In all the bitter struggles they had to pass
through they discerned but the labour and pain—the
Heble Mashiah (' Messianic Pangs ')[36]—which, as
already envisaged by the Talmudic Sages, are inseparable from the process working towards the fulfilment
of Israel's messianic hopes of world-redemption, and
the consummation of the divine purpose among the
sons of men.

Nor has the Jewish hope of millennia been left entirely
unvindicated. The rise of the Jewish State, after the
submergence of two thousand years, is one of the
greatest miracles of the ages. Israel is once more to-day
an incontestable reality; and the Jewish State a living
fact. The astonishing successes that have crowned
Israel's struggles for national independence, and the
amazing sequence of events that has led to this consummation, will remain, to the unbiased historian,
one of the inexplicable episodes in the annals of man-

kind. Whilst acknowledging the selfless devotion and heroic sacrifices of those men and women who were responsible for these unprecedented and unparalleled achievements, those who see into the heart of things cannot but perceive in this miraculous transformation of the Jewish scene the hand of God stretched out to rehabilitate His dispersed people in their ancestral homeland, in fulfilment of His purpose. In the light of these happenings, Jewish sufferings, the expulsions from Spain, the Inquisitions, the Chmelnizki massacres, the Hitler ' liquidations ', all gain a new significance. They all form episodes in a divine drama which has been unfolding itself through history in the fulfilment of the purpose of God for His People and humanity. In the words of Mr. Churchill at a Parliamentary debate on Palestine, in 1949, ' The coming into being of a Jewish State in Palestine is an event in world history, to be viewed in the perspective, not of a generation or a century, but in the perspective of one thousand, two thousand, or even three thousand years. That is a standard of temporal values or time-values which seems very much out of accord with the perpetual click-clack of rapidly changing moods and of the age in which we live. This is an event in world history.'[37] True, the end of the story is not yet. The purpose for which the Jewish people have, for millennia, struggled and suffered, lived and died, is not something already accomplished; and its fulfilment, inasmuch as it is to be worked out through the medium of conflicting wills and emotions of sinful men, may be subject to setbacks and delay; but the whole pattern of divine purpose, as it reveals itself in the context of history, and especially in the history of the Jewish people, is beginning more and more to assume definite shape; and the goal and direction towards which things are tending and moving, are gradually becoming clearer to the discerning eye. Such is the vision which Jewish faith inspires. Given this vision, the Jewish people will move forward with the growing conviction that they have been called upon to play a unique part in the building of a new civilisation, which is destined to redress and finally transform the present materialistic civilisation, with its hates and strifes, wars and rancours, and in the establishment of a new social order of free men and women, liberated in body, mind and spirit, and knit together in living co-operation under God, for the advancement and self-realisation of all peoples of the earth.

NOTES

[1] Quoted by John E. McFadyen in *Hibbert Journal*, XXI (4), 1923, p. 753.

[2] See *supra*, pp. 124f. Cf. also Norman H. Snaith, *The Distinctive Ideas of the Old Testament* (1944), p. 141: ' God has always done that which is required by any ordinary, proper and reasonable basis for all sons of men, but He has done more than was required on behalf of Israel. If He had not done this, then such a small nation as Israel would never have survived all the vicissitudes of centuries.'

[3] See I. Epstein, *Bible Teachings in our Times* (1944), pp. 3-4.

[4] See *supra*, p. 244.

[5] G. F. Moore, *Judaism* I, p. 480, paraphrases this verse, ' Everything that man devises in his mind is evil, from his youth on.' There is thus no notion of original sin, which in fact is totally alien to the Old Testament teaching. See *supra*, p. 228, n. 23.

[6] For the following pages, see I. Epstein, *Jewish Way of Life*, pp. 141ff.

[7] B.T. Taanit 7a.

[8] See C. S. Lewis, *Miracles* (1947), p. 141. The idea of selectiveness in Nature and in history is one of the dominant themes in Judah Halevi's *Kuzari*.

[9] See *supra*, p. 162, n. 22.

[10] See *supra*, p. 30. John Macmurray, *op. cit.*, points out with deep insight that the real moral problem is not so much the discovery of the good, as the discovery that it is the good that the self really wants. It is this which distinguishes the religious from the non-religious consciousness. 'For the religious consciousness, the problem that arises is not why do men not do what they ought to do, but why do men not do what they want to do ? Why do we persist in refusing to be ourselves and fulfil our own nature even when we recognise what it is ? ' (p. 62). Cf. the Rabbinic invocation: ' O Lord of the Universe, it is revealed and known before Thee that it is our will to perform Thy will, but what prevents us ?—the leaven that is in the dough (man's evil disposition).'—B.T. Berakot 17a.

[11] W. H. Lecky, *History of European Morals* (ed. 1877), I, p. 292.

[12] On the pages which follow, see I. Epstein, *Jewish Way of Life*, pp. 152ff., and *Judaism of Tradition*, pp. 81ff.

[13] ' That the physical organism, as material, is evil *per se*, sense the origin of error, the appetites and passions the source of moral evil—these ideas, for which prevalent philosophies had gained wide currency in the Hellenistic world, have no counterpart in Palestine Judaism.'—G. F. Moore, *op. cit.*, I, p. 485.

[13a] See *The Times*, December 24th, 1952, First Leader, ' Christian Duty ', reporting the Archbishop Temple as having said that ' in discharging his duties in the world a Christian cannot consciously remember God for most of the day. The distinctive quality of his service and, therefore, the influence of Christianity on the world will be determined by the comparatively rare moments in which Christian discipline obliges him to remember God.'

[14] *Ethics of the Fathers*, II, 17; see also Maimonides, *Eight Chapters*, V: ' If you will examine these brief words of the rabbis, you will find that they convey more than is contained in many voluminous works.' כשאתה תבחן קוצר המלות איך ספרו זה הענין הגדול והעצום כלו אשר חברו חבורים ולא השלימוה תדע שנאמר בכח אלהי בלא ספק והוא אמרם בצואותיהם. וכל מעשיך יהיו לשם שמים. Particularly noteworthy is Macmurray's statement that whereas other peoples have a religion, ' the Jews are the only people who were and are religious ' (p. 19), ' in that they alone conceived religion not as ' a particular sphere of human activity, but as the synthesis of all ' (p. 28, and see *supra* 73.) Macmurray makes no attempt to account for this peculiarity of what he designates as the ' Hebrew consciousness,' but it is undoubtedly the product of the Torah, with its religious observances. But, however that may be, this appreciation of the Hebrew consciousness lies behind the explanation given by Maimonides for the validity ascribed by Jewish law to a good act performed under duress, it being assumed that the doing of good corresponds to the Jew's real nature, which must assert itself once that which is opposed or contrary to it is suppressed or eliminated. To quote the words of Maimonides: ' We say [that an act was done under duress] only in the case where a man was forced or compelled to perform something not prescribed by the Torah, as for example, where he was beaten until he agreed to sell or make a gift; but where he was induced by his evil inclination to disregard a positive command or to commit a transgression, and he was beaten until he performed the deed he was obliged to perform, or abstained from the deed forbidden to him, he cannot be considered to have acted under duress; quite the reverse, it was he who had forced himself at first into an evil state of mind ' (*Yad, Gerushin* II, 19): אין אומרים אנום אלא למי שנלחץ ונדחק לעשות דבר שאינו מחויב בו מן התורה, כגון מי שהוכה עד שמכר או עד שנתן אבל מי שתקפו יצרו הרע לבטל מצוה או לעשות עברה והוכה עד שעשה דבר שחייב לעשותו או עד שנתרחק מדבר האסור לעשותו אין זה אנוס ממנו אלא הוא אנס עצמו בדעתו הרעה.

[15] Cf. Maimonides, *Guide*, III, 52 (see *supra*, p. 286). See also J. Albo, *Ikkarim* III, 31: ' It is very difficult for man to attain the required degree of fear, love and service [of God] with all heart and

soul. Hence God made it easier for man. He commanded him instead to observe merely His statutes and commandments and thereby attain that disposition which he would get from service with all heart and soul.' The positive commandments are generally regarded as conducive to the love of God, and the negative commandments to the fear of God. See Nahmanides, *Commentary on the Pentateuch*, Exodus xx. 8; also Yalkut Shimeoni, Deuteronomy, 837, and Tanna de-be Eliyyahu xxxi; cf. also J.T. Berakot 9, 5: ' Act out of love, so that should you come to hate, know that you are a lover, and no lover hates. Act out of fear, so that should you come to rebel know that you are a fearer, and no fearer rebels.'

עשה מאהבה, שאם באת לשנוא דע כי אתה אוהב, ואין אוהב שונא, עשה
מיראה שאם באת לבעוט דע שאת ירא, ואי ירא מבעט.

16 See Obadiah Sforno (1475-1550) on Exodus xix. 5-6. ' Then shall ye be Mine own treasure from among all peoples: Although the whole human race is precious unto Me more than any other existing inferior beings . . . as those of blessed memory have said: " Beloved is man, for he was created in the image (of God)," nevertheless, you shall be Mine own treasure from among them all; for all the earth is mine: and the difference between you is only one of degree (lit. a little more or a little less): for indeed all the earth is Mine, and the pious among the nations of the world are undoubtedly precious unto Me. And ye shall be unto Me a kingdom of priests: [that is to say,] Ye will be Mine own treasure from among them all, in that you shall be a kingdom of priests, charged with the task to instruct and teach the whole of mankind, in order that they may call upon the name of God and serve Him with one consent . . .'

17 The principal meaning of the term ' Torah ' is ' direction ', and it is to be understood as God's instruction in His way, and therefore not as a separate *objectivum*, as the Greek mistranslation ' *nomos* ' implies: ' Without the change of meaning in the Greek, objective sense, the Pauline dualism of law and faith, life from works and life from grace, would miss its most important conceptual presupposition.'—M. Buber, *Two Types of Faith* (1951), p. 57.

18 See Trude Weiss-Rosmarin, *Judaism and Christianity* (1943), pp. 81ff.

309

W

THE FAITH OF JUDAISM

[19] On the attitude of Paul to the Law and the inconsistencies it presents, see W. D. Davies, *Paul and Rabbinic Judaism* (1948), pp. 69ff. See also *supra*, p. 168, n. 56.

[20] בראתי יצר הרע בראתי תורה תבלין, B.T. Baba Bathra 16a, and Kiddushin 30b, and cf. Sifre on Deuteronomy xi. 18. See also Midrash Proverbs xxiv. 31: ' All the time that the words of the Torah find entrance into the chambers of the heart, the words of the Torah can rest there and the evil urge cannot rule over them, and no man can expel them. It is like a king who went into a steppe, and found dining halls and large chambers and went and dwelt in them; so it is with the evil urge, if it does not find the words of the Torah ruling in the heart, you cannot expel it from the heart.'

כל הזמן שדברי תורה נכנסין ומוצאין חדרי לב פנויין הן נכנסין ושרויין בתוכו: ואין יצר הרע שולט בהן ואין אדם יכול להוציאם מתוכו. משל למלך בשר ודם שהיה מהלך במדבר ומצא שם טרקלין וחדרים גדולים. נכנס ושורה בתוכן, כך יצר הרע אם אין מוצא דברי תורה שולט ביניהן ואין אתה יכול להוציאו מתוכו. See also Midrash Deuteronomy Rabbah, viii, 2.

' You might perhaps say that I gave you the Torah to your hurt; [know that] I have given it to you only for your benefit. תאמרו שמא לרעתכם נתתי לכם את התורה, לא נתתי אותה לכם אלא לטובתכם.

[21] Mishnah Makkot, III, 5. The word צדקו, usually rendered ' for his righteousness' sake ', is interpreted to mean ' to make him (Israel) righteous ', to justify him. See W. Bacher, *Agada der Tannaiten* (1884) II, p. 376. Cf. also Mechilta on Exodus xxii. 30: ' Whenever God gives Israel a new law He increases Israel's holiness.' כשהקב״ה מחדש מצוה על ישראל הוא מוסיף להם קדושה See also Maimonides, *Sefer ha-Mitzwot*, *Shoresh* IV, and *Yad*, *Hilekot Shabbat*, II, 3: ' The laws of the Torah are not given for vengeance in the world, but for mercy, tender love and peace in the world. אין משפטי התורה נקמה בעולם, אלא רחמים, וחסד ושלום בעולם.

[22] In Greek, *dikaioun*, corresponds to the Hebrew *tsaddek*, which in turn equals the Mishnaic *zakkeh*, to declare righteous, to justify, see N. H. Snaith, *Distinctive Ideas of the Old Testament* (1944), p. 161ff.

[23] Cf. Joseph Albo, *Ikkarim*, I, 23, and III, 29.

[24] *Ethics of the Fathers*, VI, 2.

310

[25] See I. Epstein, *Judaism of Tradition*, pp. 91-7. Another important factor which, surprisingly enough, has been overlooked by all those who deal with the attitude of the prophets to the sacrifices is the distinction between voluntary and obligatory sacrifices. Yet it is fundamental and must be taken into consideration before we can speak of an antagonism of the prophets to the sacrificial cult. An examination of the prophets' utterances cited by the critical school in support of their views on the problem, i.e. I Samuel xv. 22; Hosea vi, 6: Amos v. 21ff.; Isaiah i. 11ff; Micah vi. 6ff.; Jeremiah vii. 21ff., shows that they were all concerned with voluntary sacrifices. Unlimited in number and unattended by the confession and repentance which are inseparable from obligatory sacrifices, such as expiatory offerings, voluntary sacrifices were liable to become a source of injury to righteous life, and it was against the abuse of this type of sacrifice that the prophets launched their scathing denunciations. Not so with obligatory sacrifices. Strictly limited in number and in point of time and circumstances, and offered as atonement for sins committed *unwittingly*, they could serve only to keep alive in the people the sense of sin, and to this extent prove of inestimable value as aids to righteous living. See I. Epstein, *Introduction to Seder Kodashim*, in the *Soncino Edition of the Talmud* (1948), pp. xxiiiff., where this distinction is applied in explanation of the attitude of Maimonides to sacrifices, and in harmonizing the apparently conflicting views expressed by him on the subject. The literature on the problem of the attitude of the prophets to sacrifices is too extensive to be listed. Among the most recent works, however, might be mentioned H. H. Rowley, *The Rediscovery of the Old Testament* (1946) and *The Meaning of Sacrifice in the Old Testament* in *Bulletin of the John Rylands Library* (1950), Vol. XXX, No. 1, pp. 74-110; and to go back earlier, J. Hoschander, *The Priests and Prophets* (1938); see also I. Epstein, *Bible Teachings in our Time* (1944), pp. 16ff.

[26] J. B. Pratt, *The Religious Consciousness* (1920), p. 282.

[27] B.T. Pesahim 50b: מתוך שלא לשמה בא לשמה

[28] מצות אין צריכות כוונה   See e.g. B.T. Rosh Hashanah 28a.

[29] Cf. L. P. Jacks, *The Living Universe* (1923), pp. 22-3. ' There

is a language of action as well as of words; and of the two the language of action is the more telling, the more intelligible, the more unmistakable, and in the deepest sense the more eloquent. Some of the profoundest truths ever recorded to mankind have been conveyed through the language of action.' Similarly A. C. Welch, *Prophet and Priest in Old Israel* (1936), pp. 30-40: A professor . . . enormously overestimates the values of ideas expressed in words. . . . But the minister of a congregation soon discovers that religion, when it passes into the lives of men, is expressed not in men's words, but in the things they do day by day in consequence of their faith. . . . Religion consists in what men can do because of what they believe, and their acts are as vital as their creeds. . . . The ideas men hold of their god, of their relation to him, of the right way to approach him, of the means to maintain this relation while it exists, of the means to restore it should it have been broken, must translate themselves into acts of worship, which may take the form of words of adoration or of petition to their god, or which may appear as sacrificial rituals . . .' This is particularly true of children's education. If the religious teachings are to have lasting effect, the suggestion they convey must be transformed into action and experience of their own, as it is easier for children to imitate suggestive acts than suggestions of a mere abstract kind. See further, I. Epstein, *The Jewish Way of Life* (1946), pp. 156-7.

[30] B.T. Niddah 61b: מצוות בטלות לעתיד לבא See Joseph Albo, *Ikkarim*, III, 15.

[31] A. I. Kook, *Iggeroth Rayah* (1943), p. 173.

[32] Lewis Mumford, *Programme for Survival* (1946), pp. 61: ' Morality, in the elementary form of accepted inhibitions, is the first step toward the conscious control of the powers man now commands; without this lowest form of morality, ingrained in habit, no higher form can be practised. What Irving Babitt called the inner check—the vital restraint—is essential to our survival. Promptly we must reverse Blake's dictum—we must bless braces and damn relaxes.'

[33] The natural tendency of all artificially introduced restraints is to degenerate into mere phobias, losing thereby all their educative

effect. This is, however, not the case with the precepts of the Torah,
the value of which is derived not so much from their content, as
from the fact that they are grounded in the will of God, and adhered
to in obedience to His will. This is the reason underlying the
Rabbinical exhortation relating to the Dietary Laws: ' Let not a
man say, I do not like the flesh of the swine. On the contrary, he
should say, I like it, but what shall I do seeing that the Torah
has forbidden it to me.' (Sifra on Leviticus xx. 26 and cf. Maimonides, *Eight Chapters*, VI). See I. Epstein, *The Jewish Way of Life*,
pp. 162-3, and *Maimonides' Conception of the Law*, in *Maimonides
VIII Centenary Volume* (ed. I. Epstein), p. 73.

[34] For an exhaustive survey of the explanations given, during the
last two thousand years, of the ' Suffering Servant,' see Christopher
R. North, *The Suffering Servant in Deutero-Isaiah: a Historical and
Critical Study* (1948). For the Jewish interpretations, see A.
Neubauer and S. R. Driver, *The Fifty-Third Chapter of Isaiah
according to Jewish Interpreters*, 2 vols. (Texts and Translations).
(1876-7).

[35] Cf. *Kuzari*, II, 44: ' The trials which meet us serve to render
perfect our piety, to cleanse us, and to remove all taint from us, and
by our cleansing and perfection the " Divine Thing " will attach
itself to the world.' והצרות המוצאות אותנו סבות לתקנת תורתינו, ובור
הבר ממנו, ויציאת הסיגים מתוכנו, ובבוררנו ותקוננו ידבק העניין האלהי בעולם.
On the ' Divine Thing ', see *supra*, p. 140.

[36] On the *heble mashiah*, see B.T. Pesahim 118a, Sanhedrin 98b.
The origin of the notion is traceable to Micah, v. 1 and Isaiah xxvi.
17-19.

[37] See *The Times*, January 26th, 1949.

[See Excursus II, pp. 368-378.]

CHAPTER XV

THE KINGDOM OF GOD

DIVINE purpose is associated with the coming Kingdom of God. This is the Kingdom known, in Judaic sources, as the Kingdom of the Almighty —*Malkut Shaddai*, or the Kingdom of Heaven— *Malkut Shamayim*,[1] which has inspired some of the most impassioned and exquisite strains of the Hebrew prophets and psalmists, and with which have been intertwined the highest hopes that could be conceived for humanity. It is the Kingdom which has received its classical representation in the celebrated words: ' And the Lord shall be King over the whole earth; in that day shall the Lord be One, and His Name One ' (Zechariah xiv. 9).[2] The rule of the One and Only God, which is now owned and accepted only by isolated individuals, will then be universally acknowledged and made manifest, all men and all peoples uniting in His worship and obedient service. The blessedness of this coming Kingdom will be reflected in the world of Nature, as in human society. All that is sorrowful, unlovely and sinful will pass away, God will ' wipe away tears from all faces ' (Isaiah xxv. 8), and man will enter upon a new life in a world renovated and transformed.

This consummation is not relegated to the celestial stage of another existence. The hope of the Kingdom of God, in Jewish thought, has nothing in common with the expectations of the end of all earthly things in which all human problems will find a solution by

314

'pulling out' and retreating into another world, unconnected with the struggles, problems, hopes and aspirations of the present. This unreal conception has its source in pessimism, as against Jewish optimism. It consequently despairs of the possibilities of human evolution within the historical and social framework. It prefers to unmake Creation, and to withdraw with pessimism into a heaven which, in Jewish thought, does not exist without the earth. This is not the Kingdom of Jewish teaching. The Kingdom of God, as Judaism sees it, as Judaism originally created it, is full of life, of earthly life. It is a Kingdom which is to be built *here* on earth, under divine guidance, by the hands of man, and realised as the result of human struggles and divine discipline, which constitute the very warp and woof of the process of human history.

How marvellous is the very appearance of the Jewish conception of the Kingdom of God! No folk and no mind on earth outside Israel thought of a future of the human race within its natural and historical development. Analogies can be found, but they are foreign to the heart of these thoughts.[3] In primitive ages of awakening cultures there exists the notion of the destruction of the world—a destruction which, indeed, contains in itself the idea of world-renewal. The Hebrew prophets took over this idea, which among the peoples was associated with the 'Day of the Lord.' Some of the Prophets revel in pictures of storm, earthquake, fire, ruin, valleys splintering and mountains crumbling, pests, famine and war. Such are the judgments of God that fall upon the peoples of the earth, and no less over Israel. Out of this idea, however,

comes a higher idea—the idea of the purification and
of the guidance and moral training of the world by
God, a guidance that involves step-by-step development. Thus the 'Day of the Lord' becomes the
symbol of the Kingdom of God, entailing a regeneration
of the earth and of the peoples that dwell therein.[4] In
Joel there is the promise of the outpouring of the spirit
of the Lord on all flesh, without excepting the man-
servant and the maid-servant. The prophets of Israel
thus become the originators of the conception of a
divine purpose, moving towards fulfilment in the
transcendental reality of an earthly future.[5]

This conception of the transcendence of the earthly
future of the human race within its natural and historical development distinguishes Prophetism from
Apocalypse, that body of literature dealing with
eschatology—the doctrine of the last things—which
made its appearance in Judaism during the centuries
immediately preceding and following the rise of
Christianity. The apocalyptic writers shared with the
prophets the zeal to vindicate the righteousness of God,
despite the experiences of daily life to the contrary.
Like the prophets they had a vision of a blessed future
which would solve all the perplexities which undeserved suffering created in the mind of the faithful.
But with all this community of outlook, Prophetism
and Apocalypse conceived in fundamentally different
ways the process whereby this future was to be brought
about. The prophets laid emphasis on the present life.
They saw in the present divine forces at work for the
training of humanity in righteousness, and conceived
the future not as something unconnected with the

present, but as an organic result thereof, under divine
guidance, and as the inevitable outcome of a certain
course of human conduct. To them this world was
God's, chosen by Him to be the scene of the divine
order wherein the goodness and truth of God would
yet be vindicated, and in the realisation of which it was
man's task to co-operate. Believing in the inherent
goodness of man and in the regenerative powers inherent in the worst of sinners, they called for repentance and righteousness as the human contribution.
The Apocalyptic writers, on the other hand, despaired
of this world and of human nature. They saw
around them only misery and suffering, and could not
believe in the establishment of a divine order in any
world organically connected with the present. They
consequently directed their hopes to a future on the
celestial stage, in essential opposition to the present—
a future in which a new world will be brought into
existence, catastrophically, by divine intervention, to
take the place of the old. To this eschatological future
man can do nothing to contribute. No action of his
can serve either to speed it on or retard it. Its rise has
been predetermined from the beginning in the coun-
sels of God, and the faithful are but bidden to have
patience and trustingly await the miraculous deliverance and the reward which is to be theirs.

Judaism, with its doctrine of the inherent goodness
of man, dowering him with the moral and spiritual
energies to overcome all evil and sin, and fit himself to
become increasingly in likeness to God by the know
ledge of Him, in the pursuit of righteousness and
justice, could not accord official recognition to the

gloomy and pessimistic outlook of the Apocalyptists; and whatever Apocalyptic elements and ideas have gained a foot-hold in Judaism, these have not been able to affect the central core of Jewish teaching, which assigns to human effort a vital rôle in the establishment of the coming Kingdom.

Human endeavour as an indispensable factor in the building of the Kingdom is conceived in terms of righteousness, a conception which links the Kingdom of God with the Messianic Kingdom—*Malkut Mashiach*—which is to form its prelude.[6] This Kingdom, as depicted by the Prophets, and their spiritual successors, the Rabbis of the Talmud, is to inaugurate a golden future for Israel, established in its own homeland with ' every man under his vine and under his fig-tree ', and, through a restored Israel, for all the peoples of the earth. One might indeed think that Plato, the creator of Greek idealism, looked forward to such a future in his *Republic*, but this would be only a superficial view. The mere fact that Plato makes provision for guardians, an army of professional soldiers trained in the art of war, which he regards as an indispensable feature of the growth of his ideal state,[7] shows that there is no likeness between Plato's Utopia and Israel's Messianic Kingdom. This again is characteristic of Greek thought, which had no vision for humanity as a whole. The ideal republic in Plato consists only of Greek farmers. All the rest of mankind are barbarians and do not enter the horizon of the Greeks.[8] War, therefore, can never cease, and strife must remain unending.

How vastly different is the Jewish Messianic picture !

The chief inspiring thought of Messianism in Jewish teaching is the goodness of God, which stretches itself over all men and all peoples. ' Praise ye the Lord, all ye nations, laud Him all ye peoples, for His loving-kindness is mighty over us ' (Psalm cxvii. 1-2)—is to be the grand paean in Israel's celebration of the universal Messianic fulfilment. God is to reveal His goodness for all peoples and all nations. Gone will then be the social sins that are productive of pauperism, and the political sins that result in fratricidal warfare: ' The people will learn war no more ' (Isaiah ii. 4). Gone too will then be the present state of society, in which lust, greed, violence and passion assail every righteous endeavour, giving place to a new order, which will physically be full of satisfaction because there will be no enemy to combat, no victor, no vanquished. And not in the material sphere alone was this blissful future foreseen. It is the reign of the ' Eternal, our Righteousness ' (Jeremiah xxiii. 6), which is pictured, marking for humanity the beginning of an ever-ascending spiritual regeneration and triumph. The end and aim of Messianism is to initiate for the world at large a glorious age, undimmed by any spiritual reverses or set-backs, which through righteousness in knowledge and in action shall create a new earth and a new heaven. ' They shall not hurt nor destroy in my holy mountain, for the earth shall be full of the knowledge of the Lord, as the waters cover the sea ' (Isaiah xi. 9). Nothing is further from this conception than the sensual day-dreams of a ' perfect good time ' for everybody, or the hopes of the spiritually slothful for a Utopia beyond further possibilities of perfection. Righteousness will indeed bring peace and plenty, but without taking away the need for sacrifice on behalf of ever-widening and growing ideals. Messianism thus, far from being the end, is actually the beginning of the journey, in which humanity, freed at last from the pressure of material strife and conflict, will be able to march forward to its destiny, and devote itself without the waste of its best energies to the building of the Kingdom of God on earth.[9]

Opposed to this Jewish Messianic ideal, which pictures a future of earthly bliss and felicity for all sons of man, is the attitude of Christianity. With its overemphasis on other-worldliness and life beyond the grave, Christianity is essentially a repudiation of this hope of peace among the nations, and this longing for universal terrestrial happiness, cherished by Jews.[10]

Here is not the place to enter into a theological discussion of this particular distinction between the Jewish and the Christian outlook. But one need only think of the sufferings, horrors and cruelties that still persist, almost two thousand years after the advent of the Messiah acclaimed by Christianity, to realise how fundamental is this distinction between the Jewish and Christian religious consciousness. All the same, it might be mentioned, the Church could not escape the potent influence of Judaism. This influence is perceptible alike in the domain of *thought* and in the domain of *action*. In the domain of thought, it shows itself in the attempts made of late by Christian theologians to prove that the Christian faith ' does offer a very confident hope for the future course of terrestrial history.'[11] And in the domain of action it expresses itself in the growth of the social conscience of the Church, which has been recognised as one of the most significant phenomena in the development of Christian religious feeling at the present time.[12] And that is not all. It is generally acknowledged that the passionate strivings of modern times to realise a socialist kingdom on earth, a kingdom that is reserved for no one people but for all mankind in general, derive their inspiration from this Jewish Messianic ideal, with its passionate concern for man's terrestrial happiness. All of which serves to show how Judaism, by its very existence and refusal to bow the knee to false Messianic ideologies, serves to testify to the truth which the world is gradually perceiving and endeavouring to make its own. And it is a witness which the Jewish people, in its own quiet and unobtrusive way, will continue to give to the end of days. ' He shall not cry nor lift up, nor cause his voice to be heard in the street. A bruised reed he shall not break, and the dimly burning wick shall he not quench. He shall make the right go forth according to the truth. . . . Till he hath set the right in the earth; and the isles shall wait for his teaching ' (Isaiah xlii. 2-4).

The Messianic age will be ushered in by a descendant of the Davidic Dynasty, whose triumphs in the work of peace will be on earth, rather than in heaven. But this personage is not essential to Messianism;[13] nor is he a supernatural or divine being, having a share in the forgiveness of sin; much less is he to be confused with God. Indeed, so concerned was Judaism lest such confusion should arise, that one Talmudic teacher went so far as to deny the coming of a personal Messiah, asserting that God Himself would come to redeem His people.[14] At the highest, the Messiah is but a mortal leader who will be instrumental in fully rehabilitating Israel in their ancient homeland, and, through a restored Israel, bring about a regeneration of humanity.

It therefore betrays a profound ignorance of the Jewish conception of the Messiah to maintain, as for example, Emil Brunner does, that ' Pious Jews (having rejected Jesus as the Messiah) are still waiting for the Christ who is to come; this means . . . that they are still waiting for the revelation which we Christians believe and confess to be one that has already come.'[15] Jews are not waiting, nor have they ever waited, for any Messiah in the Christian sense. All the work of fulfilment, either for the individual or for the creation as a whole, which the Christians claim for Jesus, is left by the Jews entirely to God, who alone, without the need of a Christ or mediator, can do what He thinks best for His children, and enfold them in His eternal and gracious love.

But this passionate concern for man's terrestrial and historical destiny, which is the fundamental peculiarity of the Jewish spirit, does not contradict the expectation of an immortal life which sees the fulfilment of the highest human destiny in the sublime plane of eternity. In fact, the Kingdom of God, in its Messianic setting and terrestrial fulfilment, is, in Jewish thought, but preparatory to the consummation of the Kingdom in the Eternal World-to-Come, a world which, in Rabbinic parlance ' no ear hath heard, nor eye hath seen ' (cf. Isaiah lxiv. 3).[16] It is to that unseen world of eternity that human action and the whole social-historical process are, in the Jewish view, related.

The World-to-Come, *olam-ha-ba*, has a twofold connotation, individual and universal. On the one hand, it denotes the heavenly world we each individually enter at death; on the other hand, it stands for the world in which the universality of mankind will enter upon its over-earthly destiny. The former is the sphere of judgment and reward for our individual selves; the latter is the sphere of Resurrection and Judgment for all created beings.[17] These two worlds are not distinct but represent two phases of the same process of fulfilment, the *olam-ha-ba* awaiting the individual at death having its consummation in the *olam-ha-ba* which follows the Resurrection. The relation of these two worlds to one another has been well described by Strack-Billerbeck. ' The striking phenomenon ', they write, ' that the Rabbinic teachers have used the expression *ha-olam ha-ba* to designate both the heavenly world of the souls and also the future age of consummation would have made it clear to us, as it were, that the heavenly Aeon of the Souls and the future Aeon of Consummation on earth were regarded as one and the same great ' *olam-ha-ba* '. This great *olam-ha-ba* at present had its place in heaven (1 Enoch 71, 14ff) . . . into it the souls of the righteous enter at the hour of death for a preliminary blessedness. That is their first phase in which it serves as the world of the souls until it enters through the resurrection of the dead into its second phase in order now to become the earthly sphere of the Aeon of full blessedness.'[18]

It is true, of course, that these ideas transcend altogether the limits of the conceivable, but they are stressed by Judaism because they affirm the meaningfulness of human history and of individual human life. The question of horizon is, after all, of the first importance for the regulation of conduct. If our only horizon is the span of mortal life, then the moral value of each act can be measured only in relation to that brief span. Or, if the whole story of human history is so restricted to that of the material universe that there is no place within it for the spiritual consummation, then it is clear that all human strivings and all social progress will ultimately prove vanity.

> ' For if there were this life only, which belongeth to
>   all men nothing could be more bitter than this.
> For of what profit is strength that turneth to weak-
>   ness,
> Or fulness of food that turneth to famine,
> Or beauty that turneth to ugliness ?
>
> .   .   .   .   .   .
>
> For if a consummation had not been prepared for
> all, in vain would have been their beginning.' (*The
> Apocalypse of Baruch* xxi. 13-17).

If indeed there would be no ' consummation ', what place would there be for any morality higher than utility and pleasure ? As against such a supposition, Judaism maintains that there is a consummation reserved for both the individual and the human history. Looking beyond the earthly horizon by which man's finite existence is bound, it holds out the hope of a world to come, in which the whole of human life, in its individual patterns and its historical configurations, will, in accordance with the divine purpose of Creation, find its fulfilment.

The idea of divine purpose in Jewish teaching is thus viewed under two aspects. On the one hand, divine purpose is held to fulfil itself in the temporal realm. On the other, its true consummation is placed categorically in the realm that is eternal and spiritual. These two aspects are not regarded as mutually exclusive, or as standing in opposition to one another. Unlike other creeds, Judaism refuses to admit a real dualism between the heavenly and the earthly, the temporal and the eternal. Both are treated as organically connected, with the latter as an inevitable result and development of the former. This is the idea underlying the Rabbinic declaration that God will not enter the heavenly Jerusalem before the earthly Jerusalem is built.[19] While laying emphasis on the sublime world of eternity where alone all the ultimate values of life and the divine purpose can be fully realised, Judaism refuses to recognise the existence on earth of a dark irrational principle over which it is impossible to achieve a conclusive victory, or to admit that suffering, evil and imperfection are the inevitable lot of man. On the contrary, Judaism insists that this over-earthly consummation of divine purpose is conditioned by the course of everyday life in the historical and social context of human experience. Indeed, so concerned was Judaism to emphasise the idea of this world as being the sphere through which the divine eternal purpose is working itself out into fulfilment, that it has included in its *Credo* the doctrine of the Resurrection of the Dead.[20] Stripped of all its accidents and conceived in its essence, the implication of the doctrine of the Resurrection is clear: it relates the struggles of the present, and the human endeavours to realise goodness in history, to the eternity in which the historical process will find its consummation, thus linking the *olam-ha-ba*, the World-to-Come, with *olam ha-zeh*, this world, into a unity. It is this living relationship between the social and historical world and the unseen world, this vital union of the aspiration to realise Justice and Righteousness on earth with the consummation of a divine purpose in a world that is beyond, which forms the distinctive character of the Jewish religion, and provides at the same time the key to the understanding of Judaism in all its varied manifestations.

Immortality involves a conception of the soul of man. Such a conception has formed an element in the cultural life of all peoples at some stage or another. It has been rightly remarked that ' few conceptions can show the universality and permanence, the creative power and morphological influence, which have characterised throughout history the Idea of the Soul.'[21] But what change can be seen in the conception of the soul at different epochs ! At first the conception was essentially physical: soul was breath, life-blood.[22] With Plato, there was gradually introduced the notion of the soul as a spiritual principle. First the soul stood for thinking, for conscious-self, and thus for the principle of knowledge. Then the idea of the soul was introduced for moral problems, which leads to the Platonic definition of the soul ' as the thing in us which is of more importance to us than anything else whatever,' and which therefore it behoves us to make wise and good.[23] As soon as the soul receives the wider meaning, immortality becomes its necessary attribute. But to Plato the problem is not human. It is cosmic. The soul is the life-giving principle in all things. It is the source of all motion in the world, ' because it is the only thing in the world that moves without being itself moved by anything else.'[24] The soul is thus, according to Plato, independent of God. God indeed is, for Plato, the highest soul, the ultimate source of motion and the Supremely Good. But since there are many things in the world which are not good, and since it would be blasphemy to attribute these things to God, there must be in the Platonic view other things in the world which are, relatively at least, independent of God.[25]

It is not easy to discover the relationship in which these other souls, including the human soul, stand to God, according to Plato. But whatever the origin and nature of the soul, according to Greek philosophy its relation with God is not certain.

Opposed to the Greek attitude is that of Judaism, with its dominant conception of man's absolute relation to God. This connection is expressed in the initial teaching of Genesis, that God made man in His image. In virtue of this declaration man is recognised as a child of eternity, possessing a God-given spirit which brings him into personal relationship with God. This relationship has been variously apprehended in the Hebrew Scriptures as that of a master to a servant, of a king to his subjects, of a father to his child. But this relationship has found its highest expression in the conception of man as co-worker with God in His moral purpose for the Universe, through the advance of the human race towards righteousness.[25a] Life accordingly becomes for Judaism essentially a task for moral development and culture. And man, in his moral and spiritual capacity, has the power and the duty to fit himself to become increasingly a co-worker with God, both now and throughout eternity, by growing in likeness to Him through the knowledge of Him. All these conceptions go beyond the earthly border and illumine the horizon of another life. Death can thus no longer be regarded as merely the end of life. Death is but the home-going of the spirit of man to the further cultivation and development of the divine relationship made manifest on this stage of life. ' Then shall the dust return to the earth as it was; and the spirit shall return unto God who gave it ' (Ecclesiastes xii. 7). This gives to immortality an infinitely higher significance. It is grounded in God and His divine purpose, in which man is called upon to co-operate; and the conception of a life of co-operation with the Divine becomes an unending ideal the pursuit of which stretches beyond this earthly existence. For the existence which follows is not one of sheer inactivity. The co-operation with God in His purpose begun in this life stretches beyond the earthly life. Even after the individual has thrown off his mortal coil, the immortal spirit that is in him continues its moral progress and tasks of holiness, the origin of which is God, adding to the store of the moral forces that make for the fulfilment of God's eternal purpose. ' The disciples of the wise (the righteous) have no rest either in this world or in the world to come.'[26] Thus is the whole existence, life and after-life, the here and the hereafter, knit together, in the Jewish conception of man's relationship to God, in this unity of service.

The question of the definite form of the other life does not enter here. It may be a problem for mythology that makes primary chaos the origin of everything, including man's life. But Hebrew Monotheism gives another origin to man's life. God made man in His image. He put His spirit in man. The question of what becomes of the soul of man can only be answered in conformity with the question—where did it come from, and who gave it to man? Since God as spirit grounded the soul as spirit in man, its extinction is impossible. What has come as spirit from God will be maintained by God. The soul having its origin in God, its return to God is foreshadowed. Dust returns to dust, but the spirit returns to God who gave it. Of course, if the soul were bound to the body, the individual would remain, for all his development, bound to the conditions of matter. When the body becomes matter and is dissolved into dust, what existed as organism may cease. The individual, however, is not so exclusively bound to his organism as to make the two an identity. His own identity rests rather on his relation with God. That relation is eternal. How could it cease with the dissolution of the organism, through which it only temporarily expressed itself? And returning to God, this relation is continued for ever.

Rooted in man's relation to God, the Jewish conception of immortality is individual. Every individual as an individual has been made in the divine image, and as such stands to God in a relationship which is capable of surviving death. But as God's creature, man can never become united to God; much less can he ever become God, as in the mystery religions; he can only approximate more and more to the divine image in which he has been made. This excludes the pantheistic view which conceives immortality as absorption into the All, with complete loss of personal identity. Such a survival, whatever its philosophical validity, is of no religious significance, and can have no effect on human conduct, which is the only reason why Judaism affirms the belief in the survival after death. The only immortality which can provide the test of rightness or wrongness in conduct is the one in which the personal destiny of the individual is involved. It is this hope of personal immortality which Judaism affirms and includes in the tenets of its faith.

The doctrine of personal immortality carries with it the idea of retribution in the hereafter—reward for good-doing and punishment for evil-doing. This principle of retribution, which is fundamental to Jewish religious teaching,[27] is the inescapable sequel to the belief in the existence and the justice of God. If God is real, and His justice is real, He cannot be indifferent to human conduct, but recompenses alike the individual and the nation in accordance with their deeds. The character of this retribution is not known. Judaism, being chiefly interested in doctrines for the sake of their significance—moral and religious—is satisfied with the mere definitive establishment of the belief in retribution, without being much concerned as to the manner and circumstance in which it would be effected. In the words of the *Sepher ha-Yashar*, ' As is known,

one has to believe that if a man dies after a life of good
deeds and pious conduct, the Creator, blessed be He,
will love him, and this love is a reward than which
there is none greater . . . and we need not enquire
as to the precise character of this good reward . . .'[28]
It is true that Jewish religious teachers, trying to explain
the unfamiliar in terms of the familiar, resort to certain
material representations of the hereafter, as to the
state of the righteous in the celestial Paradise, *Gan
Eden*, and that of the wicked in Hell, *Gehinnom*. Yet,
as Moore well remarks: ' Jewish imagination did not
indulge itself in inventing retaliatory modes of torment
in hell, such as flourished in the Orphic, and the other
Greek sects, and in India. There was a Biblical warrant
for the pit of fire, and there the Jews generally left
it.'[29] The tendency, however, has been to spiritualise
the conception; and the abode of bliss in the hereafter
—the *Gan Eden*—is described as a place ' where there
is no eating, nor drinking, no begetting of children,
nor bargaining, no jealousy, no hatred, no strife, but
the righteous sit with their crowns on their heads,
enjoying the light of the *Shechinah* (the Divine
Presence).'[30]

Personal fulfilment in immortality is, however, not
to be thought of as merely individual, as it means in
the Platonic system;[31] it is to be essentially related to
the universal fulfilment at the ' End of Time ', in which
all individuals of all ages will be made to share, each
contributing to the harmony of the whole.[32] These
two aspects of fulfilment—the individual and the
universal—as well as their mutual relation to one
another, are emphasised in Jewish teaching by the

doctrine of Resurrection which is given preference in
the body of Jewish beliefs over the idea of immortality.
It was a fine insight into the heart of things that moved
the spiritual teachers of Judaism to express the hope
of everlasting life in terms of Resurrection rather than
those of immortality.[33] The doctrine of Resurrection,
as has been seen, relates the struggles and achievements
of the present to the world of eternity, in which the
whole of the historical process will be brought to
completion. As such the doctrine is concerned with
the fulfilment that awaits the universality of mankind
at the final consummation of God's creation. But side
by side with this universal fulfilment, the doctrine of
Resurrection also carries with it the hope of the fulfilment for the individual in a manner which is not
necessarily implied in the idea of immortality. By
assigning to the ' body ' some share in the final consummation, the doctrine of Resurrection asserts that
the fulfilment in which the quick and the dead are to
participate will not be an impersonal fulfilment which
bears no relation to the actual self, but a fulfilment of
the individual self as it existed in the ' body '.[34] This
principle of individuality, however, does not necessarily imply identity of the material composing the
body when alive. The fact is that even during one's
life-time the body undergoes a complete change in its
material structure and the particles composing the
body of man at one period of his life are not the same
as those composing it at any other period. What it does
imply is the existence of some unity of body and soul
which is of eternal significance in the consummation
of the life of the individual in his relation to God.[35]

It is a common fallacy to assert that the belief in personal survival after death was unknown in early Judaism, and that this belief did not emerge in Israel until two or three centuries before the rise of Christianity, and then only through the influence of Greek thought. Others, less objectively, go so far as to claim that the belief in immortality is the creation of Christianity. The early Hebrews, it is maintained, held views on the subject that did not materially differ from those of their surrounding neighbours. The religious hope of the Jew was directed only to the continuance of the people as a whole, and of individual families and tribes within it, not to the actual living-on of individuals after death. The life of the individual was to them inseparably bound up with his body, and though there was a certain survival after death, in some scattered elements of his former personality, such as the bones, the blood and the name, it was no more than a shadowy existence in an underworld known as *Sheol*, a land of ' helplessness ', ' darkness ' and ' forgetfulness '.[36] With such notions of human survival, there was no room for any idea of retribution and the hereafter. God, it is true, was the Judge who rewarded good and punished evil, but the retribution looked for was in this life, and there was none beyond the grave.

In support of this assertion much capital is made of the supposed silence of the Hebrew Scriptures on the subject of eternal life. That supposition is, however, false. Whatever notions the old Hebrews may have had concerning the soul and man's survival after death, it is certain that they had some doctrine of immortality, which in its practical bearings was not different to the one which appeared later in Jewish history. The verse which speaks of God breathing ' into man's nostril the breath of life ' (Genesis ii. 7) means, as Oesterley has already pointed out, that ' the breath breathed in by a creator who was immortal conferred thereby on man the faculty of becoming immortal.'[37]   Illuminating too, is the comment of the *Zohar* on this cited verse, ' He who breathed, breathed in of His own.'[38]   While there is much room for argument as to the precise meaning attached in early Israel to such terms as ' *Nefesh* ', or ' *Ruah*,' which are variously used in the Hebrew Scriptures to denote the vital principle in man, there is no doubt that it connoted for them some principle—material or spiritual—that was independent of the body, and continued to exist after its dissolution. Striking in this connection is the prayer of Elijah on behalf of the child of the widow of Zaraphata, ' Oh Lord my God, I pray Thee, let the soul of the child come unto him again ';—and God, we read on, answered his prayer, ' And the soul of the child returned unto him and he revived ' (1 Kings xvii. 21-2).   Here we have evidence of the conception of the human soul as an independent substance continuing to exist even after it leaves the body.

In contradistinction to the beliefs in vogue among other Semitic peoples that the soul was but the body reduced to some shadowy existence in the *Sheol*, the Jew conceived the soul as a separate entity, endowed with a permanent vitality of its own in independence of the body. That the idea of survival after death was linked in the Bible to Judgment, is evident from the verse, ' And surely your blood will I require of your

334

lives ' (Genesis ix. 5), which forbids suicide under the pain of punishment. But if death is the end of all things there would be no possibility of punishment. Likewise, the penalty of *Karet*[39] (' Cutting-off '), which is attached in the Hebrew Scriptures to specific offences, cannot be explained, in a number of places, except with reference to some punishment beyond the grave. Nor is the idea of eternal life with God unknown to early Biblical writers, as the taking away of Enoch and Elijah certainly goes to show. Many indeed are the Biblical passages which could be adduced, particularly from the Book of Psalms, which give expression to Israel's hope of immortality, whatever unsound modern Biblical exegesis may assert to the contrary. To take some examples:—

' Thou wilt guide me with Thy counsel,
And afterward receive me with glory.
Whom have I in heaven but Thee ?
And beside Thee I desire none upon earth.
My flesh and my heart faileth,
But God is the Rock of my heart and my portion for
    ever ' (Psalm lxxiii. 24-6).[40]

' For Thy lovingkindness is better than life,
My lips shall praise Thee ' (Psalm lxiii. 4).[41]

' Like sheep they are appointed for the nether-world,
Death shall be their shepherd;
And the upright shall have dominion over them in
    the morning.
And their form shall be for the nether-world to wear
    away,
That there be no habitation for it.

335

But God will redeem my soul from the power of the
nether-world,
For He shall receive me ' (Psalm xlix. 15-6).[42]

The same conviction of a life with God beyond death
breaks forth according to Welch[43] in Psalm xvi, which
forms part of the Jewish Funeral Service:

' O Lord, the portion of mine inheritance and of my
cup,
Thou maintainest my lot.'

' The lines are fallen unto me in pleasant places,
Yea, I have goodly heritage.

.   .   .   .

Therefore my heart is glad, and my glory rejoiceth,
My flesh also dwelleth in safety.
For Thou wilt not abandon my soul to the nether-
world,
Neither wilt Thou suffer Thy godly one to see the pit.
Thou makest me to know the path of life;
In Thy presence is fulness of joy,
In Thy right hand bliss for evermore ' (Psalm xvi.
5-6, 9-11).

On this Welch comments, ' Even as the heritage
which belonged to him (the Psalmist) during his life-
time was a gift of God, and was satisfying because it
came from Him, so the future, whatever it might hold,
was of divine giving, and should be no more meagre
than the past . . . God will not suffer all this to come
to an end in the *cul-de-sac* of death, for what is of real
must be of enduring worth.'[44]

But wherefore go in search for proof-texts, when

the conception of man's relation to God, which is
fundamental to Jewish teaching, carries with it inevitably the belief in individual immortality ? ' The great
thing,' writes G. A. Smith, ' is to be sure of our individual relation with God. In teaching man that life
is in Him and in nothing else, and that the term of our
days here has been given us to find Him, the Old
Testament has done more for the assurance of immortality than if it had explored the life awaiting us, or
had endowed us with strong intellectual conceptions
of its reality.'[45] This too, was the position adopted by
the author of the Book of the Wisdom of Solomon
(about 30-50 B.C.E.), who gave expression to the hope
of immortality in the famous lines, ' But the souls of
the righteous are in the hand of God, and no evil shall
touch them. . . For though in the sight of men they be
punished, their hope is full of immortality ' (Wisdom
of Solomon iii. 1-4). However much he might have
been helped by Greek psychology, he did not derive
his hope of immortality from his Greek cultural background, but founded it on the Biblical conception of
man's relation to God: ' There is a prize for blameless
souls because God created man for incorruption, and
made him an image of his own proper being ' (Wisdom
of Solomon ii. 22-23).

Yet notwithstanding this ever-present conviction, the
Bible observes a certain reticence on the question of
man's survival after death for the reason, as Neumark
puts it, ' The people had rather *too much* eschatology.'[46]
The belief in the survival of man in some form or
other was common among the nations of antiquity,
and much of their religious thought was dominated by

337

the prospect of life beyond the grave. With this belief was associated the cult of the dead and all its attendant idolatrous feasts and rites, which often served to cover up the worst and most shameful orgies. In order to wean away the Jewish people from the abominable practices then in vogue, the Hebrew Scriptures found it necessary to throw a veil more or less over the fact of man's survival after death, without, however, suppressing altogether the hope of immortality, without which there can be no vital living religion. As David Neumark rightly remarks, ' From the viewpoint of religion the reality of the individual soul of man is . . . indispensable. For you cannot do in religion without the belief in *immortality* of the soul. Some think lightly of this question. They try to hide their ignorance on the subject by displaying an air of superiority in their realisation of what they term the realities of natural law. They pretend to know something about what religion is, without the belief in immortality of the individual soul of man. But, so far, I have never met a man who was able to tell me what religion is good for without this item, nor have I ever read an argument in justification of religion without immortality that carried any weight with me.'[47]

This indeed has been well said. The first condition of a rational faith is the recognition that life is not made up of two detached existences, but of one continuous whole. Mysterious as life after death appears, it is hardly more mysterious than the experiences of the present life. If even in this world we partake of the spirit of God, then, with all that must change and perish, we become partakers of His eternity. The result of this recognition is the new value attached to conduct. Just as our conduct at any moment in this life is not without effect on us for the rest of our life, so must our conduct on earth affect for good or ill our destiny in the hereafter. The fact that we are unable to envisage the form of the life beyond, or the manner in which our actions on earth can affect our later state in the hereafter, has no bearing on this belief. We have only to think of the bundle of hereditary traits, and characteristics of generations, that are carried over at birth by a tiny cell of protoplasm, to be impressed by the claim of Judaism that there is within every one of us an indestructible spirit which takes over in the event of death the effects of all our deeds, words and thoughts, formed habits and character, into the new environment for which we are prepared.

But it might be argued, do not the facts of everyday experience, not to speak of science, make reasonable belief in immortality impossible ? The inter-relation between the mind and the brain seems to be so close as to make the mind altogether dependent on the brain. As the human brain grows old, the mind becomes enfeebled. Arrest of brain development means imbecility. Surely it follows, that when the brain is dead, the mind has ceased to be.

These arguments, however, are far from conclusive. The facts to which appeal is made can be equally well explained on the assumption that the brain is the instrument which the mind uses to control the body and to think, in the same way as the musician uses his instrument—the piano or violin—to produce his music and to play. If the instrument is defective through damp or age, or a broken string, then the music suffers. We do not jump to the conclusion that the instrument produces the musician. Rather we say that the musician expresses himself through the instrument. Similarly it is at least in consonance with all the facts to say that the brain is used by the mind or personality.

That mind is independent of brain is a conclusion to which J. B. S. Haldane is driven, in his own despite, in an article of his, quoted by M. C. D'Arcy in *Death and Life*: ' It seems to me unlikely that mind is a mere by-product of matter. For if my mental processes are entirely determined by the motions of atoms in my brain, I have no reason to suppose that my beliefs are true. They may be sound chemically, but that does not make them sound logically. And hence I have no reason for supposing my brain to be composed of atoms. In order to escape from this necessity of sawing away the branch on which I am sitting, so to speak, I am compelled to believe that mind is not wholly conditioned by matter. . . .'[48]

The point of Haldane's argument, as M. C. D'Arcy explains, is that once we assume that mind is wholly fashioned by matter, then our own judgment about matter would be conditioned as the matter about which we are judging, and that would reduce any thought to the level of matter, in fact to rubbish. If I am lying when I say I am lying, I ruin the effect of my statement; and if my judgment about matter is the same as matter, my judgment ceases to be a judgment. Thus it is that the very supposition of a mind determined by matter contains its own refutation. Mind and matter are not identical. Mind is the subject that thinks and knows; matter is the object that is thought of and is known. If therefore mind is not entirely conditioned by matter, the mind is no more dependent for its survival on the material brain than the actual life of the violinist depends on the fiddle on which he plays.[49]

Now let us examine for a moment more closely this concept of immortality. Here we have to distinguish between the idea of natural immortality—the notion that the power to survive death is a natural property of the human soul—and the idea of immortality as life eternal. The former is a quantitative concept, having reference to the *duration* of life. As such, the idea is not particularly Jewish, and for aught we know, not necessarily valid. Eternal life, on the other hand, is first and last a qualitative idea, a particular *kind* of life. Eternal life bespeaks the spiritual and aspiring, the unifying and timeless. In place of what is quantitative and repetitive and monotonous, we have here quality, intensity and timelessness, a participation in what is described in Judaic sources as *Hayye Olam*, ' Life of Eternity.' In its nature eternal life thus partakes of the qualities of prophecy which in its vivid experience of God, as already shown on a previous occasion,[50] is not subject to the limitations of time. Prophecy, in fact, yields for Judah Halevi the best proof of eternal life. Just because we see that the prophet is able to taste in this world, by his experience of God, a portion of eternal life, in its timelessness, so we realise that time is not the proper element of the spirit and its joys, and that every man who proves himself worthy can enter upon the joy of eternal life.[51]

Y

We may say that the self participates in life eternal in proportion as it absorbs some of the prophetical qualities that emancipate man from those elements in his nature that keep him tied down to the material and the earthly. These qualities are such as find expression in service—service to God and to fellow-men. Disdaining these and preferring to serve self, the self will gradually deteriorate in quality and suffer misery. If, on the other hand, life is devoted to service and spent in duty-doing, the self grows and develops and earns the reward of the life of eternity, and the infinite blissfulness of God's eternal love.

Immortality, as mentioned before, is conceived by the Talmudic sages as an existence of activity and progress—moral and spiritual.[52] There is no reason why the disappearance of evil within and without ourselves should put an end to adventure and moral progress. An analogy can be drawn between art and moral culture. The musician or painter who has nothing more to learn about the management of his bow and brush will still go on using his material for the production of beauty which is perennially new and increasingly more beautiful. The same is equally true of moral life. Even if we found ourselves in a world where there was no more evil, and where everyone was good and wise, we should still have to exercise that goodness and wisdom in the details of our lives. We should still find enough occupation in continuing what is morally of the highest importance and value in our present life. And thus there is nothing irrational in hoping for a stage in our existence in which finality may have been reached as far as the development of moral character is concerned, and yet endless room is left for the embodiment of the character so won in varied action, and for progress in the manifestation of the good life in ever varied and richer forms.[53]

Immortality as a life of activity and moral progress is but a continuation of the individual's co-operative activity begun in this life towards the fulfilment of divine purpose. This makes the doctrine of immortality but another aspect of that of the Kingdom of God. The unending development of the human race towards righteousness is the real problem which the establishment of the Kingdom presents, and the solution of which it entrusts to the individual man. And it is only to the extent to which the individual contributes to the development that his immortality is achieved. To this consummation the individual must make the highest contribution in the present. As the inevitable product of man's co-operation with the Divine, the Kingdom of God in Jewish teaching is not something yet to come. It came with the Revelation at Sinai, when Israel gladly accepted the charge of God's Kingdom, and received the Torah, which sets forth the principles of the Kingdom, and the means whereby it could be realised in their individual and corporate lives.[54] This great and unique event introduced into the world a new moral culture, which has never ceased to exercise its power and influence on the affairs of man.[55] In the words of the Talmudic sages, ' Before the Torah was given to Israel, the world was like a wilderness; once it was given, it became a civilisation.'[56] In that sense, the Kingdom of God may be said to have entered history at Sinai, waiting only upon man's continuous co-operation, in an ever-increasing measure, to bring it to its final consummation and fulfilment.[57] It is this relation of the Torah to the Kingdom of God which lies behind the declaration made by the pious Jew when about to fulfil a *Mitzvah*—to perform a religious observance: ' I am intent herewith to take upon myself the yoke of the Kingdom of Heaven.' ' I must not wait,' he means to say, ' till the Kingdom comes, not only pray for its appearance, but through my own action I must bring it forward to fulfilment.' Thus does the establishment of the Kingdom of God become for the individual Jew a reality for his sense of duty. Viewed in this light, the conception of immortality is twofold. On the one side, it is united with the unending strivings of the individual towards righteousness; on the other side, with the life of the human race and its unending variegation.

The task of righteousness, to which man is called in obedience to his destiny, beginning here and now, stretches endlessly into the future. It is the main inspiring thought of life, giving meaning and significance to existence. Without this ideal, life is but ' froth and bubble,' and existence a *Tohu wa-Bohu*. This is perhaps the great truth embodied in the mystical fantasy over which the sensitive soul of Nahman of Bratzlaw (1772-1810), the famous Chassidic Rabbi, mused, and musingly sang:

' At one end of the world there stands a mountain. The mountain crest is crowned by a Stone. From the Stone there gushes forth a Fountain. Now, everything is dowered with a heart. So has the world a

Heart. The World-Heart stands pulsating at the other end, pining and longing continually with mighty longing to get to the Fountain. The Fountain, too, in response, yearns for the World-Heart. Yet neither can the World-Heart get nearer the Fountain, nor the Fountain nearer to the World-Heart. Were they but to draw closer to one another, the Mountain crest would soon be obscured from the sight of the World-Heart. And no longer being able to behold the crest and the Fountain, the World-Heart would cease to beat, and would expire. With the World-Heart stilled, the whole World would be undone. The Heart is the life of the World, and all that it contains; and thus the World-Heart dare not approach the Fountain, but must for ever stand at a distance, and strain itself with mighty longing.'[58]

*   *   *   *

All these ideas will appear shadowy and vague; but they are not more shadowy and vague than the alternative ideas that claim to discover in man and history some inherent capacity and power, working towards the completion of life. Both the one and the other attitude are determined respectively by an act of faith. As far as the observed facts go, the natural course of the human and historical development might close in a cosmic catastrophe that would end life on this planet. To believe in a consummation which is merely the result of the natural inter-play of historical forces, is as much a creed as the belief in a consummation determined by a Divine Power, controlling and directing the whole historical process towards a supernal goal in which the individual and the race will find their fulfilment. The difference is that the materialistic creed is too much divorced from the sense of moral responsibility and moral restraint to justify the hopes of its children. The tragedy of the present-day world derives from the fact that, having lost the sense of a personal God, man has lost the sense of his own moral worth, and with it he has lost respect for other people, with the result written across the face of the globe to-day. Already long before the catastrophe of the second World War that broke upon humanity, as far back as 1932, Mr. (now Sir) Winston Churchill warned mankind of the impending danger, because of the abandonment of the ideals of religion. 'Without an equal growth of Mercy, Pity, Peace and Love, Science herself may destroy all that makes life majestic and tolerable. There never was a time when the inherent virtue of human beings required more strong and confident expression in daily life; there never was a time when the hope of immortality and the disdain of earthly power and achievement were more necessary for the safety of the children of men.'[59]

Mercy, Pity, Peace and Love are indeed the qualities for which the world is hungering to-day; but they are not to be found apart from the ' hope of immortality and the disdain of earthly power and achievement ', which characterise the outlook of the man of true religious faith. To such a man life, now and in the hereafter, is all of a piece. It is all life in co-operation with God; and death is but the portal through which he passes to continued co-operation in company with the righteous, who find in the presence of God, and in the doing of His will, their peace, their happiness and self-fulfilment. As ' co-workers with God,'[60] they are ever in the bond of life with Him, Who is the Source of all life.

A unique place amongst the co-workers with God has been assigned to Israel. As the elect people, Israel has, from the very first, been called upon to co-operate with God, and to inspire and win others to become co-workers in the building of the Kingdom. Such eminently is the claim distinctive to the Faith of Judaism. Moulded by this faith and disciplined by the Torah,[61] Israel became, in the words of the Midrash, ' the partner of God in everything '[62]—in things temporal as well as eternal—for the achievement of His purpose within humanity, the Universe and beyond, and the chief protagonist of His Kingdom. Defects there are—defects that are largely the result of millennia of persecutions; that does not change the historical fact: Israel's collective identification as a people with the purposes of God, and with the advancement of His rule of righteousness over all the sons of men.[63]

It was this collective identification of the Jewish people with divine purposes and ends, that reach beyond any immediate satisfaction and interest, which has determined Israel's unique contribution in the domain of religion and morality. Although a small people, and never possessed of any great material culture or physical power, Israel has, nevertheless, exercised a far greater influence on the moral and religious culture of the world, and on the course of history, than have the powerful empires that surrounded it and over and again seemed to have engulfed and destroyed it.

But that is not all. As Lewis Mumford in *The Conduct of Life*[64] so well observes, this collective identification of the Jewish people with a purpose, ' working over an almost cosmic stretch of time,' has brought its own fulfilment, not merely in their survival, but also in their return as a unified political group to their ancestral home, after a dispersion of two thousand years, while their conquerors and oppressors of old have long vanished from the face of the earth.

This newest attestation of history carries with it a fresh vindication of the Faith of Judaism, and at the same time also a challenge to the Jewish people everywhere —in the Land of Israel and outside: it is to remain steadfast in the Faith, which alone can ensure their survival in the future, as it did in the past, and also impart to them, individually and corporately, that dynamic of purposive development towards their God-given destiny, involving their own national salvation as well as the universal salvation of mankind:

' *Is it too light a thing that thou shouldest be my servant,*
To raise up the tribes of Jacob,
And to restore the preserved of Israel?
I will also give thee for a light to the nations
That my salvation be unto the end of the earth.'

(Isaiah xlix, 6.)

NOTES

[1] The two terms *Malkut Shaddai* and *Malkut Shamayim* are synonymous; see S. Schechter, *Some Aspects of Rabbinic Theology* (1909), p. 89.

² ' This is one of the fundamental verses for the Jewish conception of the Kingdom of Heaven ' (G. F. Moore, *Judaism* I, p. 230, n. 1). The close relation between the doctrine of the Unity of God and that of God's universal kingdom is a recurrent theme in Jewish Liturgy, e.g. the *Alenu* Prayer (*A.P.B.*, p. 76); and the Invocations of ' Kingship ', in the New Year Service (*A.P.B.*, pp. 248ff.). Apposite is the statement of Bahya ben Asher ibn Halawa (*c.* 1255-1340) in his *Kad ha-Kemah*, chapter *Yihud:* ' And it is well known that the real unity will be realised only in the days of the Messiah (see *infra*, pp. 318ff), for in the times of exile and subjection of Israel the signs of the unity are not discernible (the worship of mankind being distributed among unworthy objects), so that the denying of the truth is constantly on the increase. But with the advent of the Messiah, all nations will turn to one creed, and the world will be perfected under the Kingdom of the Almighty, all of them agreeing to the worship of the Name alone, and call upon the name of God, and serve Him with one accord. Then shall the unity of our God become known in the mouth of all nations. This is the promise the prophet made for the future: " And the Lord shall be King over all the earth; in that day shall the Lord be One and His Name One " ' (quoted by S. Schechter, *op. cit.*, p. 96).

³ It would be possible to say that the religion of Zoroaster had this kind of world view, but as Emil Brunner, *Revelation and Reason*, E.T., by Olive Wyon (1947), p. 405, n. 12, points out, the difference from the Hebrew view of the whole is that the *historical* event is not united with the goal towards which it is directed, that Ormuzd does not make himself known like the God of Israel through his prophets, ' and that the present history is not the history of a covenant which continues down the generations, and therefore not even the world of nations is regarded as the object of the Divine saving action.'

⁴ The ' Day of the Lord ' is a recurring concept in Hebrew prophecy. It was used by Isaiah (ii. 10-22, xiii. 3-22); Amos (v. 18ff.); Ezekiel (xiii. 5); Obadiah (verse 15); Zephaniah (i. 14-18); Joel (ii. 1-2); Malachi (iv). The critical school associated with the name of Wellhausen denied the existence of a developed eschatology in early

Israel, and accordingly considered the bulk of eschatological sayings in the pre-exilic prophets as post-exilic interpolations. Hugo Gressmann, however, in *Der Ursprung der israelitisch-jüdischen Eschatologie* (1905) has shown that an eschatological conception of a destruction and renewal of the world dominated Israel thought early in the pre-prophetic age; see G. W. Anderson, *Hebrew Religion* in *The Old Testament and Modern Study* (1951), ed. H. H. Rowley, pp. 303ff.

⁵ Joel iii. 1-2. The idea of the regeneration of the human race involves the disclosure of divine goodness and mercy, concerned with redemption no less than with judgment. It is this element in Hebrew Prophetism which marks it sharply off from Zoroastrianism with which it has many points of affinity. As Emil Brunner, *op. cit.*, pp. 227-8, well expresses it in his own strong theological language: ' The message of Zoroaster contains, it is true, the idea of the ethically good, but it knows nothing of forgiving, generous, grace. Even the great helper, the Saoshyant, is not the gracious and merciful One, and the last days are not the days of a new covenant, when God forgives, and in a new creation writes the law on the hearts of the faithful (see *supra*, p. 303) or gives them a new heart. The hero of the last days is only a mighty warrior who fights with the righteous and the pious, whose participation in the final struggle brings victory to their side. This means that this faith does not go farther than the moral law. . . . It lacks precisely that which transcends the moral reason . . . the paradoxical blend of holiness and mercy, which is the core of the Old Testament.'

⁶ See Pirke de Rabbi Eliezer, XI. The Messianic Kingdom is described there as universal, but temporal; the Kingdom of God, universal and eternal. See also *Targum Sheni on Esther*, i. 1.

⁷ See Plato's *Republic*, II, 375a-376e.

⁸ See Hermann Cohen, *Religion der Vernunft* (ed. 1919), pp. 280f.

⁹ See Isaac ben Moses Arama (*c.* 1420-1492), *Akedat Yitzhak*, Portal XXVIII (Warsaw, ed. 1911), p. 334, who cites a number of Biblical passages declaring that the material bliss of the Messianic times provides the physical background of the gifts of the spirit;

viz. Deuteronomy xxx. 5-6; Jeremiah, xxxii, 37-41; Ezekiel xxxvi. 24-8; etc. See also *supra*, p. 270.

10 'The hope of peace among the peoples is alien to the New Testament . . . The reign of peace belongs to metahistory, to the realm of eternal life.'—C. Garbett, Archbishop of York, *In an Age of Revolution* (1952), pp. 289-290. 'The passage of humanity (in the true Christian outlook) appears not as a passage along the line of earthly history to an ultimate goal on earth, but as a passage *across* the line of earthly history, the earth being only a platform which each generation crosses obliquely from birth to its entrance, individual by individual, into the unseen world, the world always there beside the visible one. The formation of the Divine Community in that unseen world is the supreme hope, in comparison with which everything which happens on this temporal platform, now or in the future, is of minor importance. Whenever the main stress is laid upon " building Jerusalem in England's green and pleasant land ", the Christian attitude to the world is abandoned.' E. Bevan, *The Kingdom of God and History* (1938), p. 56f., quoted by John Baillie, *The Belief in Progress* (1950), p. 197.

11 John Baillie, *op. cit.*, p. 220.

12 The late Stafford Cripps, as reported in *The Church Times*, Oct. 2, 1942.

13 This is in contrast with Christianity where the person of the Messiah it avows is an integral part of its faith, and the belief in him constitutes the very essence of the Christian religion. See Albo, *Ikkarim*, I, 1: 'the dogma of the Messiah is not a fundamental principle of the law of Moses . . . for we can conceive of the existence of the Mosaic Law without it. It is a special principle of the religion of the Christians, for their religion cannot exist without it.'
אין ביאת המשיח עקר לתורת משה . . . כי כבר יצוייר מציאותה זולתו,
ואמנם הוא עקר פרטי לדת הנוצרים שלא יצוייר מציאותה זולתו.

14 See B.T. Sanhedrin 99a, and Rashi's commentary, *a.l.* See also *Ikkarim, loc. cit.* See also Midrash Tehillim, Psalm xxxi. 2: ' The Holy One, blessed be He, said to Israel, Because your redemption hitherto had been through the hands of flesh and blood, and

your leadership through a son of man, who is here to-day and in the grave to-morrow, therefore your redemption was for the moment only; but in the future it is I even I, who live and exist for ever, who will redeem you, and therefore I will redeem you with a redemption that will endure for ever.' אמר להם לישראל הקב״ה: לפי שהיתה גאולתכם על ידי בשר ודם, והיה מנהיגיכם על ידי בן אדם שהיום כאן ומחר בקבר לפיכך גאולתכם גאולת שעה, אבל להבא אני גואל אתכם על ידי עצמי שאני חי וקיים אגאלכם גאולה קיימת לעולמים. Similarly *ibid.* Psalm xxxvi. 6: 'Israel said, We have become worn out by being enslaved, redeemed and becoming again enslaved. Now we have no desire for a redemption through flesh and blood, but our redeemer shall be the Lord of Hosts, whose name is the Holy One of Israel.' אמרו ישראל הרינו נתיגענו מהיותנו משתעבדין ונגאלין וחזרנו ונשתעבדנו עכשיו אין אנו מבקשין לגאולת בשר ודם, אלא גואלנו ד׳ צבאות קדוש ישראל. And again, *ibid.* Psalm cvii. 1: ' " Let the redeemed of the Lord say " . . . and thus Isaiah states, " the rescued of the Lord shall return " (Isaiah xxxv. 10), and not the rescued of Elijah, nor the rescued of King Messiah, but the rescued of the Lord; therefore it says, " the redeemed of the Lord." ' יאמרו גאולי ד׳ . . . וכן ישעיה מפרש, ופדויי ד׳ ישובון, ולא פדויי אליהו, ולא פדויי מלך המשיח אלא פדויי ד׳. Cf. also Midrash Tanhuma, Leviticus, *Ahare Mot,* 12, and *Ikkarim loc. cit.*

[15] E. Brunner, *Revelation and Reason*, p. 232.

[16] See B.T. Sanhedrin 99a, and Berakot 34b. It is significant that the Hebrew equivalent of the Kingdom of God is never used in Judaic sources for the world to come.

[17] In the tangled thought of Jewish sources on the subject of Resurrection there is a large variety of opinion as to the class of people who will participate in the resurrection, but there is quite considerable Talmudic warrant for the belief in individual resurrection. See *Ethics of the Fathers*, IV, 29: ' They that are born are destined to die, and the dead are to be brought to life again '. See also Pirke de-Rabbi Eliezer, XXXIV: ' All souls are in the hands of the Holy One, blessed be He, as it is said, " In whose hand is the soul of every living thing " (Job xii. 10) . . . ' And He will restore every spirit to the body of the flesh of man . . . ' Cf. Yalkut Shimeoni,

Isaiah, 428 and 499. For other views, see G. F. Moore, *Judaism*, II, pp. 302ff. and 306. See also *infra*, n. 35.

[18] Quoted by W. D. Davies, *Paul and Rabbinic Judaism* (1948), pp. 316-7; see also J. Albo, *Ikkarim*, IV, 31.

[19] B.T. Taanit, 5a.

[20] The belief in the resurrection of the dead forms the last of the thirteen articles of faith enumerated by Maimonides (1135-1204) in his Commentary on the Mishnah, Tractate Sanhedrin, chapter X, as well as in the two versions—poetical and in prose—in which these thirteen articles appear in our prayer book (see *A.P.B.*, p. 2 and pp. 89-90). This hope is also embodied in the daily *Amidah* (Prayer *par excellence*), the second benediction of which reads: ' Thou art mighty to save. Thou sustainest the living with lovingkindness, revivest the dead with great mercy . . . thou keepest Thy faith to them that sleep in the dust . . . yea, faithful art Thou to revive the dead. Blessed art Thou, O Lord, who revivest the dead.' (*A.P.B.*, p. 44). According to I. Elbogen, *Der jüdische Gottesdienst* (3rd ed. 1931), p. 29, this emphasis on the belief in the resurrection was instituted by the Pharisees to combat the denial of this doctrine by the Sadducees. See also *op. cit.*, p. 516, and L. Finkelstein, *J.Q.R.* (*N.S.*), XVI (1925-6), p. 22, and also David Neumark, *Toldot ha-Ikkarim be-Yisrael* (1917), p. 176, *contra*, D. Hoffmann, who relates it to the Samaritan schism (*Das Schmone Eszre-Gebet*, in *israelitische Monatsschrift* (1899), pp. 48ff and 1900, p. 2).

[21] A. E. Crawley, *The Idea of the Soul* (1909), p. 1.

[22] See Genesis ii. 7, ix. 4; Deuteronomy, xii. 23; Leviticus, xvii. 11.

[23] J. Burnet, in *The Legacy of Greece* (1923), p. 78.

[24] J. Burnet, *op. cit*, p. 81.

[25] See *op. cit.*, p. 82.

[25a] See *supra*, pp. 240ff.

[26] B.T. Berakot, 64a. תלמידי חכמים אין להם מנוחה לא בעולם הזה ולא בעולם הבא. See Judah Löw ben Bezaleel (d. 1609), *Netibot Olam*, section, *Netib ha-Torah*, ix.

[27] *Ethics of the Fathers*, IV, 29: '. . . Know that everything is according to reckoning, and let not thy imagination give thee hope that the grave will be the place of refuge for thee, for perforce thou wast formed, and perforce thou wast born, and thou livest perforce, and perforce thou wilt die, and perforce thou wilt in future have to give account and reckoning before the Supreme King of kings, the Holy One, blessed be He.' The belief in Retribution forms the eleventh of the thirteen articles of faith. See *supra*, n. 20.

[28] Zecharia ha-Yewani, *Sefer ha-Yashar*, V (thirteenth century): כידוע שיש לו להאמין כי כשימות האדם במעשים טובים ומתנהג בחסידות כי הבורא יתברך יאהבנו ומאחר שיאהבנו זהו הגמול שאין למעלה ממנו . . . ואין לנו לחקור איך יהיה הגמול הטוב . . . See also Maimonides, *Commentary on the Mishnah, Introduction to Sanhedrin X*. ' Know that just as a blind man can form no idea of colours, nor a deaf man comprehend sounds . . . so the body cannot comprehend the delights of the soul. Even as fish do not know the element of fire because they exist ever in its opposite, so are the delights of the world of spirit unknown in this world of flesh. Indeed we have no pleasure in any way except what is bodily, and what the sense can comprehend of eating, drinking. . . . Whatever is outside these is non-existent to us. We do not discern it, neither do we grasp it at first thought, but only after deep penetration. And truly this must necessarily be the case. For we live in a material world and the only pleasure we can comprehend must be material. But the delights of the spirit are everlasting and uninterrupted, and there is no resemblance in any possible way between spiritual and bodily enjoyments.'

[29] G. F. Moore, *Judaism*, II, p. 392.

[30] B.T. Berakot 17a. העולם הבא אין בו לא אכילה ולא שתיה ולא פריה ורביה. אלא צדיקים יושבים ועטרותיהם בראשיהם ונהנים מזיו השכינה.

[31] See R. H. Charles, *op. cit.*, p. 79, n. 1. Charles explains the individualistic character of the Greek conception of immortality as the inescapable sequence of ' its view that the soul was not only immortal but eternal, without beginning and end, and that it was capable of repeated incarnations in human and animal bodies. From this doctrine it follows that the present environment of the soul is

only one of the many in which it exists from age to age, and accordingly this community or that can have no abiding significance. . . . In Israel, however, the soul was not in itself immortal, but only won such immortality through life in God.' Whilst this may be correct as far as it goes, the statement needs the further amplification it receives in these pages.

[32] Cf. E. Bevan, *op. cit.*, pp. 58-9.

[33] See *supra*, p. 325. The idea of resurrection is one of which most modern Jewish theologians fight shy, and is generally explained away as really meaning immortality (see e.g. J. H. Hertz, *Authorised Daily Prayer Book*, pp. 133 and 255). They thus seem to regard the idea of immortality as a more plausible expression of the hope of everlasting life. But it is not appreciated, as R. Niebuhr well observes, that immortality is not easier to grasp than resurrection, either idea, as every idea which points to the consummation beyond history, being beyond logical conception; see R. Niebuhr, *The Nature and Destiny of Man*, II, p. 305.

[34] Cf. R. Niebuhr, *op. cit.*, p. 322.

[35] See A. I. Kook, *Olat Rayah*, I (1949), p. 70. For the rabbinic notions on resurrection, see G. F. Moore, *op. cit.*, II, p. 375ff. and A. Marmorstein, *The Doctrine of the Resurrection of the Dead in Rabbinic Theology*, in *Studies in Jewish Theology, Marmorstein Memorial Volume*, ed. J. Rabbinowitz and M. S. Lew (1950), pp. 144ff. For a general account of the Jewish traditional teaching on the subject see A. Löwinger, *Die Auferstehung in der jüdischen Tradition*, in *Jahrbuch für jüdische Volkskunde*, ed. M. Grunwald, Vol. 25 (1923), pp. 23-122.

[36] The etymological meaning of *Sheol* is uncertain. Some connect it with the word *sha'al*, ' to ask ', as denoting the place of enquiry *sc.* after the dead; others suggest the derivation from *sho'al* ' a hollow,' or ' pit '. For the literature, see Aubrey R. Johnson, *The Vitality of the Individual in the Thought of Ancient Israel* (1949), p. 91, n. 3. On the notions of the state of the dead in *Sheol*, see A. Lods, *Israel from its beginnings to the Middle of the Eighth Century* (E.T.S. H., Hooke, 1932), pp. 218-223.

[37] W. O. E. Oesterley, *Immortality and the Unseen World* (1921), p. 198.

[38] מאן דנפח מרוחא דיליה נפח quoted by A. B. Flahm, in *Shemen ha-Mor* (Warsaw, 1871), p. 100. See also A. I. Kook, *op. cit.*, p. 67. Cf. also Moses Nahmanides on Leviticus xxiii. 29: ' The soul of man is the lamp of God which He has breathed into man. It must thus remain in its state and cannot die, . . . its continued existence being natural and enduring for ever.' נשמת האדם נר ה' אשר נופחה באפינו מפי עליון ונשמת שדי, כמו שנאמר ויפח באפיו נשמת חיים, והנה היא בעצמה ולא תמות . . . אבל קיומה ראויה, והיא עומדת לעד.

[39] *Karet*: see Nahmanides, *loc. cit.* The explanation of this term as expulsion from the community is definitely disproved by Leviticus xx. 4, which speaks of God stepping in to cut off the evil-doer where ' the people of the land do any ways hide their eyes from that man '; and as Scripture draws a distinction between death at the hand of heaven for an offence, and *karet*, the latter must refer to some punishment beyond the grave. In the light of this we can understand the mention of the *Karet* penalty in verse 3, which appears to be subsequent to the stoning.

[40] See F. Delitzsch, *Biblischer Kommentar über die Psalmen* (ed. 1894), p. 494; and E. König, *Die Psalmen* (1927), p. 609.

[41] This beautiful verse can only mean that the lovingkindness of God extends beyond the grave. It is sheer perversity, *pace* Graetz, to emend it as he does, *Kritischer Kommentar zu den Psalmen* (1882) so as to read לחיים for מחיים, rendering it ' For Thy lovingkindness is good for life.'

[42] See C. V. Pilcher, *The Hereafter in Jewish and Christian Thought* (1940), p. 137.

[43] See A. C. Welch, *The Psalter* (1926), pp. 114-17.

[44] *Op. cit.*, p. 117.

[45] G. A. Smith, *Modern Criticism and the Preaching of the Old Testament* (1901), p. 214. Cf. also F. von Hügel, *Essays and Addresses on the Philosophy of Religion* (1921), p. 197: ' The specifically religious desire for Immortality begins not with Immortality, but with God;

it rests upon God; and it ends with God . . . the very sober but severely spiritual growth of the belief in immortality amongst the Jews . . . was entirely thus—not from immortality, of no matter of what kind of immortality, to God, but from God to a special kind of Immortality.'

[46] D. Neumark, *The Philosophy of the Bible* (1918), p. 52. This is somewhat similar to the explanation given by Judah Halevi, *Kuzari*, I, 109, and Rabbi Nissim ben Reuben (d. *c.* 1375), *Derashot ha-RaN*, *Derush* I (towards the end). For other attempts to explain the comparative silence on the reward and punishment beyond the grave, see Maimonides, Commentary on the Mishnah, Sanhedrin X (beginning), and *Yad*, *Hilekot Teshubah*, VIII, 9; Nahmanides on Exodus, vi. 2; Hillel ben Samuel of Verona (d.*c.* 1295), *Tagmule ha-Nefesh* (ed. Lyck, 1874), p. 27b; Jospeh Albo, *Ikkarim*, III, 25 and IV, 39; see also the lengthy discussion in Meir ben Ezekiel ibn Gabbai (b. 1480), *Abodat ha-Kodesh*, II, 17-19. For a strong support of the view that the doctrine of Immortality is taught by the Hebrew Scriptures, see E. König, *Theologie des Alten Testaments* (1923), p. 215-9.

[47] *Essays in Jewish Philosophy*, pp. 72-3. Cf. A. B. Davidson, quoted by J. Strachan, *Hebrew Ideals*, p. 199. ' For all that appears, the idea that any human person could become extinguished or annihilated never occurred to the prophets and saints of the Old Testament.'

[48] M. C. D'Arcy, *Death and Life* (1942), pp. 11 and 3.

[49] For the full development of the argument, see *op. cit.*, pp. 11-14.

[50] *Supra*, p. 133, n. 14.

[51] *Kuzari*, I, 103 and Hillel b. Samuel of Verona, *Tagmule ha-Nefesh*, p. 23. Similarly John Baillie, *And the Life Everlasting* (1934), p. 137, says that this argument ' is unanswerable; and it is indeed the only unanswerable argument for immortality that has ever been given or can be given . . . if the individual can commune with God, then he must matter to God; and if he matters to God, he must share God's eternity.'

[52] *Supra*, p. 328.

z

[53] A. E. Taylor, *The Faith of a Moralist* (1930), I, pp. 400ff., to whom I am indebted for this argument, makes a distinction between progress *towards* fruition, and progress *in* fruition, leading to an ever-increasing enrichment; see *ibid.*, p. 408.

[54] See Midrash Tanhuma, Yitro, 13, Pesikta de-Rab Kahana, 17, and Tanna de-be Eliyyahu, 31. See also M. Kadushin, *The Theology of Seder Eliahu*, (1932), I, p. 60.

[55] That the Old Testament has had a greater influence than the New Testament on the fundamental social ethics of Christendom is recognised by G. A. Smith, *Modern Criticism and the Preaching of the Old Testament* (1901), who declares (p. 264) that ' the Hebrew prophets have been felt by the moderns nearer to them than the Apostles.' He goes on to quote with approval the statement of F. D. Maurice that we must count ' paramount the duty of vindicating the Old Testament as the great witness for liberty . . . the witness of the sacredness of this earth.'

[56] Midrash Exodus Rabbah, xxiv. 4. עד שלא קבלו ישראל התורה היה העולם עשוי מדבר, כיון שקבלו את התורה נעשה העולם שור. שור = wall = protected habitation = civilised condition.

[57] As the inauguration of a new age, the full consummation of which is yet to come, the Sinaitic Revelation may well be described as an event of ' realised eschatology ,' to borrow the phrase coined by Prof. C. H. Dodd, in his exposition of the conception of the Kingdom of God in the New Testament (see his work, *The Parables of the Kingdom* [1935], pp. 202ff.)—a phrase which has now gained wide currency in christological circles.

[58] Quoted in Hebrew by S. A. Horodezky, *Torat Rabbi Nahman mi-Bratzlaw* (1923), p. 203.

[59] Winston S. Churchill, *Thoughts and Adventures* (2nd ed. 1947), pp. 213f.

[60] Midrash Tanhuma (ed. Buber), *Toledot*, 11: ' The righteous are partners with the Holy One, blessed be He.' הצדיקים שותפים עם הקב״ה

[61] See *supra*, p. 288.

[62] Midrash Tanhuma, *loc cit.*: ' Jacob (standing as prototype for
the people Israel) is the partner with his Creator in everything.'
יעקב שותף עם בוראו בכל דבר.

[63] Cf. the statement of Matthew Arnold, *Literature and Dogma*
(ed. 1909), p. 42: ' As long as the world lasts all who want to make
progress in righteousness will come to Israel for inspiration, as to
the people who had the sense for righteousness most glowing and
strongest.' The same thought is expressed by that great lover of
Israel, the late Rabbi A. I. Kook, *Iggerot Rayah* (1943), p. 178, in
language lyrical and mystical: ' There is no people among all the
nations of the world, in whose innermost soul there lies hidden
that precious goodness emanating from the transcendent light,
except Israel. Individual saints and sages exist everywhere, but
there is no " righteous nation " on earth but Israel.' אין עם בכל
עמי התבל שיקרת הטוב של האורה היותר עליונה תהי גנוזה במהותה של
שרש נשמתו כ״א ישראל. ישנם חסידים וחכמים יחידים, אבל אין בארץ
,,גוי צדיק" כ״א ישראל. See I. Epstein, *Avraham Yitzhak Hacohen
Kook* (1951), p. 15.

[64] Lewis Mumford, *The Conduct of Life* (1952), p. 139.

[See Additional Note, pp. 383-386.]

ARGUMENTS FOR THE EXISTENCE OF GOD, WITH SPECIAL REFERENCE TO JUDAIC SOURCES

THE argument for the existence of God from the external world of phenomena is known as the *teleological argument*, or the *argument of design*, which has been described by Kant as the ' oldest and the clearest and the most in conformity with human reason ' (see *supra*, p. 111, n. 1). This argument occurs over and over again in Rabbinic literature, of which the following passages are the most striking examples:

1. Rabbi Isaac said, ' This is to be compared to a man who was travelling from place to place and he saw a palace with lights. Is it possible, he said, that the palace has no controller ? The owner of the building looked out and said, I am the master of this palace. . . . Similarly Abraham our father said, Is it conceivable that this world is without a guide ? The Holy One, blessed be He, looked out and said to him: I am the Master of the world ' (Midrash Genesis Rabbah, xxxix. 1).

2. A heretic once came before Rabbi Akiba and said to him: ' Who created this world ? ' He replied, ' The Holy One, blessed be He.' ' Give me a clear proof,' he asked. . . . He retorted, ' What are you wearing ? ' ' A garment,' he replied. ' Who made it ? ' he further asked. ' The weaver,' was the answer. ' I do not believe you,' he retorted, ' Give me a clear proof.' ' Surely,' he replied: ' What do you wish me to show you. Don't you know that the weaver made

it ? ' ' And you don't know that the Holy One, blessed be He, created the world ? ' rejoined Rabbi Akiba. Thereupon the heretic departed. His disciples then said to Rabbi Akiba, ' What was the clear proof ? ' He replied, ' My sons, just as the house testifies concerning the builder, the garment concerning the weaver, and the door concerning the carpenter, thus the world testifies that God created it ' (*Midrash Temurah, V*). Cf. with these Midrash passages, the saying of Epictetus: ' What then, after all, is the world ? Hath it no Governor ? How is it possible when neither a city nor a house can remain ever so short a time, without some one to govern and take care of it, that this vast and beautiful system could be administered in a fortuitous and disorderly manner ? ' (*Discourses*, II. 5). This analogy of the builder is also used by Philo: ' Should a man see a house carefully constructed with a gateway, colonnades, men's quarters, women's quarters, and the other buildings, he will get an idea of the artificer, for he will be of opinion that the house never reached that completeness without the skill of the craftsman; and in like manner in the case of a city, and a ship, and every smaller or greater construction. Just so any one entering this world, as it were some vast house or city, and beholding the sky circling round and embracing within it all things, and planets and fixed stars without any variation moving in rhythmical harmony and with advantage to the whole, and earth with the central space assigned to it, water and air flowing in set order as its boundary, and over and above these, living creatures, mortal and immortal beings, plants and fruits in great variety, he will surely argue that these

361

have not been wrought without consummate art, but
that the Maker of this whole universe was and is God.
Those, who thus base their reasoning on what is before
their eyes, apprehend God by means of a shadow
cast, discerning the Artificer by means of His works '
(Philo, *Legum Allegoria*—, III, 32, E.T., F. H. Colson
and G. H. Whitaker, in the Loeb Classical Library
edition, Vol. I, pp. 367ff; See also Philo, *De Monarchia*,
I, 4).

The argument of design is also very popular with
mediaeval Jewish philosophers. Halevi (*Kuzari* III, 11,
and V. 20), Bahya ibn Pakuda (see anon), Maimonides
(*Guide* II, 20), all pressed this argument into service
for the proof of the existence of God. The following
passage from Bahya ibn Pakuda may be quoted as an
example: ' Do you not realise that if ink were poured
out accidentally on a sheet of paper, it would be impossible that proper writing should result, or legible lines
such as written with a pen? If a person brought us a
fair copy of a script that could only have been written
with a pen, and said that the ink had been spilt on paper
and these written characters had come of themselves,
we would charge him to his face with falsehood, for
we would feel certain that this result could not have
happened without an intelligent person's purpose.
Since this appears to us an impossibility in the case of
characters the form of which is conventional, how can
one assert that something, far finer in its art, and which
manifests in its fashioning a subtlety infinite, beyond
comprehension, could have happened without the
purpose, power, and wisdom of a wise and mighty
designer? ' (Bahya ibn Pakuda, *Hobot ha-Lebabot*, I, 6.

Translation, M. Hyamson.). Cf. with this Balbus' statement in Cicero's *De Natura Deorum*, II. 37: ' He who believes (the fortuitous explanation) possible, may as well believe, that if a great quantity of the one and twenty letters, composed either of gold or any other matter, were thrown upon the ground, they would fall into such order as legibly to form the *Annals* of Ennius.'

Intimately connected with the *argument from design*, is the *cosmological argument*. Briefly put, this argument, which starts from the consideration of the *cosmos* of which we are a part, is to the effect that as every natural event observed by us is the outcome of a preceding cause, we are bound, in tracing things back to their antecedent causes, to come eventually to a First Cause, itself uncaused, therefore outside and above the order of Nature—that is, to a self-sufficient and self-existing Being—God. This argument, which is essentially the same as Plato's proof of efficient causation (*Timaeus* 28), is used by Saadia (*Emunot we-Deot* I. 2), Bahya ibn Pakuda (*Hobot ha-Lebabot*, 1, 4-6), Judah Halevi (*Kuzari*, V, 18), Joseph ibn Zaddik (*Olam Katan*, III, ed. Horovitz. p. 49) as well as by Maimonides (*Guide*, II, 1), who gives it also a new form based on the observation of the ' contingent ' existence of all finite things, which makes their existence and non-existence equally possible; from this it is argued that unless there were a self-existent Being, containing within itself the necessity of its own existence from which all other things derive their contingent existence, nothing would exist (see Maimonides, *loc. cit.*, *Third Philosophical Argument*). Maimonides' treatment of the cosmological argument was taken over by Aquinas who made it the main intellectual basis of his own theism; see Étienne Gilson, *The Philosophy of St. Aquinas* (E.T., G. A. Elrington, 1924), p. 64.

The *teleological* and *cosmological* arguments have been subjected to criticisms by professional philosophers, mediaeval and modern, and particularly by Kant, who objects to the employment of ideas and principles which are valid within the world of our experience as the basis of inference for objective reality which may have laws of its own. To this we may answer that unless reason is not to be trusted at all, in which case all logical argumentation, including Kant's, becomes futile, we must assume that the laws governing the world, as we perceive it, must correspond in some objective manner to the laws that bind reality as a whole (see *supra*, p. 9). But whilst this argument precludes the supposition that the world of which we are a part was uncaused, it does not apply to the idea of a Creator who is not comprised in the cosmos, and thus is not necessarily subject to the causal laws of human experience; see Viscount Samuel, *Belief and Action* (Pelican Books) p. 33-4, n. 1. Moreover, whilst it is legitimate to ask why a finite thing has being, because it is not the essence of a finite thing to exist, it is absurd to ask whence the existence of God is derived, since in Him essence and existence are identical. ' To demand a cause for the First Cause,' as Frank Ballard observes, ' is merely to demand that what is first shall at the same time be second. It is to insist that the Great Cause of all shall, at the same time, be not the cause of all, through being in itself an effect. Such a proposition is sufficiently self-stultifying to justify its immediate and final dismissal ' (quoted by Herbert S. Box, *God and the Modern World* [1937], p. 259). For a vigorous defence of the cosmological argument against the Kantian attacks, see Otto Pfleiderer, *The Philosophy of Religion* (E.T., by Allan Menzies), Vol. III (1888), p. 257ff; E. Caird, *The Critical Philosophy of Immanuel Kant* (1889), II, p. 39ff; and especially A. E. Taylor, Hastings' *Encyclopaedia of Religion and Ethics*, XII, p. 276ff, *s.v.* ' Theism '. See also G. Dawes Hicks, *The Philosophical Bases of Theism* (1937), pp. 156ff. It should be mentioned that even Kant himself did not wish to discredit the belief in God, itself; but he was anxious that it should not be based upon unsound reasoning; and in point of fact, proceeded to argue for the existence of God from a consideration of the moral law (see *infra*).

Another objection raised by Kant and others against the *argument of design* is that the form of things can only lead to a wise designer, but not necessarily to a Creator. But as H. A. Wolfson, *Notes on Proofs of the Existence of God in Jewish Philosophy*, in *H.U.C.A.* (1924), I, pp. 582-3, has already pointed out, Jewish mediaeval philosophers never used the *argument from design* independently as proof for the existence of God, but invariably in conjunction with the cosmological argument, as evidence of divine purposiveness and other theistic doctrines regarding God, whose existence has already been demonstrated on some other ground. In this connection Wolfson, *op. cit.*, p. 583, refers to Joseph Albo's summing up of the situation, when he declares in effect, that whilst the act of Creation itself proves the existence of God, the fact that Creation was performed after a certain manner proves that it was an act of purpose and forethought; see *Ikkarim*. II, 14.

There are three more classical arguments which have been offered for the existence of God: (1) the argument of universal assent; (2) the argument of the innateness of the idea of God in the human mind—both mentioned by Cicero, *De Natura Deorum*, II, 4; (3) the ontological argument, originated by Archbishop Anselm of Canterbury (1033-1109). This last argument is an attempt to prove the existence of God from the mere idea of God: we have in our mind the idea of a perfect being, but an actually existing being is more perfect than a being that exists in the mind alone, therefore a perfect being than which nothing greater can be conceived must exist. See Anselm's *Proslogion seu Alloquium de Dei Existentia, ii.* D. Kaufmann, *Attributenlehre* (1877), p. 2, n. 4, expresses surprise that none of the mediaeval Jewish philosophers made use of either the argument of universal assent or of the innateness of the idea of God. But Wolfson, *op. cit.* pp. 575-577, rightly remarks that there was good reason for their disregard of these arguments, because the appeal to the persuasion of mankind which believed in many gods would be no proof for the existence of a one and only God. As to the ontological argument, whilst Jacob Guttmann, *Die Religionsphilosophie des Abraham ibn Daud aus Toledo* (1897), p. 121, claims to have traced it in Ibn Daud's *Emunah Ramah* (' Exalted Faith ') written in 1161, Wolfson, *op. cit.*, p. 583, energetically disputes this, and shows that Guttmann's thesis is based on a loose interpretation of Ibn Daud.

There is finally the moral argument, the best statement of which is Kant's, deriving the existence of God
from the moral constitution of human nature. The
moral law in our consciousness, it is argued, points to
a lawgiver, who is both the ground of the moral law
and the guarantor for its realisation. This moral
argument answers in a wonderful way to the Hebrew
God-consciousness which fastened more upon the
ethical attributes of God than upon His metaphysical
essence; and this method of approach (known as
' ethico-theological ', as distinct from the ' physico-
theological ', which takes the cosmological God-
conception as its starting-point) is, as D. Neumark
well observes, clearly expressed by Judah Halevi, when
he sums up his work *Kuzari* (see v, 20, especially the
six principles at the end) ' by declaring the idea of moral
freedom as the central thought of Judaism to which all
other doctrines are in relation of postulates.' See
D. Neumark, *Historical and Systematic Relations of
Judaism to Kant*, in *Essays in Jewish Philosophy*, p. 353.

THE SIGNIFICANCE OF
THE COMMANDS OF THE TORAH

THE idea set forth on pp. 288ff, that the value of the commands of the Torah lies particularly in their educative significance, is emphasised and developed by Maimonides, and applied by him to the several divine commandments, in the third book of his *Guide*, chapters 26-49. His attitude is summed up in his own words when he states: ' Every one of the six hundred and thirteen precepts serves to inculcate some truth, to remove some erroneous opinion, to establish proper relations in society, to diminish evil, to train in good manners, or to warn against bad habits ' (*Guide*, III, 31). All precepts are, accordingly, either moral law direct, or aids to moral law. They have no other significance than to be means of training men to morality; for what is not moral law is law helping thereto, although the connection may not always be clear; see *ibid.* 36, and I. Epstein, *Maimonides' Conception of the Law*, in *Moses Maimonides VIII Centenary Memorial Volume* (ed. I. Epstein, 1935), pp. 65ff.

The educative character of the precepts is already indicated in the Torah itself by the system of symbols known under the names of ' signs ' and ' remembrances ' which are used to impress them on the mind, e.g., the ' fringes ' (see Numbers xv. 37ff), and the ' frontlets ' (Deuteronomy vi. 8; xi. 18; Exodus xiii. 9, 16). Also the fact that the attainment of Holiness is made by the Torah a motive for many of the

precepts only serves to confirm their educative significance. Thus, for example, the Dietary Laws, in so
far as they are related to Holiness (see Leviticus xi.
45) are aids to moral conduct. Such too was the
view of the teachers of the Talmud, as reflected in
the statment: ' What matters it to God whether the
animal is slaughtered at the throat or at the back of the
neck ? The Torah has been given only to ennoble
mankind.' (Midrash Genesis Rabbah, xliv. 1; cf.
Midrash Leviticus Rabbah xiii. 3). Thus it is that the
mediæval Jewish Philosophers, no less than the Jewish
Hellenistic writers—Philo, the writer of the Letter
Aristeas, Aristobulus and Josephus—before them (see
I. Heinemann, *Taame ha-Mitzwot be-Safrut Yisrael*
[2nd ed. 1949], pp. 30-37, and bibliographical notes,
pp. 123-4, to which may now be added H. A. Wolfson,
Philo II, pp. 200-267), sought to rationalise the commandments of the Torah. Saadia, Bahya ibn Pakuda,
Judah Halevi, Abraham ibn Ezra, Abraham ibn Daud,
Maimonides, Levi ben Gerson, Hisdai Crescas, Joseph
Albo, Don Isaac Abrabanel—all in turn applied themselves to the problem, each employing a different
method in interpreting the inner religious and moral
signification of the precepts. An excellent account of
the attempt of these mediæval Jewish thinkers in this
direction, is to be found in I. Heinemann's cited
work, which is specially devoted to this subject. This
process has been continued ever since and among the
more recent notable efforts is that of S. R. Hirsch,
in his *Horeb* (Altona 1838). [A most valuable bibliography on the subject was compiled by Adolph Jellinek
under the title, *Kontres Taryag* (Vienna, 1878).]

Some of the precepts yield easily to treatment, whilst others, which come under the category of *Hukkim* (statutes), are admittedly hard to comprehend; yet even these, it is generally maintained, are not devoid of a practical purpose, though their reason is not so evident nor their object so clear as that of other commandments: ' Thus [the Rabbis] say [in reference to the words of Moses], " It is not a vain thing for you (Deuteronomy xxxii. 47)—it is not in vain, and if it is in vain, it is only through you." That is to say, the giving of these commandments is not a vain thing and without any useful purpose; and if it appears so to you in any commandment it is owing to the deficiency in your comprehension ' (Maimonides, *Guide*, III, 26; see also citations from Bahya ibn Pakuda and Judah Halevi, *supra*, p. 116, n. 18). Yet whilst this is generally agreed, there is a difference of opinion as to whether there is anything particularly meritorious in knowing the reason for the commandments. Here the attitudes of Halevi and Maimonides are distinctly at variance. Halevi, whilst not disputing the educative influence of the precepts nor the value of accounting, as he himself tries to do, for the reason of them, considers him ' who accepts them wholeheartedly, without rationalising them by his intellect, to be superior to him who speculates and investigates ' (*Kuzari*, ii. 26). Maimonides, on the other hand, regards the understanding of the purpose of the several precepts as an integral part of their fulfilment, and the explanation of them as an important religious need and duty which he proceeds to include in his *Code* as such; see *Yad ha-Hazakah*, *Meilah* vii. 5: ' It is proper for a man to reflect upon

370

the laws of the holy Torah and understand their purpose to the utmost of his ability.'

This difference is bound up with the estimate of the ideal content of the life with God which, it is maintained, can be won and kept through the instrumentality of the commandments, as a result of their transforming effect upon human personality and character. Maimonides, following Aristotle who holds that the end of man is the perfection of his specific form, his intellect, sets the intellectual ideal in the foreground, and considers life with God to be a kind of knowing, an activity in which reason finds its completion. This being the case, the mere practice of the laws, whether ethical or ritual, without an intellectual apprehension of their significance cannot be conducive to the highest human perfection, and the life with God which it entails.

Opposed to the Maimonidean view is that of Halevi, who without denying reason its place in man's religious consciousness, fixes the main centre of gravity in the love of God—a love which springs from a conscious communion with Him, expressed through worship and service; and the precepts of the Torah themselves are designed to serve as channels of communion, with a positive power of inspiring and deepening the love of man for his Creator, and to win for him that life with God which alone imparts the sole and absolute value to his existence and being. For a fuller discussion, see I. Epstein, *Judah Halevi as a Philosopher*, in *J.Q.R.* (*N.S.*), Vol. XXV (1935), pp. 223-4, and *The Conception of the Commandments of the Torah in Aaron Halevi's Sefer ha-Hinnuk* in *Essays Presented to J. H. Hertz,* pp. 145-6. This does not mean, however, to imply that Maimonides prized intellectual knowledge of God above the love of Him. Maimonides himself, in summing up the purpose of the commandments, states distinctly in his *Guide*, III, 52, that it is to make us acquire the fear and love of God, ' the love (being) the result of the truths taught in the Torah, including the true knowledge and existence of God.' What it does mean is that, according to Maimonides, the love of God, which is the highest of virtues, is conditioned by a correct knowledge of God and His attributes, which the precepts help to inculcate. Love of God, however, with all it implies in Jewish teaching of service and action (see *supra*, p. 67), remains in the last analysis the final goal of the precepts. It is this love which, so to speak, rounds off the knowledge of God and completes it. See I. Epstein, *Maimonides' Conception of the Law* in *op. cit.*, pp. 62ff.

Another point of difference between Halevi and Maimonides, also a matter of emphasis rather than of real divergence, is the scope of the good towards which the precepts are directed. In Maimonides, it is the individual's perfection which is put in the forefront; in Halevi, it is the perfection of the Jewish people, the ' core ' (*segulah*) of mankind, the ' heart ' of humanity (see *Kuzari*, II, 36), on which the main stress is laid throughout. The prominence which one gives to the individual and the other to the nation is simply due to the difference in aim of their respective works. Maimonides was addressing himself to the perplexed whose mind he sought to calm by harmonising the conflicting claims of Judaism and the rational philosophy of the day; whilst Halevi wrote in defence of the ' despised faith,' Judaism, and in vindication of its supremacy as against her two daughter-religions. Yet over and above the individual and national good, there is also the universal good which cannot be ignored in any proper estimate of the precepts of the Torah. This necessary corrective is supplied by Aaron Halevi of Barcelona (thirteenth century), in his *Sefer ha-Hinnuk*, where he over and again emphasises that the precepts have for their comprehensive ideal the perfection of humanity. See I. Epstein, *The Conception of the Commandments of the Torah in Aaron Halevi's Sefer ha-Hinnuk*, pp. 146ff. This too seems to be implied in the Rabbinic passage (quoted *supra*): ' The precepts have been given only to purify mankind,' the Hebrew *beriyot*, rendered 'mankind,' denoting all created human beings.

It should be mentioned that Maimonides understands this passage to mean that the precepts have been ordained merely as tests of human obedience, and that they accordingly have no other purpose beyond being the will of God. This would seem to stand in direct contradiction to the attitude espoused by Maimonides as set forth above; but he seeks to resolve the difficulty by explaining that the reference in this passage is to the details of the precepts as distinct from the precepts themselves (see *Guide*, III, 26). This, however, does not mean to imply that the details are altogether arbitrary. They may be arbitrary as far as man is concerned, but they are certainly not arbitrary as far as the divine Law-giver is concerned. Having been dictated by the divine will they have their source in the wisdom of God, and as such can admit nothing of the fortuitous or the adventitious. For a fuller exposition of this interpretation of Maimonides see I. Epstein, *Introduction to Seder Kodashim* (in the *Soncino Edition of the Babylonian Talmud in English*), pp. xxviiff, and *le-Shitat ha-Rambam be-taame ha-Korbanot, in Yad Shaul, Saul Weingort Memorial Volume* (ed. J. Weinberg, and P. Biberfeld, 1953) pp. 145ff.

A greater difficulty for Maimonides is presented by the Talmudic ruling which lays down that one who in praying uses the phrase, ' Thy mercies extend to the bird's nest,' is to be silenced because such an invocation implies that ' the measures taken by the Holy One, blessed be He, spring from compassion, whereas they are but decrees ' (B.T. Berakot 33b, and Megillah 25a). Undeterred by this, however, Maimonides does not hesitate to declare categorically that the Talmud represents but ' one of the two opinions—namely that the precepts of the Torah have no other reason save the divine will. We follow the other opinion ' (*Guide*, III, 48).

In fact, however, this Talmudic passage lends itself to a variety of interpretations some of which would bring it into accord with the Maimonidean view of the commandments. Rashi in B.T. Berakot 33b, for one, understood it to mean that the commandments have to be observed irrespective of their moral appeal and intellectual content, neither of which must ever be made the test of their validity and binding character. Again, Nahmanides explains the Talmudic passage to mean that the commandment of the bird's nest and others like it have not been ordained because of the divine compassion for animals, for in that case God would have forbidden the slaughter of them for human consumption; they were primarily decreed to train us in the quality of mercy (Nahmanides, *Commentary on Deuteronomy*, xxii. 7). Similarly, the *Sefer ha-Hinnuk* (Precept 545; Venice and Amsterdam ed. Precept 537): Divine compassion is identical with divine will, with nothing of the emotional about it, as in the case of human compassion; and it is the divine will which has decreed these commandments for our training in virtue. Maimonides was not unaware of these possible interpretations. In fact the very interpretation given by Nahmanides is already found in Maimonides' Mishnah Commentary on the Berakot passage. This would explain why Maimonides, notwithstanding his preference for his own particular attitude to the Talmudic passage, as given in his *Guide*, nevertheless embodied in his Code the ruling that ' he who says in his prayers, " May He whose mercies extend to the bird's nest, etc. . . .", is to be silenced, because these commands are divine decrees, and not due to compassion.' (*Yad, Tefillah*, IX, 7). On the Berakot and Megillah passages, see *Soncino Edition of the Talmud in English*, notes *a.l.*, and A. Marmorstein, *The Old Rabbinic Doctrine of God*, I (1927), pp. 205-6.

ADDITIONAL NOTE ON
EVOLUTION AND GENESIS

THE theory of evolution, notwithstanding its general vogue, is not so universally accepted as is often imagined. There are quite a number of eminent scientists who are opposed to the whole conception of Natural Selection, as proclaimed by Darwin. To give a few of the many examples, quoted by Arnold Lunn, *The Revolt against Reason* (1950) p. 111: Professor W. Bateson, in his Presidential Address to the British Association, in Melbourne in 1914, declared: ' To us Darwin no more speaks with philosophic authority '. F. Driesch, one of the greatest of the German biologists, categorically stated: ' For men of clear intellect Darwinism has long been dead.' Th. Dwight, Professor of Anatomy at Harvard University, wrote in 1918: ' We have now the remarkable spectacle that just when scientific men are all agreed that there is no part of the Darwinian system that is of any great influence, and as a whole the theory is not only unproved, but impossible, the ignorant, half-educated masses have acquired the idea that it is accepted as a fundamental fact.' Many more names of noted scientists, whose opinions run along the same lines, are given by Vera Barclay, *Challenge to the Darwinians* (1951), pp. 91-155, with copious extracts reproduced in support.

Twenty objections at least have been listed within recent years to the Darwinian theory, but two principal ones might be mentioned for our purpose. Not a few scientists have taken their stand against Natural Selection by directing attention to the opposite concept of

Mutual Help in the animal kingdom, and demonstrating that there exists a definite harmony in the realm of organism which showed that the struggle for existence could not afford an explanation of the origin of the species. This great manifold co-operation for existence is found not only in the animal kingdom, as Kropotkin has shown in his fascinating book *Mutual Aid* (1904), but also obtains in the domain of plant-animal relations. Many organisms, it has been shown, can maintain themselves only through co-operation of plant with plant, and plant with animal, and this co-operation has been proved to be of far greater importance to living things than any mutual struggles (see J. C. Willis, *Course of Evolution* (1940); and L. S. Berg, *Nomogenesis* (1920).

The other argument against the theory of Natural Selection is that accident and chance are quite unable to explain the co-ordination of variations necessary to adaptation. The point of the argument is that a better chance of survival on the basis of Natural Selection demands not only *one* accidental advantageous variation, but the general adaptation of all the organism to new conditions. This difficulty was already felt by Darwin himself. Speaking of the eye, he writes: ' To suppose that the eye with all its inimitable contrivances for adjusting the focus to different distances, for admitting different amounts of light, and for the correction of spherical and chromatic aberrations could have been formed by Natural Selection, seems, I confess, absurd in the highest degree ' (*Origin*, c. VI). This argument, indeed, is deemed so serious that Weissman, one of the most convinced of Darwinians, virtually admitted that it could not be got over. Applying the same argument to the human body, with its thousands of the most marvellous contrivances, one cannot fail to realize the utter absurdity of a theory which would make it all merely the product of chance.

Speaking generally, the present position as held by many of the most famous scientists seems to be that, whilst variants within the species have been observed, *the species are constant*, and that so far no evidence has been produced to the contrary. The late Rabbi A. I. Kook, writing in 1908, has indeed well expressed the sober attitude for the religious Jew to adopt in regard to the theory of evolution: ' As a whole ', he declares, ' there is no need for us to be so completely tied to the theory of evolution. This theory, no doubt, contains many sparks of truth, but there are also in it many falsehoods and fantasies. . . . Nevertheless gradual evolution is one of the myriad and illimitable ways through which " the Life of the Universe " reveals Himself '.—*Iggerot Rayah* (1943), p. 147. See also M. Kasher, *Torat ha-Beriah we-Shitat ha-Hitpathut*, in *Talpioth*, vi. (1953), pp. 205ff for a collection of Midrashic material bearing on Creation and Evolution.

ADDITIONAL NOTE ON
THE PROBLEM OF EVIL

THE presence of evil, particularly in the form of physical pain and suffering, is admittedly difficult to reconcile with the conception of a divine creator, who is both all-powerful and all-good; and yet the very fact that the world is still in the process of growth and development involves a condition of imperfection and instability, with all the suffering which this must entail (see Maimonides, *Guide*, III, 10). A greater difficulty is the apparently undeserved suffering of particular individuals. The Bible, of course, teaches that suffering is the punishment for sin, which in turn is the price man has to pay for his freedom of will. Whilst this remains the religious attitude of the present day, and it is an undeniable fact that many evils and much suffering are the consequences of sin; yet at the same time it is also an undeniable fact that it does not always go well with the righteous one and ill with the wicked. Already the prophets of Israel were oppressed by this problem, for which they sought an answer from heaven, but in vain (see Jeremiah xii. 1ff. and Habakkuk i. 13). Similarly the Rabbis of the Talmud describe Moses as having entreated for enlightenment in the matter, but only to be met with the blank reply: ' I will be gracious to whom I will be gracious ' (Exodus xxxiii. 19) —although he may not be deserving; ' And I will show mercy on whom I shall show mercy ' (*ibid.*) although he may not be deserving (B.T. Berakot, 7a). This Rabbinic attitude is well formulated in the saying

379

of Rabbi Jannai (middle of the second century): ' It is not in our power to explain either the prosperity of the wicked or the afflictions of the righteous ' (*Ethics of the Fathers*, IV. 19). The classical criticism of the doctrine that suffering is invariably the consequence of sin is found in the Book of Job, where suffering is conceived as a means of trial, whereby goodness can be perfected. Philosophy sought to explain evil away either by denying its reality, evil being only an illusion, due to man's finite nature; or by declaring it the necessary opposite of the good. Various other solutions have been suggested, and one of the profoundest discussions of the problem in recent years is by C. S. Lewis in his short work, *The Problem of Pain* (1940). But none of the explanations so far offered brings the solution any nearer. There are, however, two observations which ought to be made here. First, as W. R. Sorley, *Moral Values and the Idea of God* (1921), p. 348 points out, the fact that the existence of evil is an offence to us is something which ' may be looked upon as a special and striking expression of the cosmological argument, because, unless we assume the existence of God, we have no reason to object to the evil '. Mention should also be made of C. E. M. Joad, *God and Evil* (1942), where the author, after thirty years of agnosticism, is found driven to believe in the existence of a benevolent and participating God, precisely because of the fact of the existence of evil against which man left to his own resources can find no recourse. Secondly, if there is the problem of *evil*, there is also the problem of *good*. Why should there be goodness at all in a world originating in blind force and chance ? This problem of good, which a materialistic philosophy must find insoluble, is fully developed by Judah Halevi in his *Kuzari* (iii, 11).   After describing the marvellous gifts with which all creatures, great and small, have been endowed in accordance with their needs, he proceeds: ' He who considers the formation and use of the limbs and their relation to the animal instincts, sees wisdom in them, and so perfect an arrangement, that no doubt or uncertainty can remain in his soul concerning the justice of the Creator. When an evil thought suggests that there is injustice in the circumstance that the hare falls a prey to the lion or wolf, and the fly to the spider, Reason steps in warning him as follows: How can I charge the All-Wise with injustice, when I am convinced of His justice, and that injustice is quite out of the question ? If the lion's pursuit of the hare and the spider's of the fly were mere accidents, I should assert the necessity of accident. I see, however, that this wise and just Manager of the world equipped these lions with the means for hunting, with ferocity, strength, teeth and claw ; and that He furnishes the spider with cunning, and taught it to weave a net, which it constructs without having learnt to do so; how He equipped it with the instruments required and appointed the fly as its food, just as many fishes serve other fishes for food.   Can I say aught but that it is the fruit of a wisdom which I am unable to grasp, but that I must submit to Him who is called, " The Rock-whose-doing-is-perfect " (Deuteronomy xxxii. 4).' Whilst the phenomena mentioned by Halevi might be explained away by modern science, on the basis of Natural Selection, with its inter-related theories of adaptations and variations, there is still the need to account for the existence of unselfish goodness in a world which is fundamentally irrational and indifferent to moral values. A good book (in Yiddish) in which the various views on the problem of evil are discussed is that by Hillel Zeitlin (who fell a victim to the Nazi massacres in 1943), *Dos Problem von Guts und Schlechts bei die Yidden und andre Velker* (n.d.) The latest work on the subject is H. H. Rowley, *Submission in Suffering* (1951). An excellent account within small compass of the Old Testament attitude on the subject is W. F. Lofthouse, *A Hebrew View of Evil* (1928). See also Elias J. Bickerman in the Harvard Theological Review, October, 1951, *The Maxim of Antigonus of Socho in Pirke Avoth*; ('Do not be like servants who minister to their Master upon the condition of receiving a reward; etc.'), which he explains as a call to unconditional submission: 'The worshipper is a slave of the Deity and the divine awfulness is not measurable by man's standard of fairness.'

ADDITIONAL NOTE ON
THE RESURRECTION OF THE DEAD

THE Jewish belief in the Resurrection of the dead rests primarily on Isaiah xxvi. 19: 'Thy dead shall live, thy bodies shall arise. Awake and sing, ye that dwell in the dust, for the dew of lights (or herbs) is thy dew, and the earth shall bring shades to birth.' This verse is generally understood as expressive of the belief in personal resurrection. See G. A. Smith, *The Book of Isaiah* (1927), p. 446 and G. B. Gray in *I.C.C.* on *Isaiah* (1912), p. 438. Whether Persian eschatology had any influence on Judaism is a moot point. M. Gaster in Hastings' *Encyclopædia of Religion and Ethics s.v.* 'Parsiism in Judaism' is definitely of the view that the eschatology of Judaism was entirely unaffected by Persia for the simple reason that the rise of Zoroastrianism was subsequent to the writing of the Canonical Scriptures. Similarly N. Söderblom in the same work, *s.v.* 'Ages of the World' asserts categorically that neither religion seemed to have borrowed from the other. R. H. Charles, *A Critical History of the Doctrine of a future Life* (1899), p. 128, scommening on the cited verse from Isaiah writes: '. . . this passage of Isaiah just presents us with a truly spiritual doctrine of future life; for that life stands in organic and living relation to the present life in God, which the faithful enjoy on earth. . . . It is the genuine product of Jewish inspiration and not derived from any foreign source. For even if the

Mazdean doctrine of the resurrection of the righteous and the wicked be of an earlier date, it could not be the parent of the higher spiritual form with which we have just dealt.' Some would on that account deny the Isaiahnic authorship of this verse, but the famous prophecy in Ezekiel's ' Vision of the Valley of Dead Bones ' (xxxvii) could not have been understood by the people, even if used figuratively of the national resurrection, unless such a belief in personal resurrection had already existed in Israel. A clearer announcement of the belief is that given in Daniel xii. 2: ' And many of those that sleep in the dust of the earth shall arise, some to hope everlasting, and some to reproach and everlasting abhorrence.' As distinct from Isaiah who speaks of ' Thy dead ' (understood to refer only to Israel), Daniel includes in the resurrection the unjust as well as the just, and this leads Charles, *op. cit.*, p. 133 to detect some Mazdean influence. But in fact there is a world of difference in that, in the Mazdean religion, ' heaven was only an idealisation of earth, such as would be conceived by a people of primitive farmers. Zarathustra himself looked forward to receiving from God as his special portion in the life to come " ten men together with a stallion and a camel ".' (E. Bevan, *The Hope of a World to Come* [1930] p. 16), whereas in Daniel the bliss is spiritualised: ' And those that are wise shall shine like the brightness of the firmament, etc.' (*ibid.*, xii. 3). See also G. F. Moore, *Judaism*, II, pp. 394-5. For the literature dealing with the foreign influences—Egyptian and Persian—on the Jewish doctrine of resurrection, see L. Finkelstein, *The*

Pharisees (1938), ii., pp. 672-3, to which may be added Charles Vernon Pilcher, *The Hereafter in Jewish and Christian Thought* (1940), pp. 126-7, and Bevan's book cited above, pp. 12 and 17. Coming down to post-Biblical writings, the belief is given definite and clear expression in the story of the martyrdom of Hannah and her seven sons, as told in the *Second Book of Maccabees*; and in Rabbinic literature the belief becomes a settled article of faith, the denial of which involves the forfeiture of a share in the world to come (Mishnah, Sanhedrin x. 1). The doctrine encountered much opposition from the Sadducees, who according to Josephus, *Antiquities*, xviii, 1, 4, held that the souls and bodies perished together, thus denying both resurrection and immortality. This finds support in *Abot de-Rabbi Nathan* v, where the twin heresies of the Sadducees and the Boethusians are traced to the wrong inference which the two disciples of Antigonos of Socho (*c.* 250 B.C.E.) drew from his teaching of ' virtue for virtue's sake ' (see *Ethics of the Fathers* i. 3), to the effect that there was neither reward nor punishment after death. On the origin of these sects and their relation to one another, see the literature listed in G. F. Moore, *Judaism*, III, p. 28, n. 69 and L. Finkelstein, *op. cit.*, II, p. 663, n. 20. This generally-accepted view is, however, disputed by D. Neumark, *Essays in Jewish Philosophy*, pp. 127-8, who maintains that the Sadducees, whilst denying the belief in resurrection, held to the doctrine of immortality, and as proof he adduces the *Fourth Book of the Maccabees*, which, though written by a Sadducee, gives expression to hope of immortality, as against the doctrine of resurrection emphasised by

the Pharisean author of the *Second Book of Maccabees.*
But *IV Maccabees*, which is of Alexandrian origin, is so
largely written under Greek influence as to be of little
value as evidence for genuine Sadducean doctrine.

תם ונשלם שבח לבורא עולם

The following Hebrew texts of translated quotations which occur
in this work are additional to those included in the Notes. The
references are to the pages and notes in this volume.

P. 5.

כאב לבי על מיני מן המדברים והתעוררה נפשי לעמנו בני ישראל. ממה
שראיתי בזמני מרבים מהמדברים מהמאמינים. אמונתם בלתי זכה ודעותם
אינם ברורים. והרבה מהמכחישים מתגדלים בהפסד ומתפארים על אנשי האמת
והם התועים. וראיתי בני אדם כאלו טבעו בים הספקות, וכבר כסו אותם
מימי השבושים, ואין צולל שיעלה אותם ממעמקיהם, ולא שוחה שיחזיק
בידם וימשם.
(אמונות ודעות. הקדמת המחבר. הוצאת סלוצקי ג׳)

Pp. 19-20, n. 21.

המלמדים תנוקות בלי הסברת והרחבת הדברים להשריש ולהרחיב האמונה
בלבבם בדברים המתקבלים על הלב לפי ערך התלמיד לא יכה הלמוד הזה
שורש בלבות הנערים. וזו אחת הסבות אשר יגדלו בינינו נערים בלא אמונה
בלי תורה ובלי יראה בעו״ה. אך צריך המורה לשים לבו לדלות התועליות
היוצאות מספורי התורה הק׳ ובדברים אמונים להרחבת הענין בדברים
המתישבים על הלב.
(יצחק מלצן, פתח דבר למאמרו ״שפת אמת״)

P. 20, n. 21.

השתדלותנו והשתדלות כל איש מהיחידים חלוף ההמון, שהמון אנשי התורה
הנאה שבדברים להם והערב לסכלותם שישימו התורה והשכל שני קצוות
סותרים. ויוציאו כל דבר נבדל ומפורש מהמושכל ויאמרו שהוא מופת ויברחו
עמידת דבר על מנהג הטבע לא במה שיסופר ממה שעבר, ולא במה שיראה
מזמן העומד, ולא במה שיאמר שיארע לעתיד, ואנחנו נשתדל לקבץ התורה
והמושכל, וננהיג הדברים על טבעי אפשר בכל זה אלא מה שנתבאר בו שהוא
מופת ולא יתכן כלל נצטרך לאמר שהוא מופת.
(אגרת הרמב״ם, תחיית
המתים, קובץ תשובות הרמב״ם ואגרותיו ליפסיא תרי״ט ח״ב, י׳)

Pp. 21-22, n. 21.

כי החקירה והעיון והידיעה אי זה שתהיה לא יסירו האדם מן השלימות ולא
ימשך מידיעתם רשע ואשמה, אבל בהפך. ואם ראה נראה אנשים מה יהיו
רשעים עם למוד החכמות ההם, הנה אין החכמות ההם, הסבה ברשעותם, אבל
רוע מזגם שאם לא יהיו חכמים היו יותר רעים וחטאים — הנה כי החכמה
בשום צד אין לה להזיק אבל להועיל.
(אברהם ביבאגו. דרך אמונה. שער ג׳)

Pp. 66-67.

החסיד הוא מושל נשמע בחושיו וכחתיו הנפשיים והגופיים . . . וחסם כוחות
המתאוים ומנע אותם מן הרבוי אחר אשר נתן להם חלקם והספיק להם מה
שימלא חסרונם מהמאכל המספיק והמשתה המספיק והרחיצה . . . וחסם
הכוחות הכעסנים המבקשים לנצוח. אחרי אשר נתן להם חלקם בנצחון

המועיל . . . וגערת האנשים הרעים . . . ונתן לחושים חלקם במה שמועיל לו
ומשמש בידיו ורגליו ולשונו בענין הצורך ובחפצו המועיל וכן השמע והראות
. . . ואחר כן היצר והמחשב והזכרון, ואחר כן הכח החפצי המשתמש בכל
אלה והם משמשים עובדים לחפץ השכל.   (יהודה הלוי, כוזרי, מאמר ג׳, ה׳)

Pp. 114-115, n. 10.

והאיך היא הדרך לאהבתו ויראתו. בשעה שיתבונן האדם במעשיו ובראויו
הנפלאים הגדולים ויראה מהן חכמתו שאין לה ערך ולא קץ מיד הוא אוהב
ומשבח ומפאר ומתאוה תאוה גדולה לידע השם הגדול כמו שאמר דוד צמאה
נפשי לאלהים לאל חי. וכשמחשב בדברים האלו עצמן מיד הוא נרתע לאחוריו
ויראה ויפחד וידע שהוא בריה קטנה שפילה אפילה עומדת בדעת קלה מעוטה
לפני תמים דעות כמו שאמר דוד כי אראה שמך מעשה אצבעותיך מה אנוש
כי תזכרנו.   (רמב״ם, יסודי התורה פ׳ ב׳ ב׳)

Pp. 116-117, n. 18.

יש הבדל בין אמרנו שהנבואה למעלה מהשכל האנושי ובין אמרנו שהיא
סותרת השכל. כי שני אלו המאמרים אע״פי שיורו אצל הפתאים על ענין אחד
הנם אחר ההסתכלות הן מתחלפין חלוף אינו מעט. וזה שאמרנו שהנבואה
למעלה מן השכל הרצון בו שיש דברים רבים יודעו מצד הנבואה וא״א שיודעו
מצד מופת לא שהדברים שיחייבם השכל תכחישם הנבואה.

(ר׳ יוסף בן שם טוב בעל ס׳ כבוד אלקים בהקדמתו
לפירוש אל תהי כאבותיך בשו״ת ר׳ משה אלשקר קי״ז.)

P. 132, n. 10.

ואם יבקש אדם בזמן הזה לראות מה שהוא דומה לענינים ההם (יציאת
מצרים ומעמד הר סיני), יביט בעין האמת עמדנו בין האומות מעת הגלות
וסדור עניניו ביניהם עם מה שאנו בלתי מסכימים עמהם בסתר ובגלוי. והם
יודעים בזה, כמו שהבטיחנו יוצרנו יתברך (ויקרא כ״ו, מ״ד), ואף גם זאת
בהיותם בארץ אויביהם לא מאסתים ולא געלתים וגי׳ . . . ונאמר (תהלים קק״ד
א׳ ב׳) לולי ד׳ שהיה לנו יאמר נא ישראל בקום עלינו אדם . . .
(בחיי בן יוסף ן׳ פקודה, חובות הלבבות, שער הבחינה, ה׳)

Pp. 132-133, n. 10.

אנחנו האומה הגולה שה פזורה, אחר כל שעבר עלינו מהצרות והתמורות
אלפים מהשנים, ואין אומה בעולם נרדפת כמונו, מה רבים היו צרינו, מה
עצמו נשאו ראש הקמים עלינו מנעורינו להשמידנו לעקרנו לשרשנו. מפני
השנאה שסבתה הקנאה רבת צרריונו. גם לא יכלו לנו לאבדנו ולכלותנו. כל
האומות הקדומות העצומות אבד זכרם, בטל סברם סר צלם, ואנו הדבקים בד׳
כולנו חיים היום. . . מה יענה בזה פילוסוף חריף. המקרה עשתה כל אלה. חי
נפשי כי בהתבוננו בנפלאות אלה גדלו אצלי יותר מכל ניסים ונפלאות שעשה
השם יתברך לאבותינו במצרים ובמדבר ובארץ ישראל, וכל מה שארך הגלות
יותר נתאמת הנס יותר ונודע מעשה תקפו וגבורותו.

(ר׳ יעקב עמדי׳. סידור בית יעקב, סולם בית אל ד׳ ע״ב)

Pp. 210-211.

וזה הצלם ודמות שאמר ה׳ יתברך . . . אינו דמות תואר פנים, כי אם בדמות
מעשה אלהים ומעשה העולם, כמו שהאלוהים עליון ומושל באדם ובכל
העולם, תחת ומעלה כן האדם . . . כמו שהאלוהים יודע ומבין כן אדם שנתן
לו חכמה לידע. וכמו שהאלוהים מספיק ונותן לחם לכל בשר כן האדם מכלכל
בני ביתו, ומשרתיו ובהמתו, וכמו שהבורא עשה בנין העולם ומוסדות הארץ
ונטטית הרקיע ומקוה המים, כן האדם יכל לבנות, ליסד, לקראת ולהקוות,
ולזרוע ולצמח ולנטוע ולעשות . . . וברוב דברים ידמה האדם כמעט מזער
לאלהים לפי מיעוט הכח וקוצר החיים שנתן לו האלוהים. (שבתי דונולו,
פירוש נעשה אדם בצלמו׳ הוצאת יעללינק ח׳)

P. 222

כל מי שדעותיו ישרות ראוי לו לדעת שאף שאין כל אמת מוכרח בכל אותן
החדשות (הבאות ע״י המחקרים החדשים) מ״מ אין אנחנו חייבים כלל להכחישן
בבירור ולעמוד נגדן. מפני שאין זה כלל עיקר של תורה לספר לנו עובדות
פשוטות ומעשים שהיו. העיקר הוא התוך ההסברה הפנימית שבהענינים. וזה
יתרומם עוד יותר בכל מקום שנמצא כוח סותר שאנו מתעדדים להתגבר על
ידו . . . וכשאנו באים לידי מדה זו. אין אנו נזקקים עוד ללחום דוקא נגד
הציור המתפרסם בין החוקרים החדשים וכאשר אין אנו נוגעים בדבר נוכל
לשפוט מישרים. ועתה נוכל לבטל את החלטותיהם במנוחה במדה זו שהאמת
תורה לנו את דרכה.   (א׳ י׳ קוק, אגרות הראיה, [ירושלים, תש״ב] קס״ג,)

P. 223, n. 2.

אמר ר׳ יוחנן למה נברא אדם בצלם אלוהים . . . משל למלך שהי׳ מושל על
המדינה, והיה בונה בירניות ותיקונין לעיר וכל בני הדור משתעבדין תחתיו
יום אחד קרא לכל בני העיר ומנה עליהם שר אחד שלו אמר עד כאן הייתי
טורח בכל צרכי העיר ולעשות מגדלים ובירניות, מכאן ואילך הרי זה כמונו,
כענין זה ראה מניתי אותך על צרכי כל העולם וכל אשר בה כאשר הייתי
מושל עליה ובונה אותה ככל חפצי כך אתה תבנה ותעשה מלאכת העולם. . .
ועל כן בצלם אלוהים עשה אותו . . . לעשות כל צרכי העולם ותיקוניו כאשר
הוא עשה בתחלה.   (זהר חדש ה׳)

P. 226, n. 13.

החוברים נסתפקו למה לא ייחד השי״ת יום מיוחד לבריאת האדם . . . והשיבו
לפי שהאדם אינו נברא בעת שנברא לפי האמת כי אין שלימותו נמצא אתו בעת
הבריאה כאשר הנמצאות שמציאותם היא תכליתם וכל זה בחכמת השי״ת
להעיר אזן אדם . . . כי שלימותו תלוי בידו ובהשתדלותו להשלים עצמו.
(מעשה טוביה, א׳ א׳ הגהת בן המחבר)

Pp. 230-131.

והנה מכאן תשובת המינים . . . שטועים בדמיונם הכוזב שמדמין מעשה
שמים וארץ למעשה אנוש ותחבולותיו. כי כאשר יצא לצורף כלי שוב אין
הכלי צריך לידי הצורף כי אף שידיו מסולקות הימנו והולך לו בשוק הכלי

389

קיים בתבניתו וצלמו ממש כאשר יצא מידי הצורף, כך מדמין הסכלים האלו
מעשה שמים וארץ אך טח מראות עיניהם ההבדל הגדול שבין מעשה אנוש
ותחבולותיו שהוא יש מיש רק שמשנה הצורה והתמונה מחתיכת כסף לתמונת
כלי למעשה שמים וארץ שהוא יש מאין . . . שבהסתלקות כח הבורא מן הנברא"
ח"ו ישוב הנברא לאין ואפס ממש. אלא צריך להיות כח הפועל בנפעל תמיד
להחיותו ולקיימו.   (תניא, ליקוטי אמרים ב')

Pp. 308-309, n. 15.

לפי שזה ענין קשה מאוד שיגיע האדם אל המדרגה הראויי מן היראה ואהבה
והעבודה בכל לב ובכל נפש. הקל עליו השי"ת כי תחת כל זה צוהו לשמור
חוקות השם ומצותיו בלבד, ובזה תושג התכונה המגעת לו מצד העבודה
בכל לב ובכל נפש.   (ס' העקרים לרבי יוסף אלבו, מאמר ג' ל"א)

P. 349, n. 2.

וידוע כי עיקר היחוד לימות המשיח שהרי בזמן הגלות והשעבוד אין סימני
היחוד ניכרין . . . ותרבה הכפירה בעולם . . . אבל לימות המשיח . . . ישובו
כל האמונות לאמונה אחת ויהיה העולם מתוקן במלכות שדי ויסכימו כולם
לעבודת השם יתברך בלבד לקרא כלם בשם ד' ולעבדו שכם אחד, ואז יתפרסם
יחודו של אלוהינו בפי כל האומות והוא שהבטיח הנביא לעתיד ואמר והי'
ד' למלך על כל הארץ, ביום ההוא יהי' ד' אחד ושמו אחד.
            (רבינו בחיי, כד הקמח, יחוד)

P. 360.

אמר רבי יצחק משל לאחד שהיה עובר ממקום למקום. וראה בירה אחת דולקת
אמר : תאמר שהבירה זו בלא מנהיג : הציץ עליו בעל הבירה. אמר לו : אני
הוא בעל הבירה. כך לפי שהיה אבינו אברהם אומר : תאמר שהעולם הזה בלא
מנהיג : הציץ עליו הקב"ה ואמר לו : אני הוא בעל העולם.
            (מדרש רבה בראשית ל"ט, א')

Pp. 361.

מעשה שבא מין אין ואמר לר' עקיבא: העוה"ז מי בראו ? א"ל הקב"ה, א"ל :
הראיני דבר ברור . . . א"ל : מה אתה לובש ? א"ל : בגד. א"ל : מי
עשאו ? א"ל : האורג, א"ל : איני מאמינך, הראיני דבר ברור. א"ל : ומה
אראה לך, ואין אתה יודע שהאורג עשאו ? א"ל : ואתה אינך יודע שהקב"ה
ברא את עולמו ? נפטר אותו המין. אמרו לו תלמידיו : מה הדבר ברור. א"ל :
בני כשם שהבית מודיע על הבנאי והבגד מודיע על האורג והדלת על הנגר,
כך העולם מודיע על הקב"ה שהוא בראו.   (מדרש תמורה, ה').

P. 378.

בכלל אין אנו צריכים להיות כ"כ מאודקים לשיטת ההתפתחות, יש בה
ודאי כמה ניצוצי אמת, אבל ג"כ כמה כזבים ודמיונות . . . אלא שההתפתחות
האיטית היא אחת מרבבות אין-סוף שחי עולמים מתגלה בם. (א' י' קוק, אגרות
הראיה [ירושלים, תש"ב] קמ"ז)

INDEX TO PASSAGES CITED

This index includes references to the Hebrew Scriptures, the Talmud and Midrash, the Apocrypha, Pseudepigrapha and the New Testament

I. HEBREW SCRIPTURES

2. TALMUD AND MIDRASH

3. APOCRYPHA AND PSEUDEPIGRAPHA

4. NEW TESTAMENT

INDEX OF AUTHORS
AND THEIR CITED WORKS

The names cited in this list are those of authors whose works, statements or views are discussed or referred to in the text or notes. Articles contributed to encyclopaedias, journals or other publications are denoted by an asterisk (*).

C—2

INDEX OF SUBJECTS

*To Mrs. D. Dark and Miss C. Goldman who have been
jointly responsible for the preparation of these Indices the
Author expresses his thanks for a task ably
and cheerfully performed*

296
Ep6